A New Approach to English Grammar, on Semantic Principles

A New Approach to English Grammar, on Semantic Principles

R. M. W. Dixon

CLARENDON PRESS · OXFORD

Oxford University Press, Walton Street, Oxford OX2 6DP

Oxford New York Toronto
Delhi Bombay Calcutta Madras Karachi
Kuala Lumpur Singapore Hong Kong Tokyo
Nairobi Dar es Salaam Cape Town
Melbourne Auckland Madrid
and associated companies in
Berlin Ibadan

Oxford is a trade mark of Oxford University Press

Published in the United States
by Oxford University Press Inc., New York

First issued in paperback 1992

British Library Cataloguing in Publication Data
Data available

Library of Congress Cataloging in Publication Data
Dixon, Robert M. W.
A new approach to English grammar, on semantic principles
Includes bibliographical references and index.
1. English language—Grammar—1950–2. English language—Semantics. I. Title.
PE1106.D59 1990   425—dc20   90—7356
ISBN 0–19–824057–0

3 5 7 9 10 8 6 4

Printed in Great Britain
on acid-free paper by
Biddles Ltd.,
Guildford and King's Lynn

For Anna,
a true linguist,
who married a man called John,
and named her first child Mary.

Contents

B. THE SEMANTIC TYPES   73

Contents

C. SOME GRAMMATICAL TOPICS   205

List of tables

How to read this book

This book is, of course, designed to be read from first to last page. But other strategies are possible.

Some of Part A (at least Chapter 1) should be read before Part B. Some of Part B (at least §§3.3, 3.4 of Chapter 3) should be read before Part C. Within Part B, Chapter 3 should be read first but Chapters 4, 5 and 6 could be covered in any order. Within Part C, the chapters can be read in any order.

A reader familiar with the details of English grammar may prefer to skim over Chapter 2. Note though that §2.7, on complement clauses (which contains some original analysis), should be read before Chapter 7, on complement clauses.

Chapters 4–6 go through every semantic type associated with the class Verb. It is not necessary to study these in detail before looking at some of the discussions of grammatical topics in Part C.

Preface

When I first became interested in linguistics, in 1961, it was with the idea that it should be possible to put forward the kind of description and explanation which is attempted in this book.

I was thinking about the meanings of words and how their grammatical properties should be a function of those meanings. I thought: there really ought to be a discipline, perhaps called linguistics, which deals with such things. Then I found that there actually was a subject called linguistics. It was not immediately obvious that linguists at the time were interested in the interrelation between meaning and grammar. Nevertheless, I settled down —in a state of some excitement—to study the principles of linguistics. This was at the University of Edinburgh, under the fine tutelage of Michael Halliday and Angus McIntosh.

It seemed to me that if I wished properly to understand the methodology and theory of linguistics, I should try applying it to description of a previously undescribed language. So I went to Australia for a year (in 1963–4) to study Dyirbal. After that I became a lecturer at University College London, under Michael Halliday, and struggled for a while to find a framework in which to present the description of Dyirbal. I decided that the facts of the language were difficult enough to explain without the added impediment of an opaque jargon, and settled for a straightforward description in terms of the categories that linguists have evolved over two thousand years (with an added chapter of explanation in terms of the then-current version of transformational grammar).

I had the luck to spend 1968/9 at Harvard, at a time when striking programmes for the linking of semantics with syntax were being broached by Lakoff and Ross, McCawley, and others. I then began thinking about English (e.g. Dixon 1970, which is the genesis for Chapter 10 in the present volume). At that time I formulated the idea of 'semantic types', an outline of the semantico-syntactic framework which underlies this book (see Dixon 1977, which was first circulated in 1970).

After moving to Australia, in 1970, almost all my time was taken up with working on Australian languages—revising the grammar of Dyirbal for publication, and working with the last speakers of Mbabaram, Yidiny, Warrgamay and Nyawaygi (languages that I saw become extinct as I was writing up their grammars). I also completed a preliminary survey of the Australian language family, with reconstruction of aspects of proto-Australian (Dixon 1980).

During the 1970s I did a little work on what has always seemed to me the most fascinating topic of all in English, the semantic basis of complement choice; and gave an inchoate paper on this at a conference organised by George Miller at Princeton in 1973.

Then in 1980—during a six-month sabbatical spent at Clare Hall, Cambridge—I started working intensively on English grammar, employing the same methodology that I had used for Australian languages. That is, I began with the data, and worked out generalisations inductively. The basic data in this case were the 900 commonest verbs in English. I considered each verb in turn, examining its meaning and its grammatical behaviour (see §1.4). Writing and revising this book was my major research task in the 1980s (alongside a grammar of Fijian—see Dixon 1988).

This is not a full grammar of English, or even an exhaustive account of certain topics in the grammar of English. It attempts to put forward a semantically oriented framework for grammatical analysis, and to indicate how this framework can be applied. Many detailed studies could be undertaken, building up from the groundwork I have tried to provide. There are a number of other topics I have thought about and there are tentative plans for a second volume, at some time in the future, which might investigate the syntax and semantics of prepositions, adverbs, tense and aspect, nominalisation, and negation, amongst other topics.

Over the past twenty or thirty years I have read many descriptions of English and of other languages and have learnt something from all of them. I have also studied many accounts of 'linguistic theory' and have learnt, in different ways, from that. My personal interest is firstly in description, and only in 'theory' as it assists description and provides explanation for what has been described (not in 'theory' as an end in itself). Theoretical devices like tree diagrams and systemic network do—it seems to me—run the risk of imposing strait-jackets which languages neither deserve nor need. Language is not neat and symmetrical; it is neither necessary nor desirable to pretend that it is, or to insist that everything should be accounted for at every level. But I am convinced of the necessity for distinguishing functional categories —such as subject, predicate, object—from classes of phrases and words; and for stating the correlations which each individual language allows between functions and classes.

I have benefited from contact with many scholars—through reading their works, correspondence and discussion; the list is too long to include here. This book was greatly helped by the four semesters during which I taught the 'Advanced Syntax' course at the ANU, in 1980, 1983, 1986 and 1988. I owe a debt to the students taking these courses—for the ideas they shared, for their scepticism and criticism, and for their opinions about what they would and wouldn't say, and why.

A number of people commented on a draft of this book. Some were disappointed that I did not adhere to a current model of generative grammar, and did not provide detailed discussion of all previous literature on each topic. Most of them encouraged me to continue in my furrow. All provided helpful suggestions and comment. Thanks are due to several publishers' referees, to my colleague Tim Shopen and to my friend Lys Ford. Bernard Comrie, Rodney Huddleston and Jim McCawley have long served as mentors, with their inspiring and scholarly approaches to linguistic description and explanation; their detailed comments on this book are especially appreciated.

Anna Wierzbicka has been a colleague at Canberra for seventeen years, during which time we have been working on similar topics from similar—but by no means identical— viewpoints. I have benefited immeasurably from reading her books and papers, from attending the 'Advanced Syntax' course at the ANU when she taught it, and from many discussions. A number of her ideas have been silently incorporated into this book (which is not to say, of course, that she necessarily agrees with what I say). She read the typescript and offered many perceptive and critical comments.

Of all the people I have read and talked to, Dwight Bolinger stands out, as someone who has approached the sorts of questions which I consider interesting, in ways that are stimulating and provocative. He found time in a busy schedule to read parts of this book and, of course, provided the most pertinent counter-examples and further generalisations. He also offered a comment that encouraged me more than anything anyone else said: 'After going through Part B (Chapters 3–6) I can appreciate the heroic proportions of your undertaking. It is a conquest of the linguistic wilderness, backpacking your way through—the only way to do what other descriptions, conducted at 20,000 feet using a camera without a focus, have failed to do. The job will take a while, but this is a fine beginning.'

Canberra
November 1989

Part A

Introduction

1

Orientation

This book provides a fresh look at parts of the grammar of English. It pays particular attention to meaning, considering the different sorts of meanings words have, and showing how the varying grammatical behaviours of words are a consequence of their meaning differences.

My 'meaning orientation' stance is a little novel. In addition, some of the topics discussed here (especially in Chapters 10 and 11) are scarcely mentioned in regular grammars of English. It could be said that the present book takes off from the point where most other grammars end.

The reader will not find here any detailed discussion of the irregular inflections of verbs or plural forms of nouns, topics which are covered in standard grammars. A basic knowledge of certain aspects of English grammar is needed for understanding the later part of the book, and these are presented in Chapter 2 (which does include some original analysis).

I work in terms of the broad theoretical apparatus of linguistics that has been built up over the past two thousand years (word classes, main and subordinate clauses, underlying and derived forms, structures and systems, etc.), utilising the insights of Dionysius Thrax, Edward Sapir, Leonard Bloomfield, Kenneth Pike, Michael Halliday, Noam Chomsky and Bernard Comrie, among others. Theoretical ideas are brought in as they assist the central task, of describing the syntactic and semantic organisation of English. I have not chosen to restrict myself by casting the description in terms of any of the systems of nomenclature that are currently referred to as 'linguistic theories' and which have, in the past few decades, grown, flourished and perished with such rapidity.

The use of jargon and symbolisation has been kept to a minimum on the principle that, in a subject such as linguistics, if

3

something can be explained it should be explainable in simple, everyday language, which any intelligent person can understand. That is not to say that this book can be read through quickly, like a novel. It is a serious, scientific attempt to explain the interrelations of grammar and meaning; the reader is advised to proceed slowly and deliberately, thinking carefully about what is said and often referring back to an earlier discussion (following the cross-references given).

Many modern books on linguistics build up to a grand generalisation, something which attracts attention at the time but is found, on reflection, to be a little over-glib, to which many exceptions can be given. Language, as a pattern of human behaviour, does not yield 'laws' like those of Newton or Einstein. It is a complex phenomenon, whose parts intersect in complex ways. But it does have a principled basis and it is the purpose of this book to explore this, demonstrating that a large part of the basis concerns the meanings of words, and of grammatical constructions, and how these interrelate.

1.1. Grammar and semantics

A language consists of words and grammar. Grammar itself has two parts:

Morphology deals with the structure of words, e.g. the fact that *un-friend-li-ness* consists of four parts (called 'morphemes'), each of which has a meaning, and *laugh-ing* of two morphemes.

If a morpheme is added to a word and yields a word of a different kind this is called a **derivation**, e.g. the formation of adjective *beautiful* from noun *beauty*, noun *decision* from verb *decide*, verb *widen* from adjective *wide*, and verb *untie* from verb *tie*.

If a morpheme just adds some extra element of meaning to a word, which is required by the grammar of the language, then it is called an **inflection**, e.g. the verb *kill* inflects for past tense, becoming *killed*, and the noun *horse* inflects for plural number, becoming *horses*.

The second component of grammar, **syntax**, deals with the way in which words are combined together. In English an adjective must come before a noun and an article before the adjective—we can get *the old lion*, which is a noun phrase (or NP). A verb (or a verb phrase, such as *was sleeping*) must in English be preceded by a noun phrase—we get *The old lion was sleeping*, which is a clause.

A sentence may consist of just one clause (it is then called a simple sentence) or it can be a complex sentence, involving several clauses. There may be a main clause, and a subordinate clause, joined to it by a conjunction, which can indicate reason (*The old lion was sleeping because he was exhausted*) or temporal sequence (*The old lion was sleeping after eating the hunter*) and so on.

Underlying both words and grammar there is **semantics**, the organisation of meaning. A word can have two sorts of meaning. First, it may have 'reference' to the world: *red* describes the colour of blood; *chair* refers to a piece of furniture, with legs and a back, on which a human being may comfortably sit. Secondly, a word has 'sense', which determines its semantic relation to other words, e.g. *narrow* is the opposite (more specifically: the antonym) of *wide*, and *crimson* refers to a colour that is a special sort of red (we say that *crimson* is a hyponym of *red*).

Every morpheme has a meaning. The ending *-er*, added to a verb, derives a noun which refers either to the agent (e.g. *baker*) or else to an instrument intended for the activity (e.g. *cooker*). Some morphemes have different meanings with different kinds of word: *un-* indicates an opposite quality with an adjective (e.g. *kind, unkind*), but a reverse action with a verb (*tie, untie*).

Meaning is also associated with the way in which words are combined to make phrases, clauses and sentences. Compare *The dog bit the postman* and *The postman bit the dog*, which involve the same word meanings but quite different sentence meanings because of the different syntactic arrangements.

As language is used, meaning is both the beginning and the end point. A speaker has some message in mind. He chooses words with suitable meanings and puts them together in appropriate grammatical constructions; all these have established phonetic forms, which motivate how he speaks. A listener will receive the sound waves, decode them, and—if the act of communication is successful—understand the speaker's message.

The study of language must surely pay close attention to meaning. We consider the meanings of words, and their grammatical properties, and see how these interrelate. When a speaker of a language encounters a new word he may first of all learn its meaning, and will then have a fair idea of the morphological and syntactic possibilities. Or he may first of all learn something of how to use the word grammatically, and this will help him to work out its meaning.

If a child or adult learner hears the word *boulder* for the first time and discovers that it refers to a large rock, they will know (from analogy with *pebble, rock, stone*) that it must be able to take the plural ending *-s*, and that it will probably not take the ending *-en* (which occurs in *widen, blacken*).

Suppose that the verb *begin* is first encountered in a sentence like *He'll soon begin to understand grammar*; that is, the verb is followed by a clause introduced by *to*. Other verbs have this grammatical property, e.g. *He started to read my book, He hopes to finish it*. But the meaning of *begin* is similar to that of *start*, which is why it is scarcely surprising that it can be followed by a clause whose verb ends in *-ing* (*I began cooking dinner an hour ago*) just as *start* can (*I started writing my thesis yesterday*). And the meaning of *begin* is different from that of *hope*, which is why it should not be surprising that *begin* cannot be followed by a clause introduced by *that*, in the way that *hope* can (e.g. *He hopes that he will finish it*).

There is, as we have said, a principled interaction between the meaning of a word and its grammatical properties. Once a learner knows the meaning and grammatical behaviour of most of the words in a language, then from the meaning of a new word he can infer its likely grammatical possibilities; or, from observing the grammatical use of a new word, he may be able to infer a good deal about what it means.

1.2. Semantic types and grammatical word classes

There are many thousands of words in a language, each with a meaning; some meaning differences are large, others small. The words can be grouped together in a natural way into large classes that have a common meaning component. I will refer to these as **semantic types**. Verbs *begin, start, commence, finish, cease, stop,* *continue* and a few others all make up one type. (Rather than manufacture some high-sounding label for a type, I generally name it after one of its more important members—calling this the BEGINNING type.) Adjectives such as *big*, *broad*, *short*, *shallow* comprise the DIMENSION type. And so on, for forty to fifty more types, which between them cover the whole of the vocabulary of a language.

At the level of semantics words can be arranged in semantic types, with a common meaning element. At the level of grammar, they can be arranged in **word classes** (traditionally called 'parts of speech'), with common morphological and syntactic properties.

Languages differ in the weightings they assign to different parts of grammar. Some languages have a simple morphology but make up for this by having complex rules for the ways in which words are combined. Other languages have long words, typically consisting of many morphemes, but a fairly straightforward syntax. For every language we can recognise word classes, sets of words that have the same grammatical properties, although the nature of these properties will vary, depending on the grammatical profile of the language.

There are two sorts of word classes—major and minor. The minor classes have limited membership and cannot readily be added to. For instance, there are just seven Personal Pronouns in English (*me*, *us*, *you*, *him*, *her*, *it*, *them*—see §2.2); new pronouns do not get coined in a hurry. (As a language evolves some pronouns do disappear and others evolve, but this is a slow and natural process. Old English had *thou* for second person singular; its context of use became more and more restricted and it was finally replaced by *you*, which was originally used just for second person plural.) Most minor classes do not have any independent referential meaning (they do not correspond to any object or quality or activity) but serve just to modify words from the major classes, and link them together into phrases, clauses and sentences. Articles (*a*, *the*, etc.) and Conjunctions (*and*, *because*, *after*, and so on) are minor classes in English, whose functions and meanings should be fully covered within a comprehensive grammar of the language.

Then there are major word classes—such as Noun, Verb and Adjective—which have a large and potentially unlimited membership.

It is impossible to give an exhaustive list of the many thousands of nouns, since new ones are being coined all the time (and others will gradually be dropping out of use). Two words that belong to the same class may have almost exactly the same grammatical properties (*monkey* and *baboon*, for instance, or *black* and *red*) and will only be distinguishable through definitions in a dictionary.

For every language a number of major word classes can be recognised, on internal grammatical criteria. Latin has one class (which we can call A) each member of which inflects for case and number, another (B) showing inflection for case, number and gender, and a third (C) whose members inflect for tense, aspect, mood, person and number. Note that it is possible to give entirely morphological criteria for the major word classes in Latin. But English is much less rich morphologically and here the criteria must mingle morphological and syntactic properties. One major word class in English (which we can call X) can have the inflection *-ed* (or some variant) on virtually every member. A word belonging to a second class (Y) may be immediately preceded by an article and does not need to be followed by any other word. Members of a third open class (Z) may be immediately preceded by an article and must then normally be followed by a word from class Y.

We can make cross-language identification between classes A and Y, calling these Noun, between B and Z, calling them Adjective, and between C and X, calling them Verb. The identification is not because of any detailed grammatical similarity (the criteria employed for recognising word classes in the two languages being rather different) but because the classes show semantic congruence. That is, most nouns in Latin would be translated by a noun in English, and vice versa. (There are just a few exceptions—where English has a noun *hunger* there is a verb in Latin, *ēsurio* 'to be hungry'. Interestingly, English has a derived adjective *hungry*, formed from the noun, and Latin also has an adjective *ēsuriens* 'hungry', derived from the verb.)

There is a relationship between semantic types and grammatical word classes. Each major word class is essentially a grouping together of semantic types. The types are related to classes in similar (but not identical) ways in different languages. The Noun class always includes words with CONCRETE reference (*house, foot, grass, star, fire, hill, boy, city,* etc.). It usually also includes KIN terms, but in some languages these words belong to the Verb class (after all, *John is Tom's father* indicates a relationship between John and Tom, comparable to *John employs Tom*).

Verbs have different grammatical properties from language to language but there is always a major class Verb, which includes words referring to MOTION (*run, carry,* etc.), REST (*sit, put*), AFFECT (*hit, cut, burn*), ATTENTION (*see, hear*), GIVING and SPEAKING.

Many semantic types belong to the same word class in every language. But for others there is quite a bit of variation. Words to do with LIKING (*love, loathe, prefer,* etc.), for instance, belong to the Verb class in some languages, to the Adjective class in other languages, and even to the Noun class in a few languages.

1.3. Semantic roles and syntactic relations

A verb is the centre of a clause. A verb may refer to some activity and there must be a number of participants who have roles in that activity (e.g. *Sinbad carried the old man*); or it may refer to a state, and there must be a participant to experience the state (e.g. *My leg aches*).

A set of verbs is grouped together as one semantic type partly because they require the same set of participant roles. All GIVING verbs require a Donor, a Gift and a Recipient, as in *John gave a bouquet to Mary, Jane lent the Saab to Bill,* or *The Women's Institutes supplied the soldiers with socks*. All ATTENTION verbs take a Perceiver and an Impression (that which is seen or heard), as in *I heard the crash, I witnessed the accident, I recognised the driver's face*. AFFECT verbs are likely to involve an Agent, a Target, and something which is manipulated by the Agent to come into contact with the Target (which I call the Manip). A Manip can always be stated, although it often does not have to be, e.g. *John rubbed the glass* (*with a soft cloth*), *Mary sliced the tomato* (*with her new knife*), *Tom punched Bill* (*with his left fist*).

We are here working at the semantic level, and it should be stressed that each type has a quite distinct set of roles. There is nothing in common between Gift (that which is transferred from one owner to another) and Impression (an object or activity that is seen or heard) or Perceiver (a person who receives visual or auditory sense impressions) or Agent (a person who wields a Manip to come into contact with a Target), and so on.

There are about thirty semantic types associated with the Verb class. Some verbs, such as those in the GIVING and AFFECT types, have three semantic roles. Some, like ATTENTION, have just two. And some have just one (CORPOREAL verbs like *breathe*, and MOTION verbs like *fall*). Altogether, it is necessary to recognise forty or fifty semantic roles.

Turning now to syntax, we find that every language has a limited number of syntactic relations. Subject and Object are probably universal relations, which apply to every language. But just as the criteria for the major word classes Noun and Verb differ from language to language, so do the ways in which syntactic relations are marked. In Latin, for instance, the Subject occurs in nominative case (e.g. *domin-us* 'master-NOMINATIVE') and the object in accusative case (e.g. *serv-um* 'slave-ACCUSATIVE'). Words can occur in many different orders in a clause in Latin, so that *Dominus servum videt*, *Servum videt dominus*, *Videt dominus servum*, etc. all mean 'The master sees the slave'. In English, nouns have no case inflection and grammatical relations are shown primarily by word order, Subject before the verb and Object after it.

The roles of each type, at the semantic level, are mapped onto syntactic relations, at the grammatical level. For ATTENTION verbs, for instance, the Perceiver is grammatical Subject and the Impression is marked as Object.

There are quite often several different ways in which semantic roles may be associated with grammatical relations. With the GIVING type either the Gift may be Object, as in *Jane lent the Saab to Bill*, or the Recipient may be, as in *Jane lent Bill the Saab*; for both of these clauses the Donor is Subject. It is also possible to have Recipient as Subject, and then a different verb is used: *Bill borrowed the Saab from Jane*. *Borrow* is the semantic converse of *lend*; both verbs belong to the GIVING type and involve the same three semantic roles.

For AFFECT verbs the Agent is usually the Subject and the Target the Object, with the Manip marked by a preposition such as *with* – *John hit the pig with his stick*. But we can have the Manip in Object slot (this often carries an implication that the Manip is less strong than the Target, and likely to be more affected by the impact)— *John hit his stick against the lamp post*. Or, as a third alternative, the Manip can be placed in Subject relation—*John's stick hit Mary* (*when he was swinging it as she walked by, unnoticed by him*); use of this construction type may be intended to imply that John was not responsible for any injury inflicted.

Verbs fall into two broad subclasses—those that require only one role (intransitive verbs) and those which require two or more roles (transitive verbs). There is considerable difference between intransitive subject and transitive subject. We will need to refer a good deal to these relations so that it will be useful to employ abbreviatory letters for them, and for object:

S—intransitive subject
A—transitive subject
O—transitive object

If a verb has only one role, at the semantic level, then it must be mapped onto S relation, at the syntactic level. Some of the roles in S slot can control the activity in which they are involved (e.g. *walk*, *speak*) but other S roles exercise no control (e.g. *break*, *die*, *grow*).

If a verb has two or more roles, one will be mapped onto A and another onto O. It is the role which is most relevant for the success of the activity which is put in A relation; compare *Bill tried to borrow the Saab from Jane* with *Jane tried to lend the Saab to Bill*. And it is the non-A role which is regarded as most salient for the activity (often, the role which is most affected by the activity) which is put into O relation—compare *Mary cut the cake into slices* with *Mary cut slices off the cake*. (There is further discussion of these points beginning in §3.3.1.)

The core syntactic relations are Subject and Object. Other, peripheral, relations are in English marked by a preposition— these can refer to a place or time setting (*in the morning*, *at the races*) or to some additional participant (*for Mary*, *with a hammer*).

1.4. The approach followed

Having established the theoretical framework for this study—in terms of semantic types, semantic roles, their mapping onto syntactic relations, and so on—I worked inductively, examining the semantic and syntactic properties of a large number of individual verbs, and gradually inducing generalisations from these.

I began with a list of the 2,000 most commonly used words in English (in West 1953) and looked in detail at all those which can function as verbs (about 900 in all). Each verb was taken separately, and its semantic and syntactic characteristics investigated. The verbs were grouped into types—on the basis of semantic and syntactic similarities—and the semantic and syntactic profiles of each type were then studied. In this way—proceeding from the particular to the general—I worked out a pan-language classification of complement clauses, in Chapter 7; of transitivity, in Chapter 8; and so on.

The present volume should be regarded as the first attempt to follow through a new approach to grammatical description and explanation. It is essentially programmatic, providing a broad outline of the semantic types, and the ways in which their meanings condition their syntactic properties.

The reader will not find, in the chapters that follow, a fully articulated grammar of English from a semantic viewpoint, with the meaning of every important verb discussed in appropriate detail, and each syntactic construction dealt with exhaustively. Such a study would fill a dozen or more volumes of this size Rather, I try to provide the parameters in terms of which more detailed studies—of individual semantic types, and of individual constructions—may be carried out. This book aims to lay a foundation, upon which elegant edifices of semantico-syntactic description and explanation may be constructed.

Studying syntax in close conjunction with semantics, and in an inductive manner, differs from the approach followed by most modern linguists, both from the generative (formerly transformational-generative) and from other schools. It is most common to begin with syntax (looking for 'semantic interpretation' at a late stage, if at all) and also to begin with putative generalisations, later looking to see if there might be any counter-examples to them.

I noted above that there is a many-to-one mapping between semantic types and grammatical word classes, and also between semantic roles and syntactic relations. Textbooks of generative grammar will typically note that both *hope* and *believe* accept a THAT complement in the O slot (*Susan hopes that she will win the race*, *Susan believes that she will win the race*) and then express surprise that only *hope* takes a TO complement clause in which the subject is not stated but is understood to be the same as the subject of the main verb (*Susan hopes to win the race*, but not **Susan believes to win the race*). They appear to begin with the premiss that if two words share some grammatical properties then they might well be expected to share them all. Linguists who argue in this way generally pay only perfunctory attention to meaning.

A more rewarding approach is to commence with consideration of semantic types. *Believe* belongs to the THINKING type, together with *think*, *reflect*, *wonder*, *doubt*, all of which take THAT complements, but not TO complements of the type illustrated here. *Hope* can be semantically grouped (in the WANTING type) with *dread*, *desire* and *wish*, all of which take both THAT complements and also TO complements (with omission of a subject that is identical to the subject of the main verb).

Although there are important differences—as just illustrated—my approach does of course have many points of similarity with the work of other linguists. I have tried to build on all previous work (and add to it) rather than to ignore the insights of other scholars and strike off in some idiosyncratic direction of my own.

One idea that has been taken from the generative tradition, and adapted to the needs of the present study, is the usefulness of recognising 'underlying forms', and then general conventions for omitting or rearranging parts of them in specifiable circumstances—see §§2.11, 2.12 below. (In fact, I go a good deal further than many linguists along this path, and am consequently able to explain things that others have dismissed as perverse irregularities.)

To mention one example, there are a number of verbs in English which must take a preposition and a following NP, e.g. *decide on*, *rely on*, *hope for*, *refer to*. This NP behaves like a direct object (e.g. it may become passive subject). We suggest that *decide on*, *hope for*, and the like are each a transitive verb, involving an inherent preposition. There then appears to be a general rule of English syntax stating that a preposition must be omitted when it is immediately followed by one of the complementisers *that*, *to* and *for*. Compare (1)–(2) with (3)–(4):

(1) *Everyone in the office hoped for an English victory.*

(2) *They decided on the order of precedence*

Here there is an NP in O slot, and the prepositions *for* and *on* are retained.

(3) *Everyone in the office hoped that England would win*

(4) *They decided that Mary should lead the parade*

Here the O slot is filled by a THAT complement clause, before which *for* and *on* are omitted. The fact that there *is* an underlying preposition in (3) and (4) is shown under passivisation. The THAT clause, as object, is moved to the front of the sentence to become passive subject and the preposition again appears as the last part of the verb:

(5) *That England would win was hoped for*

(6) *That Mary should lead the parade was decided* (*on*)

But note that a THAT complement clause in subject position is typically extraposed to the end of the sentence, with *it* then occupying the subject slot. When this happens the THAT clause again follows the inherent preposition of the verb, which is omitted:

(7) *It was hoped that England would win*

(8) *It was decided that Mary should lead the parade*

There are fashions and fads in linguistic explanation. At one time it was all the rage to talk of underlying forms and deep structures and ways in which surface forms and structures could be derived from these. Nowadays some scholars are reluctant to work in such terms. My explanations in terms of underlying forms and structures could perfectly well be restated as alternations between two possibilities—saying that *hope for* is used in certain environments and *hope* in other, complementary, environments, for instance, without suggesting that *hope* is derived by prepositional omission from *hope for*; and similarly in other cases. This is essentially a matter of 'terminology', carrying no differences in descriptive or explanatory power. The approach I adopt involves shorter statements and seems pedagogically more effective; but nothing else hangs on it.

There is one respect in which I differ from the early transforma-
tionalists. They might say that *I believed him to be mad* has a 'deep
structure' something like [*I believed* [*it* [*he is mad*]]] with the third
person singular (3sg) pronoun as subject of *be mad*, but after a
'raising' transformation has applied the 3sg pronoun is now the
object of *believe*. I suggest that the 3sg pronoun bears two simultaneous syntactic relations, as object of *believe* and as subject
of *be mad* (even though it is morphologically encoded as the
unmarked and object form *him*—see §2.2).

I have tried to make this book consistent and self-sufficient. In
particular, I have *not* ventured to recapitulate every previous
attempt to deal with the syntactic questions I consider, and to
criticise aspects of these before presenting my own solution (which
is, in most cases, partly based on earlier work and partly original).
To have done this would have made the book two or three times as
long and much less easy to read. There are references to the
relevant literature at the end of most chapters.

Finally, let it be stressed that I am describing educated British
English—essentially my own dialect of it (which is based on what I
learnt as a child in Nottingham). I am fully aware that other
dialects, such as American English, differ markedly—more so
concerning the topics discussed here (e.g. the HAVE A construction
in Chapter 11) than concerning the topics dealt with in traditional
grammars. These differences should not affect the broad sweep of
conclusions reached in this book, only their detailed articulation.
It would be an interesting and rewarding task to investigate dialect
differences in terms of the framework adopted here; this remains a
job for the future.

Notes to Chapter 1

The 'semantic orientation' approach followed here has a close affinity with
the work of Apollonius Dyscolus (see Householder 1981).

§1.3. An example of a language in which KIN terms belong to the Verb
class is Yuma (e.g. Halpern 1942).

There is an important difference between my semantic roles and the
'cases' of Fillmore (1968) or the 'theta-roles' of recent work in generative
grammar (see ch. 7 of Radford 1988 and references therein). A single set
of 'theta-roles' or 'cases' is set up for a given language (or for all

languages) to cover all semantic types within that language. In contrast, I recognise a *separate* set of semantic roles for *each* semantic type in a language; semantic roles belonging to different types are related together *only* through being mapped onto the same syntactic relation.

§1.4. The *hope/believe* example is from Perlmutter and Soames (1979: 111), which is an excellent textbook of its kind.

Generative grammarians have pointed out that *hope* takes a THAT object complement clause (*They hope that a solution will be found*) but this does not have a passive (i.e. **That a solution will be found is hoped* is not grammatical) although it does have a passive when the complement is extraposed (*It is hoped that a solution will be found*)—Jacobson (1982: 65–6). I suggest, instead, that the underlying form is *hope for* (including an inherent preposition) and that this transitive verb does have a normal passive (as in *That a better solution would be found was earnestly hoped for*). It is just that *for* drops when it would be immediately followed by *that*, in consequence of a general syntactic rule for English, given in §1.4. (See also Bolinger, 1975a).

Kiparsky and Kiparsky (1970: 160) say that 'after prepositions, infinitives are automatically converted to gerunds, e.g. *I decided to go* vs. *I decided on going*'. I prefer to take the basic form of the verb as *decide on* and say that it can take a TO or an ING complement clause, with a difference in meaning; and to further say that the preposition *on* drops before *to* by an automatic rule of English syntax.

2

Grammatical sketch

This chapter outlines some of the main points of English syntax which are necessary for an understanding of later chapters (it does not go into exhaustive detail on any issue).

On a fair number of analytical issues there is currently disagreement between grammarians; only some of these disagreements are mentioned here. In a book of this size it would be impracticable to discuss all alternative proposals. What I have tried to do is provide a single, internally consistent view of the syntax of English.

2.1. Forms of the verb

It is important to distinguish between the base form of a verb, the three tense forms, and the two non-tense suffixed forms. Illustrating for one regular and three sample irregular verbs:

		regular	irregular		
	base	*discover*	*see*	*give*	*hit*
tense	present, 3sg subject	*discover-s*	*see-s*	*give-s*	*hit-s*
forms	present, other subject	*discover*	*see*	*give*	*hit*
	past	*discover-ed*	*saw*	*gave*	*hit*
non-	*-ing*	*discover-ing*	*see-ing*	*giv-ing*	*hitt-ing*
tense	*-en*	*discover-ed*	*see-n*	*giv-en*	*hit*

The tense forms are used in main clauses and must be preceded by a subject (at the least, the impersonal subject, *it*); the only circumstance in which a subject can be omitted is when two clauses with identical subject are coordinated, e.g. *John came in and sat down* (§2.10). The base form is used in the imperative, and after *to* (the so-called 'infinitive').

17

Non-tense forms are used after auxiliary verbs: *-ing* after progressive *be*; *-en* after perfect *have* and after passive *be* (e.g. *was giving; had given, was given*). *-ing* is used in varieties of complement clause, one often with *'s* on the subject (if it is stated), e.g. *I like Mary('s) playing the piano*; the other with *from* between subject and verb, e.g. *I discouraged John from going*. It can also mark the predicate of a circumstantial clause, e.g. *Having made his will, he shot himself*, and *Being absorbed in her task, she didn't notice the tiger approach*. Both *-ing* and *-en* may also function as adjectival modifiers within an NP, although only some verbs have (one or both of) their non-tense forms used in this way, e.g. *worrying news, worried expression, helping hand, informed reply*.

Unlike tense forms, the non-tense forms do not have to be preceded by a stated subject within that clause, e.g. *I like playing the piano*, and the two circumstantial clauses given in the last paragraph.

(Nouns can be derived from some verbs (§2.8) and this sometimes involves the addition of *-ing*, e.g. *the singing of the birds, the rocking of the boat*. But with many verbs a different derivational form is used, e.g. *the departure of the army*, rather than **departing*, and *decision* not **deciding*, *belief* not **believing*, etc.)

It is informative to compare the past tense form, which must have a preceding subject, with the *-en* form, which may lack a stated subject. Compare:

(1) *All students [(who were) seen in the bar last night] should report to the principal's office at noon*

(2) *All teachers [who saw students in the bar last night] should report to the principal's office at noon*

The relative clause in (1) can be shortened by the omission of *who* (a relative pronoun filling subject slot) and *were*; the non-tense form *seen* then becomes clause-initial. *Who* cannot be omitted from (2); this is because the past tense form *saw* must be preceded by a subject (see §2.6).

For all regular (and some irregular) verbs the *-en* and past tense forms fall together—both *seen* in (1) and *saw* in (2) could be replaced by *discovered*. For these verbs it is important to enquire whether a form like *discovered* is, in a particular clause, realising the past tense category (since it will then require a subject) or whether it is realising the *-en* category (when it will have different syntactic possibilities); if *discovered* is substituted for *seen* in (1) and for *saw* in (2), then we can still omit *who were* from (1) but not *who* from (2). This is parallel to the situation concerning those few nouns that have a single form for both singular and plural—there *is* still an operative category of number, which is realised in the form of accompanying demonstrative and verb; compare *this sheep is bleating* with *these sheep are bleating* (*this* versus *these* and *is* versus *are* showing that *sheep* once realises singular and once plural number).

All verbs (except *be*) have a present non–3sg form that is identical to the base form. Once again, we must know what category a plain verb form is representing, in a given clause. Compare *I know all about your children; they eat ice cream* and *I said to your children: you eat this ice cream.* The pronoun *they* cannot be omitted from the first sentence since the tensed verb *eat* must be preceded by a subject; but the subject pronoun *you* can be omitted from the second sentence since the base form *eat* (here, in imperative function) does not require a preceding subject.

2.2. Forms of the pronoun

In an earlier stage of English the function of an NP in a clause was shown by its case ending—nominative for subject, and accusative for object; there was then considerable freedom of word order. The case endings on nouns and adjectives have been lost and in modern English the function of an NP is generally shown by its place in order—subject before and object after the predicate in a simple clause.

However, the pronouns—except for *you* and *it*—still retain two case forms:

SERIES I (following preposition, and when object of clause)	*me*	*him*	*her*	*us*	*them*
SERIES II (when subject of clause unless following preposition)	*I*	*he*	*she*	*we*	*they*

Series I provides the 'unmarked' form of a pronoun. Series II occurs only in subject function, except following a preposition (in *John brought the applicants in for me to interview them, me* is subject of *interview* but also follows the preposition *for*, and thus takes a series I form); series I occurs in all other positions. If someone asks *Who wants to go?*, one could reply either *I do* (here using a series II form as subject of the verb *do*) or else just the series I form *Me* (but not just the series II form **I*).

There is a fair degree of variation in pronominal use. Some people still say *It was I who did it, She is younger than I, It is I*, where most speakers would prefer *me* in place of *I* in all three sentences. There appears to be a long-term trend towards the replacement of series II by series I (this has gone all the way with the second person pronoun where *you*, the original object form, has entirely replaced the old subject form *ye*).

In some complex constructions an NP may come between two verbs, e.g. *I know John took the ball* and *I saw John take the ball*. We may ask whether, in these sentences, *John* is object of the verb it follows, or subject of the verb it precedes, or both of these simultaneously. On substituting a pronoun for *John* we get different results: *I know he took the ball* and *I saw him take the ball*.

This information from pronominal forms is one important factor in deciding on the function of an NP in a complex sentence. We can infer that *John* is the subject of *took* in the first example, and the object of *saw* in the second. It may well *also* be object of *know* and/or subject of *take* (respectively), with other grammatical factors deciding which of two simultaneous functions determines surface form. (This question is considered in §2.7, §2.9.5 and Chapter 7.) Data on pronominal form do not provide an immediate and total answer to the question we posed in the last paragraph, but they are a most useful element in the formulation of a full answer.

2.3. Phrases

A noun phrase (NP) can be just a pronoun (e.g. *she*) or a proper name (e.g. *Shirley*). Or it can have a common noun (e.g. *mountain, boy*) as head. It is not ordinarily permissible in English to omit the noun head; if no specific head is stated the form *one* may be used (e.g. *the big one* rather than just **the big*).

A multitude of elements may precede the head of an NP:

(*a*) a predeterminer, e.g. *all* (*of*), *both* (*of*), *one-quarter* (*of*);

(*b*) a determiner, which can be an article (*the, a*), a demonstrative (e.g. *this, those*) or a possessive word or NP (*my, John's, the old man's*);

(*c*) a superlative (*tallest, most beautiful*) or a comparative (*taller, more beautiful*); and/or a cardinal number (*three*) or a quantifier (*many, few*);

(*d*) an ordinal number, e.g. *fourth*;

(*e*) one or more adjectival modifiers (see §3.2 for the ordering among adjectives);

(*f*) one or more modifiers describing: composition (*wooden, vegetable*), origin/style (*British*), purpose/beneficiary (e.g. *rabbit* in *rabbit food*).

Note that the two choices under (*c*) can occur in either order, and may carry a meaning difference, e.g. *the two cleverest girls* (the cleverest and the second cleverest) versus *the cleverest two girls* (can refer to the cleverest pair, when they were already grouped into pairs). All of possibilities (*a*)–(*f*) are unlikely all to be taken up in a single NP, although it is theoretically possible to say something like: *some of* (*a*) *the* (*b*) *best* (*c*) *fifteen* (*c*) *new* (*e*), *shiny* (*e*), *plastic* (*f*) *German* (*f*) *cat* (*f*) *baskets* (HEAD).

Following the head there can be any or all of:

(*g*) *of* followed by an NP which refers to something in syntactic relation to the head; the relation may vary, as illustrated by *the arrival of the chief*—corresponding to *The chief arrived*— *the destruction of the city*—corresponding to *Someone/thing destroyed the city*—and *the leaves of the tree*—corresponding to the possessive construction *the tree's leaves*;

(*h*) a time or place adverb, e.g. *tomorrow, upstairs*;

(*i*) any preposition plus an NP, e.g. *after lunch, in the sky*; *for Mary*;

(*j*) a relative clause (see §2.6).

An NP including all of (*g*)–(*j*) is *the* (*b*) *engine* (HEAD) *of Fred's old car* (*g*) *outside* (*h*) *in the back garden* (*i*) *which John tried to mend* (*j*). Note that (*g*) is generally incompatible with the choice of a possessor under (*b*): we may say *this old car's engine* or *John's engine* or *the engine of John's old car* but not **John's engine of the old car*. But *of* may introduce a non-possessor NP, under (*i*), which can co-occur with a choice under (*b*), e.g. *the President's promise of peace*.

I use 'verb phrase' (VP) to describe a string of verbs (an alternative use, which is not followed here, is to say that the VP also includes an object NP). A VP must include a main verb as head. This may optionally be preceded by auxiliary verbs: either *do*, or any or all of:

   (i) a modal—one of *will*, *can*, *must*, etc. (see §6.1.1);
  (ii) the perfect aspect marker *have*, which requires the following verb to be in *-en* form, e.g. *had beaten*;
 (iii) the progressive aspect marker *be*, which requires the following verb to be in *-ing* form, e.g. *was beating*;
 (iv) the passive marker *be*, which requires the following verb to be in *-en* form, e.g. *was beaten*.

It is, then, at least theoretically possible to say *might* (i) *have* (ii) *been* (iii) *being* (iv) *beaten* (HEAD).

The first word in a VP inflects for tense, e.g. *has/had broken*, *is/was breaking*, *is/was broken*. Negation is shown by *not* or *-n't*, which must follow the first auxiliary verb, e.g. *can't break*, *isn't breaking*, *hadn't broken*. If none of the auxiliary elements (i)–(iv) are present then *do* must be included with a negative, e.g. *broke*, *didn't break*. If a VP does not include a negation or any of (i)–(iv) then *do* may be included to carry emphasis, e.g. *He did go*. (Note that *do* is incompatible with any or all of (i)–(iv), except in an imperative, where one could say, for instance, *Do be sitting down when they arrive!*)

Note that for most verbs in English the so-called 'present tense' form refers mainly to a habitual activity, e.g. *He eats bananas*, and the *be* . . . *-ing* auxiliary is used for reference to a present activity, e.g. *He is eating bananas*. But certain verbs (particularly, some from the LIKING and THINKING types) are seldom used with *be* . . . *-ing* and do use the present tense form for present time reference, e.g. *He likes bananas now*, *She knows the right route*.

2.4. Main clauses

A main clause generally contains a subject and a predicate, and sometimes also an object (note that I do not consider an object to be part of the predicate, as some writers do). There are two basic types of predicate: (*a*) consisting just of a VP that has a lexical verb as head, e.g. *laughed, should have been working*; (*b*) consisting of a VP that has a copula as head, this being followed by a further constituent.

The most general and most frequent copula is *be*. This must be followed by one of a number of possibilities, which include:

(i) an NP, e.g. *She is a doctor, Mary is my mother, Susan is an evil woman*;

(ii) a *that* clause, e.g. *The point is that it is unsafe*;

(iii) an adjective, e.g. *He is happy, She is still sick*;

(iv) *for*, plus an NP referring to a beneficiary, e.g. *This bouquet is for the queen*;

(v) an adverbal expression of space or time, which can be a single word (*The meeting is here/outside/tomorrow*), or a preposition plus NP (*The meeting is in the garden/at ten o'clock*) or an adverbal clause (*The meeting is after we have finished eating*).

Many languages require a verb of rest or motion to be included with a locational expression, saying something like *She is staying in Prague* or *She is going to Vienna*. English can use just the copula to describe a position of rest, i.e. *She is in Prague*; but a verb of motion must normally be included with any specification of motion 'to' or 'from'—that is, *going* cannot be omitted from *She is going to Prague*. There is an interesting exception: the perfect auxiliary *have* plus copula *be* can be used with a *to* phrase, without a verb of motion, e.g. *She has been to Prague* (with the meaning 'she went to Prague at least once').

The other copula verbs in English include *become*, which can be followed by (i) an NP, or (ii) an adjective (*She became a doctor/my wife/sick*) and *get, come, go, grow, turn*, each of which may only be followed by a restricted set of adjectives, e.g. *get dirty, come true, go bad, grow stupid, turn green*. Whereas *become* only functions as a copula and *be* only as copula and in the progressive and passive auxiliaries, the other five also have non-copula uses; indeed, their lexical and copular uses can merge—compare *He turned/grew sad* with *He turned/grew into a sad man*. (§9.1 includes a list of the varied uses of *get*. §6.4.1 discusses verbs of the SEEM type, which also have copula-like properties.)

A main clause in English generally includes a subject, which precedes the predicate. Intransitive verbs have a single core role and this must be intransitive subject (referred to as 'S' relation). Transitive verbs have two or more core roles, and that role which is most likely to be relevant for the success of the activity is in transitive subject relation (referred to as 'A').

A transitive verb must also have a role in object (O) relation, and this will immediately follow the predicate. After an intransitive predicate, or a transitive-predicate-plus-object, a clause may include one or more peripheral NPs (each introduced by a preposition), referring to recipient (*give the book to Mary*), or beneficiary (*take the book for Mary*), or instrument (*shave with a razor*), or reason (*do it for money/kicks*) etc.; and also one or more locational or time or frequency or manner expressions (see §2.5).

2.5. Adverbal elements

Adverbal elements can refer to (i) place; (ii) time; (iii) frequency or degree; or (iv) manner of an activity or state. (For a fuller classification see Quirk and Greenbaum 1973: 210 ff.) They can comprise a word (e.g. *there*, *inside*; *today*, *already*; *often*, *always*; *slowly*, *craftily*), a phrase (*in the garden*, (*during*) *last night*, *at infrequent intervals*, *with sincerity*) or a clause (*where we had built the house*, *before she arrived*, *whenever he felt like it*, *as his mother had always told him*). Adverbal phrases are generally introduced by a preposition, although there are exceptions, e.g. *last week*, *many times*, *this way*. Adverbal clauses generally have the structure of a main clause with a preposed subordinator, e.g. *where*, *after*. There is an additional type of adverbal clause of time whose VP begins with the *-ing* form of a verb, e.g. *His mother having gone out for the day, John invited his friends in to play poker*. The subject of an *-ing* time clause will be omitted if it is the same as the main clause subject, e.g. *(After) having failed his final exam, John threw a tantrum.* (See also §2.10.)

An adverbial element is most frequently a direct constituent of the main clause, and qualifies the complete clause. The most common position is after predicate-plus-object (if an object is present). Adverbial elements and peripheral NPs referring to recipient, beneficiary, instrument, etc. can occur in any order, e.g. in *Mary hit John [with an axe] [today] [in the garden]* the final three constituents may be permuted in all six possible orders. Note that no adverbial element can occur between predicate and an NP object (although it often can between a predicate and a complement clause as object—see §2.7).

Most adverbial elements can be preposed to clause-initial position, sometimes with a contrastive intonation pattern (shown by commas in orthography), e.g. *Where we built the house, he had intended to put his bee hives.* Most can also occur in the middle of the VP—generally in any position after the first or a later auxiliary verb (if there is an auxiliary) and before the main verb, e.g. *would already have been laughing, would have already been laughing, would have been already laughing,* or (a VP with no auxiliary) *already knew.* Adverbial elements have different nuances of meaning depending on where they occur in the clause.

Place adverbials behave in two rather different ways, depending on the semantic type of the predicate head. With verbs from the REST and MOTION types and from the LOOK subtype of ATTENTION we get a place adverbial that is semantically linked to the reference of the verb—*He sat on a chair, She carried the pig to market, She stared at the picture.* Indeed, some of these verbs demand a place adverbial e.g *He put the box down/there/on the table* (**He put the box* is incomplete and thus unacceptable). Such 'inner adverbials' are almost fixed in position after the predicate; they may exceptionally occur initially (or even within the VP) but must then take a marked intonation pattern, e.g. *There, on top of the hill, he put his boundary marker.* Place adverbs occurring with verbs of other semantic types do not have the same sort of semantic link to the verb (they can be called 'outer adverbials') and may freely be moved to initial position, e.g. *In the garden Mary kissed John* is as acceptable as *John kissed Mary in the garden.*

A manner adverb derived from a VALUE adjective qualifies the activity referred to by the clause; it can occur in final but not initial or medial position, e.g. *John washed the clothes well/properly,* not **John well/properly washed the clothes* (with meaning: the activity 'John washed the clothes' was well done). In contrast, a manner adverb derived from a HUMAN PROPENSITY adjective refers just to the state of the subject; it can occur finally, initially or within the VP, e.g. *John had been washing the clothes happily/lazily* and *John had happily/lazily been washing the clothes* (with meaning: John was happy/lazy as he washed the clothes).

A time or place adverbial element—which may be a word, a phrase or a clause—can also occur as part of an NP, as in [*The noises in the night*] *upset Father*; although the noises occurred in the night, Father might not have been upset until he was told about them at breakfast, on his return from the night-shift. Compare with *The noises upset Father in the night*, which has *in the night* as a clause constituent, and implies that Father was actually upset in the night by the noises. A sentence like *We are expecting my uncle from the city* is ambiguous between the NP-modifier parsing (my uncle lives in the city, but he might be arriving today from some other direction) and the clause-adverbial reading (he is coming from the city today, although he might live somewhere entirely different). It will be disambiguated when further material is added e.g. *We are expecting* [*my uncle from the city*] *to come here today*, and *We are expecting my uncle* [*to come here from the city*] *today*.

Frequency and manner adverbial elements do not occur as such within an NP. If there is a corresponding adjective then this will be used, e.g. *eat frequently* and *frequent meals*; *decide quickly* and *quick decisions*. However, a frequency or manner adverb may modify an adjective (either when it follows a copula or when it itself modifies a noun), e.g. *occasionally dishonest*; *boringly predictable*.

Finally, there are a number of 'premodifiers' which add a qualification of degree to adjectives and to adverbs, e.g. the initial components in *very clever(ly)*, *pretty quick(ly)*, *quite happy(ly)*, *rather good/well*. A few derived adverbs also have a second sense as premodifier, e.g. *surprisingly* in *surprisingly stupid(ly)*.

2.6. Relative clauses

A relative clause is a constituent of an NP and provides a description of the referent of the head noun, parallel to an adjectival or adverbal modifier—compare *the tall man*, *the man* [*in the corner*] and *the man* [*who kicked John*].

A relative clause has the same basic structure as a main clause, with subject, tensed verb as head of the predicate, etc. It must contain an NP that has the same reference as the head of the superordinate NP in whose structure the relative clause functions, i.e. *the man* [*the man kicked John*]. A relative pronoun is placed at the beginning of the clause and the occurrence of the coreferential NP is omitted. The relative pronoun is *which* if the coreferential NP was a non-human in subject or object function or following a preposition, *who* if a human (or, for some speakers, a higher animal) in subject function, *whom* if a human in object function or following a preposition (*whom* is now being replaced by *who* in object function), *whose* if a human or non-human in possessive function, *where* if a locational and *when* if a temporal element. Thus *I saw the dog* [*which bit John*], *I watched the man* [*who hit John*], *I observed the tramp* [*who*(*m*) *John hit*], *I discovered the man/dog* [*whose house John destroyed*], *I saw the place* [*where you were born*].

Where the coreferential NP was in subject function the relative pronoun both (*a*) marks the clause as a relative clause; and (*b*) fills the subject slot (recall that a tensed VP must normally be preceded by some sort of overt subject NP). Where the coreferential NP was in non-subject function then the relative pronoun only has property (*a*).

There are two major varieties of relative clauses, illustrated by:

(3) *The firemen who the managers sacked will meet in the engine shed*

(4) *The firemen, who the managers sacked, will meet in the engine shed*

Sentence (3) implies that only some firemen were sacked by the managers, and just those fireman will meet. This is called a 'restrictive relative clause' since it restricts the reference of the head noun *firemen* (to: just those firemen who were sacked).

Sentence (4) implies that all the firemen are meeting, and that they were all sacked; it is called a 'non-restrictive relative clause' since it does not delimit the reference of the head noun.

A proper noun has unique reference and so any relative clause to it must be non-restrictive, e.g. *Amos, who I introduced you to last week, is coming to tea.* In a sentence like *My brother who lives in Athens won the lottery*, the relative clause must be non-restrictive if I have only one brother but may be restrictive if I have more than one, then indicating which of my brothers won the prize.

One can in fact usually infer from the intonation what type of relative clause is involved. A non-restrictive relative is like an inserted, parenthetical comment, and is set off by contrastive intonation (shown by commas in the written style). It could be considered as not really a part of the superordinate NP, but rather as an independent constituent in apposition with it. The relative pronoun in a non-restrictive clause is not likely to be replaced by *that*, and could not be omitted.

In a restrictive clause, a *wh*-relative pronoun (other than *whose*) may be replaced by *that* (which is here functioning as a kind of relative pronoun); or it can be omitted, so long as the coreferential NP was not in subject function in the relative clause. Thus, alternatives to (3) are *The firemen that the managers sacked . . .* and *The firemen the managers sacked . . .* (There are stylistic conditions operating—a relative pronoun is more likely to be replaced by *that* or omitted in informal talk, or when referring to some matter of little consequence, and a *wh*-form is more likely to be retained in a formal speech style, e.g. in a debate or a meeting, or when talking about some really significant happening.)

We mentioned that if the coreferential NP had been in subject slot then we can now think of this slot as being filled by the relative pronoun. This is why it cannot normally be omitted: a tensed verb must be preceded by a subject NP. Thus, if only some managers sacked firemen one could say, with a restrictive relative clause:

> (5) *The managers who/that sacked firemen have saved money*
>   *for the company*

and *who/that* cannot be omitted.

Restrictive relative clauses that have a coreferential subject NP and refer to present time can have a reduced version; the relative pronoun is omitted and the verb is put in *-ing* form. Thus, corresponding to

(6) *Those managers who/that are sacking firemen are saving money for the company*

we can have:

(7) *Those managers sacking firemen are saving money for the company*

In the case of *sack*, and other verbs which refer to present time through the *be . . . -ing* auxiliary, it looks as if (7) is derived from (6) by omission of the relative pronoun and the tensed form of *be* (with the *-ing* on the retained verb being a residue of the *be- . . . ing* auxiliary).

However, reduced relatives like (7) also occur with those verbs that use present tense, rather than *be . . . -ing,* to refer to present time (see §2.3). That is, we get *Anyone owning a gun must register it* and *People knowing the whereabouts of the diamonds are asked to keep quiet*, which relate to *Anyone who owns a gun must register it* and *People who know the whereabouts of the diamonds are asked to keep quiet* rather than to the ungrammatical **Anyone who is owning a gun must register it* and **People who are knowing the whereabouts of the diamonds are asked to keep quiet*. A related example is *Anyone having seen the diamonds should keep quiet*, which relates to the present perfect sentence *Anyone who has seen the diamonds should keep quiet* rather than to **Anyone who is having seen the diamonds should keep quiet* (as pointed out in §2.3, the auxiliary *be . . . -ing* can follow but not precede *have . . . -en*).

These reduced present-time restrictive relatives are only found when the coreferential NP was in subject function. There is no reduced counterpart of *Those firemen (who/that) the managers are sacking will meet in the engine shed*; that is, we do not get **Those firemen the managers sacking will meet in the engine shed*, parallel to (7).

A restrictive relative clause may sometimes be moved out of its NP to the end of the main clause, usually being set off from the rest of the clause by appositional intonation; this is found in colloquial styles (*That man got sacked, who you were praising yesterday*) and also in legal English (*Those persons will be prosecuted who are found in possession of illegal firearms*). Such an extraposed clause must retain its relative pronoun. (This is an example of a general preference for a 'heavy' constituent to come at the end of a main clause—see §2.11A.)

There are a number of other constructions that may relate to relative clauses; but there are varying opinions among grammarians of English about their exact syntactic status. Some scholars talk in terms of a special subtype of restrictive relative clause in which the determiner (or determiner plus head) of the superordinate NP are fused with the relative pronoun, as in the (b) sentences of:

(8a) *Those recipes which she used are marked in red*
(8b) *What recipes she used are marked in red*
(9a) *Any recipes which she used are marked in red*
(9b) *Whatever recipes she used are marked in red*
(10a) *That which he wrote was unbelievable*
(10b) *What he wrote was unbelievable*
(11a) *Our dog bites anyone who comes into the garden*
(11b) *Our dog bites whoever comes into the garden*
(12a) *He lives in the place where you'd like to live*
(12b) *He lives where you'd like to live*

The subordinate clauses in the (b) sentences of (8)–(12) have some of the properties of relative clauses but also behave in some ways like interrogatives.

Let us now return to non-restrictive relative clauses. Suppose all managers are sacking firemen; we can say:

(13) *The managers, who are sacking firemen, are saving money for the company*

We noted that the relative clause appears to be a parenthetical comment—almost an intrusion into the body of the main clause—and it is set off by contrastive intonation or commas. There are also constructions like:

(14) *The managers are saving money for the company, sacking firemen*

Now in (14) the comment *sacking firemen* is plainly non-restrictive, suggesting that (14) might be taken as derived from (13), with a reduced relative clause (*who are* being omitted) that is moved to the end of the main clause. A comment such as *sacking firemen* in (14) may sometimes be retained in its original NP or else be placed at the beginning of the main clause. Compare:

(15a) *John, who was wheezing noisily, came into the room*
(15b) *John, wheezing noisily, came into the room*
(15c) *John came into the room, wheezing noisily*
(15d) *John came, wheezing noisily, into the room*
(15e) *Wheezing noisily, John came into the room*

We also get constructions of this type where the 'host' NP, in the main clause, is a pronoun, e.g.

(16a) *He came, wheezing noisily, into the room*
(16b) *He came into the room, wheezing noisily*
(16c) *Wheezing noisily, he came into the room*

However, English does not allow a relative clause to follow a pronoun; that is, one does not get:

(16d) **He, who was wheezing noisily, came into the room*

This suggests that (16a–c) (and thus also (14) and (15b–e)) should perhaps not be regarded as involving reduced relative clauses, but instead as being a distinct construction type. The syntactic status of the 'comment clauses' in these sentences is not clear, and requires further detailed study.

There are similar constructions where a 'comment clause' relates to the object of the main clause (although here it could not normally be moved to the beginning of the main clause):

(17a) *We saw John in the garden, doing his weekly chores*

alongside the non-restrictive relative clause construction:

(17b) *We saw John, who was doing his weekly chores, in the garden*

Note that sentences of this type may be ambiguous as to whether a final comment relates to subject or to object of the main clause, e.g. *John painted Mary naked* could correspond to *John, who was naked, painted Mary* or to *John painted Mary, who was naked* (and this is in turn ambiguous between a situation in which Mary posed naked and one where she was naked only on the canvas with John having used his imagination as to what she looked like under her clothes).

2.7. Complement clauses

Every language has verbs which introduce direct speech, reporting the actual words which may have been uttered. Thus:

(18) *'Thatcher has won another election,' he announced*

(19) *She told me: '(You) pick up the towel!'*

(20) *'Put your bag in the top locker!' he instructed me*

(21) *'Is the Saab back yet?' Mary asked*

(22) *'Who left the window open?' John asked*

(23) *'Mary shall lead the parade,' Captain Smee decided*

(24) *'Jane was late again this morning,' the office boy mentioned on Tuesday*

(25) *'John is a fool,' declared Mary*

Verbs such as *announce, tell, instruct, ask, mention* and *declare* always refer to some speech event. *Decide* does not have to, but it can be used in this way, as in (23).

Many languages, including English, have alternative 'indirect speech' constructions in which what was said is coded as a subordinate clause—called a 'complement clause'—in syntactic construction with the verb of speaking. (In fact the phenomenon of complement clauses covers a good deal more than indirect speech, as we shall show.)

English has a variety of complement clauses. The most straightforward involves placing *that* before the 'speech clause', as in:

(18a) *He announced [that Thatcher had won another election]*

(19a) *She told me [that I should pick up the towel]*

(20a) *He instructed me [that I should put my bag in the top locker]*

(23a) *Captain Smee decided [that Mary should lead the parade]*

(24a) *The office boy mentioned on Tuesday [that Jane had been/was late again that morning]*

(25a) *Mary declared that [John was a fool]*

Examining these carefully we see that present tense in direct speech (*has won* in (18), *is* in (25)) becomes past in indirect speech (*had won* in (18a), *was* in (25a)) if the main clause is in past tense. Present tense would be retained if the verb of speaking were also in present—compare *'Mary is winning,' John says* and *John says that Mary is winning*. The past tense (*was late*) of direct speech in

(24) may either be retained or replaced by past-plus-perfect (*had been late*) in (24a). (This tense replacement in indirect speech can be called 'back-shifting'—see Huddleston 1984: 150 ff., Quirk and Greenbaum 1973: 342 ff.) Where the direct speech is an order or resolution, as in (19), (20) and (23), then the modal *should* is introduced in the *that* complement clause, as in (19a), (20a), (23a). Finally, deictic elements which were originally oriented to the pragmatic situation of the direct speech must be reoriented to the situation of the verb of saying: *your* in (20) becomes *my* in (20a); the optional—but always implicit—*you* in (19) becomes *I* in (19a), and *this morning* in (24) must be replaced by *that morning* in (24a).

Complement clauses which code questions begin with a *wh*-word in place of *that*, e.g.

(21a) *Mary asked [whether/if the Saab was back yet]*

(22a) *John asked [who had left the window open]*

If the direct question was of the polar variety (expecting 'yes' or 'no' as answer) then the complement clause will begin with *whether* or *if*; if the direct question began with *who, whom, whose, what, which, how, why, where* or *when* then this is retained at the front of the complement clause (see also §2.9.1). Once again, present in direct speech becomes past in indirect (*is* in (21) corresponding to *was* in (21a)) and past becomes past perfect (*left* in (22), *had left* in (22a)) if the main verb is in past tense.

A third variety of indirect speech construction is exemplified by:

(24b) *The office boy mentioned on Tuesday [Mary's having been late again that morning]*

Here the subject of the complement clause takes possessive ending *'s* and the first word of the VP is in *-ing* form (there is no tense inflection). Note that the perfect auxiliary construction *having been late* in (24b) corresponds to past tense *was late* of (24).

A further construction type involves placing *for* at the beginning of the complement clause and *to* before the VP, which loses its tense inflection (the first word of the VP appearing in base form):

(23b) *Captain Smee decided [for Mary to lead the parade]*

Note that although the direct speech in (23) includes a modal *shall*,

33

no corresponding form (*shall* or *should*) can be included in the complement clause of (23b). We refer to (23b) as a 'Modal (FOR) TO complement construction'.

The same construction type is used when a direct speech order, as in (19) and (20), is coded into indirect speech. Here the *for* must be omitted, giving a complement clause marked just by *to*; the subject of the complement clause is now also object of the main clause (here, *me*):

(19b)　*She told me to pick up the towel*
(20b)　*He instructed me to put my bag in the top locker*

If the direct speech concerns a judgement (which generally involves the copula *be*), as in (25), then this may be coded into indirect speech through a second type of TO complement clause, which we call 'Judgement TO':

(25b)　*Mary declared John to be a fool*

There is one further type of complement clause that involves *to*; it has a *wh-* word before the *to*, e.g.

(20c)　*He instructed me where to put my bag*

This is not an exact correspondent of the direct speech sentence (20), but rather a description of it.

Many verbs of speaking can have an NP, giving the content of the speech act, in object function, e.g.

(18c)　*He announced* [*the election result*]
(21c)　*Mary asked* [*a tricky question*]
(23c)　*Captain Smee decided on* [*the order of procession*]
(24c)　*The office boy mentioned* [*Mary's latest misdemeanour*]

Announce, *ask*, *decide* (*on*) and *mention* are transitive verbs. They may occur in apposition to a statement of direct speech, which is in lieu of a constituent in object function. Or they can take a syntactic object, which may be either an NP (as in (18c), (21c), (23c), (24c)) or a complement clause (as in (18a), (21a), (22a), (23a/b), (24a/b)). The verbs *tell* and *instruct* (in (19) and (20)) already have an NP object and this can be followed by direct speech or an indirect speech complement clause; it is also possible to have a further NP in place of the complement clause, e.g. *She told me my instructions*, *He instructed me in the proper procedure*.

Verbs from a number of other semantic types, in addition to the

SPEAKING type, may have a complement clause as alternative to an NP, in object or subject function, etc., e.g.

(26a) *I believed John/John's story*

(26b) *I believed that John told the truth*

(26c) *I believed John to have told the truth*

(27a) *The exam results delighted Mr Smith*

(27b) *His daughter's having gained first class honours delighted Mr Smith*

(27c) *That his daughter had gained first class honours delighted Mr Smith*

(28a) *Mary began her lunch at noon*

(28b) *Mary began eating her lunch at noon*

(28c) *Mary began to eat her lunch at noon*

It will be seen that some verbs allow several varieties of complement clause to fill a certain functional slot (sometimes with a substantial difference in meaning), e.g. *wish*, like *tell*, accepts both THAT and Modal (FOR) TO clauses; *mention* and *delight* take THAT and ING; *begin* takes ING and TO; and *plan* and *remember* take all of THAT, ING and Modal (FOR) TO. Other verbs only accept a single variety of complement clause, e.g. *ensure* with THAT, *want* with TO, and *finish* with ING.

There are of course a number of semantic types all of whose verbs demand an NP (not a complement clause) for each functional slot, e.g. *hit, take, put, break, give*. Chapters 4, 5 and 6 provide a detailed semantic and syntactic description of each verb type, stating which may occur with complement clauses.

The types which take complement clauses in object, subject, or some other functional slot are BEGINNING, TRYING, HURRYING, DARING, WANTING, POSTPONING, MAKING, HELPING, SEEM, MATTER, ATTENTION, THINKING, DECIDING, LIKING, ANNOYING, COMPARING, RELATING, ACTING, HAPPENING and of course SPEAKING. Chapter 7 deals fairly thoroughly with this topic, describing the meaning of each variety of complement clause, their syntactic statuses and the possibilities for coreferential omission etc., and the semantic basis for which verb occurs with which complements. The remainder of this section gives a preliminary sketch of the syntax of the seven varieties of complement clause in English.

(A) THAT complement clauses are exemplified in (18a), (19a), (20a), (23a), (24a), (25a), (26b) and (27c); and **(B)** WH- clauses in (21a) and (22a). Both of these have the full structure of a main clause, with obligatory subject, obligatory tense on the first word of the VP, and the full range of VP possibilities (modals, progressive *be*, perfect *have*, passive *be*). A THAT or WH-complement can have its subject coreferential with subject or object of the main clause, but it may never be omitted, e.g. *I promised you that I would go*; *I promised you that you could go*.

Besides introducing one variety of complement clause, *that* also functions as a deictic noun (*Did you see that?*), as a demonstrative determiner (*Did you see that car?*) and to introduce restrictive relative clauses, e.g.

(29)　*Everyone believed* [*the man* [*that had hired you*]]

Note that here the relative clause *that had hired you* is a constituent of the object NP *the man that had hired you*. When (29) is passivised the whole object NP becomes passive subject:

(29a)　[*The man* [*that had hired you*]] *was believed* (*by everyone*)

We mentioned in §2.6 that colloquial styles of English allow a restrictive relative clause to be moved from a subject NP to the end of the main clause, as in

(29b)　*The man was believed* (*by everyone*), [*that had hired you*]

Compare the relative clause marked by *that* in (29) with a complement clause introduced by *that*, as in

(30)　*Everyone believed* [*that the man had hired you*]

Here the clause *that the man had hired you* is object of *believe*, and can become passive subject:

(30a)　[*That the man had hired you*] *was believed* (*by everyone*)

A THAT clause in (underlying or derived passive) subject function can be extraposed to the end of the main clause, its subject slot before the predicate being then filled by the impersonal form *it*:

(30b)　*It was believed* (*by everyone*) [*that the man had hired you*]

Thus, although (29) and (30) have similar surface form, differing only in the order of *the man* and *that*, they do have entirely different syntactic structures and derivational possibilities.

Whether, *if* or a *wh-* word introducing a WH- complement clause can never be omitted. The complementiser *that* may often be omitted from a THAT clause which immediately follows the predicate, e.g. *I think (that) he's stupid*, *It was believed (that) the foreman had hired you*, or from a THAT clause which immediately follows the object NP of a verb like *promise* or *threaten* (a verb for which the main clause object is not expected to be coreferential with the complement clause subject), e.g. *I promised Mary (that) John could go*. *That* can never be omitted from a complement clause in subject relation (not from (27c) or (30a)) and is seldom omitted from a complement clause which follows the object NP of a verb for which there is an expectation that main clause object will be coreferential with complement clause subject, e.g. not from *I instructed Mary that John should go*.

That is unlikely to be omitted from a post-predicate complement clause if an adverb, a conjunction or a peripheral NP intervenes between it and the predicate—thus, *that* is generally retained in *It was believed implicitly that the foreman had hired you* and in *It was believed, however, that the foreman had hired you*. And *that* would generally be retained in (30b) if the agentive phrase *by everyone* were included. The determining factors on omission of *that* from a complement clause which immediately follows a predicate are largely stylistic—it is more likely to be omitted in casual than in formal speech, and more likely to be omitted if the reference of the complement clause is to some minor item of information rather than an important piece of reportage. Compare *He announced (that) it was eggs for breakfast*, where *that* is quite dispensable, with (18a) *He announced that Thatcher had won another election*, where it would be unusual not to include *that* (see also §2.12B). A few verbs will almost invariably include *that* in a following complement clause, and this is because they carry a formal aura of meaning, e.g. *require, propose, undertake, order, request* (note that these verbs are likely also to include *should* in their THAT clause and the *should* can be omitted—see below).

Of the verbs which take THAT complements, there are a number which typically include a modal in the complement clause. The identity of the modal depends partly on the semantics of the main verb and partly on the choice of subject for the complement clause, e.g. *I wish that I could . . .* but *I wish that you would . . .*

There is a group of verbs that commonly take *should*; indeed, the meaning of the verb implies 'should' in the complement clause. It is thus scarcely surprising that the *should* is generally omitted, producing what appears to be a tenseless, modal-less THAT clause, e.g. *order*, *command*, *suggest*, *propose*, *insist*, *require*, and:

> (31) *She demanded that he (should) empty the bin*
> (32) *He recommended that we (should) be told*

(Note that *should* is not omittable from THAT complements with other types of verbs, i.e. not from *She decided/knew/believed that he should do it*.) Partial justification for saying that *She demanded that he empty the bin* involves an underlying *should* comes from the fact that *empty* is here in base form, which would be expected after a modal. Compare this with *She says that he empties the bin*, where the verb *empties* is in tense form, and must be the initial element of its VP.

Wh- words in English may have a number of functions: (*a*) they may be used as interrogatives, e.g. *Who did you see?*, *What is that?*; (*b*) they can introduce a *wh-* complement clause, as in (21a), (22a); (*c*) they may introduce relative clauses e.g. *I rather like the man who you married*; (*d*) they can be the fusion of part of an NP and the introducer to a relative clause within that NP, e.g. *she always takes what(ever) money I earn*.

All of *who*, *whom*, *whose*, *what*, *which*, *how*, *why*, *where* and *when* have functions (*a*) and (*b*). All except *how* and *what* occur in function (*c*) (*what* is in fact used with this function in some low-prestige dialects, e.g. *I like the car what you bought*; for other dialects *which* effectively replaces *what*, functioning as NP head whereas in (*a*), (*b*) and (*d*) it is generally modifier to an NP head). In function (*d*) we find all except *whose* and *why*; *-ever* can be added to those *wh-* words that occur in (*d*), usually carrying a difference in meaning (compare (8a/b) and (9a/b)). *Whether* and *if* only have function (*d*), introducing complement clauses. *If* also functions as a clause linker—see §2.10. *Whether* is the only form in English whose sole function is to mark a complement clause.

Complement clause constructions and 'fused' restrictive relative clause constructions can appear very similar, as with:

> (33) *He ate what they put on the plate* (Relative clause construction)

(34) *He knew what they put on the plate* (Complement clause construction)

They can be distinguished on semantic grounds. *What* in (33) is a fusion of *that which*—he ate 'that', which is something concrete, and whose referent is further specified by the relative clause *which they put on the plate*. Thus, *ate* in (33) has an NP (which includes a restrictive relative clause) as object, *knew* in (34) has a complement clause *what they put on the plate* as object—the speaker knows a fact, referred to by this clause. Note that *know* could alternatively have a THAT clause as object, e.g. *He knew that they put apples on the plate*; but *eat* could not—**He ate that they put apples on the plate* is nonsensical.

(C) ING complement clauses are exemplified by (24b), (27b), (28b). The VP does not show tense inflection; instead, its first word is in *-ing* form. It may not include a modal, but can include aspect markers *have* or *have* plus *be* (but not just *be*—see §2.11C) and/or passive *be*. The subject of an ING complement clause may be different from main clause subject and is then sometimes marked by possessive ending *'s* (or, if a pronoun, it is in possessive form). But the subject can be coreferential with main clause subject, and is then usually omitted from the complement clause (since the VP in an ING clause is not tensed, it does not have to be preceded by a subject), e.g.

(35) *I remember John's/your winning the lottery*
(36) *I remember (?*my) winning the lottery*.

A fair number of verbs form a derived noun by the suffixation of *-ing*. It is important to distinguish between an NP with such a deverbal noun as head, in (37), and an ING complement clause with the corresponding verb as predicate head, as in (38):

(37) *I admired Mary's singing of 'Salty Dog' in church*
(38) *I admired Mary's singing 'Salty Dog' in church*

There is a meaning difference—(38) states that I admired the fact that she did it (Mary's temerity in giving voice to a bawdy song in a sacred place); (37) states that I admired the manner in which she sang (her syncopated style, etc.). There are concomitant syntactic differences: the object in (37) has the structure of an NP, with *Mary's* as determiner (*the* could be used instead) and with the preposition *of* introducing the post-head NP *'Salty Dog'*. In (38) *Mary* is the subject of the predicate *singing* (*Mary's* here could not be replaced by *the*), with the object *'Salty Dog'* immediately following the transitive verb. The noun *singing* in (37) could be modified by an adjective, e.g. *quiet singing*, whereas the verb *singing* in (38) would be modified by an adverb, e.g. *singing quietly*.

Of course a shorter version, *I admired Mary's singing*, is ambiguous—the NP-as-object reading implies that I admired the way she sang, and the complement-clause-as-object reading indicates that I admired the fact of her singing.

The *'s* on the subject of an ING complement clause is often omitted, especially in the most informal speech, and then the series I or unmarked form of the pronoun is used (§2.2), i.e. *him*, *her*, etc., not *he*, *she*, etc. The *'s* tends to be dropped most often from an inanimate subject, e.g. *I don't like the washing machine* (?*'s) *shuddering every time it hits 'spin' on the cycle*. The *'s* can be dropped from (24b), (27b), (35), (38) and from:

> (39) *I hate that man('s) watching Mary*

It was mentioned in §2.6 that there are constructions which appear to involve a reduced version of a restricted relative clause (although their exact syntactic status is unclear). Thus, corresponding to *I hate that man who is watching Mary*, we can have

> (40) *I hate that man watching Mary*

Examples (39) and (40) have quite different meanings: (39) states that I hate the fact of that man's watching Mary, while (40) states that I hate a particular man, whose identity is specified to the hearer by the fact that he is watching Mary—the reason I hate him may be unconnected with his watching Mary.

When the *'s* is omitted (39) coincides in form with (40) and *I hate that man watching Mary* is thus ambiguous between the readings 'NP with restrictive relative clause relating to object' and 'complement clause as object'.

The suffix *-ing* to a verbal root has a wide range of uses in English grammar, and it is important to distinguish between them. They are: (i) to mark a verb that follows the progressive auxiliary *be*, as in *she is cooking potatoes*; related to this are reduced forms of restrictive relative clauses referring to present time, as in (40), and what may be reduced forms of non-restrictive relatives, as in (14), (15b/c/d/e); (ii) to mark the predicate in an adverbal clause of time such as *Having passed his final exam, John jumped for joy* (§2.5); (iii) to mark the predicate in an ING complement clause; (iv) to mark the predicate in a further type of complement clause, FROM ING—see (G) below; (v) to mark nouns derived from some verbs e.g. *the cleaning of the stove* (§2.1); (vi) to mark adjectives derived from verbs, as in *an exhausting night*. Note that senses (i) and (iii) refer to an activity extended in time, and so too do (v) and (vi), in slightly different ways.

There are two kinds of complement clause that are similar in form but quite different in meaning. The first is introduced by *for*, includes *to* immediately before the complement clause verb and has a 'Modal-type' meaning (e.g. *I intended for Mary to win*). The complement clause subject may be omitted when it is coreferential with an NP in the main clause, and *for* is then automatically dropped (e.g. *I intended to win*). But *for* may also be omitted, in certain semantic circumstances, when the complement clause subject is retained (e.g. *I intended Mary to win*). The second kind has *to* immediately before the complement clause verb, but no *for*, and carries a 'Judgement' meaning (e.g. *I consider Mary to be beautiful*). Like ING clauses, both of these kinds of TO complement may include *have* or *be* auxiliaries, but not a modal or tense inflection.

(D) Modal (FOR) TO complement clauses are exemplified by (23b) and:

   (41) *[For John to have been so foolhardy] scares me*
   (42) *I would love it [for Mary to sing the St Louis Blues]*
   (43) *Everybody agreed [for John to give the funeral oration]*

The subject of a Modal (FOR) TO clause (together with the *for*) may be omitted when it is coreferential with a core NP of the main clause. The syntactic conditions for this omission are:

	function of complement clause in main clause	function of coreferential NP in main clause
I	object	subject
II	subject	object
III	post-object constitutent	object

Scheme I is illustrated by *I longed for Mary to win, I longed to win*; II by *For John to have to work Sundays annoyed Mary, To have to work Sundays annoyed Mary*; III by *I urged all the teachers for their pupils to take care crossing the street, I urged all the pupils to take care crossing the street.* (There is a single addition to III, which only holds in some dialects of English. *Promise* will omit the subject of a post-object complement clause when it is coreferential with main clause subject, not with main clause object, e.g. *I promised John for my charlady to clean his flat, I promised John to clean his flat.*)

A Modal (FOR) TO clause may drop the *for* with the complement clause subject still being retained; this then becomes syntactic object of the main verb. Compare:

(44) *I chose for Mary to lead the parade*
(45) *I chose Mary to lead the parade*

In (45) *Mary* is object of the main clause verb *chose* (and can become passive subject, e.g. *Mary was chosen to lead the parade*). Note the difference in meaning between (44) and (45). It would be appropriate for me to say (44) if, as organiser of the parade, I communicated my decision to other people who would in turn inform Mary. But if I stood before the participants for the parade and pointed to Mary as I made the choice, then (45) would be the appropriate construction to use. (There is fuller discussion of the semantic role of *for* in §7.2.4.)

For may only be omitted (and the complement clause subject retained) when it immediately follows a transitive verb. This correlates with the syntactic shift we have just observed—that the complement clause subject then becomes surface syntactic object of the preceding main clause verb. That is, *for* may not be omitted in any of the following circumstances:

(i)   when the complement clause is in subject relation in the main clause, e.g. *For John to be out so late worries Mary*;
(ii) when the complement clause follows a main clause object, e.g. *It worries Mary for John to be out so late, I told the captain for his men to clean the latrines*;
(iii) when the complement clause follows an adjective, e.g. *It is usual for a man to open the door for a lady* (see also the discussion of Modal (FOR) TO complement clauses with adjectives in §3.2);

(iv) when the complement clause follows *it*, e.g. *I hate it for John to pick his nose in public* (*for* may be omitted only when *it* is also dropped, e.g. *I hate John to pick his nose in public*, not **I hate it John to pick his nose in public*);

(v) when the complement clause follows an adverb, e.g. *I chose quite deliberately for Mary to lead the parade.*

Some main verbs may not omit the *for*, when complement clause subject is retained, e.g. *decide, offer, remember, know*. Some may optionally omit *for*, with a meaning difference, e.g. *choose* (as in (44/5)) and *propose, intend, mean, desire, wish*. A third set generally omit *for* when the complement clause immediately follows the main verb, e.g. *want* in *I want you to go*, but will retain it when the verb and complement clause are separated, as when an adverb comes between them, e.g. *I want very much for you to go* or in constructions such as *What I want is for you to go*; other verbs behaving like this are *need, order*, and *urge* (see also §6.2.1). A final set must always omit the *for* (and thus cannot include an adverb immediately after the main clause verb), e.g. *force, cause, allow, permit*.

There are also verbs that take what is essentially a Modal (FOR) TO complement clause but demand that the complement clause subject be identical to main clause subject and thus omitted (together with *for*), e.g. *begin* (as in (28c)), *try, hasten*.

All of the four kinds of complement clause described so far— THAT, WH-, ING and Modal (FOR) TO—may fill object slot in the main clause and can then become passive subject, as in (30a) and:

(46) [*Where he put it*] *is not known*

(47) [*John('s) winning the lottery*] *is fondly remembered by all the office staff*

(43a) [*For John to give the funeral oration*] *was agreed* (*on*)

(Many clauses with a Modal (FOR) TO clause as object, and some with complement clauses of other kinds as object, do not readily passivise. This is for semantic—and not syntactic—reasons; see §9.4.)

As already mentioned, once a Modal (FOR) TO complement drops the *for*, then its subject becomes main clause object and it is this that becomes passive subject, not the whole complement clause (see (45)).

THAT, WH- and Modal (FOR) TO clauses in (underlying or derived passive) subject function may be extraposed to the end of the main clause, with *it* filling the subject slot. Thus (30b) and:

(46a) *It is not known* [*where he put it*]
(41a) *It scares me* [*for John to have been so foolhardy*]
(43b) *It was agreed* [*for John to give the funeral oration*]

Extraposition is equally possible for a Modal (FOR) TO clause in subject relation that has its subject (and the preceding *for*) omitted under identity with the main clause object:

(48) [*To have to give the welcoming speech*] *terrified me*
(48a) *It terrified me* [*to have to give the welcoming speech*]

Note that a complement clause may not usually be extraposed over another complement clause. That is, a clause in subject relation is not open to extraposition if there is also a complement clause in object relation to the verb, e.g. corresponding to:

(49) [*That Pegasus won the race*] *indicates* [*that Bellerophon is a fine rider*]

it is not possible to say:

(49a) **It indicates* [*that Bellerophon is a fine rider*] [*that Pegasus won the race*]

ING clauses are generally not extraposable. We can get what is called 'right dislocation', in which the two clauses are set off by contrastive, appositional intonation (and *it* refers to 'Mary's singing in church'), as in:

(38a) *It was admired, Mary's singing 'Salty Dog' in church*

But this is a different grammatical phenomenon from extraposition.

(E) Judgement TO complement clauses are exemplified by (25b), (26c) and:

(50) *I noticed John to be sleeping/incompetent/badly bitten*

All Judgement TO constructions involve a transitive verb, an object NP (which is simultaneously subject of the complement clause), and *to* followed by the complement clause predicate. This predicate most often includes *be*, which can be progressive auxiliary, passive auxiliary, or copula, although other possibilities do occur (as in (26c) where the predicate begins with *have*).

Judgement TO constructions appear syntactically similar to a Modal (FOR) TO clause in object relation, with *for* omitted but complement clause subject retained, e.g. *I told John to sleep*. There is a critical semantic difference: if there is a THAT complement corresponding to a Modal (FOR) TO clause then it will generally include a modal, e.g. *I told John that he should sleep*; but if there is a THAT complement clause corresponding to a Judgement TO complement then it cannot include a modal, e.g. *I noticed that John was sleeping*. There is further discussion of this in §7.2.3.

Some verbs that take a Judgement TO clause may drop the complementiser *to* plus following *be*, e.g.

(51) *I consider John (to be) stupid*

But others do not allow this omission, e.g. *I know John to be stupid* and not **I know John stupid*. This is discussed further in §7.2.6.

To be can never be omitted from the maximal form of a Modal (FOR) TO complement, e.g. not from *I hoped for the house to be clean when I returned* or from *I asked for him to be shot*. There is, however, a small set of verbs that can omit *to be* when *for* is also omitted, e.g.

(52) *I want the house (to be) clean when I return*
(53) *I ordered him (to be) shot*

There are also just a few verbs that omit *to* from a Modal (FOR) TO complement in post-predicate position. They are *make*, *let* and the causal sense of *have* from the MAKING type (compare *They made John go* with *They forced John to go*, which retains the *to*); a subset of ATTENTION verbs, which take a complement similar in form to Modal (FOR) TO (e.g. *They saw John swim*); and just *know* from the THINKING type (e.g. *I've never known him ask such a question before*). Note, however, that the *to* must be included in the corresponding passive, e.g. *John was made to go*, *John was seen to swim*. (See also §7.2.5.)

To does of course have other functions in the grammar of English—introducing a recipient NP (*give it to John*) or an NP referring to a destination (*go to Moscow*). It is also a (preferred) short form of the clause linker *in order to* (see §2.10), as in (54), which on the surface looks similar to the complement clause construction (55):

(54) *He went to bathe*
(55) *He likes to bathe*

There are profound syntactic differences. *Go* in (54) is an intransitive verb and its clause is linked by (*in order*) *to* with the clause *bathe*. *Like* in (55) is a transitive verb (e.g. *He likes the seaside*) and here *to bathe* is a complement clause; alternatives would be *He likes bathing*, *He likes Mary to bathe*, etc. The semantic type of the first verb in a construction like (54/5) enables one to infer the kind of construction that is involved.

(**F**) WH- TO could perhaps be regarded as a sub-type of Modal (FOR) TO complements. A *wh-* word (other than *why* or *if*) simply precedes the *to* (the VP has the same possibilities as in ING, Modal (FOR) TO and Judgement TO clauses). Thus (20c) and:

(56) *I don't know who to blame*
(57) *They remembered where to look*
(58) *I'll choose when to go*

WH- TO clauses do not have any independent subject; their subject must be coreferential with the subject of the main clause or with its object (e.g. *I told John who to see*). A *wh-* element such as *who* (as in (56)) or *what* can refer to any constituent of the clause except its subject.

(**G**) FROM ING complements are parallel to a variety of Modal (FOR) TO clause, in object relation, that has the *for* omitted but complement clause subject retained. Compare:

(59) *John forced him to open the door*
(60) *John prevented him (from) opening the door*
(61) *John persuaded him to see the doctor*
(62) *John dissuaded him from seeing the doctor*

Him has the same syntactic status in all of (59)–(62); it is underlying subject of the following verb, and is also object NP for the main verb, which may become passive subject, e.g.

(59a) *He was forced to open the door*
(60a) *He was prevented from opening the door*

The VP in a FROM ING clause has its first verb in -*ing* form. It may include perfect *have*, progressive *be*, passive *be* but not a modal or any tense inflection (this is the same as for ING and the various kinds of TO complement). Interestingly, the *from* may optionally be omitted following a verb of negative causation (*prevent*, *stop*, *save*) when used in the active, but is retained in the passive—compare (60) and (60a). It can never be dropped after a verb from the SPEAKING type (*forbid*, *discourage*, *dissuade*, *prohibit*). The semantic conditioning of *from* omission is discussed in §7.2.9.

ING, FROM ING and all kinds of TO complement clause may not have tense inflection in their VP. How do they convey information about time reference, which is coded through tense in main clauses and in THAT and WH- complements? It appears that the auxiliary element *have*, which normally indicates perfect aspect, here doubles for past tense and perfect aspect; present non-perfect is marked by the absence of *have*. Compare the THAT constructions in:

(63) *I believe that Mary eats mangoes*
(64) *I believe that Mary ate the mango* (*yesterday*)
(65) *I believe that Mary has eaten the mango* (*that you brought*)
(66) *I believe that Mary had eaten the mango* (*that you left there*)

with the corresponding TO constructions:

(63a) *I believe Mary to eat mangoes*
(64a/65a/66a) *I believe Mary to have eaten the mango*

Here *have* in the TO construction corresponds to all of past (in (64)), present plus perfect (in (65)) and past plus perfect (in (66)). (This is similar to the 'back-shifting' of indirect speech, mentioned at the beginning of this section; see Huddleston 1984: 150 ff., Quirk and Greenbaum 1973: 342 ff.) An identical correspondence applies in ING clauses—all of *I mentioned that Mary ate/has eaten/ had eaten the mango* correspond to *I mentioned Mary's having eaten the mango*; see also (24b).

The auxiliary *be* carries over its progressive meaning into all varieties of complement clause, e.g. *I notice that Mary is eating mangoes* (*every time we go past*) and *I notice Mary to be eating mangoes* (*every time we go past*); see also §2.11C.

There are a number of instances in English where a verb base plus preposition effectively functions as a complete lexical verb e.g.

decide on, *hope for*, *complain about*, *rely on*, *agree on* (§1.4). The preposition is retained before an NP object or an ING complement clause as object but must be omitted—by an automatic rule of English grammar—before complementisers *that*, *for* and *to* (no verb of this kind occurs with a FROM ING complement clause). The preposition may be omitted or retained before a complementiser beginning with *wh*-. Thus (see also (43a/b) and §2.11B):

(67a) *He decided on John*
(67b) *He decided that John would be captain*
(67c) *He decided (on) who would be captain*
(68a) *She complained about the interruption*
(68b) *She complained about John's interrupting her recital*
(68c) *She complained that John interrupted her recital*
(69a) *I'm hoping for a promotion*
(69b) *I'm hoping to get promoted*
(69c) *I'm hoping that I'll get promoted*

A number of HUMAN PROPENSITY adjectives may take a preposition and then an NP or complement clause, e.g. *afraid of*, *sorry about*, *proud of*, *jealous of/about*, *careful about*. Once again, the preposition is retained before an NP or an ING complement, but dropped before *that*, *for* or *to*, e.g.

(70a) *John is afraid of the dark*
(70b) *John is afraid of going out in the dark*
(70c) *John is afraid to go out in the dark*
(70d) *John is afraid that it will be too dark*
(71a) *Mary is sorry about her mistake*
(71b) *Mary is sorry about making an error in the calculation*
(71c) *Mary is sorry that she made an error in the calculation*

In §2.5 it was mentioned that adverbal elements can occur at many positions in a clause but they may not come between predicate and an object NP. However, adverbal elements may come between a predicate and a complement clause. Consider:

(72a) *Yesterday I remembered the appointment*
(72b) **I remembered yesterday the appointment*
(72c) *I remembered the appointment yesterday*
(73a) *Yesterday I remembered that I should see Mary*
(73b) *I remembered yesterday that I should see Mary*
(73c) *I remembered that I should see Mary yesterday*

Table 2.1. *Syntactic features of complement clauses*

	THAT (A)	WH- (B)	-ING (C)	Modal (FOR) TO (D)	Judgement TO (E)	WH- TO (F)	FROM -ING (G)
1. complement clause VP is tensed	x	x	–	–	–	–	–
2. modal may be included in complement clause VP	x	x	–	–	–	–	–
3. subject NP can be omitted from complement clause when coreferential with an NP in main clause	–	–	x	x	$-^1$	x^2	$-^1$
4. when complement clause is post-predicate, its subject can become main clause object	–	–	–	x	x^1	–	x^1
5. complement clause may be in object relation, with potential to become passive subject	x	x	x	x	–	–	–
6. adverbal element may come between main clause predicate and complement clause as object	x	x	–	x	–	–	–
7. complement clause may follow object NP of main clause	x	x	–	x	$-^1$	–	$-^1$
8. complement clause may be in subject relation	x	x	x	x	–	–	–
9. complement clause may be extraposed from subject position	x	x	–	x			
10. preposition is omitted before the complement clause	x	opt.	–	x		opt.	

Key: 'x' indicates 'yes', '–' indicates 'no', a blank shows that the question was not applicable; 'opt.' = optional.

[1] Subject NP of complement clause always becomes surface syntactic object of main clause (but still functions as complement clause subject, as can be seen from reflexivisation).

[2] Subject NP must be coreferential with main clause subject or object, and omitted.

Sentences (72a), (73a) and (73b) state that I did the remembering yesterday. (73c) states that the time I was to see Mary was yesterday; (72c) (which effectively corresponds to both (73b) and (73c), since (72b) is ungrammatical) is ambiguous between the remembering being yesterday and the appointment being yesterday.

An adverbal element may readily intervene between predicate and THAT, WH- or Modal (FOR) TO complement clauses, but is at best marginally acceptable before an ING complement in object function. Compare:

(74) *I mentioned yesterday that Mary had shot Fred*

(75) ?*I mentioned yesterday Mary's having shot Fred*

Most speakers prefer *Yesterday I mentioned Mary's having shot Fred* to (75).

Table 2.1 summarises some of the more important syntactic features of complement clauses. It will be seen that (A) THAT and (B) WH- have almost identical syntax; they differ only in the minor detail, under 10, that a preposition may optionally be retained before *wh-*. Varieties (E) Judgement TO, (F) WH- TO and (G) FROM ING also show strong similarities.

ING clauses stand apart from the others. The fact that an ING clause is not readily extraposable from subject position, in 9, and that it does not easily take a preceding adverb, in 6, suggests that ING clauses function more like NPs than do other varieties of complement clause. Be that as it may, an ING clause is quite different in structure from an NP, as we saw when comparing (37) and (38).

2.8. Word derivations

English has a number of derivational affixes that change word-class membership, but each applies to a limited set of words. Nouns formed from verbs include *amusement, punishment*; *suggestion, conclusion*; *blessing, singing*; *resemblance*; *pleasure*. Among adjectives derived from verbs are *adorable, persuasive, contributory*. Verbs derived from adjectives and nouns include *purify, glorify*; *equalise, itemise*; *blacken, lighten, threaten*. Most of these derivational endings are of French or Latin origin (notable exceptions being *-en* and *-ing*).

Quite a number of English words appear to belong to more than one word class, e.g.

adjective and verb: *dirty, clean, tidy, narrow*
noun and verb: *stone, butter, bridge, cash*
verb and noun: *walk, punch, look, sleep, catch, laugh, roast*

In each case, speakers have a clear intuition that one word class membership is primary and the other secondary. *Stone* is said to be firstly a noun, although it can also be used as a verb (e.g. *Stone the Christians!*). *Walk* is regarded as a verb, which can also be used as a noun (*That walk tired me out*). In the tabulation just given, the primary word-class membership is given first (as, indeed, it generally is in dictionary entries).

There are two ways of dealing with the facts reported in the last paragraph. One is to say that *stone, butter,* etc. are nouns pure and simple, while *walk, punch,* etc. are verbs. Then to state that all nouns may be head of an NP, but a subset of nouns (*stone, butter,* etc.) may also function as head of a VP (taking appropriate verbal endings); and that all verbs can be head of a VP but that a specified subset of verbs (*walk, punch,* etc.) can also be NP head (and will then take appropriate nominal endings). The other approach is to say that the head of a VP can only be a verb, etc., and that English has derivational processes, with zero marking, that derive verbs from some nouns (verb *stone* from noun *stone*), and so on.

Evidence for preferring the second (zero derivation) alternative in the case of English comes from considerations of pairs like:

(76)	adjective	*wide*	verb	*widen*
(77)	adjective	*narrow*	verb	*narrow*
(78)	verb	*converse*	noun	*conversation*
(79)	verb	*talk*	noun	*talk*
(80)	verb	*postpone*	noun	*postponement*
(81)	verb	*delay*	noun	*delay*

The words in each pair have related meanings. In each instance the first line shows an affix marking a derivational process. By analogy, it seems most satisfactory to say that the second line also involves a derivational process, with zero marking.

In summary, English lacks a full array of productive derivational affixes; the suffixes (mostly of foreign origin) that are used each occur with a restricted set of roots. As a result there is much use of 'zero derivation', i.e. use of a noun in verb function without any change in form, etc.

Some generalisations are possible. Many verbs referring to CORPOREAL function can also be used as nouns, e.g. *bite, swallow, drink, sniff, smell, taste, laugh, cry, sob, weep, wink, kiss, hug, pee*. And many nouns referring to implements can also be used as verbs, e.g. *spear, knife, saw, hammer, whip, nail, screw*.

2.9. Clause derivations

There are a number of ways in which the basic structure of a clause in English can be transformed. Only some of the more notable processes are outlined here.

2.9.1. Questions

To form a polar question (one expecting 'yes' or 'no' as answer), the first auxiliary verb, which bears a tense inflection, is moved to the front of the clause. Corresponding to *John was eating the halva* we get *Was John eating the halva?* and alongside *John had been eating the halva* there is *Had John been eating the halva?* There must be at least one verb in the auxiliary for question formation— if the VP contains none of *have, be* or a modal then *do* must be included to take the tense inflection; thus, corresponding to the statement *John ate the halva*, we get the question *Did John eat the halva?* Note that an auxiliary, or just tense, cannot be moved over a complement clause, in subject slot; to form a question the complement clause must be extraposed and replaced by *it*. That is, we must say *Is it surprising that we lost?*, rather than **Is that we lost surprising*, corresponding to *That we lost is surprising*.

A *wh-* question (expecting a phrase or clause as answer) involves the same fronting, and in addition a *wh-* word (*who, whom, whose, what, which, how, why, where* or *when*), which refers to some constituent of the main clause, must precede the preposed auxiliary word. Compare *John was hitting Mary* with *Who was hitting Mary?*; *Mary arrived yesterday* with *When did Mary arrive?* and *John ate the halva* with *What did John eat?* If the constituent being questioned had a preposition associated with it, then this may either be moved to initial position, before the *wh*-word, or it can be left in its underlying position in the clause. Thus, corresponding to *He owes his success to hard work* we can have either *What does he owe his success to?* or *To what does he owe his success?*

There is an important difference between a straightforward question and a WH- complement clause; the latter involves an initial *wh*- element, but no fronting of the first auxiliary word. Thus *Has he come?* and *She asked whether he had come*; and *Where did she hide the money?* alongside *He enquired where she had hidden the money*. Note also that WH- complement clauses occur with many verbs that do not introduce direct speech questions, e.g. *I know who did it, She remembered why he had built the boat* (see §7.2.1).

2.9.2. Causatives

Many languages have a special 'causative' affix, deriving a transitive from an intransitive verb (and a ditransitive verb from a transitive)—when *-dür* is added to *ölmek* 'to die' in Turkish, for instance, we get *öldürmek* 'to kill'. English, with its sparse morphology, lacks this, but does have two other means of coding causation. The first is the productive use of a verb from the secondary type MAKING (§6.3.1) with an intransitive or transitive verb in a TO complement clause, as in the (b) examples below. The other involves using some (but by no means all) basically intransitive verbs in a transitive construction, with the intransitive subject (S) becoming transitive object (O), and a new 'causer' NP being brought in for transitive subject (A) function; this is illustrated in (c) below.

(82a) *The child sat on the mat*
(82b) *Mary made the child sit on the mat*
(82c) *Mary sat the child on the mat*
(83a) *The piece of metal bent*
(83b) *Mary made the piece of metal bend*
(83c) *Mary bent the piece of metal*
(84a) *The pauper bled*
(84b) *John made the pauper bleed*
(84c) *John bled the pauper*

There is a difference in each case. Sentence (82c) implies that Mary picked up the child and put it sitting on the mat; for (82b) she could have got the child to sit by telling it to, or spanking it until it did. One could use (83c) when Mary changed the shape of the piece of metal with her hands, but (83b) when she heated it over a fire, so that it changed shape. Hearing (84c) one might presume that John was a doctor who drew blood from the pauper in a scientific manner to relieve some medical condition; for (84b) John might be a blackguard who bashed the pauper with a piece of lead pipe until he began to bleed.

The (c) sentences—a basically intransitive verb used transitively —imply careful and direct manipulation, whereas the periphrastic *make* constructions imply some more indirect means. (There are also of course semantic differences between the various verbs that can be used in (b) constructions—*make*, *cause*, *force*, etc.—see §6.3.1.)

For most intransitive/transitive verb pairs with intransitive S = transitive O—such as *sit*, *bend* and *bleed*—native speakers pick the intransitive sense as primary. However, there are some S = O pairs for which the transitive sense is generally considered primary, e.g. *I broke the vase*, *The vase broke*. Further discussion of this is provided in §§8.3.2–3.

Other verbs can be used both transitively and intransitively but with S = A, rather than S = O, e.g. *He doesn't smoke* and *He doesn't smoke a pipe*; *I've eaten* and *I've eaten lunch*; *They are playing* and *They are playing hopscotch*. These could perhaps be regarded as transitive verbs that may omit an object NP under certain specific conditions. Note that some verbs (such as *take*, *hit*, *make*, *prefer*) can only omit an object NP under very special circumstances (e.g. when contrasted with another verb, as in *He takes more than he gives*), and others may do so only when the object can be inferred from the context or from the previous discourse, e.g. *You choose!* The general question of transitivity and object deletion is dealt with in §8.3.1.

2.9.3. Passives

In the passive derivation a direct object becomes subject of the derived intransitive construction; *be* is inserted immediately before the head of the VP, and the following head verb is in *-en* form. Thus, corresponding to *Fred stole the Saab*, there is *The Saab was stolen* (*by Fred*).

An underlying transitive subject may almost always be included in a passive construction, marked by the preposition *by*. This can indicate the role which was primarily responsible for the activity that has resulted in the state described by the passive verb. In fact, a *by* phrase is only included in a smallish minority of actual passive clauses, in most styles of English.

Not all NPs that directly follow a verb can be passivised (i.e. become a passive subject)—not those in *possess an expensive house*, *resemble a famous film star*, or *stand fifteen minutes in the rain*, for instance. Some NPs that are introduced by a preposition may be passivisable, e.g. *This hat has been sat on* and *Has the new audition tape been listened to yet?* Chapter 9 discusses the syntax and semantics of passive constructions.

2.9.4. Promotion to subject

That role which is most likely to be relevant to the success of an activity is generally associated with the syntactic relation A (transitive subject), in a transitive clause. For *record*, this is the person doing the recording. If a VALUE adverb, such as *well*, is included, as in (85), it implies that the activity proceeded well owing to the efforts of John McDonald (the recording engineer) in A slot:

> (85) *John McDonald recorded the Hallé Orchestra well* (*with the Beyer microphone*) (*in studio B*)

But the success of a recording venture might be attributable to the qualities of the orchestra involved, or of the microphone used, or to the acoustic properties of the recording studio. To indicate these, any of the three non-A NPs could be promoted to the A slot (displacing the original A, which cannot be included in the three sentences below). If a promoted NP was marked by a preposition, this is dropped.

> (86) *The Hallé orchestra recorded well* (*with the Beyer microphone*) (*in studio B*)
>
> (87) *The Beyer microphone recorded* (*the Hallé Orchestra*) *well* (*in studio B*)

> (88) *Studio B recorded (the Hallé Orchestra) well (with the Beyer microphone)*

Sentences (86)–(88) are still transitive. There can still be an O NP, *the Hallé Orchestra*, in (87)–(88); in (86) *the Hallé Orchestra* is in A slot, but is still understood to be the object of *record*.

There is a crucial semantic and syntactic difference between (86), a transitive clause with *the Hallé Orchestra* in A slot, and the passive of (85), which is intransitive and has *the Hallé Orchestra* in S relation:

> (89) *The Hallé Orchestra was recorded well (by John McDonald) (with the Beyer microphone) (in Studio B)*

In (86) the excellence of the recording venture is attributed to the qualities of the orchestra. In (89) (as in (85)) it is due to the skill of the underlying agent (and is so perceived even if the agentive phrase *by John McDonald* is omitted from (89)).

Non-A NPs can be promoted to A slot in the presence of a limited set of adverbs (*well, nicely, slowly, easily* and just a few more) or the negative marker, or a modal, or a combination of these. We can say *Studio C didn't record the Hallé Orchestra very well*, but plain **Studio C recorded the Hallé Orchestra* is not acceptable.

Chapter 10 discusses the conditions under which 'promotion to subject' is appropriate.

2.9.5. Reflexives

If an NP following the predicate (either an object or an NP introduced by a preposition) has the same reference as the subject NP within the same clause, then the post-predicate NP must be replaced by the appropriate reflexive pronoun, e.g. *Pablo cut himself, Agnes looked at herself in the mirror, Gonzales told a story about himself*. However, if two NPs are coreferential between different clauses in a single sentence then a reflexive pronoun is not applicable, e.g. *After John swore, Mary hit him*, not **After John swore, Mary hit himself*.

The occurrence of reflexive pronouns provides confirmation for our analysis of complement clauses (§2.7). In

> (90) *John imagined [that Mary was hitting him]*

(91) *John imagined [that he was hitting Mary]*

The *he/him* are in a different clause from *John,* and are thus not in reflexive form. But in

(92) *John imagined himself to be hitting Mary*
(93) *John imagined Mary to be hitting herself*

we can see that the NP that follows *imagined* is both object of *imagine* and in the same clause as *John* (hence *himself* in (92)), and also subject of *hit* and in the same clause as *Mary* (hence *herself* in (93)). That it is both simultaneously is shown by:

(94) *John imagined himself to be hitting himself*

The fact that *Mary* in (93) is simultaneously (*a*) object of *imagine,* and (*b*) subject of *hit,* leads to conflict of criteria over the form of a pronoun substituting for it. It should be series II (*she*) by (*b*) but series I (*her*) by (*a*). We can explain the occurrence of *her* (as in *John imagined her to be hitting Fred*) in terms of series I being the 'unmarked' form of the pronoun.

The occurrence of reflexive pronouns also confirms our analysis of relative clauses (§2.6). Consider *[the man [who cut himself]]* *bled to death*; the object of *cut* is in reflexive form since it is coreferential with *who,* the relative pronoun filling subject slot, and this is itself coreferential with determiner-plus-head of the superordinate NP, *the man.* We do not, however, get a reflexive pronoun for the object of *hit* in *Mary sacked [the man [who hit her]]* since this is in a different clause from *Mary.*

Whether or not a given verb may occur in a reflexive construction depends to a great extent on whether it is semantically plausible for the same referent to relate to both subject and some post-predicate slot. It seems a little more felicitous to say *John stopped himself from jumping in at the deep end* than ?*John prevented himself from jumping in at the deep end.* With some verbs reflexive reference is scarcely plausible, e.g. *fetch.* With others the opposite applies, e.g. for *think* the NP introduced by *to* must be coreferential with the subject, *I thought to myself* (not **yourself/*herself/* etc.).

Self pronouns can also be used with an 'intensive' or 'emphatic' function, in apposition to an NP (which is usually in subject function), e.g. *The President himself said so*, or *I myself told a story to Agnes.* An intensive pronoun from a subject NP can be

57

moved to a later position in the clause—*The President (himself) said so (himself)*, and *I (myself) told the story (myself) to Agnes (myself)*.

The contrast between reflexive and intensive pronouns is well illustrated with *sit down*, an intransitive verb that can also be used causatively, e.g. *She sat the child down*. *John sat himself down* is a reflexivised causative, whereas *John himself sat down* and *John sat down himself* are intransitive, with an intensive pronoun that relates to the subject NP.

Intensive pronouns are generally not placed in structural positions that could be filled by a reflexive pronoun. *Watch* is a transitive verb which can omit its object—*John watched Mary*, *John watched himself (on the video)*, *John watched*. In this case an intensive pronoun from the subject NP (*John himself watched*) would not be likely to be moved to a position after the verb, since it could then be mistaken for a reflexive substitute for the object NP. However, an intensive pronoun could be moved after an explicit object NP (especially if there was a gender difference), e.g. *John watched Mary himself*.

There is a very small set of transitive verbs which may omit specification of an object with it being understood to be a reflexive pronoun (i.e. coreferential with the subject), e.g. *Mary hid* (sc. herself), *My daughter is dressing* (sc. herself), *John is shaving* (sc. himself), *The Queen is washing* (sc. herself). It appears that *hide* and *dress* may only omit an NP when it is reflexive. *Shave* and *wash* have wider possibilities of object omission; *Mary is washing* is thus ambiguous between a reflexive interpretation (she is washing herself) or simple transitive use with the object left unstated (she may be doing the weekly clothes wash for her family).

A number of verbs with a fairly concrete central meaning can take on a special metaphorical sense when used with a reflexive object NP, e.g. *put yourself in his place* 'imagine yourself to be him', *pull yourself together* 'stop behaving irrationally', *try and bring yourself to do it* 'force yourself to do it'.

Reflexives are often used to achieve a casual, informal style, e.g. the reflexive causative *Just sit yourself down here* is more chatty and friendly than the plain intransitive *Just sit down here*.

2.9.6. Reciprocals

Instead of saying *John punched Mary and Mary punched John* we would normally use a reciprocal construction, *John and Mary punched each other*. Here the two participants (each of whom is both Agent and Target in different instances of punching) are coordinated as subject, and the predicate is followed by *each other*. The subject of a reciprocal can refer to more than two participants, as in *Tom, Dick and Harry like one another*. We need not even know exactly how many it does refer to, e.g. *The boys hit one another*. This last sentence does not necessarily mean that each boy hit every other boy, just that each boy hit someone, and was hit by someone. (*Each other* tends to be preferred for two participants and *one another* for more than two, although there is a degree of substitutability.)

We mentioned in the last section that just a few verbs may omit a reflexive object, e.g. *John hid* (sc. himself). There is a slightly larger set of verbs which may omit the reciprocal marker *each other* or *one another*, e.g. *John and Mary hugged* (sc. each other), *All my aunts quarrelled* (sc. with one another). We will refer to verbs such as *hug* and *quarrel* (*with*), which can omit the reciprocal marker, as 'inherently reciprocal'. Note, though, that there are many verbs describing actions that are often reciprocal, which commonly occur with *each other* or *one another*, which cannot omit this reciprocal marker. If *each other* were dropped from *John and Mary watched each other*, giving *John and Mary watched*, there is an implication that they watched something (e.g. a game, or programme on TV) together, not that they watched each other.

The 'inherently reciprocal' verbs can be grouped into sets:

(I) verbs that only omit a post-predicate NP if it is *each other* or *one another*:

    (*a*) simple transitive verbs—*adjoin*, *touch*; *hug*, *cuddle*, *kiss*, *fuck* (and synonyms); *match*;

    (*b*) verbs that include a preposition plus NP, both of which can be omitted if the NP is *each other* or *one another*—*collide* (*with*), *quarrel* (*with*), *converse* (*with*), *differ* (*from*);

note that when a verb from set I is used with no object (or no prepositional object) then it must have a subject with plural reference, e.g. *The cars collided*, not **The car collided*.

(II) verbs which may omit a non-reciprocal object NP (or preposition plus NP) but may also omit a reciprocal marker. If they occur with a plural subject and no stated object (or preposition plus NP) then the most natural interpretation is a reciprocal one:

   (*a*) simple transitive verbs—*pass*, *meet*, *fight* (here *with* may optionally be inserted before the object), *marry* (this forms a causative, see §8.3.3);

   (*b*) verbs that take preposition plus NP—*play*, *compete*, *struggle*, *speak*, *talk*, *chat*, *joke*, *argue*, *gossip*, *agree*, *disagree* (all taking *with*).

(III) *discuss* takes a direct object (the Message) and, optionally, *with* plus Addressee NP, which should be omitted if the NP is a reciprocal marker: *John discussed the accident (with Mary)*, *John and Mary discussed the accident* (sc. with each other).

(IV) *exchange* and *trade* each take a direct object (the Gift), e.g. *John exchanged his knife for Mary's dagger*. If two tokens of the same gift are involved we can say *John exchanged knives with Mary* or *John and Mary exchanged knives* (sc. with each other).

The adverb *together* is often included when the reciprocal pronoun is omitted, with *play*, *struggle*, *speak*, *talk*, *chat*, *joke*, *argue* from II*b*, *fight* from II*a* and *discuss* from III, but not with the other verbs.

Some of these verbs must have a reciprocal meaning. If it is true that *This house differs from that one* then it must be true that *That house differs from this one* and also that *This house and that one differ* (sc. from each other). Similar verbs are *match*, *converse*, *marry*, *agree*, *disagree*, *discuss*, *exchange*, *trade*. Others of the verbs in I–IV refer to an activity that is normally entered into by both (or all, if more than two) participants, but need not necessarily be, e.g. *meet* (discussed in §9.2), *chat*, *hug*, *fuck* (there is a verb to describe this normally reciprocal activity being entered into freely by only one of the parties—*rape*).

There are odd anomalies. For instance, *resemble* has a symmetrical meaning just like *differ* (*from*) and yet it cannot omit *each other* or *one another*, e.g. *John's ideas and Mary's ideas resemble each other* but not **John's ideas and Mary's ideas resemble*. (The predicate *be similar* (*to*) is very close in meaning to *resemble*, and here *each other/one another* can be omitted.)

2.9.7. HAVE A VERB, GIVE A VERB and TAKE A VERB

As an alternative to *John ran* (*in the park before breakfast*) we can say *John had a run* (*in the park before breakfast*), with a slight difference in meaning. *Have* replaces an intransitive verb and this verb, preceded by the indefinite article *a*, becomes head of the NP that follows *have*. However, parallel to *John arrived* (*from town before breakfast*) it is not permissable to say **John had an arrive* (*from town before breakfast*). Some verbs can occur in HAVE A VERB constructions but others, with similar meanings, cannot. Why can we say *have a cry* but not **have a die; have a yawn* but not **have a breathe; have a sit-down* but not **have a settle-down; have a think* but not **have a reflect?*

Similar to HAVE-A-plus-intransitive-VERB is GIVE-A-plus-trans-itive-VERB. *John kicked the door* could be rephrased, with a slight meaning difference, as *John gave the door a kick*. But it is not possible to say, alongside *John broke the door*, the sentence **John gave the door a break*. Similarly, *John gave the silver ornament a polish* is acceptable, but not **John gave the silver ornament a wrap*; and *Mary gave John a kiss* is fine, but not **Mary gave John a kill*.

HAVE A constructions occur primarily with intransitive and GIVE A constructions primarily with transitive verbs, but there are exceptions. *Laugh* is intransitive; one can *have a laugh* and also *give a laugh*, with a meaning difference. *Stroke* is transitive; one can *give the cat a stroke* or *have a stroke of the fur coat*. And, alongside *Mary looked at John* we can have both *Mary had a look at John* (with no implication that he knew he was being looked at) and *Mary gave John a look* (with the expectation that he did receive it, and that it was a meaningful gesture).

There are also TAKE A VERB constructions such as *take a stroll*, *take a look*, *take a kick*, which have a recurrent meaning difference from *have a stroll, have a look, have a kick*. It appears that in British English a subset of those verbs which occur with HAVE A also occur with TAKE A. (American English is significantly different, with *take a walk* etc. being used instead of *have a walk* etc. It is likely that the same general semantic principles hold, but are applied in a slightly different way.)

Chapter 11 considers the meanings of HAVE A VERB, GIVE A VERB and TAKE A VERB constructions, and the semantic motivation for which verbs may occur in these construction types and which may not.

2.10. Clause linking

There are a number of ways of linking clauses in English, including (*a*) by coordinate linkers such as *and*, *but*, *or*; (*b*) by temporal subordinate linkers such as *after*, *before*, *while*; (*c*) by logical subordinate linkers such as *since*, *because*, *if*; (*d*) by the purposive linker *in order*.

Linked clauses often share a coreferential NP. It is infelicitous to repeat the same word several times in a sentence, and there are grammatical conventions in English for omitting a repeated NP, or replacing it by a pronoun.

A repeated NP can be omitted under two circumstances, one involving coordinate and the other involving temporal subordinate linkers. Firstly, if two coordinated clauses share an NP which is in subject (S or A) function in each clause, then it may be omitted from the second clause in sequence. From *Mary* (S) *came in* and *Mary* (A) *saw John* (O) can be formed the complex sentence *Mary came in and saw John*. But if the shared NP is in non-subject function in either clause then omission is not possible—from *John* (S) *came in* and *Mary* (A) *saw John* (O) it is not permissible to form **John came in and Mary saw*. (We do have available the passive construction, which puts an underlying O into derived S function. *John* (S) *came in* can be linked with *John* (S) *was seen by Mary* and the second *John* may now be omitted, giving *John came in and was seen by Mary*.)

A temporal subordinate clause may have the structure of a main clause, preceded by a subordinate marker such as *after* or *while*, e.g. *After he took off his hat, John sat down*; no omission of a coreferential NP is possible here. Alternatively, we may have a VP whose initial verb is in *-ing* form; the subject of such a clause must be omitted if it is coreferential with the subject of the main clause, e.g. *After taking off his hat, John sat down*. Note that such a temporal clause can come before, after, or in the middle of the main clause, e.g. *John was, while waiting for Mary, deciding what he would say to her* and *Fred always washes his hands before eating*. We find, in addition, that *after* and *while* (but never *before*) can be omitted under specific circumstances. *After* can be dispensed with before a VP commencing with *having* (it appears that the perfect auxiliary *have* sufficiently conveys the idea of prior time, without requiring *after* as well), e.g. *(After) having taken off his hat, John sat down*. Note that *after* cannot be omitted if there is no *have*, e.g. not from *After taking off his hat, John sat down*. *While* may be—but perhaps less often is—omitted when the VP begins with a lexical verb in *-ing*, e.g. *(While) sitting in the garden, John studied the birds*. (As noted in §2.5, there are also temporal clauses, whose VP begins with an *-ing* form, that have a different subject from the main clause, e.g. *His mother having gone out for the day, John had a party*.)

Another important device—which is much used when a complex sentence includes two underlying occurrences of the same NP —is to replace one of them by the corresponding third person pronoun. This is possible whatever the syntactic functions involved, e.g. *Mary* (S) *came in and she* (A) *saw John*, or *Mary* (S) *came in and John saw her* (O). Pronominalisation can only apply 'forwards' within coordinate constructions, e.g. *She came in and Mary saw John* is not a possible paraphrase of *Mary came in and she saw John*. (If *She came in and Mary saw John* were heard, *she* would have to be taken to refer not to *Mary* but to someone else, previously mentioned in the discourse.)

Pronominalisation can apply forwards or backwards into a subordinate clause, whether introduced by a temporal connective such as *after* or *while*, or a logical connective such as *since* or *if*, e.g. *If he comes here, John will get a shock* and *After she lost her keys, Mary couldn't get into the house*. Backwards pronominalisation is not possible from subordinate clause to main clause; it is not acceptable to say *He will get a shock if John comes here*, with the *he* referring to *John* (the *he* would have to be taken as referring to someone else).

Two clauses linked by *if* or the non-temporal sense of *since* must
—just like two clauses linked by *and* or *but*—each have the
structure of a main clause. The fourth type of clause linker, *in
order*, is quite different; it must occur with a main clause and be
followed by a THAT, FOR-TO or TO complement clause (the main
clause usually comes first although, as with *since* and *if* constructions, the order can be reversed), e.g. (54) and

(95) *John told the children to keep quiet in order that he/Mary
     might work*

(96) *John kept the children quiet (in order) for Mary to be able
     to work*

(97) *Mary went to her study (in order) to work*

A THAT clause, as in (95), may have the same or different subject
as the main clause, while a FOR-TO complement, as in (96), will
normally have a different subject. A TO complement used after *in
order*, as in (97), has the same subject as the main clause, and this
subject cannot be stated in the TO clause. *In order* may be—and
usually is—omitted from *in order to*; it may also be omitted (but
less often is) from *in order for . . . to*; it is possible—but less usual
—to omit *in order* from *in order that*.

When a complement clause occurs after *in order*, any verb may
fill the predicate head slot in the accompanying main clause
(subject to semantic plausibility of the complete sentence). The
term 'complement clause' is perhaps not appropriate here, but it
shows that a clause which follows *in order* does have the same
structure as a complement clause that can fill a subject or object
slot for semantically determined types of predicates, as described
in §2.7 and Chapter 7.

There is a further convention in English grammar, concerning a
VP that recurs in two clauses of a complex sentence. This is: if two
coordinated clauses have the same predicate but different subjects,
objects and other peripheral constituents, then the predicate can
simply be omitted from the second clause (this is called 'gapping'),
e.g. *John likes apples and Mary (likes) pears; Fred is sitting in the
lounge and Jane (is sitting) in the garden; Peter has been looking at
the Cézannes and Julius (has been looking) at the Renoirs.*

We mentioned that it is in English considered infelicitous to
repeat the same word several times within a single sentence or,

indeed, too closely together within a discourse. It is a feature of 'good style' to employ lexical substitution, using synonyms and near-synonyms rather than keep repeating a given word. This applies more in written than in spoken language, and more in literary than in scientific work—but it is to some extent a feature of every variety of English. Rather than employ the word 'use' several times in one paragraph a writer may alternate 'use' with 'utilise' and 'employ' (I first began this sentence with 'Rather than use the word "use" . . .' but then substituted 'employ' for the first 'use' since writing 'use' twice in four words seemed ugly.) In the third paragraph of this section I alternated 'can', 'may', 'is possible' and 'is permissible' to save having too many occurrences of 'can'.

It was mentioned in §2.6 that restrictive relative clauses may be introduced by a *wh-* word or by *that*. These will often be alternated for stylistic effect, so as not to have too many occurrences of *that*, or too many of *which* or *who*, in close proximity. And in an NP beginning with *that* as demonstrative one would generally prefer *wh-* over *that* for introducing a relative clause—*that man who you saw* sounds much more felicitous than *that man that you saw*.

The topic of lexical substitution belongs to the domain of stylistics. It has an obvious semantic basis and is most deserving of systematic study. I have not attempted this here; it remains an important topic for future research.

2.11. Syntactic preferences and constraints

There are a number of general surface syntactic preferences and constraints in any language. Those in English include:

A. Placing a heavy (i.e. long) constituent at the end of its clause

There is a preference for stating the shorter constituents first, before a heavy constituent (whatever its syntactic function). This accounts for the frequency with which a complement clause in subject function is extraposed, and replaced by impersonal *it* in the subject slot, e.g. *It appears definite that the show has been postponed* and *It annoys Frances to have to say grace before meals* (see §2.7). There is also the tendency in some colloquial styles to extract a restrictive relative clause from a pre-predicate NP and move it to the end of the main clause, e.g. *The watch broke, which you gave me for Christmas* (see §2.6). And the prepositional element of a phrasal verb is likely to be moved leftward over a heavy object NP, so that this can occur clause-finally—compare *The doctor brought my father to*, where *to* follows the object NP, and *The doctor brought to* [*that thin man with grey hair who was brought in from that terrible smash-up ten miles down the Pacific Highway*] where *to* precedes the bracketed object NP.

B. Omission of a preposition before complementisers *that*, *for* or *to*.

This has already been mentioned in §§1.4 and 2.7. It is a definite constraint. There are a number of verb-root-plus-preposition combinations which together function as a transitive verb; the preposition is retained before an NP or an ING complement clause, but must be omitted before a complement clause introduced by *that*, *for* or *to* (and may optionally be omitted before a complement clause beginning in *wh-*). Thus: *He boasted about his victory in the tournament*, *He boasted about winning the tournament* but *He boasted (*about) that he had won the tournament*.

Note that if a THAT or Modal (FOR) TO object complement clause becomes passive subject, the underlying preposition may be stated, since it is not then immediately followed by *that* or *for*. Compare (cf. §§1.4, 2.7):

    (98) *They decided on John*
    (99) *They decided (*on) that John would be captain*
    (99a) *That John would be captain was decided (on)*

But if the THAT clause is extraposed, it will again follow the (passive) predicate, and the preposition is normally suppressed:

    (99b) *It was decided (*on) that John would be captain*

Note also *I was surprised by the fact that the plumber came* where *by* is followed by two constituents in apposition, the NP *the fact* and the complement clause *that the plumber came*. *The fact* can be omitted, and the preposition *by* must then be dropped from its position before *that*, i.e. *I was surprised (*by) that the plumber came*.

C. Constraint against successive verbs in -ING form within a VP

There are two circumstances in which the general grammatical rules of English would be expected to generate a VP in which successive verbs were in *-ing* form. In both instances an ungrammatical string results, apparently because of a proscription on successive verbs being in *-ing* form *within* a VP. Both circumstances relate to the fact (reported in §2.7) that, unlike a main clause or a THAT or a WH- complement clause, an ING or TO complement cannot include a modal, or tense inflection.

(i) We describe in §6.1.1 the partial semantic equivalence between some semi-modals and some modals, e.g. *be able to* and *can*, *be going to* and *will*. The former may be used in place of the latter in functional possibilities where modals are not permitted, e.g. after another modal (if it is semantically plausible to replace modal by semi-modal in this context), as in *He will be able to tell you*, rather than **He will can tell you*.

The semi-modal *be able to* may be used in a TO or ING clause corresponding to the modal *can* in a THAT clause:

(100a) *I assume that John can climb the tree*
(100b) *I assume John to be able to climb the tree*
(100c) *I assume John's being able to climb the tree*

The same should apply to the semi-modal *be going to* vis-à-vis modal *will*. We do get *be going to* in a TO complement, as in (101b), but not in the ING complement at (101c); this is because of the constraint against two successive *-ing* verbs within a VP:

(101a) *I assume that John will climb the tree*
(101b) *I assume John to be going to climb the tree*
(101c) **I assume John's being going to climb the tree*

(ii) We mentioned in §2.7 that the VP of a TO complement clause can include auxiliary *have* (corresponding both to past tense inflection and to *have* in a main clause or a THAT clause) and/or auxiliary *be* (corresponding to *be* in a main or THAT clause), e.g. *I noticed John to have laughed/to be laughing/to have been laughing*. The VP of an ING complement can also include *have*, e.g. *I mentioned John's having laughed*. However, it cannot include *be* as the sole auxiliary element; if it did so there would be successive verbs in - *ing* form (the initial *be* taking the *-ing* which marks this variety of complement, and the following main verb taking the *-ing* specified by the progressive auxiliary *be*), which is not permitted, i.e. **I mentioned John's being laughing*. We can, however, have *be* together with *have*, since there is then a verb (*be*, plus the *-en* ending demanded by *have*) between the two *-ing* forms, i.e. *I mentioned John's having been laughing*.

Note that it is perfectly permissible to have successive verbs in *-ing* form so long as they belong to the VPs of different clauses, e.g. *He is enjoying painting the garage* (where *enjoying* belongs to the main clause and *painting* to the object complement clause—§2.7) and *He's coming rubbing his eyes* (where *coming* belongs to the main clause and *rubbing* to a relative-clause-like comment clause, as in (15) of §2.6).

There is a set of 'in-between' cases. Many languages code concepts like 'begin' and 'try' as affixes to a main verb. English uses lexical verbs that take an ING or TO complement clause; the complement must have the same subject as the BEGINNING or TRYING verb. There are some similarities between verbs of the BEGINNING and TRYING types and modals (in §§3.4 and 6.1 we group them all together as 'Secondary-A' verbs). Although *begin to walk* is best regarded syntactically as two VPs (main clause *begin* and complement clause *walk*) linked by *to*, it is semantically quite similar to *ought to walk* or *be going to walk*, each of which is syntactically a single VP.

Speakers vary in judgement as to whether a BEGINNING or TRYING verb preceded by the *be* progressive auxiliary (which puts an *-ing* on the following main verb) may or may not be followed by an ING complement clause, i.e. as to whether *He is beginning walking*, *She is trying eating less*, *It is continuing raining* are grammatically acceptable. This reflects the Janus nature of such constructions— in some ways like two VPs and in others like a single VP.

2.12. Summary of omission conventions

The approach to grammatical description followed here involves relating together two constructions that differ only in that one includes and the other omits some minor element(s), and which appear to have essentially the same meaning. It generally seems appropriate to take the longer construction as more basic, and say that certain omissions are involved in the shorter.

It will be useful at this stage to summarise the major conventions for omission:

A. Omission of subject NP

A1. Under coordination. If two coordinated clauses share an NP which is in subject function in each, then this NP can be omitted from the second clause in sequence.

A2. In subordinate time clause. One variety of temporal clause has its VP beginning with an *-ing* verb; if the subject of this clause is coreferential with the main clause subject then it must be omitted, e.g. (*While*) *lying on the beach, Mary got sunstroke* (§2.10).

A3. From an ING complement clause. If the subject of an ING complement clause in object slot is coreferential with the main clause subject, or if the subject of an ING complement clause in subject slot is coreferential with the main clause object, then it is omitted, e.g. *Mary hates having to wash up* and *Having to wash up annoys Mary*. (An exception concerns ATTENTION verbs as head of the main clause predicate. Coreferentiality is rare, but if it is encountered then omission of the complement clause subject is not possible, e.g. *John watched his fighting the tiger on a video replay*.) (§2.7C.)

A4. From a Modal (FOR) TO complement clause. The subject of a Modal (FOR) TO clause, in post-predicate position, must be omitted if it is coreferential with main clause subject, following one class of verbs, e.g. *I need to mow the lawn*; or if it is coreferential with main clause object, following another class of main verbs, e.g. *I persuaded Mary to go*. If the subject of a Modal (FOR) TO complement, in subject function, is coreferential with the main clause object, then this subject (and the preceding *for*) may optionally be omitted, e.g. (*For her*) *to be expected to wash the car infuriated Mary* (§2.7D). A WH- TO clause must have its subject coreferential with the main clause subject or object, and omitted (§2.7F).

B. Omission of complementiser *that*

The initial *that* may often be omitted from a complement clause when it immediately follows the main clause predicate (or predicate-plus-object-NP where the predicate head is *promise* or *threaten*). The *that* is more often omitted in casual speech (e.g. chatting between friends) than in formal communication (e.g. in court or parliament). And it is more often omitted if the complement clause refers to some minor item of information than if it describes something of significance; this can be inferred from the meaning of the main verb used, and the NPs, and the context of utterance. Thus, in the (a) sentences below it would sound infelicitous to omit the *that*; in the (b) sentences *that* could be included but might be more likely to be omitted (§2.7A):

    (102a) *He promised that he would lend me two million dollars*
    (102b) *He promised (that) he'd buy me an ice-cream*
    (103a) *He mentioned that the king had died*
    (103b) *He mentioned (that) Mary was coming to tea*

C. Omission of relative pronoun *wh-/that*

A relative pronoun *that* or *who*, *which*, etc. may be omitted from a restrictive relative clause if the coreferential NP was not in subject function in the relative clause, e.g. *the chair (that/which) you bought is the one (that/which) I sold last week*. Once again, omission is more likely in a casual speech style, and when referring to something that is not of huge importance (§2.6).

D. Omission of *to be* from complement clause

Some verbs taking a Judgement TO complement clause, whose VP begins with *be*, may omit *to be*, e.g. *I thought him (to be) crazy*. In addition, just a few verbs taking a Modal (FOR) TO complement whose VP begins with *be* may omit *to be*, e.g. *I need my wound (to be) dressed* (§2.7 and see §7.2.6).

E. Omission of predicate

If two coordinated clauses have the same predicate but different subject, object, etc. then the predicate may be omitted from the second clause (this is called 'gapping'), e.g. *John dug a long trench and Freddie (dug) a tiny hole* (§2.10).

F. Omission of modal *should* from a THAT complement

There is a class of verbs which carry an implication of obligation, similar to that of *should*. This modal may be omitted from a THAT complement clause following such a verb e.g. *He ordered that I (should) do it*, and *She suggested that John (should) propose the vote of thanks* (§2.7A).

G. Omission of preposition before complementisers *that, for* and *to*

Certain transitive verbs which have a preposition as the last element in their lexical form may take a complement clause in object function. The preposition is omitted before *that, for* or *to*, although it is retained before an ING complement clause or a plain NP as object (and may optionally be retained before a WH- clause), e.g. *He confessed to the crime, He confessed to strangling Mary*, but *He confessed (*to) that he had strangled Mary* (§§2.7, 2.11B).

H. Omission of complementiser *to*

This must be omitted following a subtype of ATTENTION verbs, and following *make, have* or *let*; it can optionally be omitted following *help* or *know*. For example, *He let Mary (*to) go; They heard John (*to) sing in the bath; She helped John (to) wash up*. Note that *to* is not omitted from the corresponding passive, e.g. *John was heard to sing in the bath* (§§2.7-D and 7.2.5).

I. Omission of *after/while*

A time clause whose VP begins with an *-ing* verb may omit the initial *after* if the first word of the VP is the perfect auxiliary *have*, e.g. *(After) having dug the garden, John had a shower*. Similarly, an initial *while* may be—but less often is—omitted if the VP begins with a lexical verb, e.g. *John caught a bad cold (while) waiting for the bus* (§2.10).

J. Omission of *in order*

The clause linker *in order* is usually omitted before *to*, e.g. *Fred rose early (in order) to get to work on time*, and it may occasionally be omitted before *for* or *that* (§2.10).

Notes to Chapter 2

Further details on many of the points discussed here will be found in the standard grammars of English, e.g. Sweet (1891–8); Jespersen (1909–49); Poutsma (1926–9); Curme (1931, 1935, 1947); Quirk, Greenbaum, Leech and Svartvik (1985) (and the shorter version: Quirk and Greenbaum 1973); Huddleston (1984).

§2.6. There are illuminating discussions on the alternations of *that*, *wh*-words and zero in relative clauses in Quirk (1957).

§2.7. McDavid (1964) has a useful discussion of the omission of *that* from complement clauses; see also Borkin (1984).

§2.8. For a full account of word derivation in English see Adams (1973).

§2.11C. The constraint against consecutive verbs ending in *-ing* is discussed in Ross (1972), Pullum (1974), Bolinger (1979) and Wierzbicka (1988: 89–93), among others.

Part B

The Semantic Types

3

Noun, adjective and verb types

The lexical words of a language can be grouped into a number of semantic types, each of which has a common meaning component, and a typical set of grammatical properties. One of the grammatical properties of a type is its association with a grammatical Word Class, or Part of Speech. (See §1.2.)

Chapters 4–6 contain brief sketches of the semantic and syntactic characters of those semantic types which are in English associated with the Verb class. Following chapters discuss the occurrence restrictions on specific syntactic constructions, providing explanations for these that link the meanings of the constructions with the meanings of semantic types. In this chapter I provide a brief summary of the semantic types associated with the Noun and Adjective classes in English and introduce the division into Primary and Secondary verb types.

One preliminary point should be stressed: semantic types are not mutually exclusive. The central representatives of a type tend to be frequently used words with a simple, general meaning; these do have unequivocal membership. But words of more specialised meaning may combine the semantic properties of more than one type. *Offer*, for instance, relates both to GIVING (the most frequent kind of offer is an offer to give something) and to SPEAKING (the person offering will usually employ words, although gestures could be used instead). *Bite* is basically a CORPOREAL verb, alongside *eat*, *chew* and *swallow*, but it can also be used—like *cut*—as an AFFECT verb, e.g. *He bit/cut through the string*. Generally, when a verb shares the semantic characteristics of two types, it will also blend their syntactic properties.

75

3.1. Types associated with the Noun class

There are five major types associated with the grammatical class Noun in English:

1. CONCRETE reference, e.g. *youth, horse, foot, piece, grass, star, fire, hill, city, table*. This type can be divided into HUMAN; other ANIMATE; (body and other) PARTS; INANIMATE. INANIMATE may be further subdivided into: FLORA; CELESTIAL and WEATHER (e.g. *sun, wind, shade*); ENVIRONMENT (*air, water, stone, oil, gold, forest*); ARTEFACTS (*building, market, door*). One subgroup of HUMAN relates to RANK (*lady, lieutenant, chief*); another to SOCIAL GROUP (*nation, army, crowd, company*); and another to KIN terms (*father, daughter, uncle, wife*).

Members of this type are almost all basic noun roots, although there are a few which are derived from verbs (e.g. *building*).

2. ABSTRACT reference. Subtypes here include: TIME (*time* itself, as well as words referring to position in time, e.g. *future, yesterday*, and units of time, e.g. *month, moment, night, summer*); PLACE (*place*, together with words referring to position or direction, e.g. *front, edge, north*, and to units of measurement, e.g. *mile*); QUANTITY (*number, amount, age, size, length*, etc.); VARIETY (e.g. *type, character, shape* and types of shape such as *circle, line*); LANGUAGE (*sound, word, sentence, noun*); and general abstract terms such as *idea, unit, problem, method, result, truth*.

Members of this type are also predominantly basic noun roots, although there are some derived stems, e.g. *distance, height, truth*.

3. STATES (and PROPERTIES). This covers both the mental (*pleasure, joy, honour*; *ability, sagacity*) and the corporeal (e.g. *ache; strength*) domains. Some are basic nouns (e.g. *anger, hunger*) but many are derived from adjectives (e.g. *jealousy*) and a few from verbs (e.g. *delight*).

4. ACTIVITIES. Some are basic nouns, e.g. *war, game*, but most are derived from verbs, e.g. *decision, speculation, whipping, sale*. For almost every activity noun there is a corresponding verb, even if it is not always cognate, e.g. *play* for *game*.

5. SPEECH ACTS, e.g. *question, order, report, description, talk, promise*. In each case there is a related verb; this is usually cognate, e.g. *answer, congratulat(ion)*, although there are some exceptions, e.g. *question/ask*.

Every language has words of these five types, but they do not always belong to the Noun class. In the Australian language Dyirbal, for instance, almost all nouns are CONCRETE. Dyirbal has an ample supply of words dealing with states, properties, activities and speech acts, but they all belong to the Verb and Adjective classes; that is, the English words *anger*, *game* and *question* must be translated into Dyirbal through adjectives ('angry') and verbs ('play', 'ask'). Dyirbal has only a few words with ABSTRACT reference, including some nouns like 'summer', 'night', 'word'. Reference to size is through DIMENSION adjectives, and general reference to number through the interrogative 'how many?' There are in Dyirbal no words—of any word class—directly corresponding to English *time*, *past*, *idea* or *problem*. (There is also a distinct word class which includes specific Time words such as 'long ago', 'yesterday', 'always', 'not yet'.)

In a fair number of languages it is appropriate to recognise KIN terms as making up a distinct type. Sometimes KIN is associated with the Verb class (i.e. 'X fathers Y'). In other languages KIN functions as a grammatically marked subset of Noun, in that a kin term must take an obligatory possessive affix (that is, one cannot just say 'mother', but must specify 'my mother', 'her mother', etc.).

In English almost all the CONCRETE, ABSTRACT and SPEECH ACT nouns have a plural form (exceptions include those referring to non-discrete material, e.g. *mud*, *milk*). ACTIVITY nouns that refer to a discrete act may form a plural, but others, referring to a mode of activity, sound infelicitous in the plural (compare *many mistakes* with *lots of ineptitude*, rather than **many ineptitudes*). STATE nouns seldom have a plural form—one does not hear **many hungers* or **three jealousies*. (*Pleasure* has a plural used in restricted contexts, e.g. *It is one of my few pleasures*, but note *It gave me much pleasure*, not **It gave me many pleasures*.)

The main significance of the five Noun types lies in the verbs with which they can occur. Thus, the object of *experience*, used in its literal sense, is generally a STATE noun, or an ACTIVITY noun derived from an AFFECT verb (*He experienced hunger/a whipping*). The object of *postpone* will normally be an ACTIVITY or SPEECH ACT noun (*They postponed the sale/the order*). *Punch* requires a CONCRETE object. But *discuss* can have any type of noun as head of its object NP.

3.2. Types associated with the Adjective class

The following semantic types are associated with the grammatical class Adjective in English:

I. DIMENSION, e.g. *big, great, short, thin, round, narrow, deep*.

2. PHYSICAL PROPERTY, e.g. *hard, strong, clean, cool, heavy, sweet, fresh, cheap*; this includes a CORPOREAL subtype, e.g. *well, sick, ill, dead*; *absent*.

3. SPEED—*quick, fast, rapid, slow, sudden*.

4. AGE—*new, old, young, modern*.

5. COLOUR, e.g. *white, black, red, crimson, mottled, golden*.

6. VALUE, e.g. (*a*) *good, bad, lovely, atrocious*; (*b*) *odd, strange, curious*; *necessary, crucial*; *important*; *lucky*.

7. DIFFICULTY, e.g. *easy, difficult, tough, hard, simple*.

8. QUALIFICATION, with a number of subtypes:

   (*a*) DEFINITE, a factual qualification regarding an event, e.g. *definite, probable, true*;

   (*b*) POSSIBLE, expressing the speaker's opinion about an event, which is often some potential happening, e.g. *possible, impossible*;

   (*c*) USUAL, the speaker's opinion about how predictable some happening is, e.g. *usual, normal, common*;

   (*d*) LIKELY, again an opinion, but tending to focus on the subject's potentiality to engineer some happening, e.g. *likely, certain*;

   (*e*) SURE, as for (*d*), but with a stronger focus on the subject's control, e.g. *sure*;

   (*f*) CORRECT, e.g. *correct, right, wrong, appropriate, sensible*. These have two distinct senses, commenting (i) on the correctness of a fact, similar to (*a*) (e.g. *That the whale is not a fish is right*), and (ii) on the correctness of the subject's undertaking some activity (e.g. *John was right to resign*).

9. HUMAN PROPENSITY, again with a number of subtypes:

   (*a*) FOND, with a similar meaning to LIKING verbs (§5.5), e.g. *fond* (taking preposition *of*);

   (*b*) ANGRY, describing an emotional reaction to some definite happening, e.g. *angry* (*about*), *jealous* (*of*), *mad* (*about*), *sad* (*about*);

(*c*) HAPPY, an emotional response to some actual or potential happening, e.g *anxious, keen, happy, thankful, careful, sorry, glad* (all taking *about*); *proud, ashamed, afraid* (all taking *of*);

(*d*) UNSURE, the speaker's assessment about some potential event, e.g. *certain, sure, unsure* (all taking *of* or *about*), *curious* (*about*);

(*e*) EAGER, with meanings similar to WANTING verbs (§6.2.1), e.g. *eager, ready, prepared* (all taking *for*), *willing*;

(*f*) CLEVER, referring to ability, or an attitude towards social relations with others, e.g. *clever, stupid*; *lucky*; *kind, cruel*; *generous*.

10. SIMILARITY, comparing two things, states or events, e.g. *like, unlike* (which are the only adjectives to take a direct object); *similar* (*to*), *different* (*from*) (which introduce the second role—obligatory for an adjective from this type—with a preposition).

Almost all the members of DIMENSION, PHYSICAL PROPERTY, SPEED, AGE, DIFFICULTY and QUALIFICATION are basic adjectives (*dead*, derived from a verb, is an exception). Many of the less central COLOUR terms are derived from nouns, e.g. *violet, spotted*. There are a fair proportion of adjectives derived from verbs in the VALUE type (e.g. *interesting, amazing, desirable*) and some in the HUMAN PROPENSITY and SIMILARITY types (e.g. *thankful, prepared, different*). A few words in VALUE and HUMAN PROPENSITY are derived from nouns (e.g. *angry, lucky*).

These ten Adjective types do have rather different grammatical properties. The prefix *un-* occurs with a fair number of QUALIFICATION and HUMAN PROPENSITY adjectives, with some from VALUE and a few from PHYSICAL PROPERTY and SIMILARITY, but with none from DIMENSION, SPEED, AGE, COLOUR or DIFFICULTY. The verbalising suffix *-en* is used with many adjectives from types 1–5 but with none from 6–8 (*toughen* and *harden* relate to the PHYSICAL PROPERTY sense of these lexemes) and with none save *glad* and *like* from 9 and 10 respectively. Derived adverbs may be formed from almost all adjectives in SPEED, VALUE, QUALIFICATION, HUMAN PROPENSITY and SIMILARITY and from some in PHYSICAL PROPERTY and DIFFICULTY but from none in AGE; adverbs based on adjectives in DIMENSION and COLOUR tend to be restricted to a metaphorical meaning (e.g. *warmly commend, drily remark, darkly hint*). When adjectives co-occur in an NP then the unmarked ordering is: 10–8–7–6–1–2–3–9–4–5. (For a fuller discussion of these and related points see Dixon 1977, reprinted as Dixon 1982*b*: ch. 1.)

An adjective will typically modify the meaning of a noun, and can be used either 'attributively', as modifier within an NP (*That clever man is coming*) or 'predicatively', following a copula (*That man is clever*); only a few adjectives show just one of these syntactic possibilities (see Quirk and Greenbaum 1973: 121 ff.).

DIMENSION, PHYSICAL PROPERTY, COLOUR and AGE adjectives typically relate to a CONCRETE noun. SPEED can modify a CONCRETE or an ACTIVITY noun. HUMAN PROPENSITY adjectives, as the label implies, generally relate to a HUMAN noun. DIFFICULTY and QUALIFICATION adjectives tend to refer to an event, and may have as subject an appropriate noun (e.g. *Cyclones are common at this time of year*) or a complement clause. VALUE adjectives may refer to anything; the subject can be any kind of noun, or a complement clause. There is a tendency for a THAT or Modal (FOR) TO complement clause in subject function (which is a 'heavy constituent') to be extraposed to the end of the main clause, and replaced by *it*—compare *The result was strange*, with *It was strange that Scotland won*, which sounds a little more felicitous than *That Scotland won was strange*. SIMILARITY adjectives relate together two things that can be CONCRETE, ABSTRACT or ACTIVITIES (but should normally both come from the same category).

VALUE adjectives may take as subject an ING or THAT complement clause (a THAT clause will generally be extraposed), e.g. *Mary's baking a cake for us was really lovely, It is lucky that John came on time*. Subset (*b*) of the VALUE type may also take a Modal (FOR) TO subject complement, e.g. *It was necessary/odd for John to sign the document*. DIFFICULTY adjectives may take as subject a Modal (FOR) TO clause, again generally extraposed, e.g. *It is hard for Mary to operate our mower*. Both VALUE and DIFFICULTY types can also take in subject relation a complement clause which has no subject stated (it is understood to be 'everyone/anyone'). This applies to ING clauses for VALUE adjectives, e.g. *Helping blind people is good*, and to both Modal (FOR) TO and ING clauses for DIFFICULTY adjectives, e.g. *Operating our mower is hard, It is hard (sc. for anyone) to operate our mower*.

VALUE and DIFFICULTY adjectives occur in a further construction, one in which what could be object of a complement clause functions as subject of the adjective, with the rest of the complement clause following the adjective, introduced by *to*, e.g. *That picture is good to look at, Our mower is easy to start.* For the DIFFICULTY type it is tempting to derive *Our mower is easy to start* from *It is easy to start our mower*, by 'raising' the complement clause object to become main clause subject. However, this derivation is not available for some adjectives from the VALUE type which do not take a Modal (FOR) TO clause in subject slot. (See also §10.2.)

The various subtypes within QUALIFICATION differ in the kinds of complement clause they accept. The overall possibilities are:

  (i) a THAT complement as subject, often extraposed, e.g. *That John will win is probable, It is probable that John will win*;

 (ii) a Modal (FOR) TO complement as subject, normally extraposed, e.g. *It is unusual for a baby to be walking at twelve months*;

(iii) a variant of (ii), where the complement clause subject is raised to fill main clause subject slot, replacing *it* (and *for* is then dropped), e.g. *A baby is likely to walk by twenty-four months, John was wrong to resign*;

(iv) an ING complement clause (often with the subject omitted) in subject slot, e.g. *(Your) taking out accident insurance was sensible.*

The QUALIFICATION subtypes occur with subject complements as follows:

8*a*	DEFINITE	i	—	—	—
8*b*	POSSIBLE	i	ii	—	—
8*c*	USUAL	i	ii	—	—
8*d*	LIKELY	i	—	iii	—
8*e*	SURE	—	—	iii	—
8*f*	CORRECT	i	ii	iii	iv

Some pairs of QUALIFICATION adjectives which might appear to have similar meanings do in fact belong to different subtypes, and show distinct syntactic properties. Compare *definite* (from 8*a*) and *certain* (from 8*d*):

(1a) *It is certain that the King will visit us this month*
(1b) *It is definite that the King will visit us this month*
(2a) *It is certain that the monsoon will come this month*
(2b) **It is definite that the monsoon will come this month*

Sentence (1b) implies that an announcement has been made; the speaker uses *definite* to report this. In contrast, (1a) presents an opinion (albeit a very strong one)—from all the signs of preparation, the King must be about to make this visit. One can say (2a), using *certain* to qualify an inference made from study of meteorological charts etc. But (2b) is an inappropriate sentence, simply because there is no ordinance that rains will come at a particular time.

Now compare *possible* (from 8*b*), *likely* (from 8*d*) and *sure* (8*e*):

(3a) *That John will win the prize is possible*
(3b) *That John will win the prize is likely*
(3c) **That John will win the prize is sure*
(4a) **John is possible to win*
(4b) *John is likely to win*
(4c) *John is sure to win*

Both *possible* and *likely* may comment on the chance of some event happening, as in (3a/b). *Likely* differs from *possible* in that it can focus on the outcome as due to the efforts of the subject— hence (4b) but not *(4a). When *sure* is used with a human subject it always focuses on the subject's effort, hence the unacceptability of *(3c).

HUMAN PROPENSITY adjectives normally have a HUMAN noun as subject. They can be followed by a preposition introducing a constituent that states the reason for the emotional state; this may be an NP or a complement clause, e.g. *John was sorry about the delay*, *John was sorry about being late*, *John was sorry that he was late*, *John was sorry to be late*. The preposition drops before *that* or *to* at the beginning of a complement clause, but is retained before an ING clause.

The various subtypes of HUMAN PROPENSITY have differing complement possibilities:

9*a*. FOND only accepts an NP or ING complement, e.g. *I'm fond of watching cricket*.

9*b*. ANGRY takes an NP or a THAT or ING clause, e.g. *She's angry* *about John('s) being officially rebuked, She's angry that John got the sack.*

9c. HAPPY takes an NP or THAT or ING or Modal (FOR) TO (complement clause subject, and *for*, is omitted when coreferential with main clause subject), e.g. *I'm happy about the decision, I'm happy about (Mary('s)) being chosen, I'm happy that Mary was chosen, I'm happy (for Mary) to be chosen.*

9d. UNSURE takes an NP or a THAT clause for its positive members *certain (of)* and *sure (of)*, e.g. *I'm sure of the result, She's certain that John will come*; but an NP or a WH- clause after those members that indicate uncertainty, *unsure (of)* and *curious (about)*, e.g. *I am unsure of the time of the meeting, She is curious (about) whether John will attend* (or after positive members when *not* is included, e.g. *I'm not certain whether he'll come*).

9e. EAGER takes an NP or a THAT or Modal (FOR) TO complement, e.g. *I'm eager for the fray, I'm eager that Mary should go, I'm eager (for Mary) to go. Ready* may only take an NP or a Modal (FOR) TO clause (not a THAT complement) while *willing* must take a THAT or Modal (FOR) TO clause, i.e. it cannot be followed by preposition plus NP.

9f. CLEVER shows wide syntactic possibilities. Firstly, like other HUMAN PROPENSITY adjectives, a member of the CLEVER subtype may have a HUMAN noun as subject, and a post-predicate prepositional constituent, e.g. *John was very stupid (about ignoring the rules/in the way he ignored the rules)*. Alternatively, there may be a complement clause as subject, with *of* introducing an NP that refers to the person to whom the propensity applies— either a THAT clause, e.g. *That John came in without knocking was very stupid (of him)*, or a Modal (FOR) TO clause, e.g. *For John to come in without knocking was very stupid (of him), To come in without knocking was very stupid of John, It was very stupid of John (for him) to come in without knocking, It was very stupid for John to come in without knocking.* (Note that *of John* and *for John* can both be included—with the second occurrence of John pronominalised—or either of these may be omitted.) As with some QUALIFICATION subtypes, the subject of an extraposed Modal (FOR) TO subject complement can be raised to become subject of the main clause, replacing impersonal *it*, e.g. *John was stupid to come in without knocking.*

SIMILARITY adjectives have similar meaning and syntax to COMPARING verbs (§5.7). There may be NPs or ING complement clauses, with comparable meanings, in subject slot and in post-predicate slot, e.g. *John is similar to his cousin, Applying for a visa to enter Albania is like hitting your head against a brick wall.*

Semantic explanation for the differing complement possibilities of the various adjectival types is given in §7.4.5.

Some adjectives have two distinct senses, which relate to distinct types. We have already mentioned *tough* and *hard* which belong to both PHYSICAL PROPERTY (*This wood is hard*) and to DIFFICULTY (*It was hard for John to bring himself to kiss Mary*). *Curious* is in one sense a VALUE adjective, taking a THAT complement in subject function, e.g. *The result of the race was rather curious, That Mary won the race was rather curious.* In another sense, *curious* (*about*) belongs to the UNSURE subtype of HUMAN PROPENSITY, e.g. *John was curious about the result of the race, John was curious* (*about*) *whether Mary won the race.* *Sure* and *certain* belong both to QUANTIFICATION (*That Mary will win is certain*) and also to the UNSURE subtype (*John is certain that he/Mary will win*).

As mentioned above, many adjectives from the DIMENSION, PHYSICAL PROPERTY, SPEED, AGE and COLOUR types form derived verbs by the addition of *-en*. These generally function both intransitively, with the meaning 'become', e.g. *The road widened after the state boundary* 'the road became wide(r) . . .', and transitively, with the meaning 'make', e.g. *They widened the road* 'they made the road wide(r)'. The occurrence of *-en* is subject both to a semantic constraint—in terms of the types it can occur with—and also to a phonological constraint—only roots ending in p, t, k, f, s, $\int$, θ, d take *-en* (see Dixon 1982b: 22). Adjectives from the appropriate types which do not end in one of these permissible segments may have the root form used as a verb, e.g. *narrow* can function as an adjective, as an intransitive verb 'become narrow' and as a transitive verb 'make narrow'; *clean* and *dirty* may function both as adjectives and transitive verbs 'make clean/dirty'. The two main VALUE adjectives, *good* and *bad*, have suppletive verbal forms *improve* and *worsen*, which are used both intransitively 'become better/worse' and also transitively, 'make better/worse'. (Further discussion of transitive verbs derived from adjectives is in §8.3.3.)

Whereas all (or almost all) languages have major word classes that can be labelled Noun and Verb, some do not have a major word class Adjective. A fair number of languages have a small, closed Adjective class, which generally comprises DIMENSION, AGE, VALUE and COLOUR. In such languages the HUMAN PROPENSITY type tends to be associated with the Noun class ('cleverness', 'pride' etc.) and the PHYSICAL PROPERTY type with the Verb class. (See Dixon 1982*b*: ch. 1.) Many languages do not have words for QUALIFICATION as members of the Adjective class; they may be adverbs, or else grammatical particles.

3.3. Introduction to verb types

3.3.1. Subject and object

Each semantic type associated with the verb class takes a number of semantic roles. A GIVING verb involves Donor, Gift and Recipient; a SPEAKING verb can demand reference to Speaker, Addressee, Message and Medium. Not every verb from a type necessarily requires all of the roles—some MOTION verbs take just one role, the thing Moving (e.g. *John is running*), while others also take a second role, the Locus with respect to which motion takes place (e.g. *Mary passed the school*).

As described in §1.3, semantic roles are mapped onto syntactic relations. If a verb has only one core role this always corresponds to S (intransitive subject) at the level of syntax. S has a wide semantic range—compare *JOHN ran away, THE STONE rolled down the hill, FRED is winking, FRED is sleeping.*

If a verb has two or more semantic roles then one will be mapped onto A (transitive subject) and one onto O (transitive object) syntactic function. There is a semantic principle determining which role corresponds to which function. Basically: that role which is most likely to be relevant to the success of the activity will be identified as A—this is the Speaker for SPEAKING verbs, the Agent for AFFECT verbs like *hit*, and the Perceiver for ATTENTION verbs (e.g. *JOHN tried to watch Mary*).

Where there are just two core roles, then that which is not mapped onto A will become O, e.g. *John* in all of *The nurse sat John up, Fred kicked John, Mary watched John.* If there are more than two roles, that which is most saliently affected by the activity will be mapped onto O. A role that is not identified as A or O will be marked by an appropriate preposition.

Some semantic types include alternative lexemes which differ (only, or largely) in that one focuses on a particular non-A role as most salient (and in O function) while the other focuses on a different role (which is then O). *Mention* and *inform* both belong to the SPEAKING type, requiring Speaker, Addressee and Message. But *mention* focuses on the Message (and the consequences of telling it) whereas *inform* focuses on the Addressee (and the consequences of telling them the message). Compare:

> (5) *John* (A) *mentioned the decision* (O) *to Mary* (*and there was then no going back on it*)
> (6) *John* (A) *informed Mary* (O) *of the decision* (*with the result that she fainted away*)

Some verbs from semantic types that have three core roles appear in two kinds of construction, with alternative roles being mapped onto O, e.g. *John* (Donor: A) *gave all his money* (Gift: O) *to Mary* (Recipient) and *John gave Mary* (O) *all his money*. The two constructions have different semantic implications—the role identified as O is focused on, as particularly salient in this instance of the activity. Only an NP which has definite and specific reference is likely to be suitable to be O. Thus, one might say *John gave all his money* (O) *to good causes* but scarcely **John gave good causes* (O) *all his money*, simply because *good causes* is too vague and general to be a suitable candidate for the syntactic function O.

It is important to stress that there is nothing mechanical about 'alternative syntactic frames' such as those just illustrated for *give*; semantic conditions always apply. Compare (cf. §8.2.4):

> (7a) *Mary sent* (O) *a present to the doctor*
> (7b) *Mary sent the doctor* (O) *a present*
> (8a) *Mary sent John* (O) *to the doctor*
> (8b) **Mary sent the doctor* (O) *John*

Send actually straddles the GIVING and MOTION types. *The doctor* in (7a/b) is in recipient role, and can be coded into O syntactic slot, as in (7b). But in (8a/b) *send* is being used as a MOTION verb, with *the doctor* simply a destination (parallel to *Mary sent John to Geneva*). Such a destination NP is not saliently affected by the activity, and is thus not a candidate for O slot. (Sentence (8b) could only be used if John were being sent to the doctor as something like a present, as in *Mary sent the doctor a slave/a new assistant*.)

3.3.2. Grammar versus lexicon

What is done by morphology in one language may be achieved through syntax in another. Latin (a language with fairly free word order) marks subject and object by nominative and accusative cases, respectively. English puts the subject before the verb and the object after it.

Some languages have derivational morphemes that correspond to separate lexemes in other languages. Consider the following:

(*a*) Warao, from Venezuela, has a verbal suffix -*puhu*- corresponding to the modal verb *can* in English. From *ruhu*- 'sit' is derived *ruhu-puhu*- 'can sit', which takes the full range of tense-aspect verbal inflections (Osborn 1967). To achieve the same semantic result, English must use the two verbs *can* and *sit* in syntactic construction within a VP.

(*b*) Dyirbal, from north-east Australia, has a verbal affix -*yarra*- 'start'. Thus *jangga-yarra-nyu* ('eat-START-PAST') is a single word, with the same meaning as *started eating* in English, a construction that has *started* as main verb and *eating* as a complement clause to it (Dixon 1972: 249).

(*c*) The Uto-Aztecan language Luiseño has derivational affixes -*viču*- 'want to' and -*ni*- 'make, force to'. From *ngéé* 'leave' can be derived *ngéé-viču* 'want to leave', *ngéé-ni* 'make leave' and even *ngéé-viču-ni-viču* 'want to make want to leave' (Langacker 1972: 76–7). Luiseño can achieve by a single verb what in English requires constructions involving one, two or three complement clauses.

Many other examples could be given of a concept that is expressed by a derivational process in one language but only as a separate lexical verb in another.

It is not, however, the case that *anything* which is a verb root in one language may be a derivational morpheme in another. Ideas like 'lean', 'stir', 'swallow', 'discuss' and 'remember' are always expressed by separate lexical verbs, in every language. This question will be taken further in the next section.

3.4. Primary and Secondary verbs

Verbal concepts naturally divide into two sorts:

PRIMARY—those directly referring to some activity or state, i.e. verbs which can make up a sentence by themselves with appropriate NPs filling the various semantic roles, e.g. *I HIT her, She SWAM across the river, He MUNCHED the apple, They WATCHED it.* These are lexical verbs in every language.

SECONDARY—those providing semantic modification of some other verb, with which they are in syntactic or morphological construction, e.g. the verbs printed in capitals in *I MAY hit her, She TRIED to swim across the river, We STOPPED him munching an apple, I LET them watch it.* Some or all of these may be realised as verbal affixes in languages that show a complex morphology (as exemplified in the last section). They are likely all to be realised as lexical verbs in languages, like English, which have a relatively sparse morphology.

Various subdivisions can be recognised within the two main divisions of Primary and Secondary verbs in English. We now list these, and the semantic types that correspond to them. The following three chapters consider the verb types one at a time, outlining their semantic and syntactic characteristics.

PRIMARY-A verbs must have NPs (not complement clauses) in subject and object slots. The semantic types with this property are:

MOTION, e.g. *run, return, take, pull, throw, fall, spill*
REST, e.g. *sit, stay, put, hang, surround, hold*
AFFECT, e.g. *hit, punch, cut, sweep, cover, twist, burn*
GIVING, e.g. *give, lend, pay, present, donate, exchange*
CORPOREAL, e.g. *eat, taste, kiss, laugh, sleep, bleed, die*
WEATHER, e.g. *rain, snow, thunder, hail*
COMPETITION, e.g. *beat, win, attack, lose, compete*
SOCIAL CONTRACT, e.g. *appoint, govern, manage, join, marry*
USING, e.g. *use, employ, operate, wear, waste*
OBEYING, e.g. *obey, process, deal with, grant, perform*

These verbs take CONCRETE nouns as heads of their subject and object NPs, when used in a literal sense. There are some metaphorical uses of individual verbs that can involve nouns of other types, but these are in the nature of idiosyncratic extensions of meaning, e.g. *I hit on a good idea* (but not **I punched/cut on a good idea*, or even **I hit a good idea*), *She tasted the joys of victory* (but not **She ate/kissed the joys of victory*).

PRIMARY-B verbs may have NPs filling subject and object slots but they also allow—as an alternative—a complement clause to fill one of these slots, e.g. *I understand my father*, *I understand that he refused to sign the document*; and *My father surprised me*, *That he refused to sign surprised me*.

One semantic type may have a complement clause or an NP as subject:

ANNOYING, e.g. *please, satisfy, amuse, anger, disgust, surprise*

A number of types may have a complement clause as an alternative to an NP in object (or, sometimes, in a post-object) slot:

ATTENTION, e.g. *see, hear, notice, discover, watch*
THINKING, e.g. *think (of/about/over), imagine, assume; know, learn, understand, realise; believe, suspect*
DECIDING, e.g. *decide (on), choose, resolve, elect*
SPEAKING, e.g. *shout, state, remark, propose, inform, tell, order, ask, promise, describe*
LIKING, e.g. *like, love, hate, loathe, prefer, envy*
ACTING, e.g. *act, behave, copy, imitate; reproduce*
HAPPENING, e.g. *happen, take place, commit, experience, undergo*

There are also two types that may have complement clauses in both A and O slots:

COMPARING, e.g. *resemble, differ (from); compare, measure, cost*
RELATING, e.g. *depend on, relate to, imply, be due to*

Note that ATTENTION, ACTING, HAPPENING, COMPARING and RELATING straddle Primary-A and Primary-B, each including some verbs that do—and some that do not—take a complement clause.

The object of a verb from ANNOYING, and the subject of a verb from ATTENTION, THINKING, DECIDING, SPEAKING, LIKING and ACTING (that is, the function which cannot be realised by a complement clause for those types) will generally be a HUMAN noun.

SECONDARY verbs all provide semantic modification of some other verb. That is, in each of *Mary continued eating the pudding*, *Mary wants to eat the pudding*, *John made Mary eat the pudding*, *It seems that Mary is eating the pudding*, the underlying event is 'Mary eat the pudding'. *Eat* is the central verb, from a semantic point of view. But at the level of syntax it is *continue, want, make* and *seem* which are predicate head within the main clause, with 'Mary eat the pudding' being a complement clause in syntactic relation with this predicate.

There are four different kinds of semantic (and syntactic) link between a secondary verb and the verb it semantically modifies:

SECONDARY-A verbs have the same subject as the verbs they modify, and the same object too, if the verb is transitive. That is, modification by a Secondary-A verb does not involve the addition of any semantic roles. The semantic types with this property are:

> MODALS, e.g. *will, can, should, might, ought to, must*
> SEMI-MODALS, e.g. *be going to, be able to, have got to*
> BEGINNING, e.g. *begin, start, finish, complete, continue (with)*
> TRYING, e.g. *try, attempt, succeed, fail, practise*
> HURRYING, e.g. *hurry (over/with), hasten (over/with), dawdle (over)*
> DARING—*dare, venture*

For the MODALS, syntax is congruent with semantics, since they occur as auxiliary in the same VP as the verb they modify.

A verb from BEGINNING, TRYING, HURRYING or DARING must occur as syntactic main verb, with the verb that is semantic focus being predicate head of a TO or ING complement clause, e.g. *She stopped hitting him, She attempted to hit him*. The complement clause verb may, in certain circumstances, be omitted, yielding a sentence that has the superficial appearance of the BEGINNING, TRYING or HURRYING item being the only verb. Consider

> (9) *Mary began (cooking/to cook) the pudding at six o'clock*
> (10) *Mary began (eating/to eat) the pudding at six o'clock*

The bracketed portion from sentences like (9) and (10) could only be omitted if the addressee could be expected to infer it, on the basis of the contextual knowledge he shares with the speaker. If Mary were known to be a cook then *Mary began the pudding at six o'clock* would be understood in terms of (9). If Mary were known to be a lady who employs a cook and never goes near a stove herself, then it would be understood in terms of (10). If the addressee could not be expected to have this sort of information about Mary, then no omission should be made from (9) or (10).

It is interesting to note that only certain verbs may be omitted after a BEGINNING or TRYING form. We can shorten the following, if the bracketed information could be expected to be inferred by the addressee: *John finished (making) the bricks before lunch, Mary started (learning) French at fifteen*. But we cannot normally omit the complement clause verb from: *John finished fetching/counting the bricks before lunch, Mary started liking/forgetting French at fifteen*. §§6.1.2–4 discuss the question of which verbs can be omitted after a BEGINNING or TRYING or HURRYING verb (there being a slightly different answer for each type).

Sentences such as *John has begun the potatoes* and *Fred has begun the carrots* are each at least five ways ambiguous. John could have begun planting, harvesting, peeling, cooking or eating, and Fred likewise. Now if *begin* in these two sentences was a simple transitive verb, we would expect the coordination *John has begun the potatoes and Fred (has begun) the carrots* to be $5 \times 5 = 25$ ways ambiguous. It is not—it is only five ways ambiguous. Whatever John is understood to have begun doing to the potatoes, Fred is understood to have begun doing a similar thing to the carrots.

This provides justification for our position that a sentence like *John has begun the potatoes* has an underlying complement clause verb, which can be omitted when certain linguistic and pragmatic conditions are satisfied. In a coordinate structure, such as *John has begun the potatoes and Fred (has begun) the carrots*, this omission applies in tandem in the two clauses, omitting verbs that have the same or similar meaning (e.g. *peeling* from before *the potatoes* and *scraping* from before *the carrots*, since these both refer to modes of preparation).

Further support for this syntactic treatment of BEGIN verbs is provided by evidence from passivisation, discussed in §9.3.

SECONDARY-B verbs introduce an extra role, the Principal or the Timer (which is subject of the main verb), in addition to the roles associated with the semantically central verb, which is predicate head within the complement clause, e.g. *Jane wants Jim to drive the Saab, Fred dreads Mary's seeing that photo*. However, the subject of the Secondary-B verb is often identical with the subject of the complement clause and the latter is then generally omitted, e.g. *Jane wants to drive the Saab, Fred dreads seeing that photo*. The semantic types with this property are:

WANTING (with a number of subdivisions, see §6.2.1), e.g. *want, wish (for); hope (for); need, require; expect; intend; pretend*
POSTPONING, e.g. *postpone, delay, defer, avoid*

(In some languages WANTING verbs must have the same subject as the verb they semantically modify; WANTING is then a Secondary-A type.)

The complement clause verb may be omitted after certain WANTING verbs if it has the general meaning 'get' (i.e. *get, receive, have*, etc.). Thus, *I want (to get) a rabbit for my birthday, He needs (to get/have) a haircut*. Some verbs from this type include a preposition in their basic form, e.g. *hope (for), wish (for)*; this is omitted before a TO complement but retained when immediately followed by an NP, e.g. *Fred hoped to receive a slice of your pudding, Fred hoped for a slice of your pudding*.

SECONDARY-C verbs must introduce a further role over and above the roles of the complement clause verb. This is subject of the main verb; it is the Causer or Helper role, and is generally HUMAN. Thus, *Harry forced Mary to eat the snail*. It is unlikely that main clause and complement clause subjects will be identical; if they are, neither can be omitted, e.g. *Harry forced himself to eat the snail* (not **Harry forced to eat the snail*). The types are:

MAKING, e.g. *make, force, cause, tempt; let, permit, allow; prevent, spare, ensure*
HELPING, e.g. *help, aid, assist*

SECONDARY-D verbs may optionally add a role (introduced by preposition *to*) to the roles required by the verbs they modify, e.g. *It seems likely (to Mary) that John voted for Thatcher*, and *That Chris can't understand algebra doesn't matter (to Karen)*. There are two semantic types with this property:

SEEM, e.g. *seem, appear, happen, look*
MATTER—*matter, count*

The *to* NP marks the person who makes the inference (for SEEM) or who attaches importance to the happening (for MATTER). If it is omitted, then, according to the pragmatic context, the statement of the complement clause will be taken to seem/matter 'to me', or 'to us' or 'to everyone'.

Secondary-D verbs take a complement clause in subject slot. Verbs from the SEEM type occur with one of those adjectives that may take a subject complement clause (VALUE, DIFFICULTY, QUALIFICATION and the CLEVER subtype of HUMAN PROPENSITY). There is further discussion of the semantics and syntax of Secondary-D verbs in §6.4.

Each Secondary verb modifies some other verb. The verb modified may be a Primary verb, or a further Secondary verb—in which case there must be a third verb which it in turn modifies. Thus:

(11) *The invalid wants* (Sec-B) *to eat* (Prim-A)
(12) *The nurse wants* (Sec-B) *to try* (Sec-A) *to force* (Sec-C) *the invalid to eat* (Prim-A)

A Primary-B verb may involve nothing but NPs as arguments, or it can take a complement clause, which can have any kind of Primary or Secondary verb as predicate head, e.g.

(13) *John remembered* (Prim-B) *the swindle*
(14) *John remembered* (Prim-B) *Mary's starting* (Sec-A) *to like* (Prim-B) *ordering* (Prim-B) *her jockey to appear* (Sec-D) *to try* (Sec-A) *to win* (Prim-A) *certain races*

Such a grammatical chain may carry on indefinitely; when it finishes, the final clause must contain a Primary-A verb, or a Primary-B verb with all argument slots filled by NPs.

4

Primary-A verb types

This chapter deals with literal meanings of Primary-A verbs, with roles filled by NPs that have CONCRETE heads. As mentioned before, some Primary-A verbs do have secondary, metaphorical meanings, with other kinds of NP (or even a complement clause) as subject or object (e.g. *John's having got the job quite threw me* i.e. 'discomfited me'). However, these are almost all idiosyncratic to particular verbs so that no generalisations are possible across a type or subtype.

4.1. MOTION and REST

These two types have a number of subtypes which show pervasive semantic and syntactic parallels, so that they can usefully be considered together.

The role common to all MOTION verbs is (thing) Moving (e.g. *Mary ran*) and to all REST verbs (thing) Resting (e.g. *John knelt*). There may also be specification of Locus—the place of rest, or place with respect to which motion takes place. For some verbs specification of Locus is obligatory, e.g. *He resides in town*; for others it is optional, e.g. *John stood (on the stone)*.

An NP in Locus role is most often marked by the appropriate preposition. As noted in §2.5 such place adverbial NPs are semantically linked to the MOTION/REST verb and should be placed after the predicate (whereas place adverbs with verbs from other types may occur sentence-initially or medially). Certain MOTION verbs may allow the preposition to be omitted, a slight semantic difference then resulting, e.g. *He jumped (over) the river*, *She climbed (up) the mountain*. It is also possible in certain circumstances to omit a preposition before a measure phrase, e.g. *He ran (for) a mile*. Conditions for omitting the preposition, and the status of the final NP in these constructions, are taken up in §§8.2.4–5.

A fair proportion of MOTION and REST verbs are intransitive. Some of these may be used transitively in a causative sense (i.e. with S = O); thus, *The horse trotted around the ring, He trotted the horse around the ring*, and *The plant stood on the window-sill, He stood the plant on the window-sill.* (See §8.3.)

Others are basically transitive, e.g. *take.* Only some of these may omit an object NP if it can be inferred from context and/or surrounding dialogue, e.g. *We followed (him) as far as the minefield.* Transitivity is largely determined by the meaning of a verb; that is, by the subtype to which it belongs.

We can recognise seven subtypes of MOTION and six of REST. Taking these one or two at a time:

MOTION-a, the RUN subtype, refers to a mode of motion, e.g. *run, walk, crawl, slide, spin, roll, turn, wriggle, swing, wave, rock, shake, climb, dive, stroll, trot, gallop, jog, dance, march, jump, bounce, swim, fly* and one sense of *play* (as in *The child is playing in the sand*).

REST-a, the SIT subtype, referring to a stance of resting, e.g. *sit (down), stand (up), lie (down), kneel, crouch, squat, lean, hang (down), float.*

Verbs in these two subtypes are basically intransitive. Since they describe a mode of motion or stance of rest the only obligatory role is Moving/Resting. A Locus can be included, but this is optional, e.g. *He loves strolling (in the park), Mary is sitting down at last (in her favourite armchair).*

There exists the potential for any verb from RUN or SIT to be used transitively, in a causative sense. The Moving or Resting role (which is S in an intransitive construction) becomes O, and an additional role—the Causer, normally HUMAN—is introduced in A syntactic function, e.g. *The dog walked, He walked the dog*; *The log slid down the icy track, He slid the log down the icy track*; *The child lay down on the couch, She laid the child down on the couch*; *The raft floated on the stream, He floated the raft on the stream.*

Some RUN and SIT verbs are commonly used in transitive constructions, e.g. *spin, roll, rock, trot, march, fly, sit, stand, lean, hang.* Others seldom or never are, e.g. *climb, dive, stroll, kneel,*

crouch. This is simply because people do not often make someone
or something climb or dive or kneel, as they do make them march
or roll or sit (and this often relates to the activity, that it is
something which is not easy for an outsider to control). But the
potential exists for any verb from these types to be used
causatively if the appropriate circumstances should arise. Suppose
that someone chose to train a possum to climb high, for some
marsupial Olympics; in such circumstances one could say, side by
side with *The champion possum climbed to the top of a kauri pine*,
the sentence *He climbed the champion possum to the top of a kauri
pine*.

Ride and *drive* can be considered members of the RUN subtype
which are only used in causative form, e.g. *John rode the mare*.
Since there is no corresponding intransitive (e.g. **The mare rode*)
it is permissible to omit specification of the object NP, in
appropriate circumstances, e.g. *John rides every morning* (cf.
§8.3.1).

MOTION-b, the ARRIVE subtype, deals with motion with respect to a
definite Locus, e.g. (i) *arrive, return, go, come*; (ii) *enter, cross,
depart, travel, pass, escape*; *come in, go out*; (iii) *reach, approach,
visit* (which spans the MOTION and ATTENTION types).

REST-b, the STAY subtype, deals with rest at a definite Locus, e.g.
stay, settle (down), live, stop, remain, reside; *attend*.

Since verbs from these two subtypes refer to motion or rest with
respect to a Locus, the Locus must normally be stated, either
through an NP or an adverbal, e.g. *He has remained outside/in the
garage*, *She hasn't yet travelled to Spain/there*.

STAY verbs are almost all intransitive, and include a preposition
before the Locus NP, e.g. *stay on the farm*. Some ARRIVE verbs
have similar syntax, e.g. *arrive at the station, return to Sheffield, go
to the cowshed, come into the kitchen*. *Go* and *come* include in their
meanings a Locus specification 'to there' and 'to here' respectively; in
view of this, *here* can be omitted from *come here* and *there* from *go
there*, although these adverbs often are retained. *Arrive* and *return*
may also be used without a Locus NP or adverb, and 'here' is then
implied. (A Locus NP may also be omitted after these verbs when
it could be inferred from the previous discourse, e.g. *He cycled all*

the way to town. Oh, what time did he arrive (sc. in town)*?* and
She's driven over to Brighton. How long is she staying (sc. in
Brighton)*?*)

Set (ii) of ARRIVE verbs could also be regarded as intransitive,
with the Locus marked by a preposition; but this preposition may
be omitted in appropriate circumstances. *Enter* would generally
omit the preposition, e.g. *enter (into) the room. Cross* can equally
well retain or omit it, e.g. *cross (over) the road. Depart* may omit
the preposition in some styles of speech, e.g. *depart (from) the
city. Travel* can occur with a variety of prepositions; just *over* can
be omitted, from a sentence like *He travelled ((all) over) Africa
from coast to coast. Pass* can omit *by*, as in *pass (by) the church*,
but not *through*, e.g. *pass through the tunnel/funfair*. In all of these
instances omission of a preposition carries a semantic difference
(see Chapter 8). This can clearly be seen with *escape*—a
preposition is required with the meaning 'get away from a place,
where one was confined', e.g. *escape from prison*, but not for the
meaning 'avoid (confinement, or some other ill fortune)', e.g.
escape (being sent to) prison, escape punishment.

A few ARRIVE verbs are basically transitive, e.g. *approach, visit*
and *reach*, as in *They won't reach the lake tonight.* (There is also
reach (to) 'extend to', as in *The road reaches to the coast*; this sense
relates to the STRETCH subtype of AFFECT.) From the STAY subtype,
attend is transitive and generally has a non-CONCRETE noun as
object, e.g. *He attended the meeting/play/wedding*.

ARRIVE and STAY verbs can generally not be used in a causative
construction, but there are some exceptions. *Settle* may be used
causatively and then the Causer will generally be in position of
authority, e.g. *Baby settled down for the night, Mother settled baby
down for the night; Ex-servicemen settled on the plains; The
government settled ex-servicemen on the plains*; see §8.3.2. *Return*
would normally have an animate NP in S function, e.g. *Fred has
returned to work*; it can be used causatively, generally with a non-
human O NP, e.g. *John returned the book to the library*. If the
Moving role for *pass* is a manipulable object the verb can then be
used transitively, e.g. *They passed the port around the table*
alongside *The port passed around the table.* (Compare *The
procession passed around the front of the palace*, where the Moving
role is non-manipulable, and a causative construction is implausible.)

MOTION-C, the TAKE subtype, refers to causing something to be in motion with respect to a Locus, e.g. (i) *take, bring, fetch*; (ii) *send*; (iii) *move, raise, lift, steal*.

These are all transitive verbs with a Causer (normally HUMAN) in A function. Set (i) involves double realisation of the Moving role —both A and O NPs normally refer to something in motion, e.g. *John* (Causer; Moving) *brought his dog* (Moving) *to the party*. For sets (ii) and (iii) the Causer need not be Moving but of course the O NP must be.

Most TAKE verbs are like ARRIVE in requiring specification of the Locus. However, *take* and *bring*, the transitive correspondents of *go* and *come*, have as part of their meaning the specifications 'to there' and 'to here' respectively, so that *there* can be omitted after *take* and *here* after *bring*. *Fetch* is a combination of *go* (to where something is) and *bring* (it back to the starting point); again 'here' is implied and can be omitted. *Send* involves a Causer arranging for a Moving thing to go, not normally accompanying it. Here a Locus should be specified, e.g. *I sent the cow to market* (unless it could be inferred from the preceding discourse, e.g. *Have you got in touch with Phoebe yet? Well, I sent a letter* (sc. to her) *yesterday*).

Take, bring, fetch and *send* may be used with the additional implication of 'giving'—compare *take the pig to market* (a destination) with *take the pig to/for Mary* (*for* is likely to imply a recipient, and *to* could mark recipient).

Move may be intransitive or transitive; the former use could be assigned to the ARRIVE subtype, the latter to TAKE. This verb does not denote a general mode of motion (like RUN) but rather motion with respect to various Locuses, e.g. *Mary moved from Seattle to Vancouver*. *Move* can be used with a general adverb, or with no overt specification of Locus, e.g. *He's always moving* (*about*), *She's continually moving the furniture* (*around*), but the meaning of the verb still provides a clear implication of 'from this place to that place to another place . . .'. *Raise* and *lift* behave similarly.

Steal is a more specific verb, relating to *take* and transitive *move*, where the Moving role (in O function) refers to something that does not belong to the Causer and should not have been taken/ moved by him. Here the focus is on the nature of the referent of the Moving role, and a Locus NP, while often included, is not obligatory, e.g. *He stole ten dollars* (*from Mary's purse*).

REST-c, the PUT subtype, refers to causing something to be at rest at a Locus, e.g. (i) *put, place, set, arrange, install, put NP on, sow, plant, fill, load, pack*; *hide*; *beach, land, shelve*; (ii) *leave, desert, abandon, take NP off*.

These are also transitive verbs, with the Causer (normally HUMAN) in A and the thing Resting in O function. The Locus must be specified, by a prepositional NP or an adverb, e.g. *She put the box down/outside/there/on the table*. Some hyponyms of *put* have Locus specified as part of the meaning of the verb, e.g. *land* 'put on land', *beach* 'put on a beach', *shelve* 'put on a shelf'.

The transitive verbs *leave, desert* and *abandon* involve an intersection of MOTION and REST. They have two senses: (i) the subject (Moving) goes away, and does not take a person or thing (Resting or conceivably Moving) which he might have been expected to take with him, or else expected to remain with, e.g. *John* (Moving) *abandoned his car* (Resting or Moving) *on the highway*, or *Mary* (Moving) *left her husband* (Resting); or (ii) the subject (Moving) goes away from a place (Locus) where he had been for some time and might have been expected to remain longer, e.g. *Trotsky left Russia in the twenties*. In (i) the Moving participant has a kind of Causer role (i.e. did *not* take, did *not* stay with); this does not apply for (ii).

MOTION-d, the FOLLOW subtype, refers to motion with respect to something which is moving, e.g. (i) *follow, track, lead, guide, precede*; *accompany*; (ii) *meet*.

These are all transitive verbs with the Moving role in A and Locus (typically, also Moving) in O function, e.g. *Mbfira tracked the car/Mary, Fred met the train/Jane. Follow* has a further sense in which the O NP is a geographical feature extended in space, e.g. *They followed the river*. A further extension of meaning, applying to both *follow* and *meet*, has geographical features in both A and O slots, e.g. *That road follows the spur of the hill, Those two rivers meet at the foot of the mountain. Lead* may have a variety of non-human NPs in A function, in extensions from its central meaning e.g. *The path/Those tell-tale noises/Her sense of direction led Mary to the robbers' lair*.

Verbs of set (i) are particularly susceptible to omission of the object NP if this is inferable from the context or from previous dialogue, e.g. *You go and I'll follow* (*you*); *I'll lead* (*you*) *and you follow* (*me*). *Meet*, of set (ii), is typically reciprocal—see §§2.9.6 and 9.2.

An additional non-moving Locus is often specified, but is not obligatory, e.g. *John followed Mary* (*to the cave*), *John and Mary met* (*in town*).

REST-d, the CONTAIN subtype, describes relative position of two things, both at rest, e.g. *contain, enclose, encircle, adjoin*; *surround*.

These verbs are transitive. Both roles are Resting, and each is effectively a Locus with respect to the other; they typically have INANIMATE reference. *Adjoin*, like *meet*, is inherently reciprocal (§2.9.6). *Surround* straddles this subtype and also the WRAP subtype of AFFECT (§4.2).

MOTION-e, the CARRY subtype, refers to motion in juxtaposition with some moving object (prototypically, a person's hand), e.g. *carry, bear, transport, cart*.

REST-e, the HOLD subtype, refers to position of rest with respect to, prototypically, a person's hand, e.g. (i) *hold, handle*; (ii) *grab*; *grasp, clutch, catch, gather, pick up*; *capture, trap*.

These are all transitive verbs with the Moving/Resting role mapped onto O function. The subject maps a Causer role (normally HUMAN) and the Locus is likely to be some part of the human's body; the actual body part involved can be specified by a prepositional NP, e.g. *John carried/held the banana in/with his hand/teeth*. (If no body part is specified it is taken to be the unmarked one, hand.)

The CARRY subtype includes some more specialised verbs whose meaning involves specification of the Locus, e.g. *cart* 'carry on a cart' (cf. *land* 'put on land'). Here Causer and Locus are distinct, although the Causer will move with the Locus (i.e. John goes with the cart in *John carted the potatoes* (*to market*)). (Nowadays, *cart* is also used to describe carrying something unwieldy or heavy, by any means.)

Whereas *hold* refers to being in a position of rest in juxtaposition with a person's body, the verbs in set (ii)—*grasp, grab, catch, pick up* and the like—refer to something being brought into such a position, e.g. *John grabbed/picked up the axe (and then held it tightly)*.

As with FOLLOW, an additional non-moving Locus may be specified, but is entirely optional, e.g. *John held the baby (in the nursery)*; *John carried the baby (to the bathroom)*. *John held/carried the baby* are self-sufficient sentences, in the same way that *John ran/sat down* are.

MOTION-f, the THROW subtype, describes causing something to be in motion, e.g. *throw, chuck, fling, pour, spray, water*; *push, press*; *pull, jerk, drag, tug*, one sense of *draw* (e.g. *draw sword from scabbard*).

These are transitive verbs with the thing Moving as O and the Causer (which need not be moving) as A. The meanings of individual verbs describe both the mode of motion and the way in which it was caused.

As with RUN, a specification of Locus is possible, but quite optional, e.g. *Mary pushed the bed (out from the wall) (into the middle of the room)* and *John threw the javelin (towards the grandstand)*. (Note that *throw* and *chuck* can take an adverb *away* or *out* and then have the additional sense of abandon, e.g. *Mary threw away all John's love letters to her*.)

REST-f, the OPEN subtype, refers to causing something to be in a particular position of rest, e.g. *open, close, shut* (the verb *lock* appears also to relate to this subtype).

These verbs are used transitively with the thing Resting in O and Causer (normally HUMAN or WEATHER) in A function, e.g. *John/the wind closed the door*. They also occur in what appears to be an intransitive construction, but most examples of this are in fact either copula plus a participial form of the verb (functioning as an adjective, and describing a state), e.g. *The door is closed*, or else a 'promotion to subject' construction, e.g. *This door opens easily* (see Chapter 10).

In the literal use of OPEN verbs the thing Resting is limited to a small set of PART nouns, e.g. *window, door, lid*. The Locus is inferable from meanings of noun and verb and is unlikely to be stated (*The door was shut into the door-frame* sounds unbearably pedantic).

These verbs, especially in their participial use, also have a metaphorical sense, e.g. *His mind is open/closed/shut to new ideas.*

MOTION-g, the DROP subtype, refers to unwanted motion, e.g. *fall, drop, spill, tip (over), upset, overturn, capsize, trip, slip.*

These verbs may be used intransitively, with the Moving thing in S function. The motion may be due to a combination of natural forces such as gravity (*The apple fell from the tree*) and weather (*The boat overturned in the storm*). All DROP verbs, with the sole exception of *fall*, are also used transitively, with the thing Moving as O. The A NP is Causer—either a natural force responsible for the movement (*The storm overturned the boat*) or some HUMAN who brought the movement about either through planned action (*John deliberately dropped the vase*) or—and this is the unmarked circumstance—through miscalculation (*John (accidentally) dropped the vase*). S = O intransitive pairs such as this are discussed further in §8.3.2.

It is interesting that *fall*, perhaps the most common verb of this subtype, is the only member that is exclusively intransitive. (There is the transitive *fell* but this is only used of trees—and, sometimes, people—and refers to deliberate action, whereas *fall* normally describes uncontrolled motion towards the ground.)

Locus NP(s) may be added, but are not obligatory, e.g. *The milk spilt (out of the jug) (onto the ground).*

4.2. AFFECT

AFFECT items are prototypical transitive verbs (according to the criteria set out by Hopper and Thompson 1980). They involve three basic semantic roles—an Agent moves or manipulates something (referred to as the Manip role) so that it comes into contact with some thing or person (the Target role). Either the Manip or the Target (or, occasionally, both) will be physically affected by the activity.

These roles can be mapped onto syntactic relations in three distinct ways:

I. *John* (Agent)   *hit the vase* (Target)   (*with the stick* (Manip))

II. *John* (Agent)   *hit that stick* (Manip)   *on/upon/against*
                                                    the table (Target)

III. *That stick* (Manip)   *hit the vase* (Target)

The most characteristic AFFECT verb construction is I, in which the Target is affected by the Manip being brought into contact with it—John swings that stick against the vase so that the vase breaks; the Manip is, in this instance of the activity, stronger than the Target. The Manip will either be an object held by the Agent (usually, in his hand) or else some body part of the Agent. The *with* instrumental phrase in construction I need not be stated, although it could always be supplied. (Neither A nor O can be omitted from any of the three construction types.)

Construction II is likely to be used when the Manip is less strong than the Target, so that it is the Manip which is physically affected by impact of Manip on Target—John swings that stick against the table and the stick breaks. That role which is physically affected is most salient in this instance of the activity and is coded onto O syntactic relation (§3.3.1)—this is the Target in I and the Manip in II. In II the Target is marked by a preposition *on*, *upon*, *against*, etc. It is noteworthy that this prepositional phrase cannot be omitted from II. (If it were, then *John hit that stick* would be taken to have *that stick* as Target, i.e. an instance of construction I where the *with* phrase has been omitted. This confirms I as the unmarked construction for AFFECT verbs.)

It is also possible to say, as an alternative to I, *John's stick hit the vase* (*when he was swinging it to test its weight, not aware that there was a vase nearby*) or just *That stick hit the vase* (*when John swung it*), as in III. To put the Manip into A (transitive subject) slot in this way may disclaim the Agent's responsibility for the result of the activity—true, he was swinging that stick, but he did not intend to hit the vase (and wouldn't have dreamt of swinging it if he'd known the vase was there). For III the Target must, as in I, be in O slot. The Agent has no obligatory syntactic coding in III, but it is usually hovering somewhere in the sentence, e.g. as possessor to Manip within the A NP (*John's stick*) or as A within a subordinate clause (*when John was swinging it*). Pattern III is, like II, a marked construction for AFFECT verbs; it is used to achieve a certain semantic effect.

(Sentences such as *The falling coconut hit Mary* (*as she sat under the palm tree*) can also be classified as III. The Manip role in this sentence, *the falling coconut*, is something moving due to a natural force—here, gravity.)

It will be seen that 'patient' and 'instrument' are not appropriate labels for the semantic roles associated with AFFECT verbs. That role which is affected by the hitting is the patient and is mapped onto O syntactic relation—this is the Target in I and the Manip in II. The role which engenders the affect on the patient is the instrument—this is the Manip in I; the Target could conceivably be called an instrument in II.

There are two other construction types applicable to some AFFECT verbs. The first is a variant of I, with a preposition inserted before the Target:

> IV *John* (Agent) *kicked at the door* (Target) (*with his hob-nailed boots* (Manip))

In Chapter 8 we discuss the syntactic status of *the door* in IV—whether or not it is still in O relation.

The other construction type is also a variant of I. An adverb may replace the O NP, indicating that the activity was indulged in rather wildly (rather than being directed, in a controlled fashion, at a specific Target):

> V *John* (Agent) *hit out* (*with that stick* (Manip))

It is not possible to include *the door* either before or after *out* in V. However, *at the door* is acceptable, yielding a blend of IV and V, where the Agent hits out wildly, but in the direction of a Target, i.e. *John hit out at the door* (*with that stick*).

Note that there is no necessary connection between IV and V. Some verbs can take a preposition before the Target, in IV, but cannot accept an adverb, in V, e.g. *He hammered at the door*, but not **He hammered out*. (*He hammered the message out* is different both syntactically—an O NP is included—and semantically.)

A number of AFFECT verbs may include an adjective after the Target NP (when this is in O function) in construction I or III, describing the state in which the Target was put by the activity, e.g. *Mary knocked John unconscious* (*with her stick*), *Mary's stick knocked John unconscious*.

AFFECT, like MOTION and REST, is a large type, involving hundreds of verbs. It can usefully be divided into eight subtypes, each of which has its special semantic and syntactic characteristics. (Note that all AFFECT verbs are transitive; verbs in some subtypes (noted below) may also function intransitively.)

AFFECT-a, the TOUCH subtype, refers to Manip minimally coming into contact with Target, with no disturbance of the Target, e.g. *touch*, *stroke*.

These verbs occur in the first three constructions, e.g. I *She stroked the fur* (*with her left hand*), II *She stroked her left hand on/ over the fur*, III *Her left hand stroked the fur* (*although she wasn't aware of it*). Note that *feel* only occurs in construction I; it is most appropriately regarded as a member of the ATTENTION type (§5.1).

AFFECT-b, the HIT subtype, refers to Manip being brought through the air to impact on Target, e.g. *hit*, *strike*, *punch*, *bump*, *kick*, *knock*, *tap*, *bash*, *slap*, *spank*; *whip*, *belt*, *stone*, *cane*, *hammer*; *shoot*.

All occur in constructions I, II and III. Those like *hit*, *strike*, *punch*, *kick*, which refer to some vigorous activity that can be done quite wildly (just moving the Manip without controlled focus on a particular Target), also occur in V and in IV. Verbs such as *knock*, *tap*, *bash*, *slap* and *spank* carry an implication that Manip should make contact with a specific Target—they occur in I, II and III, and also in IV, e.g. *He knocked on/at/against the door* (*with his stick*), but not in V. Then there are verbs derived from nouns—such as *whip*, *belt*, *stone*, *hammer*—which have more restricted syntactic possibilities (as verbs derived from nouns often do have). They may all occur in I, just *whip* in III (*The rope which John swung whipped my face*) and just *hammer* in IV. The meanings of these verbs include specification of an archetypical Manip (e.g. the central meaning of *hammer* is 'hit with a hammer') and because of this it would be implausible for the Manip to be in O slot, in II. (Note, though, that these verbs may be used with a non-cognate Manip, which can be O in II, e.g. *He hammered his fists upon the door*.)

Shoot is an unusual verb in that there are effectively two Manips —the Agent operates a gun or bow ($Manip_1$) which sends on its way a projectile ($Manip_2$) that impacts on the Target. Either 'gun' or 'projectile' may fill the Manip slot in I/IV and III, with the 'other Manip' being introduced in I/IV by *using*; thus: I/IV *John shot (at) the pig with pellets using his shotgun/with his shotgun using pellets*, and III *John's shotgun/pellets accidentally shot the pig*. The 'gun', however, is unlikely to occur in O slot in II, simply because use of the verb *shoot* implies a gun as Manip—we may say *John shot pellets at the pig using his shotgun*, a II construction with the 'projectile' in O slot, but scarcely **John shot his shotgun at the pig using pellets*.

Some verbs from the HIT subtype may include an adjective after the Target role when it is in O function, describing a state engendered by the action, e.g. *kick/punch/knock unconscious*, *shoot dead*.

AFFECT-c, the STAB subtype, refers to a pointed or bladed Manip penetrating below the surface of the Target, e.g. *pierce*, *prick*, *stab*, *dig*, *sting*, *knife*, *spear*; *cut*, *prune*, *mow*, *saw*, *slice*, *chop*, *hack*.

All of these verbs occur in constructions I and III (although it is not terribly common for something to slice or chop or—especially —to saw or prune accidentally, in III). Construction II, with the Manip as O, is more marginal for most STAB verbs simply because their meanings focus on the affect on the Target, which should thus be in O slot (however, it is possible to say *He stabbed his dagger into the ground*, with focus on the dagger, since here the Target, the ground, is not critically affected by the activity). Construction II is least likely with *spear* and *knife*, verbs derived from nouns, since the meaning of the verb includes specification of an archetypical Manip; however, the Manip can be in O slot when it is not cognate with the verb, e.g. *She speared the garden fork through her foot*.

AFFECT-d, the RUB subtype, refers to the Manip being manipulated to affect the surface of the Target, e.g. *rub*, *wipe*, *scrape*, *scratch*, *mark*; *sweep*, *brush*, *shave*, *rake*; *polish*; *lick*. *Wash* has a slightly different meaning, referring to the effect on the Target ('make clean using liquid') but can be regarded as a divergent member of this subtype.

Rub, the prototypical member of the subtype, can occur in constructions I, e.g. *He rubbed the table with that cloth*, and II, e.g.

He rubbed that cloth over/on the table. Construction III is just possible: *His trousers rubbed the table* (*as he squeezed by*). Construction IV is also plausible (*He rubbed at the table with a clean cloth*) but not V.

We also get variants of I where the head of the O NP refers to something on a surface, whose relationship to the surface is affected by the activity:

Ia. *John rubbed* [*the polish into the table*] (*with that cloth*)
Ib. *John rubbed* [*the mark* (*off the table*)] (*with that cloth*)

It is interesting to note that, although prepositional NPs can usually occur in any order after a verb, *with that cloth* could not felicitously intrude between *the polish* and *into the table* in Ia, or between *the mark* and *off the table* in Ib.

Note that instead of *off* in Ib we could have *on*, describing just where the mark is, rather than where it should go. *On* must be used when *at* is inserted before the O NP, giving:

IVb. *John rubbed* [*at the mark on the table*] *with that cloth*

Wipe, *scrape* and *scratch* may—like *rub*—be used in I–IV and Ia, Ib, IVb. *Sweep*, *brush*, *shave* and *rake* all have meanings that focus on the Target—they occur in I, Ib, IV and IVb, less convincingly in III, and scarcely in II, where the Target is not in O function. *Polish* is even more limited, being effectively restricted to I and IV; since the meaning of the verb includes reference to the substance rubbed into a surface, the Target can only be the surface (i.e. *the table* in I, and not *the polish* in Ia). *Lick* occurs in I, Ib, IV and IVb but is scarcely plausible in II (?*The possum licked its tongue over the leaf*)—because the meaning of the verb includes specification of the Manip (a tongue) which is unlikely to be focused on and placed in O slot—or III—because tongues do not lick things accidentally (although, in one metaphorical sense of the verb, flames do).

Verbs from the RUB subtype may typically take an adjective after the Target when it is in O slot, e.g. *rub/wipe/scrape/brush/lick clean*.

AFFECT-e, the WRAP subtype, refers to the Manip moving into juxtaposition with the Target, e.g. *wrap*; *cover*; *butter, roof, veil, clothe, dress, grease*; *plaster, paint, coat*; *surround, frame*; *put NP on*.

Wrap, the key member of this subtype, occurs in:

  I. *John* (Agent) *wrapped the box* (Target) *in/with the paper* (Manip)
 II. *John* (Agent) *wrapped the paper* (Manip) *around the box* (Target)

That role which is specifically focused upon is in O slot. Construction II talks about a piece of paper and what was done with it—the paper was wrapped around the box (no matter that perhaps it didn't cover all six sides). Construction I describes what was done to the box—it was well and truly wrapped in the paper (ready for mailing).

Cover, another verb from this subtype, occurs in I *John* (Agent) *covered the box* (Target) *with leaves* (Manip), and in III *Leaves* (Manip) *covered the box* (Target) but not in II (one would scarcely say **John covered leaves over the box*). Interestingly, *wrap* is not used in a straightforward III construction, simply because it is not possible for 'the paper wrapped the box' to happen without an Agent intervening; there is, however, *That sheet of newspaper* (Manip), *blown by the wind, wrapped* (*itself*) *around my legs* (Target).

There are a number of hyponyms of *cover* and *wrap* (mostly derived from nouns) which occur only in construction I—*butter, roof, veil, clothe, dress, grease*. For these the Target is the focus of attention (in O slot) with the general nature of Manip being specified as part of the meaning of the verb.

Paint can be noun and verb but the Verb class membership is diachronically and synchronically prior; it may occur in I *He painted the door with emulsion*, and II *He painted emulsion onto the door*. *Plaster* and *coat* were historically verbs derived from nouns but in the present-day language they function as full members of the WRAP subtype, occurring in I *He plastered his bread with butter*, II *He plastered butter on his bread*, and even III *Mud plastered everything after the flood, Dust coated the window-sills*.

Surround involves intersection of the CONTAIN subtype of REST (*Those hills surround the waterhole*) and WRAP, appearing in I *The general* (Agent) *surrounded the city* (Target) *with his army* (Manip) and III *The army/floodwater* (Manip) *surrounded the city*.

(Target). *Frame* has a similar meaning with primary membership of WRAP, and perhaps a metaphorical extension to CONTAIN (*The clouds and hills frame the sunset tonight*).

Only *paint*, from this subtype, commonly takes an adjective after the Target in O slot, e.g. *paint the door red*.

There is a set of verbs describing an action the reverse of WRAP; this includes *un-* derivatives of some WRAP verbs, e.g. *unwrap, uncover, unroof, undress*, as well as *take* NP *off* and its hyponyms *peel* 'take peel off' and *shell* 'take shell off'. They are virtually restricted to a single construction, which is similar to Ib for RUB, e.g. *He took the lid off the pan with his left hand*.

AFFECT-f, the STRETCH subtype, refers to the Agent using a Manip to change the shape or state of a Target, e.g. *stretch, extend, compress, bend, curl, fold, coil; twist, pinch, squeeze; fade; vaporise, liquefy, solidify, melt; dissolve; freeze, cool (down), warm (up), heat (up), burn, singe*.

The first set of verbs refer to changing the shape of a Target—in one dimension (*stretch, extend, compress*), in two dimensions (*bend, curl, fold, coil*), or in three dimensions (*twist, pinch, squeeze*). These focus on the change in the Target, which must be in O slot. Thus, construction II is not available, only I (III is implausible, since such changes are unlikely to be accidentally engendered). The Manip used to effect the change can be stated (e.g. *stretch it on a rack, curl them with a curling iron, squeeze it with pincers, twist it with his bare hands*) but need not be.

All these verbs are transitive. The one-dimensional and two-dimensional items (and perhaps *twist* of the three-dimensional) may also be used intransitively, with the Target as S, e.g. *Leaves curl in late summer, That patch of desert extends further each year*.

Related to change-of-shape verbs are those describing a change of state—*vaporise, liquefy, solidify* (all derived from nouns), *melt* —and a change of temperature—*freeze* (which may also involve change of state), *cool (down), warm (up), heat (up)*. These occur in constructions I and III (*She froze the mixture with solid carbon dioxide, John's bar heater/the hot weather melted the butter*), and may also be used intransitively, with O = S (*The butter melted*).

Burn and *singe* belong in this subtype. They can be used intransitively (*The fire/house is burning*) and transitively in I *Mary burned John with that hot poker*, III *That hot poker burned John*, and Ib *Mary burned the paint off the door with a blow-torch*.

Some STRETCH verbs may take a state adjective or an adverb after the Target role when in O relation, or after the verb used intransitively with Target in S relation, e.g. *John froze it solid*, *It froze solid*; and *bend double, fold over*.

AFFECT-g, the BUILD subtype, refers to manufacture and cooking. These verbs involve an Agent manipulating Manip so as to create something (called the Product role), e.g. *build, knit, tie, weave, sew, shape, form, stir, mix, knead; fry, bake, cook*.

The roles can be mapped onto syntactic relations in two ways:

	A	O	Peripheral
VI.	*Mary* (Agent)	*built those bricks* (Manip)	*into a wall* (Product)
VII.	Mary (Agent)	*built a wall* (Product)	*with those bricks* (Manip)

That role out of Manip and Product which is the focus of attention is placed in O relation. Construction VI directs attention to 'those bricks', which may have been left over from another job so that Mary wondered what to do with them—then she hit upon the idea of building them into a wall. Construction VII is concerned with 'a wall', that was perhaps badly needed; it is likely that sufficient bricks were purchased to build it.

Knit behaves in a similar way: VI *Mary* (Agent) *knitted the wool* (Manip) *into a jumper* (Product); and VII *Mary knitted a jumper from/with the wool*. The verb *tie* combines the syntactic possibilities of *knit* and of the WRAP subtype—thus VI *Mary* (Agent) *tied the string* (Manip) *into a knot* (Product); VII *Mary tied a knot* (Product) *with the string* (Manip); and I *Mary tied the box* (Target) *with the string* (Manip); II *Mary tied the string* (Manip) *around the box* (Target).

Besides *make* (in the sense 'bake' or 'build', a different lexeme from the Secondary-C verb in *John made Mary eat it*), *weave, sew, shape* (with sculptor as Agent), *form*, and so on, this subtype also contains *stir* and *mix* (e.g. *She mixed the flour and water into a paste, She mixed a paste from the flour and water*).

Many cooking verbs have quite simple syntax, with Manip in O relation, e.g. *She fried a steak*; there is no special name for the product here, just *fried steak*. With *bake* it is possible to have a simple list of ingredients (the Manip) in O slot, as an alternative to the Product, e.g. *She baked the flour* (Manip) *into a damper* (Product), *She baked a damper with the flour*. But generally it is the Product role that is syntactic O, e.g. *She baked a chocolate cake* (*with/using flour, sugar, cocoa, milk, eggs, butter and vanilla essence*). We mentioned that in *She built those bricks into a wall* the focus is on *those bricks*—what is to be done with them. It would be implausible to focus in the same way on a complex list of cake ingredients, which is why this is not found in O slot, i.e. *?She baked the flour, sugar, cocoa, milk, eggs, butter and vanilla essence into a chocolate cake* sounds very odd.

Two other sets of verbs can be assigned to the BUILD subtype—*mend, repair*; and *draw, write, sign, forge*. Both sets focus on the product and are confined to construction VII, e.g. *John mended the radio with some tape, Timmie drew a horse with the crayons you sent*.

AFFECT-h, the BREAK subtype, involves an Agent causing some object (the Breaking role) to lose its physical unity, e.g. *break, crush, squash, destroy, damage, wreck, collapse; tear, split, chip, crack, smash, crash; burst, explode, blow* NP *up, let* NP *off, erupt*.

It is useful to compare BREAK with HIT. *Hit* describes a type of action, a Manip being brought into contact with a Target; there often is, but there need not be, damage to either Manip or Target —we can say *John hit the vase with that stick but it didn't even chip*, or *John hit that stick on the table but it didn't break*. In contrast, *break* describes the resultant effect of some action on an object (the Breaking).

BREAK verbs occur in constructions I, II and III (but not IV or V). The Breaking role is focused on (as part of the meaning of these verbs) and must be in O slot; it can be identified with either Target or Manip:

    I. *John* (Agent) *broke the vase* (Target = Breaking) (*with that stick* (Manip))

    II. *John* (Agent) *broke that stick* (Manip = Breaking) (*on the table* (Target))

    III. *John's stick* (Manip) *broke the vase* (Target = Breaking)

Like such verbs as *bend* or *burn*, from the STRETCH subtype, *break* may also be used intransitively (with Breaking as S), either to describe something which appears to happen spontaneously (*It just broke*) or to describe the effect of a HIT activity. Sentences I, II and III above could be rephrased *John hit the vase* (Target) *with that stick and the vase* (Breaking) *broke*; *John hit that stick* (Manip) *on the table and that stick* (Breaking) *broke*; *John's stick hit the vase* (Target) *and the vase* (Breaking) *broke*.

Breaking may also be identified with roles from other types, e.g. with Moving from the THROW subtype of MOTION, as in *John* (Causer) *threw the vase* (Moving) *down and it* (Breaking) *broke*, which could be restated with *break* as transitive verb in the first clause, *John broke the vase* (Breaking) *by throwing it* (Moving) *down*.

Crush, *squash* and *destroy* all describe a massive distintegration of physical form, which can only be achieved if Breaking is Target (not Manip); they are not used intransitively and only in transitive constructions I and III. *Damage* and *wreck* occur in I, II and III but are not used intransitively, since there must be some identifiable agent for the effects referred to by these verbs. *Tear*, *split*, *chip*, *crack* and *smash* are like *break* in occurring in I, II and III and in an intransitive construction. *Burst* shows similar possibilities—*John burst the balloon with a pin* (i.e. he moved the pin to the balloon), *John burst the balloon on a nail* (he moved the balloon to the nail), *A nail burst the balloon* (when the balloon happened to touch it) or just *The balloon burst*. *Explode* and *blow up* occur in I and also intransitively; *let off* has a meaning similar to the transitive sense of *explode*, and is confined to I. *Erupt* only occurs intransitively, simply because people have not yet found a way of causing volcanoes to erupt.

Chip and *tear* also occur in construction IV (with *at* before the Target) indicating that something is done bit by bit until a result is achieved, e.g. *He kept tearing at the wrapping paper until it was all removed*.

Native speakers have clear intuitions that *break* and *smash* are primarily transitive verbs, which can also be used intransitively, but that *explode* and *burst* are basically intransitive, with the transitive constructions being causative (e.g. *The bomb exploded*, *The army disposal squad exploded the bomb*). We return to this question in §8.3.2.

Some BREAK verbs may have an adjective inserted after the Breaking role in O relation, or after the verb when used intransitively with Breaking in S slot, e.g. *He broke it open, It broke open, She squashed it flat.*

4.3. GIVING

Verbs of this type involve three semantic roles—a Donor transfers possession of some Gift to a Recipient. There are two basic construction types, both with Donor in A syntactic relation; one has the Gift and the other the Recipient as O:

A	O	Peripheral
I. *John* (Donor)	*gave a book* (Gift)	*to Tom* (Recipient)
II. *John* (Donor)	*gave Tom* (Recipient)	*a book* (Gift)

There is a variant of construction II in which the preposition *with* is inserted before the post-O Gift NP:

IIw. *John* (Donor) *supplied the army* (Recipient) *with bully beef* (Gift)

Some verbs occur in both I and II, others only in one of these constructions. Some verbs must take *with*, for some *with* is optional—shown as II(w)—and for a third set *with* is not permissible in construction II. Thus:

I and II—*give, hand* (*over*), *lend, sell, rent, hire, pay, owe, bequeath*
I and II(w)—*serve, feed, supply*
I and IIw—*present*
I only—*donate, contribute, deliver, let*
II only—*tip*
IIw only—*reward, bribe*

Construction I focuses on the Gift, which is then in O slot; these sentences centre on 'giving a book' (or other Gift). Constructions II and IIw focus on the Recipient, in O slot; they centre on 'giving Tom' (or some other Recipient). Suppose John wanted to sell his Caxton Bible to raise money; this would be described with the Gift as O, e.g. *John sold his Caxton Bible* (*to Tom, or whoever*). But suppose instead that Tom begs to be allowed to purchase the

Bible; John doesn't need to sell it but he likes Tom and is prepared to oblige him—in this circumstance it would be appropriate to say *John sold Tom his Caxton Bible*, with the Recipient as O.

As mentioned in §3.3.1, an instance of a particular role should have specific reference in order to be a candidate for the O syntactic slot. One could say *John gave the Red Cross a hundred dollars* alongside *John gave a hundred dollars to the Red Cross*, but scarcely **John gave good causes a hundred dollars* (since *good causes* is too vague to be an acceptable O), only *John gave a hundred dollars to good causes*.

Donate and *contribute* focus on the Gift that the Donor makes available (others will also be giving to that Recipient). These verbs only occur in I, with the Gift as O. (*Bequeath* is most used in I, again with focus on the Gift, although for many speakers II is also possible.) *Reward* 'give in appreciation for some achievement', *bribe* 'give in recompense for doing something illegal' and *tip* 'give in return for some service' focus on the Recipient and are restricted to II or IIw; the important point is that this person is being rewarded, bribed or tipped, with the actual nature of the Gift being of secondary interest.

In §8.2.4 we suggest that construction II is derived from I by putting the Recipient role in O syntactic relation, with Gift being retained as 'second object' (many speakers can passivise on either Recipient or Gift in II, e.g. *Tom was given a book (by John)*, *A book was given Tom (by John)*). Besides *give*, verbs which occur in II include *hand (over)* 'give by hand', *lend* 'give for a limited period', *sell* 'give in exchange for a sum of money', *pay* 'give money in exchange for some service', *owe* 'have an obligation to give, according to social conventions', *bequeath* 'arrange to give on the Donor's death', *rent* and *hire* 'give for a limited period in exchange for a sum of money'. *Let*, which has a meaning similar to *rent* and *hire*, is essentially an abbreviation of *let have*, with the implication that monetary compensation is involved. It can occur only in frame I, i.e. *John let the house to Tim*, not **John let Tim the house* (although we find *let have* in a construction similar to II *John let Tom have the house (for a highish rental)*).

Construction II is used for the direct transfer of ownership of some specific Gift. Construction IIw tends to be used to describe a more general act, along the lines of 'make available'—compare

The ladies gave the soldiers warm socks (each soldier might have been given a pair by one lady) with *The ladies supplied the soldiers with warm socks* (the ladies might here have delivered a large box, from which the soliders could choose socks as they wished and needed). Some verbs occur in both II and IIw, enabling us to draw out a semantic contrast. Thus *They fed us with junk food at that camp* (*but most of us didn't eat it*) and *They fed us lots of vitamins*. The last sentence—without *with*—carries a definite expectation that the vitamins were transferred to (i.e. consumed by) the Recipients.

Construction IIw can be used with *supply* 'give as much as needed of some commodity', *feed* 'supply with food; make eat' and *serve* 'give food and/or drink, in a culturally acceptable manner'; IIw is also employed with *present* 'give in a formal manner', *reward* and *bribe* because here the focus is on the type of giving that the Recipient experiences, with the nature of the Gift being to some extent inferable from the verb (something valuable with *present*, and either a sum of money or something that can easily be converted into money with *reward* and *bribe*).

Note that IIw may also be used with a verb like *pay* when the Gift is something non-typical for that verb; here *with* highlights the unusual nature of the Gift, e.g. *Mary paid John with a kiss* (not **Mary paid John a kiss* or **Mary paid a kiss to John*).

As mentioned in §4.1, some transitive MOTION verbs may, with appropriate NP referents, add a 'giving' sense to their basic meaning, e.g. *take/throw an apple to Mary*. The syntactic consequence of this is that these verbs may, just when they do carry an implication of giving, occur in construction II (which is not normally available to MOTION verbs), e.g. *take/throw Mary an apple*. (See §8.2.4.)

For *give*, all three roles must normally be stated—no constituent can be omitted from *John gave a book to Tom*, or from *John gave Tom a book*. However, an adverb such as *out* or *away* may be added, indicating a general giving activity, and the Recipient can then be omitted, e.g. *John gave out/away lots of books* (*to his pupils*). Other, more specific verbs can allow one role (other than Donor) to be omitted. Thus, *lend*, *sell*, *rent*, *hire* and *supply* can all omit reference to a Recipient; the focus is on the commodity that the Donor sells, supplies, etc—it is assumed that he'll do this to any potential Recipient (e.g. *She sells stamps*). The Gift need not be stated for *pay*, *bribe*, *tip*, *reward*, *contribute*, *feed*. Here the verb indicates the nature of the giving activity; the unmarked Gift is a sum of money for all of these verbs save *feed*, for which it is food. *Serve* may, in different senses, omit either Gift (*We'll serve the Queen first*) or Recipient (*They serve a lovely quiche in the corner café*) but not both at once. Perhaps only *contribute* may simultaneously omit reference to both Gift and Recipient, and then only when it can be inferred from context or previous dialogue, e.g. *How much are you going to give to the restoration appeal? I've already contributed.*

Market has the meaning 'put on sale', with no particular Recipient in mind; there are only two roles for this verb, e.g. *John* (Donor) *marketed his produce* (Gift). *Exchange* and *trade* describe reciprocal activities, where several people are both Donor and Recipient and are grouped together as referents of the A NP, e.g. *John and Mary* (Donors and Recipients) *exchanged hats* (Gifts).

A further set of GIVING verbs, including *borrow*, *buy*, *purchase*, *accept*, *receive*, *rent* and *hire*, occur in the construction:

> III. *Tom* (Recipient) *bought a book* (Gift) (*from John* (Donor))

Borrow is the converse of *lend*, *buy* and *purchase* of *sell*, and *accept* and *receive* are close to being converses of *give*. *Rent* and *hire* function as converses of themselves—*John hired a boat to Mary* implies *Mary hired a boat from John*, and vice versa.

If the A relation is filled by Recipient, as in III, then the O relation must be Gift. The Donor role can be a peripheral constituent marked by *from*; but it can freely be omitted.

There is also the OWN subtype, related to GIVING, which includes *have*, *lack*, *get*, *obtain*, *come by*, *gain*, *own* and *possess*. These verbs require two roles—Owner and Possession. The Possession corresponds to Gift, while Owner can relate to both Donor and Recipient, e.g. *John* (Owner) *had a Saab* (Possession), *then he* (Donor) *gave it* (Gift) *to Mary* (Recipient) *so now she* (Owner) *has a Saab* (Possession).

Have refers not to an activity but to a general relationship between two roles; it has a very wide semantic range, e.g. *I have a stereo/a daughter/a headache/a wonderful idea/a good dentist.*

Lack, the complement of *have*, is used to draw attention to someone's not having a thing that he might be expected to have. *Get, obtain* and *come by* carry a meaning of becoming, i.e. 'come to have'—compare *I have a Ford* and *I got a Ford yesterday. Gain* is often used for getting something in addition to what one had before, e.g. *gain weight, gain promotion, My shares gained fifteen cents. Own* implies legal or official right to a thing—*Now that the mortgage is paid off, I really own this house. Possess* indicates that there is a strong emotional or mental connection between Owner and Possession—*She possesses a good sense of humour/a fine brain*, or *He doesn't possess a single suit* (*possess* is used here partly to draw attention to what this lack tells about his character). Compare the use of *own* and *possess* in *His father owns an old sedan but John possesses a fine new red sports car*—the verb *possess* implies that John is proud of his car, almost that it is an extension of his personality. (Note that the passive use of *possess*, as in *She is possessed by the devil*, seems to be a separate, homonymous, lexeme.) In §9.2 we explain the different passivisation possibilities of OWN verbs in terms of these differences of meaning.

Have can substitute for most (perhaps all) instances of *possess*, but only for *own* in general statements (*John owns/has two cars*), not in deictically referring expressions (*John owns that car*, scarcely **John has that car*). The general relationship indicated by *have* can alternatively be expressed by the clitic *'s* (which goes onto the last word of an NP), by the preposition *of*, or by the verb *belong to*. Whereas the other verbs of the OWN subtype have Owner as subject, *belong to* has Possession as subject, e.g. *John owns that car, That's John's car, That car belongs to John*.

(*Have* and *get* also have a causative sense, e.g. *She got him to run, She had him running*. These belong to the MAKING type; see §6.3.1.)

The verb *lose* has a number of related senses—it can be the opposite of *gain*, e.g. *lose money*; or of *find* from ATTENTION (§5.1), e.g. *lost my wallet*; or of *win* from COMPETITION (§4.6), e.g. *lose the big game*.

4.4. CORPOREAL

This type covers verbs dealing with bodily gestures. All involve a Human role (which may be extended to higher animals), that is in Subject relation. There may be a second role, some Substance that is taken into or expelled out of the Human's body—thus *eat*, *suck*, *smell*, *taste* on the one hand, and *spit*, *pee*, *vomit*, *fart* on the other. Other CORPOREAL verbs refer just to bodily postures and states—*dream*, *think* (both of which also belong to the THINKING type), *laugh*, *ache*, *die*, etc. There is no clear division between the subclasses—one can swallow a pill or some water or just swallow, much in the way that one blinks; and one can cough, or cough something up.

Some of these verbs may have the Substance in O relation, but this is always omissible—*She has eaten* (*lunch*), *She is vomiting* (*up*) (*her dinner*), *He is shitting* (*blood*).

A number of CORPOREAL verbs may be followed by an NP that has a head noun cognate with the verb, e.g. *He sneezed the most tremendous sneeze I have ever heard*, *I dreamt a really horrid dream*, *She died the most awful death*. It would not usually be felicitous to use a cognate NP that did not include some adjectival modification—*He sneezed a sneeze*, *I dreamt a dream* are only likely to occur in the most extreme rhetorical style. Sometimes the description of a bodily gesture can be achieved through an adverb, e.g. *He laughed raucously* (as alternative to *He laughed a raucous laugh*) but English grammar has much more restricted possibilities for adverbal modification of verbs than for adjectival modification of nouns—hence the usefulness of cognate NPs (one would not say **She died awfully* or **He sneezed* (*most*) *tremendously*, and even *?She died most awfully* sounds a little odd). These cognate NPs have few of the properties of direct objects; for instance, they can only in fairly specific circumstances be the subject of a passive construction—one would scarcely say, **The most awful death was died by her*, although *The same dream was dreamt by all of my brothers* is acceptable.

It is hard to draw boundaries within this type. There do appear to be a number of subsets but these tend to merge into each other:

(*a*) verbs that can be followed by a direct object but not by a cognate NP: *eat*, *chew*, *suck*, *drink*, *smoke*;

(*b*) those that can be followed by a direct object or by a cognate NP: *bite* (e.g. *He bit off a piece of pie, He bit off a huge bite*), *nibble, sip; smell, feel, taste, sniff, swallow, breathe, smile, fart, burp, cough, spit, shit, pee, vomit* (and their synonyms); *live*;

(*c*) those that can only be followed by a cognate NP: *yawn, sneeze, laugh, leer, wink, blink, sob, sleep, dream, think, die*;

(*d*) those that cannot be followed by any NP: (d₁) verbs that are solely intransitive, e.g. *weep, cry, shiver, faint, pass out, wheeze, sweat, rest, ache, suffer, come to, recover, be born*; (d₂) those that also exist in causative form with the Human role (the original S) as transitive O, e.g. *wake, waken, grow, swell, hurt, bleed, heal, drown*.

A number of comments are in order about how individual verbs fit into this classification:

(i) *drink* and *smoke* exist as verbs and as independent nouns—*He drank a drink (of tea)* and *She smoked (that whole packet of/some) smokes* involve a Substance role in O slot, not a cognate NP;

(ii) we can *dream a horrid dream* or *dream a horrid nightmare*. *Nightmare* is not cognate with the verb *dream* but it is a hyponym of the cognate noun *dream*, and behaves like a cognate NP (e.g. *a horrid nightmare* can scarcely be passivised);

(iii) *laugh* and *cry* can take a reflexive pronoun, followed by *to*-plus-verb or a result adjective, e.g. *John cried himself to sleep, Mary laughed herself silly*. These constructions are similar to *John sang Timmie/himself to sleep, Mary talked Jane/herself into going,* where the object can be, but need not be, identical to the subject. Note that the natures of the activities referred to by *laugh* and *cry* are such that one could not laugh or cry anyone else into anything (as one can sing or talk them); these verbs may be used transitively, but are then obligatorily reflexivised;

(iv) *live* is mostly used intransitively, or else with a cognate NP (*He lived a full and happy life*). There are also limited possibilities for non-cognate NPs, e.g. *He lived a dream/an illusion of reality/a lie*. Jespersen (1909–49: part iii, p. 301) quotes *His whole life seemed to be lived in the past*, suggesting that for *live* (but perhaps not for other CORPOREAL verbs) the cognate NP should be considered a direct object (since it is passivisable), similar to non-cognate NPs such as *a lie*;

(v) *blink* would not normally be followed by a cognate NP, as *wink* might be (*He winked a comradely wink at me across the room*), but it surely could be, if the circumstances were right (e.g. *She blinked a rapid series of staccato blinks, before dying*) and so is placed in set (*c*);

(vi) in its literal sense *swell* is intransitive and should belong to (d_1), but it does have a causative when used metaphorically (*The new arrivals swelled the crowd*), indicating membership of (d_2).

Native speakers have intuitions that set (*a*), and *bite*, *smell*, *feel* and *taste* from set (*b*), are basically transitive, and that all the remainder are basically intransitive. As already mentioned, the subject is normally the Human role, except that for *ache* and *hurt* it is a body part of the Human (for *bleed* and *grow* the subject can be either a person or a body part). CORPOREAL verbs such as *grow* and *die* may be extended as appropriate to animals and plants.

There are a number of transitive verbs which have the Human role in O slot and a meaning something like 'make recover', e.g. *bring to* (the causative correspondent of *come to*), *comfort*, *console*, *cure*, *soothe*, *ease*, *nurse*, *doctor* (the last two derived from nouns). Related to them are *kill* 'make dead'—and its hyponyms such as *murder* 'kill with premeditation' and *assassinate* 'kill a political figure for political reasons'—*beat up*, *injure*, *wound*, *poison*. All of these can be classified with the causatives of set (d_2), as can *give birth to*, the transitive correspondent of *be born*.

Finally, there are a number of verbs which typically describe corporeal interaction between two people—*kiss*, *embrace*, *hug*, *cuddle*, *fuck* (and its many synonyms). These are basically symmetrical verbs: either Human can be in A with the other in O slot in a transitive construction, or else both may be covered by the subject NP of a reciprocal sentence, e.g. *John kissed Mary*, *Mary kissed John*, *John and Mary kissed* (*each other*); see §2.9.6.

Smell, *taste* and *feel*—referring to three of the human senses—involve intersection with two other types. They function in one way as ATTENTION verbs (e.g. *I tasted that it had gone off*), §5.1; and in another way like verbs of the SEEM type (*It tasted burnt*), §6.4.1.

4.5. WEATHER

A number of WEATHER verbs—notably *rain, snow, hail* and *thunder*—effectively have no semantic roles at all. The verb makes up a complete clause, but the impersonal subject *it* has to be added, to satisfy the requirement of English syntax that each clause have some constituent in the subject slot (see §2.4), e.g. *It is raining, It snowed in the night, Listen to it thundering out there.*

It is possible to include with a WEATHER verb an NP that contains a cognate noun, e.g. *It thundered the most ear-splitting cracks of thunder that I've ever heard*, or a noun that is a near synonym of the cognate noun, e.g. *It rained an absolutely tremendous storm while we were on holiday.* The 'cognate' NP is not properly either an object or an extraposed subject in such clauses—it is just an appositive mechanism for commenting on the nature of the weather event. As was noted above, when discussing cognate NPs with CORPOREAL verbs, there are much wider possibilities for modification of a noun in an NP (by adjectives, etc.) than there are for adverbial modification of a verb (e.g. we could not say **It thundered ear-splittingly*, or **It rained (absolutely) tremendously*).

4.6. Others

A number of other Primary-A types are surveyed here quite briefly, since they generally do not have critical properties in terms of the syntactic topics discussed in Chapters 7–11. The types listed below— unlike MOTION, REST, AFFECT, GIVING and CORPOREAL—do permit non-concrete nouns (mostly, ACTIVITY nouns) in core syntactic relations.

COMPETITION refers to some Competitor (who is invariably HUMAN) trying to establish his superiority, whether in fighting a battle or playing a game. These verbs are generally transitive, with the A relation filled by a Competitor role. With *conquer, beat, overcome* and *race (against)*, the O relation relates to another Competitor (and generally may not be omitted), e.g. *John beat Fred at Scrabble/in battle.* For *resist, fight* and *play* the O can be either another Competitor or else an ACTIVITY noun such as *attack*, e.g. *The French resisted the Germans/the attack/the attack of the Germans.* For *win* or *lose* the O will be either an ACTIVITY noun, or else a noun referring to some prize that is transferred as a result of the competition; an object of the first kind can be omitted but one of the second kind may not be. In addition, an NP referring to a second Competitor may be introduced by a preposition. Thus *Argentina lost* (*the battle of the Falkland Islands*) (*to Britain*), and *John won the book* (*from Mary*). With *win* and *lose* an NP that provides a general description of some kind of activity may be introduced by a preposition, whereas an NP referring to a specific instance of activity would be in O slot, e.g. *John won/lost that game of chess*, but *John wins/loses at chess* (see §8.2.3). For *attack*, *guard*, *shield* and *surrender* the O NP can refer to a place or to people, e.g. *They attacked the city/army*, *They surrendered the city/hostages/themselves* (*to the enemy*), while for *defend* it must be a place or thing, e.g. *They defended the city* (*against enemy attack*), *They defended their company* (*against take-over bids*). Finally, there are a number of 'symmetrical' verbs, as *John competed with Mary*, *John struggled against Mary* and *John and Mary competed* (*with each other*), *John and Mary struggled* (*against each other*); *fight* and *play* may be used in the same manner (see §2.9.6).

Race can be used in a causative construction, e.g. *The tortoise raced against the hare*, *John raced the tortoise against the hare*. *Win* and *lose* form unusual causatives where the 'reason' for winning/losing (which may, in the plain construction, be introduced by *because*) becomes transitive subject and the original transitive subject is now introduced by *for*, e.g. *We lost/won the match because of that error* and *That error won/lost the match for us*. The NP governed by *for* can be moved into direct object slot (with the *for* dropping), e.g. *That error won/lost us the match*.

SOCIAL CONTRACT refers to the ways in which some human societies are organised. Most of these verbs are transitive, and require a HUMAN in A relation. Some may have an O NP referring to one person or to a group of people, e.g. *appoint*, *employ*, *dismiss*, *sack*, *fire*, *promote*, *nominate*, *convert*, *arrest*, *prosecute*, *impeach*, *punish*. For others the O must refer to a group of people (often organised in units like a nation or company), e.g. *govern*, *rule*, *civilise*, *missionise* and *join*. *Manage* may have the O NP referring either to a group of people or to some activity, e.g. *manage the pupils/the school/the organisation of sports day*. There are also

SOCIAL CONTRACT verbs that involve an inherent preposition introducing an NP that refers to some job or position, e.g. *apply for*, *qualify for*, *resign from*, one sense of *withdraw (from)* and one sense of *work (at)*. A further kind of social contract is described by the inherently reciprocal verb *marry* (see §2.9.6).

USING verbs are all transitive. The verb *use* can take a wide range of O NPs; it means 'do with that thing whatever is most appropriately done with it, in the circumstances, doing this in a productive manner', thus *He used all the potatoes* might refer to cooking them; *She always uses flowers from the garden* could refer to picking them and putting them in vases through the house. *Use* will often be followed by a subordinate clause specifying the appropriate activity, e.g. *use the flour to make a cake*, *use the money to buy a dress*, *use the stick to hit Fred*, *use the bus to get to work*, *use those allegations of misconduct to get John to resign*. There are also hyponyms of *use* such as *operate, manipulate*, one sense of *work*, one sense of *employ*, *wear* (e.g. clothes); and there are *waste* 'use non-productively' and *fiddle with* 'play at using'.

OBEYING verbs are also transitive. The verb *obey* can have as referent of the O NP either a specific kind of SPEECH ACT (e.g. *order, instruction*) or else the person who issued such a speech act. For *execute* (in the 'obey' sense) the O must be a speech act. *Process, deal with, grant* and *refuse* (in one of its senses) take as head of the O NP another kind of SPEECH ACT noun (e.g. *request, application*). *Perform* requires an activity noun (e.g. *task, plan*). The O NP may be omitted after *obey* (e.g. *John always obeys*), but not after the other, more specific, verbs.

Notes to Chapter 4

The question of alternative syntactic frames (see especially §4.2) and their meaning differences was explored in a pioneering paper by S. R. Anderson (1971). Foley and Van Valin (1984: 57 ff., 82 ff.) provide useful discussion of this question; they also demonstrate—in terms of the possibilities of adverb placement—that both *Bill* and *the book* should be considered objects in *John gave Bill the book* (see §4.3 and also §9.2).

5

Primary-B verb types

Primary-B verbs can, like Primary-A, be the only verb in a sentence, with all their roles filled by NPs (e.g. *John saw Mary*). But they can also, unlike Primary-A, have a complement clause as alternative to an NP in one syntactic relation (e.g. *John saw that Mary had won*). Whereas most Primary-A verbs, when used in a literal sense, take CONCRETE NPs, many Primary-B verbs may take any type of NP in O relation, e.g. an ACTIVITY noun as in *John witnessed the incident*.

The sections below outline the variety of complement clauses that the various types and subtypes of Primary-B verbs take. We return to this topic in Chapter 7, there providing semantic explanation for the occurrences.

5.1. ATTENTION

Verbs of this type have two core roles. A Perceiver (which is HUMAN or higher animate) finds out something about an Impression through use of eyes, or ears, or nose, or the taste-buds in the tongue, or the tactile feelings in the skin. The Perceiver is always mapped onto A and the Impression onto O syntactic relation (except for *show*—see below). Most subtypes of ATTENTION are Primary-B, in that the Impression can be an NP or a complement clause; one subtype must have the impression realised through an NP and is thus Primary-A.

People gather more kinds of information by their eyes than by other sense organs, and many ATTENTION verbs imply vision, e.g. *see*, *watch*, *look* (*at*), *stare* (*at*), *peep* (*at*), *inspect*. The only verbs specifically referring to audition are *hear* and *listen* (*to*). The other human senses are each represented by a single verb—*feel*, *smell* and *taste* (these are also classified as CORPOREAL—§4.4). There are, however, a number of general verbs of ATTENTION which—while most frequently being used for something which is seen—can be used to refer to any of the senses, e.g. *notice, recognise, study*, as in *I noticed, on tasting it, that he'd put in too much curry powder*; *She recognised John's voice*; *He is studying the various smells produced in a Thai kitchen.*

The subtypes that can be recognised are:

(*a*) The SEE subtype, involving straightforward description of an act of perception (which can be involuntary)—*see, hear, smell, taste, feel*. Also *observe*, which refers to seeing or hearing something happening; *notice*, seeing or hearing something which stands out from its background; and *perceive*, which implies picking out some particular thing or state or event from its background (and is also used as a high-flown alternative to other verbs from this subtype).

(*b*) The SHOW subtype, describing how one person assists another to an act of perception. The main verb in this subtype, *show*, is lexical causative of *see/notice/observe*. There will be a Causer in A slot, and either Perceiver or Impression will be in O relation, according to which is focused on in this instance, e.g. *John picked up the book and showed it* (Impression: O) *to Mary* (Perceiver), or *John brought Mary over and showed her* (Perceiver: O) *the book* (Impression).

When *show* has NPs realising all roles it implies visual perception, e.g. *John showed the parrot to Mary* implies that she saw it, not that she heard it. But when the Impression is a complement clause, then *show* may imply use of the eyes—*John showed Mary how to mend a fuse* can imply that he did it, and she observed this—or of the ears—*John showed Mary how to make a uvular trill* implies that he made the sound, and she heard it. (*Demonstrate* is a near synonym of this sense of *show*.)

(*c*) The RECOGNISE subtype, referring to perception of something (by any sense) and then knowing what it is, or what its significance is—*recognise, spot*.

(*d*) The DISCOVER subtype, referring to perception of something that was not previously apparent, e.g. *discover* 'perceive something (which may be surprising) for the first time'; *find* 'perceive something that was either looked for, or which is familiar from the past'.

(*e*) The WITNESS subtype, referring to observation of some definite unit of activity; *witness* may be the only member.

(*f*) The LOOK subtype, referring to the Perceiver directing his attention in order to connect with some Impression, e.g. *look* (*at*), *listen* (*to*) and the more specific verbs *stare* (*at*), *glare* (*at*), *peep* (*at*), *peer* (*at*), *squint* (*at*); *eavesdrop* (*on*); also *search* (*for*), *look* (*for*), *hunt* (*for*); *inspect, study, investigate, scan, scrutinise, examine, check, view*; *explore, survey*; *visit* (which involves intersection of MOTION and ATTENTION).

(*g*) The WATCH subtype, similar to (*f*) but referring to deliberate perception over a period of time. *Watch* may be the only verb uniquely belonging to this subtype; the contrast with *look* (*at*) can be seen in the acceptability of *I watched John eat his dinner*, but not **I looked at John eat his dinner*. *Listen* (*to*) has two senses, one parallel to *look* (*at*), belonging to subtype (*f*) (cf. *Look at this picture!*, *Listen to this noise behind the skirting!*) and the other parallel to *watch,* in subtype (*g*), e.g. *I listened to John say his prayers*.

The subtypes have differing grammatical properties:

(i) Omission of object NP

All ATTENTION verbs are basically transitive. Some involve an inherent preposition but the following NP has the same syntactic properties as for those items where it immediately follows the verb root—compare *The repairman hasn't yet looked at our washing-machine* and *The foreman hasn't yet inspected that new switchboard*, and their passives, *Our washing-machine hasn't yet been looked at*, and *That new switchboard hasn't yet been inspected*.

An O NP, coding the Impression role, may be omitted after verbs in the LOOK and WATCH subtypes (a preceding preposition will then also drop). A sentence such as *He is listening/looking/ staring/hunting/checking/exploring/watching* simply focuses on the way in which the Perceiver is directing his attention, without noting any specific Impression to which it may be directed.

LOOK verbs, especially when the O NP is omitted, may take a place adverbal which is semantically linked to the verb, and thus must come after the predicate (§2.5), e.g. *He is exploring to the north, She is hunting in the forest*. An O NP could always be included, e.g. *He is exploring the country to the north, She is hunting (for) rabbits in the forest.*

Look (at) and *look (for)* are distinct lexemes—compare *She is looking at a millionaire* and *She is looking for a millionaire.* This contrast is neutralised when the O NPs (and preceding prepositions) are dropped, e.g. *She is looking under the table.* But, once again, an O NP could always be stated, e.g. *She is looking at the hole in the carpet under the table,* or *She is looking for spilt peanuts under the table* (in each sentence, the two prepositional NPs could occur in either order).

For three verbs in the SEE subtype—*see, hear* and *notice*—an O NP can be omitted if it could be inferred from the preceding discourse or context, e.g. *Mary hit John on the temple! Yes, I saw* (sc. the blow), or *John gave his pudding to the dog; Yes I noticed* (sc. John('s) giving his pudding to the dog). An O NP cannot be omitted after *observe* or *perceive*; here one must include at least *it*, e.g. *Did you know there was an eclipse of the sun today? Yes, I observed it. Smell, taste* and *feel*, in the senses corresponding to subtype (*a*), also require an O NP to be stated. These verbs are used less frequently than *see, hear* and *notice*, which may be why no convention for omitting an *it* NP has yet evolved.

Show, of subtype (*b*), must include either Perceiver or Impression in O slot, e.g. *Mary showed John her ring* or *Mary showed her ring to John.* It can freely omit a non-O Perceiver, e.g. *John and Mary showed their wedding presents* (sc. (say) to the guests). And *show* can omit a non-O Impression NP where this is inferable from previous discourse, e.g. *Does Mary know where the key is? She should, I showed her.*

(ii) Realisation of Impression role

All ATTENTION verbs can have a CONCRETE NP realising Impression, except for *witness*, which must relate to an activity, e.g. *He witnessed the battle, She witnessed John's signature on the document* (note that *signature* is an ACTIVITY noun—a paraphrase would be *She witnessed John's signing his name on the document*). All ATTENTION verbs can have an ACTIVITY noun as Impression (e.g. *They noticed/discovered/viewed the football match*) except perhaps *explore* and *survey*, which in their central meanings relate to some geographical feature.

Most verbs in the LOOK subtype may only take an NP in O slot (and are thus Primary-A); some LOOK verbs can take a WH- clause, e.g. *examine, investigate, study*. All other subtypes allow complement clauses for the Impression role. We now discuss the various kinds of complement one at a time.

(iii) THAT and WH- complements
These two varieties of complement clause can fill the O slot for subtypes (*a*)–(*e*) and (*g*). Thus, *I noticed/smelt/recognised/discovered that the meat was off/where the cheese was hidden*. A THAT clause with *see* can refer to an inference from direct observation (*I saw that his leg was broken*) or to a general mental assessment (*I saw that it was pointless to continue*). *Feel* has similar properties, e.g. *I felt that the dough was sufficiently kneaded* (tactile observation) and *I felt that she was the right person for the job* (intuition). A THAT clause with *hear* almost always refers to something the Perceiver has been told, e.g. *I heard that John had cursed*; for reporting direct observation a different variety of complement would be preferred, e.g. *I heard John curse, I heard John('s) cursing*.

Subtype (*g*), with *watch* and one sense of *listen* (*to*), may take THAT and WH- clauses which directly describe some activity, e.g. *I watched that he crossed the road safely*, and *She listened that he locked all the doors before going to bed*.

(iv) TO complements
A smallish number of ATTENTION verbs may take a special variety of Modal (FOR) TO complement clause: the *to* is obligatorily omitted in an active construction, but obligatorily included in the passive, e.g. *Everyone saw John kick Mary, John was seen to kick Mary*.

It is important to distinguish this TO complement construction, with the *to* omitted, from a THAT complement clause, which can omit the *that* when it comes directly after the predicate, e.g. *I noticed (that) John kicked Mary (every time he went past)*—here the verb *kicked* shows tense inflection, indicating that it is in a THAT clause—and *I noticed John kick Mary (when no one was looking)*—here the verb is in base form, as it always is in a TO clause. (For a verb like *hit*, which makes no distinction between the base and past tense forms, these would fall together, i.e. *I noticed John hit Mary* is ambiguous between THAT and TO readings.)

This variety of TO complement, where *to* is omitted in the active, occurs with *see*, *hear* and *notice* and, less readily, with *feel*, *smell*, *observe* and *perceive* from the SEE subtype (but not with *taste*). It is also attested with subtype (*g*), WATCH, but only in the active, e.g. *I watched John hit Mary*, *I listened to him sing* (here *to* comes from *listen to*, rather than being the complementiser); there are no acceptable passives of these sentences. (Van Ek (1966: 68) also mentions examples with *find*, from subtype (*d*), but these seem somewhat archaic; Bolinger (1975*b*) quotes examples with *show* and *look at*, e.g. *Can you show it happen?* and *Look at him run!* The *look* example is only possible in the active.)

In addition, verbs in subtypes (*a*)–(*d*) may take a 'Judgement' TO complement clause. As mentioned in §2.7, Judgement TO clauses most frequently have their VP beginning with *be* (although other possibilities do occur, e.g. *I noticed John to have lost some weight since last Christmas*). When *be* is the copula, then *to be* can be omitted only after verbs of the DISCOVER subtype, e.g. *I found John* (*to be*) *dead*, but *We noticed John to be dead*, where the *to be* must be retained. When *be* is the progressive auxiliary, *to be* may be omitted after verbs from DISCOVER, SEE or SHOW, e.g. *I noticed/ discovered John* (*to be*) *singing a hymn*.

(v) ING complement

This occurs with verbs from the SEE, SHOW, WITNESS and WATCH subtypes, e.g. *We observed/watched/witnessed John('s) stealing those apples*; *I can't hear John('s) playing the trumpet*. The subject of the complement clause can take possessive marking, but this is most frequently omitted. (ATTENTION verbs seem particularly prone to loss of a complementiser; we just described a type of TO clause where *to* must be omitted in the active.)

A construction like *John noticed that tall man watching Mary*, with the complement clause subject followed by a verb in *-ing* form, can be derived in two ways: by omission of possessive marker from the subject of an ING clause, or by omission of *to be* from a Judgement TO complement whose VP begins with the progressive auxiliary *be*. With some verbs there is no problem of ambiguity. *Watch* and *witness* may only take an ING, not a Judgement TO clause, and so *I watched/witnessed that tall man('s) saying his prayers in church* (*from two until four, so he couldn't have committed the burglary which took place at three o'clock*) must be an ING complement, describing some durative event. Similarly, *discover* only takes a TO, not an ING, complement, and so *I discovered that tall man* (*to be*) *saying his prayers* (*just when I'd decided he must be an atheist*) is also unambiguous, referring to the perception of some fact that was not previously known. But verbs from the SEE and SHOW subtypes can take both ING and TO complement clauses; an abbreviated sentence such as *I noticed that tall man saying his prayers* is thus ambiguous between the readings of the *watch/witness* and of the *discover* sentences just given.

There is still further room for ambiguity. In the discussion of relative clauses, in §2.6, we mentioned a reduced form of restrictive relative clause referring to present time which, for verbs that take the *be . . . -ing* auxiliary, effectively involves omission of the relative pronoun and the form of *be*. Thus *I noticed that tall man* (*who was*) *watching Mary* (*he looks just like the picture on the 'wanted' poster*), where (*who was*) *watching Mary* helps restrict the reference of the O NP. This has a quite different meaning from the ING complement construction *I noticed that tall man('s) watching Mary* (*all afternoon, and took great offence at his ogling my wife for such a long time*), where what I noticed was not the identity of the tall man, but the fact of his watching Mary. The abbreviated sentence *I noticed that tall man watching Mary* would thus be ambiguous between these two readings.

Table 5.1 summarises the more important syntactic properties of these ATTENTION verbs.

Complement clauses with ATTENTION verbs have one special property. The complement clause subject is generally distinct from the main clause subject, for the straightforward reason that one would not normally *see* or *hear* etc. oneself (or, perhaps more to the point, one would not normally report doing so). It is possible for the two subjects to have the same reference, but under no circumstances can the complement clause subject be omitted, e.g. *myself* cannot be dropped from *I saw myself on the video*, *I finally recognised myself to be middle-aged*. This contrasts with verbs

Table 5.1. *Syntactic properties of the main* ATTENTION *verbs*

	Is O omittable?	Complement varieties allowed in O slot				
		THAT	WH-	Modal (FOR)TO[1]	Judgement TO	ING
(*a*) SEE subtype						
see, hear, notice	yes	yes	yes	yes	yes	yes
smell, taste, feel	no	yes	yes	some	yes	yes
observe, perceive	no	yes	yes	yes	yes	yes
(*b*) SHOW subtype						
show	no	yes	yes	yes	yes	yes
(*c*) RECOGNISE subtype						
recognise, spot	no	yes	yes	no	yes	no
(*d*) DISCOVER subtype						
discover, find	no	yes	yes	some	yes	no
(*e*) WITNESS subtype						
witness	no	yes	yes	no	no	yes
(*f*) LOOK subtype						
look (at)	yes	no	yes	yes[2]	no	no
listen (to) etc.	yes	no	some	no	no	no
(*g*) WATCH subtype						
watch, listen (to)	yes	yes	yes	one[2]	no	yes

[1] *To* omitted in active, retained in passive.
[2] Only in the active.

from a number of other subtypes, where coreferential omission is normal, e.g. *I want (?myself) to eat an avocado.*

There are three further sets of ATTENTION verbs:

(i) *ignore, disregard, overlook, pass* NP *over* refer to the Perceiver not making contact with a certain Impression (either accidentally or on purpose). These verbs are transitive, with either an NP or an ING complement clause in O slot, e.g. *She walked by and ignored me/ignored my waving at her.*

(ii) *appear, disappear* are intransitive and refer to an Impression (in S relation) being available or not available for the visual attention of a potential Perceiver. A Perceiver can be included with *appear*, marked by preposition *to*, e.g. *An angel appeared to Mary.* (With *disappear* we can say *The angel disappeared from the scene/from (Mary's) view*, but not **The angel disappeared from Mary.*) *Appear* is also a member of the SEEM type—§6.4.1.

(iii) *look*, *sound*; *smell*, *taste* and *feel* are also intransitive verbs, with the Impression in S slot; the Perceiver may be included, marked by *to*, e.g. *This violin sounds good* (*to me*) (*now that it has been tuned*), *That chicken tasted really lovely* (*to all of us*). Note that there is one verb in this set corresponding to each of the five senses. *Smell*, *taste* and *feel* are identical in form to the corresponding transitive verb, e.g. *She felt the fur* (transitive), *It felt soft and silky* (*to her*) (intransitive). Intransitive *look* corresponds to transitive *see* and *look* (*at*), e.g. *He saw/looked at the painting* and *The painting looks good*. Only *sound* (derived from the noun) is not cognate with a corresponding transitive verb from the ATTENTION type. (There is of course a transitive verb *sound* with a meaning entirely different from *hear* and *listen* (*to*), and with quite restricted use, e.g. *sound the trumpet* 'make it sound out'.)

Both semantically and syntactically these five verbs behave like the SEEM type; they involve an intersection of this type with ATTENTION (and, for *smell*, *taste* and *feel*, also with CORPOREAL). They are normally followed by an adjective from the VALUE, DIFFICULTY or QUALIFICATION types, or the CLEVER subtype of HUMAN PROPENSITY, e.g. *It looks difficult*, *It sounds definite*—see §6.4.1. Interestingly, *bad* can be omitted after *smell*, i.e. *It smells* implies *It smells bad*. (Note that the derived adjective *smelly* refers to 'a bad smell' while *tasty* means 'a good taste'. One might expect, on a principle of analogy, that *good* should be omissible from *It tastes good*. It cannot be; languages seldom work on so symmetrical a pattern as this.)

5.2. THINKING

This type covers verbs of thinking, knowing, believing and the like. There are always two roles—a Cogitator (who is generally HUMAN) has in mind some Thought. THINKING verbs are basically transitive, with Cogitator in A and Thought in O syntactic relation. The Thought may be realised by an NP, or by one of a variety of complement clauses; the syntactic possibilities vary somewhat across subtypes.

The following subtypes can be distinguished:

(*a*) The THINK subtype, referring to the Cogitator's mind just focusing on some person, thing, state or happening. The most general verb is *think* (*of/about/over*). Others include *consider* 'think about some actual or possible state of affairs (and its consequences)'; *imagine* 'think of something as if it were true, although the Cogitator is aware that it may not be true (and that it might be surprising if it were)'.

(*b*) The ASSUME subtype, when there is some doubt as to whether the Thought is true, e.g. *assume* 'think of something as true when the Cogitator realises that it is only likely—not certain —that it is'; and *suppose* 'think of something as true when the Cogitator realises that there is insufficient evidence to be sure that it is'.

(*c*) The PONDER subtype, referring to different modes of thinking, e.g. *ponder* (*on/over*), *meditate* (*on/about*), *brood* (*on/over*), *speculate* (*on/about*), *wonder* (*at/about*), *reflect* (*on/about*), *dream* (*of/about*), *contemplate*.

(*d*) The REMEMBER subtype, referring to the Cogitator having in mind, or trying to get in mind, something from the past, e.g. *remember* 'think about something from the past, or about something arranged in the past which is to take place in the present or future', and *forget* 'fail to think of something that one should have thought about, or that one should have been able to think about'.

(*e*) The KNOW subtype, referring to the Cogitator being aware of some fact, or body of information, or method of doing something. The most general verb is *know*. There are also *sense* 'know some fact intuitively' (one meaning of *feel* may also belong here); *realise* 'suddenly think in an appropriate way, so as to know some fact', *learn* 'come to know something by (often, diligent) effort', and *understand* 'know something, and also the reason for it'. *Teach*, a lexical causative related to *know/understand*, also belongs in this subtype; it has the meaning 'Causer tries to help Cogitator know/understand some Thought'. Causer must be in A relation. If Cogitator and Thought are both NPs then either may be focused on, and placed in O syntactic relation, e.g. *John taught geometry to Mary, John taught Mary geometry*. If the Thought is expressed by a complement clause then it will follow the Cogitator, which must be in O slot, e.g. *John taught Mary that the square on the hypotenuse is equal to the sum of the squares on the other two sides*.

(*f*) The CONCLUDE subtype, referring to using the mind to think about the consequences of certain facts, observations, assumptions, suppositions, etc., e.g. *conclude, infer, reason*, one sense of *argue, prove*, one sense of *demonstrate*, one sense of *show, guess*.

(*g*) The SOLVE subtype, referring to the mind thinking in such a way as to achieve some end, e.g. *solve, work* NP *out; devise, make* NP *up; analyse*.

(*h*) The BELIEVE subtype, referring to thinking of something as true. The verb *believe* means 'think of something as true (when in fact it may not be, but the Cogitator will not accept that it may not be)'. There are also *suspect* 'think that something is likely to be true' and *doubt* 'think that something is unlikely to be true'.

Dealing now with the grammatical properties of THINKING verbs:

(i) NP as object, and object omission
Verbs in all subtypes typically take a complement clause in O slot. An NP is a possible alternative, but for many verbs this must have non-CONCRETE reference, e.g. *She learnt weaving, We assumed his cooperation, He proved the truth of the theorem*. Some verbs may have a CONCRETE noun as head of the NP, but this leaves something unsaid about that thing, which the addressee may be assumed to be aware of, e.g. *We considered Mary (for promotion), She understands John* (i.e. the reason he acts as he does), *They speculated about the house* (what price it would fetch at the forthcoming auction). The most common verbs from the THINKING type may more frequently have a concrete NP in Thought role, e.g. *think (of/about), remember, forget, believe*, but even here some amplification may be implicit, e.g. *I am thinking of Odette* (of how much I love her), *I forgot John* (i.e. forgot to invite him to my party). *Know* has a special sense 'be acquainted with a person or place', e.g. *I know Paris/Peter Trudgill well*, which is rather different from the 'be aware of something' meaning, which it shares with *sense, realise*, etc. *Believe* also has a special sense, marked by the preposition *in*—compare *I believed Mary* (i.e. what she said) with *I believe (in (the existence of) the Christian god)*, and *I believe in (the wisdom and goodness of) my boss*.

Most verbs in the PONDER subtype take a preposition before a Thought NP (this does, of course, drop before *that*, e.g. *I reflected on John's deciding to withdraw, I reflected that John had decided to withdraw*). It is a difficult decision whether to regard these as transitive verbs with an inherent preposition, or as intransitive verbs which can take a peripheral NP referring to the Thought. In favour of the transitive alternative is the fact that these NPs passivise relatively easily, e.g. *That decision by the Vice-Chancellor has been wondered at in every committee room of the university*. But, as some support for the intransitive analysis, the preposition-plus-NP can be freely omitted after most PONDER verbs, e.g. *She is meditating/brooding/reflecting*.

Both *dream* and *think* have cross-membership of the CORPOREAL type. Like many other CORPOREAL verbs they may be followed by a cognate NP, e.g. *I dreamt a perfectly lovely dream*, *She has a tendency to think really evil thoughts*. Note that these cognate NPs, which may not have the full syntactic status of 'object', immediately follow the verb. *Think* (*of/about*) and *dream* (*of/about*), as THINKING verbs, involve an inherent preposition before the O NP (which can readily be passivised, e.g. *That change in the plans has been thought about for an awfully long time*).

Some THINKING verbs, such as *think*, *dream* and *learn*, may omit an object NP only in the habitual or progressive, e.g. *I dream every night*, *I'm learning* (*gradually*). Others, such as *infer* and *prove*, are seldom used in the progressive and must always have an O NP stated. Verbs from subtype (*d*) and some of those from (*e*)—*remember*, *forget*, *know* (in the 'be aware of something' sense) and *understand*—can omit an O NP if it can be inferred from the context, e.g. *Mary won the prize. I know* (sc. that she did) and *Fred won't come to the door. Oh, I understand* (sc. why he won't). (*Believe* can occur with no object only when used in a religious sense, e.g. *He believes* (*in the Christian god*).)

Verbs from subtypes (*a*), (*b*) and (*g*) (excluding the negative verb *doubt*) may use *so* in place of the Thought role where this could be inferred, e.g. *Does John know? I assume so* (sc. that he knows). For *guess* the *so* may optionally be omitted in some dialects, e.g. *Will she win? I guess* (*so*).

(ii) THAT, WH- and WH- TO complements

All THINKING verbs may take a THAT complement in O slot except perhaps for some from the PONDER subtype (e.g. *brood*, *meditate*). Only the ASSUME and BELIEVE subtypes, and certain members of

SOLVE, do not accept some instance of WH- or WH- TO (*doubt* is an exception—it takes a WHETHER clause as a near-paraphrase of a THAT complement, e.g. *I doubt that/whether John will win*—see §7.2.1).

(iii) ING complements

Verbs from THINK, PONDER and REMEMBER may have an ING clause for the Thought role; the subject of the complement clause can be identical to the subject of the main clause and will then be omitted, e.g. *I thought of/imagined/speculated about/remember (Mary's) being attacked when on holiday in Nigeria. Understand*, from the KNOW subtype, may also have an ING clause in O slot. Here the complement clause subject is unlikely to be the same as the main clause subject; if it is, it would not normally be omitted, e.g. *I understood Mary's/my being denied promotion*.

(iv) Judgement TO complements

All except the PONDER and SOLVE subtypes and *doubt* (and the causative *teach*) can take a Judgement TO complement, e.g. *I guessed/supposed/knew/inferred/suspected John to be clever*. (*Forget* only takes Judgement TO in limited circumstances; some speakers accept *I'd forgotten him to be so fat*.) The *to be* can often be omitted, just after *think, consider* and *imagine*, e.g. *We considered him (to be) stupid, I think it (to be) very unlikely*. Other verbs allow the *to be* to drop only in certain circumstances, e.g. *I supposed him (to be) dead/sick* but only *I supposed him to be clever/tall/rich/alive*, with the *to be* retained. (See §7.2.6.)

Show and *prove* have the special property that, with a TO complement, the A and O NPs can be coreferential—compare the regular construction *John showed Fred to be stupid (by analysing his behaviour)* and the special one *Fred showed himself to be stupid (by the way he behaved)*. *Prove*, but not *show*, has an even more abbreviated construction type, with the reflexive pronoun and *to be* omitted, e.g. *Our guide proved (himself) (to be) useless*.

(v) Modal (FOR) TO complements

Remember, forget, know, learn and *teach* may take a Modal (FOR) TO complement. This will often have its subject coreferential with the main clause subject, and then omitted, e.g. *I remembered/*

Table 5.2. *Complement clause possibilities for* THINKING *verbs*

	THAT	WH- and WH- TO	ING	Judgement TO	Modal (FOR)TO
(*a*) THINK subtype					
think (of/about/over)	yes	yes	yes	yes	yes
consider, imagine	yes	yes	yes	yes	no
(*b*) ASSUME subtype					
assume, suppose	yes	no	no	yes	no
(*c*) PONDER subtype					
ponder (on/over) etc.	some	yes	yes	no	no
(*d*) REMEMBER subtype					
remember	yes	yes	yes	yes	yes
forget	yes	yes	yes	limited	yes
(*e*) KNOW subtype					
know, learn	yes	yes	no	yes	yes[1]
sense, realise	yes	yes	no	yes	no
understand	yes	yes	yes	yes	no
teach	yes	yes	no	no	yes
(*f*) CONCLUDE subtype					
conclude, infer, etc.	yes	yes	no	yes	no
(*g*) SOLVE subtype					
solve, work out, etc.	yes	some	no	no	no
(*g*) BELIEVE subtype					
believe, suspect	yes	no	no	yes	no
doubt	yes	yes	no	no	no

---

[1] With *know*, the *to* may be omitted in the active, but must be retained in the passive.

forgot/knew/learnt to stand up when the judge enters the room; or, the subjects can be different (and then *for* must be retained), e.g. *I remembered for Mary to take her pill. Think* may also take a Modal (FOR) TO complement but only, it appears, in the past tense and in a negation or question, e.g. *Did you think to lock the door?, I didn't think to lock the door.* (*Remember, know* and *learn*—and *think*, in restricted circumstances—are thus numbered among the very few verbs to accept both Modal and Judgement varieties of TO complement. See §7.2.3.)

Alone of THINKING verbs, *know* may take a Modal (FOR) TO complement with both *for* and *to* omitted, similar to a small set of ATTENTION verbs (§5.1). This usage appears always to involve past tense or perfect aspect, and very often includes a negator such as *never* or *not*, e.g. *They'd never known him hit her.* As with ATTENTION (and MAKING) verbs, the suppressed *to* must be used in the passive, e.g. *He had never been known to hit her.*

The complement clause possibilities for THINKING verbs are summarised in Table 5.2.

5.3. DECIDING

This type involves two roles: a Decision-Maker (who is generally HUMAN) thinks to himself that he will follow a certain Course (of action). DECIDING verbs are basically transitive; the Decision-Maker is always in A and the Course in O syntactic relation.

We can recognise two subtypes:

(*a*) The RESOLVE subtype, focusing on one particular Course, e.g. *decide (on), determine (on), resolve; plan* (which intersects with WANTING).

(*b*) The CHOOSE subtype, preferring one Course out of a number of alternatives—*choose* and its hyponyms such as *select, pick* NP (*out*); *appoint, elect; vote (for/on).*

Verbs of the RESOLVE subtype may have the Course role realised as a THAT, or WH-, or Modal (FOR) TO or WH- TO complement clause (the subject of a FOR TO complement is most often identical to the main clause subject, and is then omitted, together with the *for*), e.g. *Tom resolved that he would not be beaten, Father will decide whether we have lunch inside or out, The headmaster decided (for the girls) to go in front, John will determine where to erect the marquee. Decide (on)* and *determine (on)* may also take an ING complement, which normally has its subject identical to main clause subject, and then omitted, e.g. *He decided on pruning the roses this weekend.*

There are two kinds of NP possible, as Course. *Decide (on)* and *determine (on)*—but not, it seems, *resolve* or *plan*—may take a CONCRETE NP in O slot, e.g. *Fred decided on a red shirt, John decided on the theatre this evening.* But this NP is effectively the O (or other post-predicate constituent) of a complement clause, and is used as main clause O when the verb of the complement clause could be inferred by the addressee from the context—thus, Fred may have decided to wear, or to buy, a red shirt, and John may have decided to go to the theatre this evening.

Decide, determine and *resolve* have a further, related meaning (similar to one sense of *settle*), referring to someone indicating an appropriate Course where there had been some difficulty or doubt, e.g. *John decided the dispute, Mary determined the order of precedence, Einstein resolved the paradox* (see §8.2.1). Note that in this sense they take an ACTIVITY or other abstract NP in O slot, with no preposition *on*. (When used in this sense, verbs from the RESOLVE subtype may have a non-human NP in A slot, e.g. *That final speech determined the result of the debate, Fred's penalty kick decided the match.*)

Choose has similar syntactic properties to *decide* (*on*) (excluding that mentioned in the last paragraph), occurring with THAT, WH-, Modal (FOR) TO, WH- TO and ING complement clauses, e.g. *I chose that we should have Christmas dinner in the evening this year, I chose (for) Mary to give the vote of thanks, You choose who to give it to!* There can be a CONCRETE NP as O but this always does imply some suppressed complement clause, e.g. *Mary chose a teddy bear* could in appropriate contexts be understood by the addressee to state that she chose to buy one, or to make one in her soft toys evening class, or to receive one out of the list of possible presents her grandmother had offered.

The other verbs in the CHOOSE subtype are hyponyms of *choose* (that is, *choose* could almost always be substituted for an occurrence of any of them). *Select, pick (out), appoint* and *elect* must have a CONCRETE NP, not a complement clause, in O slot. (There will often be included in the sentence some specification of what the choice is related to, e.g. *Mary selected a teddy bear (as the Christmas gift from her grandmother), I appointed John (to be sales manager).*) *Vote (for/on)* may take a THAT, or a WH- or a Modal (FOR) TO or a WH- TO complement or a concrete NP, e.g. *I would have voted for Nixon to be impeached, I would have voted to impeach Nixon, I didn't vote on whether to impeach Nixon, I would not have voted for Nixon (in any election).*

Only *decide* and *choose*, the two most general and most frequently used verbs from the DECIDING type, may omit specification of the Course when it could be inferred from the context, e.g.

I don't think we should attack the enemy today, sir. It's too late Sergeant, I've already decided (sc. to attack them today) and *Why don't you ask for that stereo set? No, I've already chosen* (sc. something else). *Vote* can occur without specification of Course, which is then taken to refer to the casting of a ballot, e.g. *Are you going to vote this time around?* (which might be said in election year).

5.4. SPEAKING

English—like other languages—has many verbs in the SPEAKING type, reflecting the important role that language activity has in our lives. There are four semantic roles associated with SPEAKING verbs —the Speaker, the Addressee(s), the Message, and the Medium (language or speech-style used). Speaker, Addressee and Medium are realised as NPs; the Message can be an NP or complement clause or direct speech.

Speaker role is in every case mapped onto subject (A or S) syntactic relation. There is considerable variation in how the other three roles are associated with semantic relations—see the summary in Table 5.3. Many verbs have the Message as O, e.g. *She reported John's illness* (*to the chairman*), while many others have Addressee as O, e.g. *She reminded the chairman of John's illness.* The verbs *speak* and *talk* may have the Medium in O slot, e.g. *They speak French here.*

If the Addressee is not in O slot it is generally introduced by the preposition *to*; if the Medium is not in O slot it is generally introduced by *in*. There are a variety of means for grammatical marking of the Message, which are discussed below.

Verbs in five of the eight SPEAKING subtypes may introduce direct speech, e.g. *'It's Christmas day,' he shouted/said/informed Mary/told the children/instructed the alien.* The other subtypes describe kinds of vocal activity (e.g. *speak, discuss, slander*) and generally do not occur in apposition to direct speech.

Thought is often considered internalised speech, and a verb like *think* may occur with an utterance in quotation marks (really referring to direct thought rather than direct speech), e.g. *'Maybe I'll win the lottery,' John thought.* People are sometimes repres-

Table 5.3. *Syntactic coding of semantic roles for* SPEAKING *verbs*

Speaker is always mapped onto subject (S or A) relation.

Medium is generally introduced by *in*; the *in* can be omitted, with Medium then appearing to be in object (O) relation, for some verbs from subtype (*a*).

The possibilities for coding Message and Addressee are:

Subtype	Message	Addressee
(*a*) TALK	*about/concerning*	*with/to/at*
(*b*) DISCUSS	O	*with/to*[1]
(*c*) SHOUT	O	*to/at*
(*d*) REPORT		
sets (i)–(vii)	O	*to*
set (viii)	post-O	O
(*e*) INFORM	*of/on/about*	O
(*f*) TELL	{ *about/of*	O
	{ O	*to/of/from*
(*g*) ORDER	post-O	O
(*h*) FORGIVE	preposition	O[2]

[1] Addressee not normally statable with *refer to*.
[2] Addressee introduced by *to* with *apologise*.

ented as making decisions aloud, or thinking aloud in various ways, and a number of verbs from the DECIDING and THINKING types are sometimes used to introduce direct speech, as in (23) from §2.7 and '*I ought to spray the apple trees,*' *he reflected/ remembered/concluded/decided/resolved*. (Note that the use of such verbs to introduce direct speech occurs much more often in written, literary English than in colloquial styles.)

The Message, if it is not shown by direct speech, may have two components, as in [*the news*] *about* [*the murder*], [*an announcement*] *concerning* [*the picnic*]. The first part, which we can call the Message-Label, is an NP whose head is a SPEECH ACT noun (e.g. *announcement, question, proposal*) or a noun referring to some language unit (e.g. *news, message*). The Message-Label is linked by a preposition to the second component, which we can call the Message-Content. This may be an NP, or an ING, WH- or THAT complement clause; thus *the news about the murder, the news about Mary's shooting John, the news about who Mary shot, the news that Mary had shot John* (as always, a preposition drops before *that*). (The Message-Content can alternatively be a full Message, consisting of Label, preposition and Content, e.g. *the news about* [[*the announcement*] *concerning* [*the election*]].

A Message can consist of Label-preposition-Content or just Label or just Content. The possibilities are summarised in I–III. In each sentence the Message is in O slot. For Ia it consists just of a Label; in Ib–e it is Label followed by preposition plus Content, which is NP or ING, WH- or THAT clause. Constructions IIa–c show a Message that is just Content—NP, ING or WH- clause. Frame IIIa again shows just Content, here a THAT clause, while IIIb involves direct speech. (The possibilities are grouped in this way since some verbs show all I, some all II, some both of III, and some combinations of I, II and III).

   Ia. *Fred reported the sad news*
   Ib. *Fred reported the sad news about the murder*
   Ic. *Fred reported the sad news about Mary('s) shooting John*
   Id. *Fred reported the sad news about who Mary shot*
   Ie. *Fred reported the sad news that Mary had shot John*
   IIa. *Fred reported the murder*
   IIb. *Fred reported Mary('s) shooting John*
   IIc. *Fred reported who Mary shot*
   IIIa. *Fred reported that Mary had shot John*
   IIIb. *Fred reported: 'Mary has shot John'*

We can now discuss the individual subtypes within the SPEAKING type (their occurrence in the various syntactic frames is summarised in Table 5.4):

(*a*) The TALK subtype simply refers to an activity of vocal communication, e.g. *speak, talk, chat, gossip, converse, communicate, quarrel*, one sense of *argue* (that corresponding to 'have an argument'); *joke* involves intersection of the TALK and REPORT subtypes.

These verbs are basically intransitive and can occur with just the Speaker role filled. *In* may introduce a Medium NP and *about* or *concerning* a Message in frame I or II (that is, *speak about, talk about*, etc. can be substituted for *report* in I and II). Frame III is not possible—TALK verbs do not take a THAT complement or introduce direct speech.

Table 5.4. *Main grammatical frames for* SPEAKING *verbs*

	I	II	III	IV	V	VI	VII	Used intransitively
(a) TALK subtype								
e.g. *talk, speak*	prep[1]	prep[1]	no	no	no	no	no	yes
(b) DISCUSS subtype								
discuss, refer to,	yes	yes	no	no	no	no	no	no
describe	no	yes	no	no	no	no	no	no
(c) SHOUT subtype								
e.g. *shout, call*	yes	no	yes	no	no	no	no	yes
(d) REPORT subtype								
(i) *say* set	limited	no	yes	some	no	no	no	no
(ii) *state* set	yes	no	yes	most	no	no	no	no
(iii) *announce* set	yes	yes	yes	most	no	no	no	no
(iv) *remark (on)* set	yes	yes	yes	no	no	no	no	no
(v) *boast (about/of)* set	yes	yes	yes	no	no	no	no	yes
(vi) *suggest* set	no	yes	yes	some	no	no	no	no
(vii) *undertake* set	no	yes	yes	no	yes	no	no	no
(viii) *promise* set	no	yes	yes	no	yes	no	no	no
(e) INFORM subtype								
e.g. *inform, lecture*	prep[1]	prep[1]	yes	no	no	no	no	no
(f) TELL subtype	yes/prep[2]	prep[2]	yes[2]	no	no	no	no	no
(g) ORDER subtype								
(i) *order* set	no	no	yes[3]	no	no	yes	no	no
(ii) *forbid*	no	no	yes[4]	no	no	yes	yes	no
discourage, dissuade	no	no	yes[4]	no	no	no	yes	no
(h) FORGIVE subtype								
e.g. *forgive, accuse*	no	no	some[4]	no	no	no	no	some

[1] Preposition is required before Message.
[2] There are two possibilities: (i) Addressee as O, with following Message introduced by a preposition (see text for details of preposition inclusion); or (ii) Message, which includes Message-Label, as O, in frame I only, followed by *to* plus Addressee.
[3] Message as THAT clause following Addressee (which is in O relation).
[4] Only direct speech (IIb), not THAT complement clause (IIIa).

Chat, gossip, converse, communicate, quarrel and *argue* generally refer to reciprocal activity; they should either have a plural
Speaker NP or else an Addressee NP introduced by *with* (rather
than *to*), e.g. *John and Mary chatted* or *John chatted with Mary*.
Talk and *speak* may also be used reciprocally, taking *with*, but they
may alternatively have an Addressee introduced by *to*; *speak* has,
as a further alternative, *at*.

The meaning of *speak* focuses on the fact that the speaker is
using a language (one asks *How many languages does he speak?* in
preference to *How many languages does he talk?*) whereas *talk*
refers to how the language is used, in what circumstances and on
what topics (e.g. *Don't talk in church!* and *What shall I talk about
with your father?*). *Speak* tends to be used for one-way communication and may be employed where there is a difference of rank
(*The King spoke to/with me!*) whereas *talk* carries an expectation
of reciprocity and equality (*The King talked with the Queen*). We
can say, focusing on the speaker's activity: *He spoke the truth, She
spoke her mind*, but not **He talked the truth, *She talked her mind*.
(*Write* can be used in the same contexts as *speak*, referring just to a
different medium, e.g. *She wrote the truth in that letter*, but it also
had a wider range, e.g. *She wrote (to say) that she'd been ill*.)

Both *speak* and *talk* (but not other verbs from this subtype) may
omit preposition *in* before the Medium NP, which then appears to
be in O syntactic relation since it freely passivises, e.g. *They are
talking Swahili, Spanish is spoken here* (see §8.2.4). Again, there is
a difference between *talk* and *speak*—*Ken talked Navaho to Clyde*
implies that Clyde can understand him; one could say *speak
Navaho* with a similar interpretation but there is also *Ken spoke
Navaho at Sally*, where the preposition *at* indicates that she
probably didn't comprehend it.

There are examples of Message-Content (when it is a single
noun) dropping its preposition and filling O slot, e.g. *The old men
are talking politics and the young mothers are talking babies, A lot
of linguistics was talked at that party last night* (*which made it
extremely boring for the spouses*). This is possible with *talk*, which
deals with what the language is used for, but not for *speak*, which
centres more on what the speaker is doing. Some of the other
verbs may also, in specially marked circumstances, drop the
preposition before a Message-Content NP, e.g. *They are arguing*

(*about*) *politics*. (One also hears *He is speaking/talking rubbish/ double Dutch*, where the NP refers to the lack of comprehensibility of the Message; note that one could add specification of the Medium, e.g. *in Spanish*.)

(*Talk* also occurs in an idiomatic causative, e.g. *We talked Mary into going* 'We talked to Mary until we persuaded her to go'.)

(*b*) The DISCUSS subtype refers to vocal activity that focuses on a specific message, e.g. *discuss, refer to, describe*.

These are strictly transitive verbs, with O slot filled by the Message role. *Discuss* and *refer to* may occur in frames I and II while *describe* is restricted to II, where the O NP is Message-Content, e.g. *John described the battle* (but scarcely frame I *John described the news* (*about the battle*)). None of these verbs may be used in III, with a THAT clause or introducing direct speech.

DISCUSS verbs could be regarded as transitive correspondents of TALK—in fact *talk about* may substitute for most occurrences of *discuss, refer to* and *describe*. *Discuss* has a reciprocal meaning; there should be either a plural Speaker NP or else an Addressee introduced by *with* (not *to*). *Describe* takes the normal *to* before the Addressee while *refer* would not generally include any mention of Addressee (at least partly because the appropriate preposition *to* is already present, as an inherent component of this transitive verb).

(*c*) The SHOUT subtype refers to manner of vocal production, e.g *shout, call, cry, roar, swear, pray, preach, narrate, recite, intone, read, sing*. Related to this subtype are *whistle* and *warble*. (*Shout, call, cry* and *read* often take the adverb *out*.)

These verbs may be used intransitively, or else transitively with the Message in O relation (see §8.3.1). They occur in frame III, with a THAT complement or with direct speech, e.g. *John called out that the pirates were approaching* or '*The pirates are approaching,*' *John called*; or in Frame I, where the Message NP begins with a Label, e.g. *Fred read the message* (*about the murder*). The Label can be omitted from the Message constituent, but the following preposition must be retained, so that we get a variant of frame I:

I′a. *Fred read about the murder*
I′b. *Fred read about Mary('s) shooting John*

Note that this is distinct from frame II, which is not possible with SHOUT verbs, i.e. **Fred read the murder*.

All SHOUT verbs introduce the Addressee by *to* except *swear*, which takes *at* (*swear at the dog*), and *shout, roar, cry*, which can take *to* (when raising one's voice the better to communicate, e.g. *shout to the children that dinner is ready*) or *at* (when raising the voice in annoyance e.g. *shout at the children* (*to go away*)).

A number of other verbs are marginal members of this subtype. *Translate* shares all syntactic properties except that it does not take a THAT complement. *Pronounce, mispronounce* and *utter* take an O NP that begins with an appropriate label and may be followed by quotation of the sound or word or sentence which this label refers to, e.g. *pronounce the letter 's', utter the name 'Jehovah'*.

Name, and one sense of *call*, have rather different syntax (and could perhaps be regarded as a separate small subtype). They have in O slot an NP referring to a person or thing or place, and this is followed by the name (which may be in direct or indirect speech), e.g. *She called him 'my little doll', She called him her little doll*, and *They named the baby 'Imogen'*.

(*d*) The REPORT subtype refers to the manner of presenting a message. We can distinguish a number of sets of verbs within this subtype, with sample members:

  (i) *say, declare, assert*, one sense of *observe*, one sense of *joke*; *put* NP *about*, *give* NP *out*, *let* NP *out*, *put* NP *across*, *let on about* NP (see §8.2.2 for this method of citing phrasal verbs);
 (ii) *state, affirm, rumour* (mostly used in the passive, cf. §9.4);
(iii) *announce, proclaim, mention, note, report*; *regret* (also in LIKING);
 (iv) *remark* (*on*), *comment* (*on*); *explain*;
  (v) *boast* (*about/of*), *brag* (*about/of*), *complain* (*about/of*), *grumble* (*about*);
 (vi) *suggest, claim*; *acknowledge, admit, confess* (*to*); (*repute*, which is confined to the passive, may also belong here, cf. §9.4);
(vii) *undertake, offer, propose*; one sense of *agree* (*with*);
(viii) *promise, threaten*.

Sets (i)–(vii) are basically transitive, with the Message in O slot. *Promise* and *threaten* are ditransitive with Addressee as O (although this can freely be omitted), followed by the Message. For all REPORT verbs the Message may be a THAT clause or direct speech (frame III), e.g. *'New York is the finest city in the world,' she announced/ remarked/ boasted/suggested/proposed* and *She announced/remarked/ boasted/ suggested/proposed that New York is the finest city in the world.*

All sets except (i) and (ii) may have the Message-Content as O (frame II), e.g. *He mentioned/complained about/suggested/offered/ promised a dinner-party.* Sets (ii)–(v) occur in frame I, with Message-Label (optionally followed by preposition plus Content) as O, e.g. *They stated/announced/complained about/regretted the message* (*concerning our having to work on Sundays in future*). *Say* has somewhat unusual properties—if there is no direct speech or THAT complement it can take a Message whose first element is some qualification, e.g. *He said a lot/something/nothing* (*about the picnic*); there is also a very limited set of nouns that can occur in the label slot, e.g. *say a prayer* (*for/about . . .*), *say grace.*

A Judgement TO complement may occur with most verbs from sets (ii) and (iii), as well as *declare*, *admit* and *claim* (and *say* only in the passive, §9.4). Thus:

IV. *The Judge declared/reported/admitted him to be insane*

Sets (vii) and (viii) may take a Modal (FOR) TO complement, e.g.

Va *I offered/undertook/promised/threatened for my charlady to clean your house*

The subject of the complement clause will often be coreferential with main clause subject and then omitted (together with *for*):

Vb. *I offered/undertook/promised/threatened to clean your house*

Speakers tend to accept the full FOR TO construction (in Va) with only some of these verbs; for the remainder they require coreferential subjects, as in Vb.

As already mentioned, *threaten* and *promise* have Addressee in O relation. This can be followed by Message-Content (introduced by *with* in the case of *threaten*) or by a THAT clause or by direct speech. Imagine a scenario in which I have the authority to transfer Mary and in which John has strong feelings about her; to taunt him I may either promise a transfer (if I want to please him) or threaten it (if I wish to annoy him):

> (1) *I promised John a transfer for Mary/I threatened John with a transfer for Mary*
>
> (2) *I promised/threatened (John) (that) I/Bill would transfer Mary*
>
> (3) *I promised/threatened (John): 'I/Bill will transfer Mary'*

When the Addressee is omitted these verbs may take a Modal (FOR) TO complement (with complement clause subject coreferential to main clause subject and thus omitted):

> (4) *I promised/threatened to transfer Mary*

In many dialects of English *promise* (but never *threaten*) may take a Modal (FOR) TO clause—with subject coreferential with main clause subject and thus omitted, together with *for*—even when the Addressee is retained:

> (5) *I promised John to transfer Mary*

However, speakers of other dialects (e.g. contemporary Australian English) do not accept (5) as grammatical, and must instead say (2), i.e. *I promised John that I would transfer Mary*. When confronted by (5) these speakers can only interpret it with the complement clause subject coreferential with main clause object (i.e. John arranges the transfer, the whole sentence then meaning perhaps that I let him transfer her); that is, they interpret (5) as having the syntax of a verb from the ORDER subtype.

Of this subtype only set (v)—*boast, brag, complain* and *grumble*—may be used intransitively; the meanings of these verbs indicate the Speaker's attitude towards some Message, which need not be specified, e.g. *She's complaining again. Confess* may omit the Message only when this could be inferred from the context, e.g. *Did you steal the Saab? Okay, I confess* (sc. that I did steal it). All other verbs in sets (i)–(vii) must include a Message, which can be a THAT clause, or else introduce direct speech. Of set (viii), *threaten* should have either Message or Addressee stated, e.g. *He's threatening John, She's threatening to blow up the plane*; but *promise* is like *confess* in that it may omit both Addressee and Message when they could be inferred, e.g. *Will you really mend the window? Yes, I promise* (sc. you that I will mend it).

Offer and *promise* are both very frequently used to convey a Message of giving (where the subject of *give* is coreferential with main clause subject); the verb *give* can then be omitted, with the Donor, Recipient and Gift roles being coded as surface constituents of the SPEAKING verb. Thus *She offered/promised me an apple/ an apple to me* are paraphrases of *She offered/promised to give me an apple/an apple to me*.

Note also that *offer* (especially in relation to giving) and *threaten* —and perhaps other REPORT verbs—need not necessarily involve language activity but could just refer to some gesture. The verbs can still be used in their full syntactic range to describe these gestures (except for the direct speech option), e.g. *The dumb giant threatened to hit her* (*but then she handed over the keys, and so he didn't*).

(*e*) The INFORM subtype refers to the way in which a Message (which is not an order or instruction) is conveyed to the Addressee, e.g. *inform*, *lecture*, *agree* (*with*); *remind* has cross-membership of the INFORM and ORDER subtypes.

These verbs are transitive and have the Addressee role in O syntactic relation. This is followed by the Message introduced by a preposition—*of* (for *inform* and *remind*), *on* (for *lecture* and *agree*) or *about* (for all four verbs). The varieties of Message illustrated in frames I and II (with a preposition inserted) and III are all applicable, e.g. I *I informed John of the announcement* (*about the picnic*); II *I informed John of the picnic*; IIIa *I informed John that there will be a picnic tomorrow*; IIIb '*There will be a picnic tomorrow,*' *I informed John.*

The Addressee NP is obligatory with *inform* and *remind* but can be omitted after *lecture* and *agree* when inferable from the cotext, e.g. *Mary's father thought that she should resign and her mother agreed* (sc. with her father that she should resign). Statement of the Message may be omitted after any of the verbs when inferable, e.g. *Does Mary know about the picnic? She should, I did inform her* (sc. about the picnic).

(*f*) The TELL subtype contains verbs which relate both to Message (particularly its Label component) and to Addressee; they may have either of these roles in O relation. The subtype includes *tell*, *ask, request* and *beg* (note that all these verbs also have cross-membership of the ORDER subtype).

Tell combines something of the syntactic properties of the last two subtypes. Compare:

Message as O

    (*d*) REPORT   *I reported the news (to John)*

    (*e*) INFORM   **I informed the news to John*

    (*f*) TELL   *I told the news to John*

Addressee as O

    (*d*) REPORT   **I reported John (of/about) the news*

    (*e*) INFORM   *I informed John of/about the news*

    (*f*) TELL   *I told John (of/about) the news*

There are, however, important differences. The Message, as O of *report*, can be Label, Label-preposition-Content or just Content, e.g. *I reported the news/the news about the accident/the accident (to John)*. For *tell* the Message, if in O slot, must include a Label—thus *I told the news (about the accident) to John* but not **I told the accident to John*. In addition, a THAT complement or direct speech cannot be included with *tell* if the Addressee is marked by *to*.

The basic syntactic frame for *tell* appears to be with Addressee as O. The Message—which can be Label, Label-preposition-Content or Content—is then introduced by a preposition, e.g. *I told John about the news/about the news concerning the accident/about the accident*. The initial preposition may be dropped only if the Message begins with a Label, e.g. *I told John the news (about the accident)*, but not **I told John the accident*. (There is, of course, a semantic difference between *tell John the news* and *tell John about the news*. And there can, in the Addressee-as-O frame, be a THAT clause or direct speech, e.g. *I told John that the bus had crashed*, and *'The bus has crashed,' I told John*.)

Ask, request and *beg* have similar syntactic properties, with some differences of detail. With Message as O the Addressee is introduced by *of* with *ask* and by *from* with *request* and *beg*, e.g. *She asked a question (about the accident) (of John), He requested information (about the accident) (from John)*. When Addressee is O, *ask* does not include a preposition before a Message Label, e.g. *She asked John (a question) (about the accident)* whereas *request* and *beg* require *for*, e.g. *They begged John for information* (*about the accident*). *Enquire*, and one sense of *demand*, are semantically similar to *request* but may only have a Message (beginning with a Label) in O slot, e.g. *She enquired directions* (*about how to get to the station*) (*from John*).

Ask can omit specification of Message and/or Addressee if these could be inferred from the context, e.g. *I'll ask Mary where the key is. No, don't, I've already asked* (sc. her where it is). *Tell* can omit the Message in similar circumstances, e.g. *Does Mary know where it is? She should, I've told her* (sc. where it is), and it may omit the Addressee when the Message is being particularly focused on, e.g. *I don't want to tell that story again, I've already told it a hundred times*. But Message and Addressee may generally not both be omitted at once with *tell* (except perhaps in a style of children's English, where one child may sometimes be heard accusing another with: *Oh, you told!*).

Answer is an unusual verb in that there are effectively two Messages—the question which was asked, and the answer that may be given (*reply to* is similar, except that it can be used for the response to a question or as a comment on some statement). The question may be coded as an NP in O slot (sometimes with the Addressee as 'possessor' to the Label), e.g. *He answered the/ Mary's question* (*about the accident*). Or the Addressee may be in O relation, e.g. *He answered Mary*. Or the answer may be shown by a THAT complement or by direct speech, e.g. *He answered that the accident was in Pall Mall*; '*The accident was in Pall Mall,' he answered*. Note, though, that question and answer may not both be coded in the same clause (e.g. one cannot say **He answered Mary's question that the accident was in Pall Mall*) simply because the conventions for interpreting apposition in English syntax would then imply that *Mary's question* and *that the accident was in Pall Mall* are coreferential, which they aren't. Instead, one might say *To Mary's question he answered that the accident was in Pall Mall* or *He answered Mary's question by saying that the accident was in Pall Mall*. *Answer* and *reply to* may, like *ask*, be used without any Addressee or Message where the relevant information is supplied by context, e.g. *Have you asked him about the accident? Yes, but he won't answer* (sc. my question about the accident).

(g) The ORDER subtype refers to a Message (generally an order or instruction) directed at an Addressee, e.g. (i) *order, command, urge, instruct, encourage*; *warn, caution, persuade, invite, recommend* (*to*); senses of *tell, remind, ask, request, beg*; (ii) *forbid, discourage, dissuade, prohibit*.

All these verbs are transitive, with the Addressee in O slot. It is followed by the Message, which can only be direct speech (often, an imperative) or—for set (i)—a THAT complement (generally including a modal *should* or *would*) or a Modal (FOR) TO complement. The subject of the complement clause (or of the direct speech) may be different from the main clause subject:

IIIb. *I instructed the lieutenant: 'Your platoon should be ready at dawn!'*

IIIa. *I instructed the lieutenant that his platoon should be ready at dawn*

VIa. *I instructed the lieutenant for his platoon to be ready at dawn*

Or the subject of the complement clause can be coreferential with the main clause object, and then omitted from a direct speech imperative or from a Modal (FOR) TO complementiser:

IIIb'. *I instructed the lieutenant: 'Be ready at dawn!'*

IIIa'. *I instructed the lieutenant that he should be ready at dawn*

VIb. *I instructed the lieutenant to be ready at dawn*

(Speakers vary as to which verbs from this subtype may be used in frame VIa. For those that may not, we simply have to say that the subject of a Modal (FOR) TO clause *must* be coreferential with main clause object.)

The only verbs that may not omit the Addressee (in the presence of a THAT complement or direct speech) are *tell* and *remind*. As with their other senses—*remind* in subtype (e) and *tell* in (f)—these two verbs focus on the Addressee role, which must be stated. *Persuade* does not involve an order or instruction but refers to an attempt to get the Addressee to do something voluntarily; it is not used with direct speech (except perhaps if *try* is also included, e.g. '*You go there, and you'll really enjoy it,*' we tried to persuade him). *Warn* and *caution* may occur in IIIa/b and VIb (often, with the complement clause or direct speech including *not*), or with the negative preposition *against* plus an ING complement that lacks the negative particle (the ING clause will generally have its subject identical to the Addressee, and then omitted), e.g. *I warned him not to go*, *I warned him against going*.

We have already mentioned that, for all verbs in set (i), the subject of a reduced TO complement, in frame VIb, is understood to be identical to the O NP of the main verb (the Addressee role). All verbs except *ask*, *beg* and *request* must include an O NP in VIb; these three verbs can omit the Addressee and the subject of the Modal (FOR) TO clause is then understood to be identical to main clause subject, i.e.

> VIa. *John asked Bill to watch Mary* (i.e. Bill will watch Mary)
> Va. *John asked to watch Mary* (i.e. John will watch Mary)

(The second sentence could perhaps be regarded as an abbreviation of *John asked to be allowed to watch Mary*.) *Ask*, *request* and *beg* appear to be the only verbs in English whose complement clause subject is taken to be coreferential with the main clause object if there is one, and with main clause subject otherwise.

Recommend has a meaning difference from the other verbs in set (i) in that it involves offering advice, not issuing an order, instruction or request. It has the regular syntactic possibilities of the subtype (except that *to* introduces the Addressee, but is dropped before a TO complement), e.g. *'Use brushbox for the steps,' he recommended (to me)*; *He recommended to me that I should use brushbox for the steps*, *He recommended me to use brushbox for the steps*. *Recommend* may also code the Message-Content through an ING complement clause, e.g. *He recommended (to me) (my) using brushbox for the steps*. And there is an abbreviated construction in which a concrete NP may fill the O slot, e.g. *He recommended brushbox (to me)*; a sentence like this could only be used where further necessary details could be inferred by the listeners (e.g. they know that I have been looking for a suitable timber to repair my steps).

The verbs in set (ii) involve negative instruction or advice (i.e. telling the Addressee not to do something that he may have intended to do). They can take direct speech, or a FROM ING complement, e.g.

> VII. *I discouraged John from going*

Discourage and *dissuade* only take a FROM ING, not a TO, clause.

Forbid occurs in both frames with no difference in meaning (*John forbade Mary to go/from going*); speakers differ as to which frame is 'most correct'.

(*h*) The FORGIVE subtype refers to the Speaker saying something to the Addressee which reveals the Speaker's attitude, such as his approval of the Addressee or of something the Addressee has done (or which the Addressee or some other person thinks reveals such an attitude), or saying something which satisfies a social convention (such as greeting), e.g. (i) *insult, slander, curse, abuse, scold, blame, rebuke, forgive, pardon, praise, thank, congratulate, compliment; tell* NP *off, pick on* NP; (ii) *accuse, excuse*; (iii) *greet, welcome, introduce*; (iv) *cheer, applaud, apologise*.

All the verbs in sets (i)–(iii) are strictly transitive, with Addressee as O. *Cheer* and *applaud* are also transitive, but may omit the O; *apologise* is intransitive, but *to*-plus-Addressee may optionally be included.

Accuse and *excuse* must have a Message following the Addressee (unless it could be inferred from the context); this will be an NP or ING clause, introduced by *of* after *accuse*, and by *for* or *from* (with very different meanings) after *excuse*, e.g. *He accused Mary of fiddling the books; She excused John for overlooking the mail/from dealing with the mail*.

Verbs from sets (i)–(ii) and (iv) may add specification of the way in which the attitude was revealed or the greeting effected, using *by* plus an NP or ING clause, e.g. *He insulted me by mispronouncing my name; She thanked me by making a very sweet speech*. Set (i) may also specify the reason for the Speaker's adopting this attitude, using *for* or *on* plus an NP or ING clause, e.g. *He thanked me for saving his life*. It follows from the meanings of these verbs that the subject of a clause introduced with *by* is taken to be coreferential with Speaker (main clause subject) while the subject of a clause introduced by *for* is taken to be coreferential with Addressee (main clause object), e.g. on hearing *John congratulated Tom by shaking his hand on/for winning the race* a listener will infer that John did the shaking and Tom the winning.

Actually using one of these verbs may constitute an instance of the activity it refers to—that is, the verb is being used as a 'performative'—e.g. '*I greet you, stranger*', '*I forgive you, darling*';

this may be referred to in a *by* constituent, e.g. *He congratulated me just by saying 'I congratulate you, my boy' in that posh voice and didn't even shake my hand.* These verbs generally do not introduce direct speech in the ways that the SHOUT, REPORT, INFORM, TELL and ORDER subtypes do. But—like some THINKING and DECIDING verbs—they may be used with direct speech, especially in a bad literary style (and may then omit the Addressee), e.g. *'Oh, you are so wonderful,' she praised.*

Some FORGIVE verbs may of course refer to an activity that involves no speech at all, e.g. *The dumb giant greeted me by clutching my shoulders.* Or the subject may not even be human, e.g. *My cat greets me when I get home.* Syntactic possibilities remain unchanged.

SPEAKING is probably the most varied subtype, both semantically and syntactically. There are many more marginal properties, and differences of detail between verbs, than have been mentioned. But this abbreviated account has dealt with the major parameters which will be needed for the discussion in Chapters 7–11.

5.5. LIKING

Verbs of this type have two roles—an Experiencer (who must be HUMAN or a higher animal) gets a certain feeling about a Stimulus. The meaning of the verb expresses the nature of the feeling.

LIKING verbs can roughly be divided into the following sets: (i) *like, love, hate, prefer*; *fear*; *dread* (also in WANTING); (ii) *dislike, loathe, abhor, admire, value*; *regret* (also a member of the REPORT subtype of SPEAKING); *rejoice at*; *(don't) mind (about)*, *(don't) care (about)*; (iii) *enjoy, favour, object to, approve of* (the adjective *fond*, in *be fond of*, patterns with set (iii), see §3.2); (iv) *worship, fall for*.

These verbs are transitive with the Experiencer in A relation and the Stimulus—which cannot be omitted—in O relation. The only exceptions are *(don't) care (about)* and *(don't) mind (about)*, which may freely omit *about*-plus-Stimulus and are perhaps best regarded as basically intransitive.

The Stimulus may be realised in a variety of ways. It can be a straightforward concrete NP, as in I, or an ING complement, as in

II. The subject of an ING clause will be omitted when it is coreferential with main clause subject, as in IIb.

    I. *Fred likes horses/Mary/your uncle/the wet season*
    IIa. *Fred likes John's playing baseball*
    IIb. *Fred likes playing baseball*

Or the Stimulus can have two components (similar to those of the Message role for SPEAKING verbs)—a Stimulus-Label, generally a SPEECH ACT or other abstract noun—linked by a preposition to a Stimulus-Content, which can be an NP, or an ING, THAT, or Modal (FOR) TO complement. Thus:

    IIIa. *Fred likes the proposal*
    IIIb. *Fred likes the proposal about baseball*
    IIIc. *Fred likes the proposal about (our) playing baseball instead of cricket on Saturdays*
    IIId. *Fred likes the proposal that we should switch to baseball*
    IIIe. *Fred likes the proposal for us to switch to baseball*
    IIIf. *Fred likes the proposal to switch to baseball*

(Following a general rule of English, the preposition drops before *that*, *for* or *to* in IIId/e/f.)

As described in §5.4, a Message role may include just Label, or Label-preposition-Content, or—for some SPEAKING verbs—just Content. The Stimulus role shows different possibilities. It may just comprise a Label, as in IIIa. But it may not omit the Label from IIId. That is, one cannot say, in most dialects of English **Fred likes that we now play baseball*.

It is possible, however, to substitute the impersonal pronoun *it* for the Label in frame IIId. The Label may be omitted from IIIf, with no substitution, and it may be omitted from IIIe with substitution of *it*. (Omitting the Label plus preposition from IIIc gives IIa.)

    IIId'. *Fred likes it that we now play baseball*
    IIIe'. *Fred would like (it for) us to switch to baseball*
    IIIf'. *Fred would like to switch to baseball*

We can first focus on the inclusion of the impersonal pronoun in IIId'/e'. It is clear that the substitution of *it* does engender a semantic difference. The Stimulus-Label may be one of a number of nouns, with different meanings, e.g. *proposal*, *idea*, *suggestion*, *fact*. When *it* replaces the Label the Stimulus has a meaning rather close to that with *fact*—*I like the fact that he stands up to the boss* is a near paraphrase of *It like it that he stands up to the boss*. A Stimulus with *it* certainly has a different sense from one with *the proposal* (which is why I changed the verb phrase of the complement clause in IIId', in order to maintain a felicitous sentence). The sequence *it for* can be omitted from IIIe', with a definite semantic effect—see §7.2.4.

Stimulus-Label and Stimulus-Content essentially make up one syntactic component, in O slot. An adverb may follow the complete statement of Stimulus, e.g. *I like the suggestion that we should disarm an awful lot, I'd like it for us to disarm very much.* But the Content component can be moved to the end of the clause, and an adverb may then come between the Label (which remains in O slot) and the Content, e.g. *I like the suggestion an awful lot that we should disarm, I'd like it very much for us to disarm.* (The longer the Content is, the more likely it is to be moved to the end of the clause; cf. §2.11A.) Extraposition of Content applies in almost exactly the same manner for ANNOYING verbs, described in the next section, and is then more visible. (See also the discussion of phrasal verbs, in §8.2.2, for further confirmatory data.)

No *it* can come before *to* in IIIf' but an adverb may still come before or after the TO clause (as it may come before or after THAT and FOR TO complements in IIId'/e') e.g. *I would like very much to switch to baseball, I would like to switch to baseball very much.* The question of why *it* should be obligatory in IIId', optional in IIIe' (speakers vary in their judgements here) and obligatorily absent in IIIf' is an interesting one, to which no answer is at present known.

Turning now to the syntactic behaviour of different LIKING verbs, it appears that they can all occur with an NP or ING clause as Stimulus but may not all be equally happy with THAT and (FOR) TO complements. There are no hard and fast divisions (which is why we do not talk of subtypes), rather a scale of relative acceptability.

Set (i) are at home in all the frames discussed, with ING, THAT and (FOR) TO complements. Set (ii) are found with ING and THAT clauses but appear awkward with FOR and TO complements (IIIe/f and IIIe'/f'). One hears *I like/hate to go* but scarcely *I dislike/ loathe to go*; they become more acceptable if *would* is included, e.g. *I would dislike/loathe to go.* (We do get *I don't care to go,* meaning 'don't want to', but this is a different meaning of *don't care* (*about*) from that in *I don't care about the proposal that we should go*, where the sense is 'be indifferent to'.) Set (iii) are almost restricted to NP and ING codings of Stimulus. They sound most odd with (FOR) TO and TO complements, and the possibilities for THAT clauses (frames IIId/d') are very limited—one might accept *I enjoy it that John cooks* and perhaps ?*I favour the idea that Mary* (*should*) *organise the picnic*, but scarcely ??*I enjoy the fact that John cooks* or ??*I favour it that Mary should organise the picnic*. Set (iv) appear restricted to an NP Stimulus. (§7.4.5 attempts a semantic explanation for the varying syntactic possibilities of LIKING verbs.)

Object to and *approve of* each include an inherent preposition and (*don't*) *care* (*about*) includes a preposition before the Stimulus, if this is stated. These prepositions must be included in frames I, II, IIIa–f. In IIId' *about it* is omitted after *don't care*, e.g. *I don't care* (*about it) *that we may switch to baseball* and—to the extent that *object to* and *approve of* are used in frame IIId'—the *to it* and *of it* may either be omitted or retained, e.g. *I object* (*to it*) *that John wants to play cricket*; *I approve* (*of it*) *that John adores baseball*.

With (*don't*) *mind* the preposition may be included or omitted in all of I, II, IIIa–e. In fact it carries a semantic difference: *don't mind* implies that the speaker is stoical about something that may adversely affect him, whereas *don't mind about* indicates indifference, similar to *don't care about*. Compare *I don't mind Mary* (let her insult me all she wants, I've got a thick skin) with *I don't mind about Mary* (couldn't give a damn what happens to her); and *I don't mind the proposal that my salary should be cut* (sure it'll affect me, but I do have a private income) with *I don't mind about the proposal that my salary should be cut* (since I know it's just hot air, they wouldn't dare actually do it). The contrast should be neutralised in frame IIId', since a preposition must drop before *that*; but in fact *I don't mind that my salary will/may be cut* has the clear sense of *don't mind* (not *don't mind about*).

Rejoice at appears to belong to set (ii), but is unusual in that it does not include *it* before a THAT complement (e.g. *I rejoiced that he had returned unharmed*).

Fear and *dread* have rather different meanings from the other

LIKING verbs. They occur in frames I, II, IIIa–e and, typically IIIf′, but not in IIIe′, where the Stimulus is realised as a FOR TO clause with no preceding Label. Both occur in IIId′ but here *dread* may omit the *it* and *fear* would generally omit *it*, e.g. *I dread (it) that she may return home*, *I fear (?it) that she may return home*. (It is interesting that *rejoice* and *fear*, two verbs which do not take *it* before a THAT clause, appear to be the only LIKING verbs to occur in parentheticals—see §7.1.)

Two further verbs may be regarded as divergent members of this type. *Envy*, but not *pity*, can occur in frames I and IIa, e.g. *I envy Mary's luck*, *I envy Mary's getting promoted.* But *envy* is more felicitously used—and *pity* must be used—in a quite different frame, where the verb is followed by an NP referring to a person (who is the object of the envy/pity), optionally followed by a constituent stating the reason for this emotional attitude—this can be an NP, or a Label followed by preposition and ING or THAT clause, or just an ING or THAT clause:

IVa. *I envy Mary her promotion*
IVb. *I envy Mary (the fact of) her husband('s) being such a good cook*
IVc. *I envy Mary (the fact) that she got promoted*

Note that the subject of an ING complement (*her* in IVb) may optionally be omitted if it is coreferential with main clause object (e.g. *I envy Mary being so quick at figures*).

(The adjective *jealous* (*of*) has a very similar meaning to *envy* but different syntactic possibilities—we cannot say **I was jealous of Mary her promotion*, only something like *I was jealous of Mary because of her promotion*.)

5.6. ANNOYING

This type has the same two roles as LIKING—an Experiencer gets a certain feeling about a Stimulus—but they are mapped differently onto syntactic relations, Stimulus becoming A and Experiencer O, e.g. *frighten, terrify, scare, shock, upset, surprise; offend; delight, please, satisfy, entertain, amuse, excite, inspire; impress, concern, trouble, worry, grieve, dismay, depress, sadden; madden, infuriate,*

annoy, anger, disappoint; confuse, bewilder, perplex, puzzle;
interest, distract, bore; attract; embarrass, disgust; tire, exhaust,
bother.

All ANNOYING verbs are transitive. Some do have meanings
similar to those of LIKING verbs (e.g. *please* and *delight* are almost
converses of *like* and *love*—if *X pleases Y* it is likely that *Y likes X*,
and vice versa) but most have meanings rather different from
those of the LIKING type.

The syntactic frames we outlined for LIKING apply almost exactly
to ANNOYING verbs, with A and O reversed, e.g

> I. *Horses/Mary/your uncle/the wet season annoy(s) Fred*
> IIa. *John's playing baseball annoys Fred*
> IIb. *Playing baseball annoys Fred*
> IIIa. *The proposal annoys Fred*
> IIIb. *The proposal about baseball annoys Fred*
> IIIc. *The proposal about (our) playing baseball instead of*
>   *cricket on Saturdays annoys Fred*
> IIId. *The proposal that we should switch to baseball annoys*
>   *Fred*
> IIIe. *The proposal for us to switch to baseball annoys Fred*
> IIIf. *The proposal to switch to baseball annoys Fred*

In §5.5 we presented evidence—from adverb placement—that a
THAT, or Modal (FOR) TO clause, as the Content part of Stimulus,
may be extraposed to the end of the clause, with the Label
remaining in its original syntactic slot. This happens very plainly
for ANNOYING verbs, where the extraposition is from A slot, i.e.

> III′d. *The proposal annoys Fred that we should switch to*
>   *baseball*
> III′e. *The proposal annoys Fred for us to switch to baseball*
> III′f. *The proposal annoys Fred to switch to baseball*

(It should be noted that speakers differ over the acceptability of
III′d–f).

LIKING verbs also occur in IIId″/e″/f″ where the Label is either
omitted or replaced by *it*; the complement clause can again be
transposed. These possibilities are once more clearly distinguished
for verbs from the ANNOYING type:

> IIId′. *That we now play baseball annoys Fred*
> IIIe′. *For us to switch to baseball would annoy Fred*

IIIf′. *To switch to baseball would annoy Fred*
III′d′. *It annoys Fred that we now play baseball*
III′e′. *It would annoy Fred for us to switch to baseball*
III′f′. *It would annoy Fred to switch to baseball*

A minor syntactic difference is now revealed. Most LIKING verbs take *it* before a THAT clause and also have *it* before a full (FOR) TO complement (but omit *it* when the *for* is dropped). ANNOYING verbs retain *it* in subject slot for all three complement types when they are extraposed, but cannot include *it* when the complement clause stays in A slot. The inclusion of *it* when extraposition has taken place is necessary to satisfy the surface structure constraint that there be something in the subject slot for every main clause in English. The omission of *it* when there is no extraposition is also due to a surface syntactic constraint—no sentence in English may begin with *it that*, *it for* or *it to*.

(It is in keeping with the general syntactic structure of English (§2.7) that an ING complement can generally not be extraposed; there can be what is called 'right dislocation', a quite different syntactic phenomenon, which is marked by contrastive intonation, shown in writing by a comma, e.g. II′a *It annoys Fred, John's playing baseball.*)

Not all verbs from this type occur equally freely with all kinds of complement; Modal (FOR) TO constructions may be especially rare for some. This relates to the meanings of the complement constructions and the meanings of the verbs (see Chapter 7). No hard and fast occurrence restrictions are evident, as a basis for establishing subtypes.

Most verbs in this type do not allow an O NP to be omitted (even if it has a very general meaning, e.g. *He amuses everyone*). There are just two or three that occasionally occur with no Experiencer stated, in marked contexts, e.g. *He always offends, She does annoy, He can entertain, can't he!* A small subset of ANNOYING verbs may also be used intransitively, with S = O (i.e. the Experiencer is then in S relation). These include *worry*, *grieve* and *delight*, e.g. *The behaviour of his daughter worries/grieves John, John worries/grieves a lot (over the behaviour of his daughter); Playing golf delights John, John delights in playing golf.* (Note that there is semantic difference here: used transitively these verbs imply that it is the Stimulus which engenders the feeling in the Experiencer; used intransitively they imply an inherent propensity, on the part of the Experiencer, to the feeling.)

The passive participle—which is still a verbal form although it behaves in some ways like an adjective—and the past participle—which is a derived adjective—coincide in form (e.g. *broken* in *The window was broken by Mary* and in *the broken window*). With ANNOYING verbs it is not an easy matter to distinguish between a passive construction and a copula-plus-past-participle construction. Consider:

(1a) *John's winning the race surprised me*
(2a) *The result surprised me*
(1b) *I was surprised at/by John's winning the race*
(2b) *I was surprised at/by the result*

Sentences (1b) and (2b) have the syntactic appearance of passives except that the preposition may be *at* or *by* (carrying a slight meaning difference) whereas in a normal passive the underlying A can only be introduced with *by*. Note that we can have *at* or *by* after *surprised*, *about* or *with* or *by* after *pleased*, *in* or *by* after *interested*, *of* or *by* after *terrified*, etc. There is in each case a meaning difference, e.g. *terrified by a noise* (something specific), *terrified of strangers* (a general phenomenon). *By* is always one possibility, suggesting that this alternative could constitute a passive construction, with the other alternative (featuring *at* or *about* or *with* or *of* or *in*, etc.) marking an adjectival construction.

Adjectives from the ANGRY and HAPPY subtypes of HUMAN PROPENSITY have similar meanings to past participles of some ANNOYING verbs. These can introduce the Stimulus role by a preposition, e.g. *angry about*, *jealous of*, *sorry about*, *ashamed of*. It appears always to be a preposition other than *by*, lending support for the position that (1b) and (2b) with *surprised by* are passives, while (1b) and (2b) with *surprised at* are not passives but parallel to a construction with copula plus HUMAN PROPENSITY adjective.

One syntactic test for distinguishing between verbal and adjectival forms is that only the latter can be modified by *very*, e.g. we can say *This hat is very squashed*—where *squashed* is a derived adjective—but not **This hat was very squashed by Mary* or **Jane* *was very seen by her brother*—where *squashed* and *seen* aɪe passive verbal forms. Most speakers accept *very* with *surprised at, pleased with, interested in* (supporting our contention that these are adjectival constructions) but are less happy when *very* is used with *surprised by, pleased by, interested by* (supporting our treatment of these as passive constructions).

There is one apparent counter-example. The prefix *un-* can be added to some verbs from the AFFECT type with a reversative meaning (e.g. *untie, uncover*), and to some adjectives from HUMAN PROPENSITY, QUALIFICATION, VALUE, SIMILARITY and PHYSICAL PROPERTY (see §3.2) forming an antonym (e.g. *unkind, impossible, unlike*). The antonymic sense of *un-* never occurs with a verb. Thus we get verb *impress*, derived adjective *impressed*, and negative adjective *unimpressed* (but not a negative verb **unimpress*). However, *unimpressed* can be followed with *by*, e.g. *I was (very) unimpressed by his excuses*. How can it be that *by* occurs with *unimpressed*, something that is not a verbal form?

This apparent counter-example can be explained. We have seen that a passive construction takes *by*, whereas a derived adjective (the past participle) may take one of an extensive set of prepositions; which preposition is chosen depends on the meaning of the past participle and of the preposition. This set of prepositions does include *by*, and it is this which is used with the adjectival forms *impressed* and *unimpressed*. Thus:

	In verbal passive construction	In adjectival past participle construction
surprised	*by*	*at*
pleased	*by*	*with* or *about*
terrified	*by*	*of*
satisfied	*by*	*with*
dissatisfied	—	*with*
interested	*by*	*in*
uninterested	—	*in*
impressed	*by*	*by*
unimpressed	—	*by*

We see that *dissatisfied, uninterested* and *unimpressed* (which must be adjectival forms) take the same preposition, in the right-hand column, as *satisfied*, *interested* and *impressed* (which can be verbal or adjectival). It is just that *impressed* and *unimpressed* take *by* in the right-hand column, the same preposition that occurs with all verbs in a passive construction, as shown in the left-hand column. *Unimpressed* is an adjective, which takes *by* in the same way that *uninterested* takes *in*.

Since *impressed* has *by* in both columns a sentence such as *John was impressed by the report* is ambiguous between passive and past participle interpretations. We also encounter ambiguity when a THAT or Modal (FOR) TO complement clause is involved. Compare:

(3a) *That John won the race surprised me/It surprised me that John won the race*

(3b) *I was surprised that John won the race*

Sentence (3a) is a normal active construction with an ANNOYING verb; (3b) could be either the passive of (3a) or a copula-plus-past-participle construction. Since, by a general rule of English, a preposition is automatically dropped before complementiser *that* (or *for* or *to*) we cannot tell, in the case of (3b), whether the underlying preposition is *by* or *at*.

Past participles of many ANNOYING verbs may—like adjectives—occur in construction with a verb of the MAKE type, e.g. *make confused*, *make depressed*. It is instructive to compare:

(4a) *The pistol shot in the airport frightened me*

(4b) *The stories I've heard about pistol shots in airports have made me frightened (of ever visiting an airport)*

The transitive verb *frighten,* in (4a), refers to the Stimulus putting the Experiencer directly in a fright. *Make*-plus-past-participle-*frightened*, in (4b), refers to the Stimulus causing the Experiencer, less directly, to get into a fright. (See also §8.3.3.)

Some verbs of the ANNOYING type are morphologically derived from adjectives, e.g. *madden* and *sadden*, from *mad* and *sad*, members of the ANGRY subtype of HUMAN PROPENSITY (here we would say *make mad/sad*, parallel to *make frightened* in (4b); we would not say *make maddened/saddened*). Quite a number of verbs from this type also function as nouns, with the same form, e.g. *scare*, *shock*, *upset*, *surprise*, *delight*, *concern*, *trouble*, *worry*, *puzzle*, *interest*, *bore*, *bother*. Some have nouns derived from them, e.g. *amusement*, *offence*, *satisfaction*, *confusion*; and a few are verbs derived from nouns, e.g. *frighten* from *fright*, *terrify* from *terror*.

5.7. Others

A number of other Primary-B types are here surveyed quite briefly since—like those mentioned in §4.6—they do not have critical properties in terms of the syntactic topics discussed in Chapters 7–11. All of these types include some verbs which take complement clauses and some which do not.

The ACTING subtype refers to a manner of behaving. *Act* and *behave* are intransitive, generally with a HUMAN subject, and normally receive adverbal modification that expresses a value judgement about the activity, e.g. *He is acting like a fool, She is behaving well*. (If no adverbal element is included with *behave* then 'well' is implied, i.e. *She is behaving* is an abbreviation of *She is behaving well*. When *act* is used without adverbal modification it takes on a quite different sense, akin to 'behaving falsely'.)

Transitive verbs *adopt* (e.g. habits), *copy, imitate, mimic, mime* and *reproduce* have a similar, very general potential reference; their A NP is likely to be HUMAN and the O NP should refer either to a person or to some activity (either through an NP or—except for *adopt*—an ING complement clause), e.g. *She copied John, She adopted his manner of walking, They reproduced the fight, She imitated John's trying to button his shirt when he was drunk*.

HAPPENING verbs describe some event taking place and generally have an ACTIVITY noun in S or O slot. *Happen* and *take place* are intransitive, and carry no implication that an 'agent' was involved, e.g. *The fight just happened*. The transitive verbs *organise, arrange* and *bring* NP *about* will have a HUMAN as A and either an ACTIVITY noun or a THAT or ING clause as O, e.g. *He arranged the fight/that they should fight after school/their fighting after school*. There are transitive verbs with more specific meanings which are only likely to have an NP as O—*commit* (e.g. a crime), *attend to/neglect* (e.g. the arrangements), *put* NP *on* (e.g. the concert), *take* NP *on* (e.g. the responsibility of organising something), *do* (e.g. the organising), *tie* (e.g. the concert) *in with* (e.g. the prize-giving), one sense of *change* (e.g. the arrangements), *devise* (e.g. a new hierarchy).

Experience and *undergo* are transitive verbs with a different semantic profile—here the A NP is a HUMAN who is generally not in control of what happens. In O relation we can have an ACTIVITY or STATE noun or an ING complement clause (often in the passive, as befits the meanings of *experience* and *undergo*), always with the same subject as the main clause, e.g. *I experienced being shot at/a bloody battle/her jealousy*

COMPARING verbs are all transitive (some having inherent prepositions). *Resemble* and *differ* (*from*) must have NPs or subjectless complement clauses with comparable meanings as fillers of A and O slots, e.g. *John differs a lot from his brother* (*in work habits*), *Being kissed by Zelig resembles being licked by an elephant.* The phrasal verb *take after* NP is restricted to NPs in A and O relation, e.g. *He takes after his mother* (*in being deeply religious*). Adjectives *like*, *unlike*, *similar* (*to*) and *different* (*from*) have similar semantics and syntax to *resemble* and *differ* (*from*).

A second set—*distinguish* (*between*), *compare*; *class*, *group*, *cost*, *grade* (the last four derived from nouns); *match*, *balance*, *measure*, *weigh*, *time* (e.g. a race) and *count*—describe the human activity of comparing and quantifying. They normally take a HUMAN noun as head of the A NP and an O that refers to several comparable things or activities (which can be described through NPs or ING complement clauses linked by a preposition), e.g. *He compared Hadlee and/with Botham, She found it hard to distinguish between John's nodding his head and his shaking his head. Fit* and *suit*, which can refer to natural connections between things, belong in the same type, e.g. *Yellow suits Mary, That dress fits you, Going in first wicket down suited Don Bradman. Equal* is most frequently used with numerical quantities, e.g. *The square on the hypotenuse equals the sum of the squares on the other two sides.*

The verbs *include*, *comprise*, *consist of* and *be made up of* may have NPs or complement clauses in A and O relations, e.g. *That book includes four maps, Mailing a letter consists of buying a stamp, sticking it on the top right corner of the envelope, and then dropping it into the mail box.*

RELATING verbs are all transitive (again, some include an inherent preposition) and refer to a natural or logical relationship between two states or activities. A and O can each be a plain NP (generally, with an ACTIVITY or STATE noun as head) or a THAT or WH- or ING complement clause, e.g. *Whether John will agree to go depends on the weather/on who is appointed leader, Mary's refusing to eat dinner results from the fact that her dog just died, The fact that the dog died indicates that it wasn't properly cared for* (see the discussion in §7.4.6).

Verbs in this type, besides *depend* (*on*), *result* (*from*) and *indicate*, include *relate* (*to*), *imply*, *be due* (*to*) and particular senses of *show*, *demonstrate* and *suggest*. Note that these verbs, together with some from the COMPARING type (such as *resemble*, *differ from*, *include*, *comprise*) and some from MAKING (§6.3.1) and HELPING (§6.3.2) appear to be the only verbs in English which can take complement clauses in A and O slots simultaneously.

6

Secondary verb types

6.1. Secondary-A types

None of the Secondary-A verbs have any independent semantic roles. Basically, they modify the meaning of a following verb, sharing its roles and syntactic relations.

6.1.1. MODALS and SEMI-MODALS

Many tens of thousands of words have been written about the English modals. Only some of the main points of their grammatical and semantic behaviour are indicated here.

There are two, syntactically different but semantically related, types, MODALS and what we can call SEMI-MODALS:

MODAL	SEMI-MODAL	central meaning
will/would (*shall/should*) }	*be going to*	prediction
should *ought to* }	—	obligation
must	{ *have to* *have got to* }	necessity
can/could	*be able to*	ability
—	*be about to*	imminent activity
be to	—	scheduled activity
may/might	—	possibility
—	*get to*	achievement
—	*be bound to*	inevitability

We mentioned at the end of §3.4 that a clause may contain a chain of verbs, each in syntactic relation with its neighbours, e.g. *She will soon be able to begin telling John to think about starting to build the house.* A modal must occur initially in such a chain—that is, it cannot be preceded by any other verb. Semi-modals behave like other Secondary verbs in that they can occur at the beginning or in the middle of a chain, but not at the end. A VP can contain only one modal, but it may involve a sequence of semi-modals, e.g. *He has to be going to start writing soon.*

Modals and semi-modals in the same row of the table have similar, but by no means identical, meanings; combinations of modal and semi-modal are acceptable. Thus, in place of the ungrammatical **will can* and **could will*, one might say *will be able to* and *could be going to* respectively.

A semi-modal can occur in initial position; it does not then have exactly the same import as the corresponding modal. Semi-modals often carry an 'unconditional' sense, while modals may indicate prediction, ability, necessity, etc subject to certain specifiable circumstances. Compare:

(1a) *My sister will get married on Tuesday if I go home on that day*

(1b) *My sister is going to get married on Tuesday, so I'm going home on that day*

(2a) *John can do mathematics, when he puts his mind to it*

(2b) *John is able to do mathematics, without even having to try*

(3a) *The boat must call tomorrow, if there aren't any high seas*

(3b) *The boat has to call tomorrow, even if there are high seas*

However, this is very much a tendency; there is a great deal of semantic overlap between the two sets of modals.

The first word of the auxiliary component of a VP plays a crucial syntactic role in that it takes negator *not* ~ *n't*, and is moved before the subject in a question (§§2.3, 2.9.1). Modals (the *ought* and *be* elements in the case of *ought to* and *be to*) fulfil this role, e.g. *Will he sing?*, *He shouldn't run today*, *Are we to go tomorrow?* When a semi-modal begins a VP then the *be* of *be going to*, *be able to*, *be about to*, and *be bound to* and the *have* of *have got to* will take the negator and front in a question, e.g. *Is he going to sing?*, *You haven't got to go*. The *have* of *have to* behaves in the same way in some dialects, e.g. *Has he to go? He hasn't to go*; but other dialects include *do* (effectively treating *have to* as a lexical verb in this respect, and not as an auxiliary), e.g. *Does he have to go?*, *He doesn't have to go*. The *get* of *get to* never takes the negator or fronts in a question—one must say *I didn't get to see the Queen*, not **I gotn't to see the Queen*.

Each modal has a fair semantic range, extending far beyond the central meanings we have indicated (they differ in this from the semi-modals, which have a narrower semantic range). There is in fact considerable overlap between the modals (see the diagram in Coates 1983: 5). The central meaning of *can* refers to inherent ability, e.g. *John can lift 100 kilos* (*he's that strong*), and of *may* to the possibility of some specific event happening, e.g. *We may get a Christmas bonus this year*. But both verbs can/may refer to a permitted activity, e.g. *John can/may stay out all night* (*his mother has said it's all right*) and to some general possibility, e.g. *The verb 'shout' can/may be used both transitively and intransitively*.

It is usually said, following what was an accurate analysis in older stages of the language, that four of the modals inflect for tense, as follows:

present	*will*	*shall*	*can*	*may*
past	*would*	*should*	*could*	*might*

A main justification for retaining this analysis comes from indirect speech. Recall that a sentence uttered with present tense is placed in past tense when it becomes indirect speech to a SPEAKING verb in past tense (§2.7), e.g. *'I'm sweating,' John said* and *John said that he was sweating*. We do get *would*, *could* and *might* functioning as the past tense equivalents, in indirect speech, of *will*, *can* and *may*, e.g. *'I will/can/may go,' he said* and *He said that he would/could/ might go*. *Shall* is little used by most speakers nowadays, except perhaps with the negative, e.g. *I shan't go*; there is a preference nowadays to use *would* as the past tense equivalent of *shall* here (*I said that I wouldn't go*) since *should* has taken on an independent status as an 'obligation' modal. *Must* is not used in the past by most speakers and the past form of the corresponding semi-modal *had to* may fill the gap, while *should* and *ought to* function as both present and past, e.g. *'I must/should/ought to go,' he said* and *He said that he had to/should/ought to go*.

Would, *could* and *might* nowadays have semantic functions that go far beyond 'past tense of *will*, *can* and *may*'. *May* and *might* are often used interchangeably, e.g. *He may/might come tomorrow* (speakers vary in their opinion as to whether one of these indicates a stronger possibility than the other, and if so which one). *Would* can mark a 'likely hypothesis', e.g. *I saw John embrace a strange woman; Oh, that would be his sister. Could* is often a softer, more polite, alternative to *can*—compare *Could you pass the salt?* and *Can you pass the salt?* (in both cases what is literally a question about ability is being used as a request). And so on.

There is a clear semantic difference between the 'necessity' forms *must/have to/have got to* and the 'obligation' forms *should/ought to*:

(4a) *I should/ought to finish this essay tonight (but I don't think I will)*

(4b) *I must/have to/have got to finish this essay tonight (and I will, come what may)*

It is hard to discern any semantic difference between *should* and *ought to*, these two modals being in most contexts substitutable one for the other (see the discussion in Erades 1959/60, Coates 1983: 58–83). However, *ought to* is a little unwieldy in negative sentences—where the *ought* and the *to* get separated—so that *should* may be preferred in this environment; thus *You shouldn't dig there* seems a little more felicitous than *You oughtn't to dig there* (although the latter is still acceptable). The same argument should apply to questions, where *ought* and *to* would again be separated; interestingly, the *to* may optionally be dropped after *ought* in a question, e.g. *Ought I (to) go?*

Parallel modals and semi-modals from the two columns can be combined—*will be going to* could refer to 'future in future', e.g. *He will be going to build the house when he gets planning permission (but even then I doubt if he'll do it in a hurry)* while *could be able to* combines the 'possibility' sense of *could* (as in *That restaurant could be closed on a Sunday*) with the 'ability' meaning of *be able to*, e.g. *John could be able to solve this puzzle (let's ask him)*.

There are a few other verbs that have some of the characteristics of modals. *Used to* must be first in any chain of verbs but—unlike other modals—it generally requires *do* in questions and negation, e.g. *Did he use(d) to do that?*, *He didn't use(d) to do that* (although some speakers do say *Used he to do that?* and *He use(d)n't to do that*). It could be regarded as an aberrant member of the MODAL type.

Then there is *had better*, as in *He had better go*. Although the *had* is identical with the past tense of *have*, *had better* is used for present reference, and without any inflection for person of subject (coinciding in this with all modals except *be to*); it can also be used where a past form would be expected in indirect speech, e.g. *I told him he had better go*. Sometimes the *had* is omitted—*You better (not) go!* This is perhaps another, rather unusual, modal.

Need (from the WANTING type) and *dare* (from DARING) have two patterns of syntactic behaviour. They may be used as lexical verbs, with a TO complement clause, taking the full set of inflections for tense, including 3sg subject present ending -*s*, and requiring *do* in questions and negatives if there is no other auxiliary element present, e.g. *Does he dare/need to go?*, *He doesn't dare/need to go*. But these may also be used as modals (with no *to*), fronting in questions and taking the negative directly, e.g. *Dare/need he go?*, *He daren't/needn't go*. Note that in their modal use *dare* and *need* do not take the 3sg present inflection -*s* (behaving like all modals except *be to*) but they also lack past tense inflection (like *must* but unlike *will*, *can*, *may*). There is a semantic contrast between the two uses of *need* and *dare*—§§6.1.5, 6.2.1; because of this, the modal uses are almost restricted to questions and negatives.

6.1.2. BEGINNING

Semantically, the verbs of this type divide into three groups: (i) *begin*, *start*, *commence*; (ii) *continue (with)*, *keep (on (with))*; *go on (with)*; (iii) *finish*, *cease*, *stop*, *complete*, *discontinue*.

We suggested in §3.4 that a BEGINNING verb should be followed by another verb, which it modifies and which may in certain circumstances be omitted, e.g. *The choir started (singing) 'Messiah' at two o'clock, Mary continued (with) (writing) her book after a short holiday, Tommy has finished (shelling) the peas, I've completed (grading) these assignments*. This statement of usage will be expanded and refined below.

There are two kinds of verbs that may readily be omitted after a member of the BEGINNING type:

(i) verbs concerned with making or preparing or performing something, such as *cook*, *knit* and *tell*, e.g. *He began (cooking) the supper*, *She began (knitting) a sweater*, *My uncle began (telling) another joke*. Other verbs of similar meaning that may be omitted include: *build, perform, write, copy, type, print, bind, weave, sew, mend, cook, boil, peel, scrape, shell, chop*; *clean, wash, polish, sweep*;

(ii) verbs concerned with consumption, such as *read, eat, drink* and *smoke*, e.g. *I started (reading) 'Great Expectations' last night, John began (eating) the chocolate cake.*

Note that when a verb is omitted after a BEGINNING item its object NP is left behind. This NP should be something that is a typical object of the omitted verb, so that the nature of the verb can with a degree of probability be inferred from it. From *John began building Mary's house last February* it is permissible to omit *build*, since *house* is a prototypical object of that verb. However, from *Mary began liking her new house after she'd been living it it for six months* it is not possible to omit *liking* since this is a verb that can take any sort of object. As mentioned before, there may be more than one verb that is omissible before a given object NP, e.g. *John began (building/painting) Mary's house, Hosanna began (reading/writing) a new detective novel, Junior began (shelling/ cooking/ eating) the peas*; a speaker will not normally omit a verb unless he thinks the addressee has enough background knowledge to be able to retrieve it, e.g. it might be known that John is a painter and not a builder, that Hosanna writes detective stories but seldom reads them.

The verbs which can be omitted after a BEGINNING item mostly come from the AFFECT, CORPOREAL and SPEAKING types (but are only a selection of verbs from these types, e.g. omission is quite impossible from *John began caning the children*). It would be highly unusual to omit a verb that belongs to MOTION, REST, GIVING, THINKING, DECIDING, LIKING or ANNOYING—that is, from sentences like *The old lady started fetching the firewood, Mary began choosing dresses, The army finished crossing the river.*

Verbs that are omitted normally have two stated NPs (in A and O syntactic relations) and both are retained. It is interesting that a verb for which three roles are stated is not open to omission, e.g. no GIVING items (not even from *She started giving alms to the beggars*). *Telling* may not be omitted from any sentence where all of Speaker, Addressee and Message are stated, e.g. not from *He began telling another joke to the delegates (although they hadn't laughed at the previous one*) nor from *He began telling the delegates another joke* (. . .). But it may be omitted from *He began* (*telling*) *another joke* (. . .), where there are just two roles stated.

If the subject NP is a description of a person such that it indicates their habitual activity then it may be possible to omit an object NP together with a transitive verb, or to omit an intransitive verb. Parallel to *Mary started* (*cooking*) *the dinner at four o'clock*, we can have *The chef started* (*cooking*) (*the dinner*) *at four o'clock*. In the *Mary* sentence the NP *dinner* should be included to enable the listener to retrieve the verb *cook*; but if *the chef* is subject NP this is not necessary. Similarly, on hearing *The juggler finished two minutes before the conjuror appeared* one would assume that the juggler had finished juggling; if the message to be conveyed were that he had finished eating then the verb should not be omitted and/or an object NP should be retained, e.g. *The juggler finished* (*eating/his dinner/eating his dinner*) *two minutes before the conjuror appeared*. (It goes without saying that more drastic omission is possible if relevant circumstances are known to all participants in the speech activity, e.g. *Mary has finished* may be said if everyone knows what Mary has been doing. My point is that *Mary has finished the jumper* or *The choir started five minutes ago* could be said in neutral circumstances, with the verbs *knitting* and *singing* being understood, as implied, by a stranger.)

When a BEGINNING verb modifies an intransitive verb, or a transitive verb that has no object stated, then this verb may often be replaced by an ACTIVITY or SPEECH ACT noun derived from the verb, e.g. *John began the apology before you arrived* corresponds to *John began apologising/to apologise before you arrived*, and *Mary started her swim at two o'clock* corresponds to *Mary started swimming/to swim at two o'clock*. There is a recurrent meaning difference—the noun may refer to some unit of activity (it might be a cross-Channel swim, for instance) and the verb just to the fact that the activity happens.

A BEGINNING verb may also appear in an intransitive construction where the subject is an ACTIVITY, STATE or SPEECH ACT noun, e.g. *The game continued after tea, John's jealousy first began when he saw Mary out with Tom, The offer finishes on Friday*. For each of these sentences there is a near-paraphrase that includes a related verb or adjective in a complement clause—(*Some*) *people continued playing the game after tea, John first began to be jealous when he saw Mary out with Tom, (Someone) finishes offering (something) on Friday* (the constituents introduced by *some* here could be replaced by more specific NPs, on the basis of information shared by speaker and hearer). There are some peripheral members of the BEGINNING type which can only be used intransitively, with an ACTIVITY noun in subject slot, e.g. *set in* and *break out* as in *The rains have set in for the monsoon season, Fighting broke out at midday.*

Some nouns with CONCRETE reference refer to things extended in space. A river moves in space, and it is appropriate to refer to the place where it begins moving, e.g. *The Murrumbidgee River rises on the Dividing Range*, or *The Murrumbidgee River starts on the Dividing Range*. A road does not move but, by analogy with river, one can say *The Bruce Highway starts/begins in Brisbane and finishes at Cairns* (or, depending on one's ethnocentric focus, *The Bruce Highway starts/begins at Cairns and finishes in Brisbane*). *Begin, start* and *finish* cannot here be related to any underlying verb, and such 'extended in space' usages of items from the BEGINNING type have to be considered additional senses of the verbs.

Turning now to semantic analysis, we can first note a clear contrast between *finish* on the one hand and *stop* and *cease* on the other:

(1a) *John finished (painting) the wall on Tuesday*
(1b) *John stopped/ceased painting the wall on Tuesday*

Finish has 'object orientation'; sentence (1a) implies that the activity terminated because the wall was fully painted. *Cease* and *stop* have 'subject orientation'; the activity terminates (perhaps only temporarily) because of something to do with the person doing it—it could be that on Tuesday John decided he'd had enough of painting, irrespective of the job not being completed. *Cease* and *stop* most often refer to the volition of the subject, but need not always do so, e.g. *His heart stopped beating, He ceased breathing*. It is because of their subject orientation that *cease* and *stop*—unlike other verbs in this type—scarcely allow a following verb to be omitted. These verbs mark the involvement of the subject in the activity referred to by the verb (here, *painting*) and because of this that verb should be retained.

The difference in meaning between these two verbs is that *stop* tends to refer to something happening suddenly (often, unexpectedly) while *cease* may describe a general winding down to nothing, e.g. *The clock stopped* (*going*) *at five past three* (it had been going perfectly until then) and *My starter motor finally ceased to work* (it had been in poor shape for months).

There is a meaning contrast of a different sort between *begin* and *start*. Consider

(2a) *The marathon race begins at Santa Monica*
(2b) *The marathon race starts at three o'clock*

Start tends to refer to a time and *begin* to a place—*He'll start the public reading from his new book after dinner, and I can assure you that he'll begin at page one, right at the beginning, and he won't stop until he's finished the whole book.* Another example combining several of these verbs is *The three o'clock race began at the 500 metre mark* (place); *it started ten minutes late* (time); *James Donoghue finished first* (i.e. he finished the course—'object orientation') *and Tubby Arbunckle stopped racing* ('subject orientation') *a hundred yards from home because his horse lost a shoe.*

Wierzbicka (1988: 78 ff.) has pointed out that the noun *start* refers to the first moment of some activity—which relates to my observation that the verb *start* tends to refer to a time—and the noun *beginning* to the first segment—see also Freed (1979: 77). Note that for a race we have both a *starting time* and a *starting point* (not a **beginning time* or **beginning point*).

In many sentences *start* and *begin* may be substituted one for the other with little or no change in meaning (as may *finish* and *stop* and *cease*). But there do appear to be semantic preferences for each verb, which motivates their use to an appreciable extent.

Both *commence* and *complete* tend to be used for some definite and significant piece of work, not just any everyday job, e.g. *He has commenced* (*writing*) *his new symphony, John should complete the wall tomorrow.* One would be less likely to say *They commenced breakfast at 8.30* or *John has completed the peas* (to say this implies that it was a fairly significant event!). *Commence* has orientation to time, similar to *start*—note that we can say *re-start* or *re-commence* (i.e. at a new time), but not **re-begin*.

Complete is like other verbs in the type (except *stop* and *cease*) in that it may omit a following verb referring to making, preparing or performing, but *complete* differs in that a verb referring to consumption would not normally be omitted, e.g. *They completed the meal* implies that they finished cooking it, not eating.

Continue (*with*) is often used when someone has stopped doing something and then starts again; *keep on* (*with*)) and *go on* (*with*) imply no cessation of activity. *Keep* (*on*)—without the *with*—can be used to describe relentless (and, often, unreasonable) repetition of some activity, e.g. *He kept on mowing the grass* could be used to refer to someone cutting his lawn twice a week, even though the grass had scarcely grown during that interval. All three verbs may optionally omit their preposition(s) before an ING complement but must include them before an NP, e.g. *John kept* (*on* (*with*)) *building the wall*, but *John kept on with the wall*. *Discontinue* implies a temporary cessation, e.g. *They discontinued* (*having*) *the daily paper* (*delivered*) *while they were away on holiday*.

Start, *stop* and *keep* can all be used causatively (see §8.3.3)— *The official started the jockeys racing* implies *The jockeys started racing*; *The official started the race on time* implies *The race started on time*; *Peter stopped John chopping wood* implies *John stopped chopping wood*; *Mary kept her horse galloping at full pelt across the plain* implies *Her horse was galloping at full pelt across the plain*. *Begin* may also be used causatively, e.g. *The master began the boys racing as they passed the copse*; but it is used in a causative construction less often than the other three verbs.

The fact that *stop* has a causative use whereas *finish* doesn't is related to their semantic orientation. *Stop* generally refers to something done at the subject's instigation, and this can be transferred to a Causer, e.g. *John stopped chopping firewood* (he was tired) and *Fred stopped John chopping firewood* (Fred considered that John was tired). But *finish* refers to the referent of the O NP being fully satisfied, e.g. *Jack finished chopping firewood* (all the wood was chopped up); it would not be plausible to transfer this 'reason for termination' to a Causer; hence we do not get **Fred finished John chopping firewood*. It is mildly surprising that there is no causative use of *cease*; this may relate to its meaning of 'gradually falling away'; if a Causer makes someone halt in a task he is likely to do it reasonably abruptly, and *stop* is then the appropriate verb.

A sentence like *The parents started the game at three o'clock* is ambiguous between a non-causative use of *start* with the verb of the complement clause omitted, e.g. *The parents started (playing) the game at three o'clock*, and a causative sense, which could be an abbreviated version of *The parents started the children playing the game at three o'clock* (i.e. gave the signal to start). This ambiguity does not apply to *stop*, simply because that verb generally does not permit omission of a complement clause verb, i.e. *playing* cannot be dropped from *They stopped playing the game*, thus, *They stopped the game at three o'clock* has only a causative sense.

BEGINNING verbs are restricted to ING and Modal (FOR) TO complement clauses with subject omitted, e.g. *Mary began to like John*, *Mary began liking John*. *Mary* and *John* are in the same semantic roles and syntactic relations for *begin to like* and *begin liking* as they would be for *like*. *Begin to like* and *begin liking* are each, in one sense, a single syntactic unit. (But there is a difference —an adverb may intervene between a BEGINNING verb and *to*, e.g. *John began, after breakfast, to load the truck*, but not between a BEGINNING verb and a following verb in *-ing* form, e.g. we cannot say *John began after breakfast loading the truck*, only something like *John began loading the truck after breakfast*.)

All BEGINNING verbs may take an ING complement; just some of them also accept a Modal (FOR) TO clause:

ING and modal (FOR) TO complements—*begin, start, continue (with), go on (with), cease*

only ING complements—*commence, keep (on (with)), finish, stop, complete, discontinue*.

§7.3.2 attempts a semantic explanation of these syntactic possibilities.

We should also note the verb *begin on*, which can be used in some circumstances where *begin* is appropriate. But *begin on*— unlike *begin*—also has a special anaphoric sense, referring back to the verb of a previous clause. In *The compère described the new season's fur coats and then began on the new winter dresses*, the *began on* in the second clause is equivalent to *began describing* (that is, the *on* of *begin on* signals a kind of gapping—cf. §2.10). In contrast, a sentence like *He began the winter dresses* would be taken to have an underlying verb of making, etc., such as *design* or *produce* (but certainly not *describe*). *Begin on* can make anaphoric reference to any sort of verb, within the limits of discourse organisation and semantic plausibility.

6.1.3. TRYING

Semantically, verbs of this type divide into four groups: (i) *try, attempt*; (ii) *succeed (in/at), manage*; (iii) *miss, fail*; (iv) *practise, repeat*. (We are here referring to the senses of *manage* and *succeed* in *He managed to solve the problem, She succeeded in solving the problem*, not those in *She manages the business, He succeeded his father*.)

Like the BEGINNING type, a TRYING verb is followed by another verb which it modifies semantically, but which is syntactically in a complement clause to it, e.g. *He attempted to open the safe, He succeeded in opening the safe*. Like BEGINNING, TRYING verbs are restricted to ING and Modal (FOR) TO complements with the subject omitted. The syntactic behaviour of individual verbs is:

ING and Modal (FOR) TO complements—*try;*
most used with Modal (FOR) TO, can also take ING—*attempt, manage;*
only Modal (FOR) TO—*fail;*
only ING—*succeed (in/at), miss, practise, repeat.*

Try has two distinct but related senses, as can be seen in:

(1a) *John tried to eat the cake*
(1b) *John tried eating the cake*
(2a) *John tried to travel by train*
(2b) *John tried travelling by train*

The (a) alternatives indicate that John wanted to engage in the activity, but may well not have been able to; the (b) alternatives indicate that he did engage in it for a sample period. Thus (2a) could be used if he went to the station but found that the train was full. Sentence (2b) implies that he did travel by train for a while (for long enough to decide whether he preferred it to the bus). Another pair is *John tried to catch the ball* (but missed) and *John tried catching the ball* (during the team's two-hour fielding practice).

Note that the first sense requires a Modal (FOR) TO and the second an ING complement clause. Chapter 7 provides an explanation for this, and for the other complement possibilities of TRYING verbs.

Attempt is basically a synonym of the (a) sense of *try*. Like *commence* and *complete*, it implies a fairly significant task, with a degree of difficulty involved—compare *He tried to climb to the top of that hill* with *He attempted to climb Mt. Everest.* (For simple, everyday things, e.g. *She tried to eat all the pudding*, it is scarcely felicitous to substitute *attempt* for *try*.)

Both *manage* and *fail* are likely to imply that a certain result was obtained only after considerable perseverance, in contrast to *succeed* (*in/at*) and *miss*, e.g.

(3a) *Fred managed to solve the puzzle* (after weeks of trying)
(3b) *Fred succeeded in solving the puzzle* (perhaps at once, perhaps after a little effort)
(4a) *John failed to hit the target* (despite twenty attempts)
(4b) *John missed hitting the target* (perhaps, with the only bullet he had)

Miss (to a greater extent than *succeed*) can be used where there was no effort at all—something can be missed by chance. Compare *I failed to see Mary* (despite looking all over the place) and *I missed seeing Mary* (I didn't know she was calling in, and just happened to arrive after she'd left).

In the last section we mentioned that just verbs of making, preparing, performing and consuming can be omitted after a BEGINNING verb. No such simple categorisation can be given for verbs that may be omitted after a TRYING item. There is, however, a basic rule for omission after *try*, the central member of the type: a verb may be omitted when followed by a typical object, i.e. if its identity could be inferred from that object. Thus, on hearing *She tried a new book*, one would understand *She tried reading a new book* (since many more people read books than write or print or bind them); *He tried the chocolate cake* implies *He tried eating the chocolate cake* (not baking it). Some uses of *try* are semi-idiomatic —but do conform to the rule—e.g. *He tried (to open) the door*, *She tried (to solve) the problem*, and *She tried (putting on) the pink dress (to see how it looked on her)*. *Try out* is a little different; this generally has an implement as object and substitutes for *try using*, e.g. *He tried out the new axe.*

Virtually any verb (except one from the LIKING or ANNOYING types) may be omitted after *try* if it could be recovered by an addressee from the specific context and/or from previous dialogue, e.g. *Where is the post office? I don't know, you'd better try (asking) Mary.* There is also *I offered Mary an apple but she refused it, Well, why don't you try (offering her) a pear?* where verb-plus-NP (*offering her*) is omitted. Note in fact that only one NP may follow *try*—that is, one could not say **Well, why don't you try John an apple*, with *offering* omitted.

Omission of a verb is much rarer after *attempt* or *manage*, but is possible with an appropriate object, e.g. *I'm going to attempt Everest next year* or *I managed the problem in the end* (there is only one verb that could plausibly be substituted in each case—*climb* and *solve* respectively). With *fail* we get only *He failed the exam/test*, where *pass* is implied. *Miss* freely omits a wide range of verbs, e.g. *miss (seeing) Mary, missed (hitting) the target, missed (experiencing) that cyclone.* *Succeed (in/at)* may, like *fail*, omit *pass*, e.g. *I succeeded in (passing) the mathematics exam*, and just a few other verbs, as in *She succeeded at (playing) golf (well).*

Practise refers to a continuous activity, typically described by the *-ing* form of a verb; deletion possibilities are virtually limited to *playing*, e.g. *He practised (playing) the clarinet.* *Repeat* describes a delimited activity being done more than once—it may take an ING complement and the verb is likely to be omitted if its identity could be inferred from the object, e.g. *Johnnie repeated (reciting) that poem all morning*, and *He repeated (making) the same old mistake.*

Like the BEGINNING type, a TRYING verb may take an ACTIVITY or SPEECH ACT noun as object; in most cases there is an equivalent construction with a complement clause whose verb is related to the noun, e.g. *Karen tried an apology (to Auntie Daphne) (but she ignored her)* and *Karen tried apologising (to Auntie Daphne) (but she ignored her).*

One difference from the BEGINNING type is that TRYING verbs are not used intransitively, with an ACTIVITY, STATE or SPEECH ACT noun as subject (parallel to *The game continued, The offer finishes on Friday*). This is because TRYING verbs relate to volition on the part of a HUMAN, who must be referred to, whereas in the world-view of speakers of English things may begin, continue and finish spontaneously, e.g. *That fight just started* (i.e. no one was really responsible for starting it), and *My boring old life just continues on*.

6.1.4. HURRYING

This is a small type, consisting of verbs that describe the speed with which an activity is performed; *hesitate* falls naturally into the same type.

Complement possibilities are:

Modal (FOR) TO and ING complements—*hurry* (*over/with*), *hesitate* (*over/with*)

most used with Modal (FOR) TO, can also take ING—*hasten* (*over/ with*)

ING complement only—*dawdle* (*over*).

The prepositions are, as usual, retained before an ING clause or an NP, but dropped before *to*, e.g. *He hurried over finishing the job*, *He hurried to finish the job*.

Hurry and *hasten* have a very similar meaning 'do quickly', with *hurry* having stronger overtones of 'motion' than *hasten*. Thus both of *He hurried/hastened to change the lock on the door* can mean either (i) he moved quickly to the door, to change the lock when he got there, or (ii) he was quick about taking the old lock off and putting a new one on; but interpretation (i) is more likely with *hurry* and (ii) is more likely with *hasten*.

Hurry can freely take either a Modal (FOR) TO or an ING clause, e.g. *He hurried over* (*eating*) *his meal* (ate quickly the whole time), and *He hurried to finish his meal* (ate quickly towards the end). *Hasten* is found quite rarely with an ING clause. *Dawdle*, with the opposite meaning 'do slowly', only takes an ING complement.

Hesitate accepts both complement types. An ING clause implies that there was initial uncertainty but that the subject did it, in the end (unless the contrary is explicitly stated), e.g. *She hesitated about/over going*. A Modal (FOR) TO complement with *hesitate* indicates that the subject couldn't make up his mind whether or not to do it (and probably didn't do it, in the end), e.g. *She hesitated to go.* (There is further comment on the semantics of these complement choices in §7.3.2.)

As with *try*, a verb may be omitted after *hurry* or *dawdle* if its identity could be inferred from the nature of subject and object and shared socio-cultural knowledge of speaker and hearer, e.g. *She hurried/dawdled over (arranging) the flowers, The doctor hurried/dawdled over (examining) the last patient.* Verb omission is also possible with *hesitate*, e.g. *Auntie Daphne hesitated over (choosing) a present for Karen*, but is rare after *hasten.* Any of these four verbs may be used alone (i.e. just with a subject) in an appropriate context, e.g. *Hurry up!, Don't dawdle!*; and we get omission triggered by the surrounding text, e.g. *Mary hesitated (over going) before (in fact) going.*

Hurry and *hasten*, but not the other two verbs, form causatives, e.g. *John hurried/hastened Mary out of the house*, corresponding to *Mary hurried/hastened (to go) out of the house.* (See §8.3.3.)

6.1.5. DARING

The verbs *dare* (and one sense of *venture*) indicate that the subject had enough courage to do something; they are often found in the negative *doesn't dare, doesn't venture.* *Dare* and *venture* take a Modal (FOR) TO complement and have no roles additional to those of the verb of the complement clause—compare *John didn't dare to enter the lion's cage, John didn't enter the lion's cage.*

Dare can be used causatively with a rather special meaning 'say to someone that you think they haven't enough courage to do something', e.g. *Fred dared John to enter the lion's cage.* This use of *dare* is similar in meaning and syntax to *challenge.* (Note that the causative use of *dare* is not parallel to a Secondary-B verb like *want. Tom wants Bill to go* becomes *Tom wants to go* when the subjects of the two clauses coincide. However, *John didn't dare to go* ('lacked sufficient courage') has a quite different meaning from *John didn't dare himself to go* ('didn't challenge himself to go').)

Like *need* (§6.2.1), *dare* can be used as a lexical verb—taking tense and 3sg -*s* inflection, and complementiser *to*, and requiring *do* in questions and negatives when there is no other auxiliary element present—and it can also be used as a modal—with no inflections and no *to*, and itself acting as an auxiliary in questions

183

and negatives. Compare: *John didn't dare to go, Did John dare to go?* and *John daren't go, Dare John go?*

The two syntactic uses of *dare* carry a semantic difference. The lexical-verb sense tends to refer to an inner state of the subject, as in (1a), and the modal use to some external circumstance, as in (1b).

> (1a) *He doesn't dare to touch Mary* (he hasn't the courage, since she is so beautiful and he is too shy)
> (1b) *He doesn't dare touch Mary* (for fear of catching AIDS)

Corresponding to its 'external' meaning, the MODAL sense of *dare* (as of *need*) is found almost exclusively in questions and negative sentences.

6.2. Secondary-B types

Secondary-B verbs introduce one role (the subject of the Secondary-B verb) in addition to the roles of the verb in the complement clause, e.g. *John* in *John wanted Fred to congratulate Mary*. However, the subject of the main clause often is identical to the subject of the complement clause, and the latter is then generally omitted, e.g. *John wanted to congratulate Mary*, although it can be retained for contrastive emphasis, e.g. *John wanted himself to congratulate Mary* (*not* (*for*) *Fred to congratulate her*). Note that *John wanted to congratulate Mary* has the same semantic roles, in the same syntactic relations, as *John congratulated Mary* (and is then similar to the Secondary-A construction *John began to congratulate Mary*).

6.2.1. WANTING

This type has one independent role, the Principal, who has a certain attitude (described by the WANTING verb) towards some event or state (described by the complement clause) that is not (yet) real. The Principal is always syntactic subject of the WANTING verb.

Verbs of this type divide into a number of semantic sets (some of which have special syntactic properties): (i), *want, wish* (*for*), *desire, crave, long (for), pine (for)*; (ii) *hope (for)*; (iii) *demand*; (iv) *need, require, deserve*; (v) *expect, wait (for)* and *dread* (which has cross-membership of LIKING); (vi) *intend, plan (for)* (which has cross-membership of DECIDING), *aim (for)*, one sense of *mean, prepare (for)*; (vii) *pretend*.

We mentioned in §3.4 that a verb with a meaning similar to *get, receive* or *have* can be omitted from a complement clause after *want*; the NP following the 'get' verb then becomes surface object to *want*. This applies to all verbs from sets (i)–(iv) and to *expect* (but probably not to *dread*), e.g. *I need (to get) a new pen, She deserves (to receive) a medal, I'm hoping to get/for a bit of peace this afternoon, She is expecting (to get/to be given) a horse for her birthday*. Note that this omission is only possible when main clause and complement clause share the same subject, which is then omitted from the complement clause—thus, *to get* can be omitted from *I want (to get) a new Honda*, but not from *I want Mary to get a new Honda*.

Expect and *dread* may take a surface object NP in two further ways. Firstly, if main and complement clauses have different subjects then a verb with the meaning 'come/arrive' can be omitted from the complement clause, e.g. *I expect John (to come) tomorrow, Mary always dreads the cyclone season (arriving)*. Secondly, there can be an ACTIVITY verb in O slot, e.g. *I expected a beating* (which corresponds to a passive complement clause with the same subject as *expect, I expected to be beaten*).

Some WANTING verbs, especially those from set (vi), may also have an activity verb in surface object slot, e.g. *We're planning a game (at the weekend), They're planning a surprise for Mary, She's preparing for the climb (up Everest)*. In most cases there is a corresponding complement clause construction, e.g. *We're planning to play a game (at the weekend), They're planning to surprise Mary, She's preparing to climb (up Everest)*.

The role of the preposition *for* with verbs from the WANTING type is particularly interesting. *Hope, long, pine, wait, plan, aim,* and *prepare* take *for* before an NP object (*I'm hoping/aiming for an invitation to her party*), and also retain *for* before the subject of a Modal (FOR) TO complement (*I'm longing/aiming for Mary to invite me to stay over Christmas*). There is a second group of verbs —*crave, demand, deserve* and *dread*—which do not include *for* before an NP object but do require it before the subject of a Modal (FOR) TO clause, e.g. *He demanded a drink, He demanded for Mary to bring him a drink.* (*Dread* may take *it* before a Modal (FOR) TO or before a THAT clause, by virtue of its cross-membership of the LIKING type—§5.5.) The third group consists just of *wish*, taking *for* before an object NP and allowing the *for* to be either omitted or retained (with a meaning difference—see Chapter 7) before the subject of a Modal (FOR) TO clause, e.g. *I wish Mary to go, I wish for Mary to go.* The fourth group—made up of *desire*, *intend*, *mean* and *pretend*—do not have *for* before an NP object but, like *wish*, may include or omit *for* before the subject of a Modal (FOR) TO complement, e.g. *I intended Mary to win, I intended for Mary to win.* The other verbs in the type (*want*, *need*, *require* and *expect*) do not include *for* before an O NP or a complement clause subject when this immediately follows the verb, e.g. *I want an apple, I want Mary to give me an apple.* But a *for* may become evident under other syntactic conditions, such as when an adverb is inserted between main clause predicate and complement clause, e.g. *I want very much for Mary to give me an apple* and *I need more than I can say for Mary to nurse me.* Another example involves optional inclusion of *for* when there has been anaphoric omission of the predicate, as in the sentence quoted in the first paragraph of §6.2, *John wanted himself to congratulate Mary, not (for) Fred to congratulate her.*

All WANTING verbs may take a Modal (FOR) TO complement clause. As just described, some retain the *for* before the complement clause subject, some may omit or retain it, and others normally omit it. When the subject is coreferential with main clause subject it is generally omitted (together with *for*)—*I'm hoping for promotion, I'm hoping for Mary to promote me, I'm hoping to be promoted.*

There is a kind of syntactic abbreviation that applies with *order* from the SPEAKING type and with most verbs from sets (i) and (iv) of the WANTING type. If a Modal (FOR) TO complement has (*a*) an explicit subject, and (*b*) predicate consisting of copula plus the past participle of a verb or an adjective, then *to be* may be omitted, e.g. *I want her (to be) shot, I need the whole house (to be) cleaned thoroughly before the visitors arrive.* Note that the complement clause subject can be coreferential with main clause subject, but may not be omitted, e.g. *I wished myself (to be) invisible* but only *I wished to be invisible* not **I wished invisible*. Only a limited set of participles and adjectives can occur in the complement clause of such a construction, e.g. *killed, cooked, taken away, put away, begun, finished, explained, dead, well, well-dressed, tidy*.

Most verbs from the WANTING type can also accept a THAT complement clause (preposition *for* is again omitted before *that*). Since WANTING verbs refer to a state or event that is not (yet) real, it is normal for a modal to be included in a THAT complement clause. Different verbs prefer different modals, e.g. *I wish that he would/I could sing, I dread that my children might leave home one day, I expect that I/he will die soon, She planned that he should stay the night, I hope that she will/may go* (*hope* is unusual in that it commonly also occurs without a modal, e.g. *I hope she goes.*)

A THAT complement does not appear possible for *want, need* or *prepare*, and is rather marginal with *crave, long, deserve* and *aim*. It might be thought surprising that *want* and *need*—which are among the most frequently used WANTING verbs—do not take a THAT complement; a semantic explanation for this lack is provided in §7.3.3.

An ING complement clause is only possible with some verbs from set (vi) (and then only if complement clause subject is coreferential with main clause subject, and omitted), e.g. *She intends qualifying within three years, He plans going abroad after he has finished his exams. Aim* must include *at* before an ING clause, e.g. *She aims at finishing her thesis before Easter*.

A quite different variety of *-ing* construction occurs just with a number of verbs that are frequently found with a passive complement clause—they comprise *need, require* and *deserve*, and also a sense of *want* that is almost synonymous with *need*. This *-ing* construction has similar meaning to a passive TO clause with coreferential subject omission, e.g. *That meat requires cooking* corresponds to *That meat requires to be cooked*; and *This brat needs/wants spanking* corresponds to *This brat needs/wants to be spanked*. The syntactic status of *cooking* in *That meat requires cooking* is hard to ascertain. It is not an NP since we cannot insert an article, e.g. **That meat requires a cooking*. (It is possible to say *This brat needs/wants a spanking*, with an NP object that refers to a unit of activity, e.g. going to the headmaster's study for an institutionalised punishment, but this has a different meaning from *This brat needs/wants spanking.*) And *cooking* might not be a clause since it sounds rather odd with an adverb as in ?*That meat requires cooking well*—it is surely preferable to use a Modal (FOR) TO clause when an adverb is included, i.e. *That meat requires to be cooked well.*

A special syntactic property of some verbs from the WANTING type is that they occur with the modal *be to* only in the passive (and then only when no agent is stated), e.g. *It is to be hoped/expected that she will win.* This applies to *hope* (*for*), *expect* and *desire* and —with more marginal acceptability—to *wish* and *dread.* With verbs from other types *be to* may be used in the active or in the passive (with or without an agent stated), e.g. *The bishop is to crown him tomorrow, He is to be crowned (by the bishop) tomorrow.*

Need is basically a Secondary-B verb but has a further sense as a MODAL, and then shows quite different syntax. When used like a member of the WANTING type, *need* inflects for tense, takes *do* in negatives and questions if there is no preceding auxiliary element, and it cannot omit the *to* complementiser, e.g. *He needs to go, Does he need to go?, He doesn't need to go.* When used as a MODAL it does not inflect for tense or show *-s* for 3sg subject, it acts like an auxiliary verb in questions and negatives, and it does not take complementiser *to*, e.g. *Need he go?, He needn't go.* There is a semantic difference—the Secondary-B sense relates to some inner state of the Principal (in subject relation), as in (1a), whereas the MODAL sense relates to some external circumstances as in (1b) (see also Leech 1971: 96):

(1a) *I don't need to go to the toilet* (my bladder isn't full)
(1b) *I needn't go to the toilet* (no one is telling me to go)

Corresponding to its 'external' meaning, the MODAL sense of *need* is found almost exclusively in questions and negative sentences. (*Dare* also has modal and non-modal senses, with the same syntactic contrast and a similar meaning difference—see §6.1.5.)

Most verbs from the WANTING type must have a following complement clause or NP. *Wish, hope* and *pretend* may be used without one in a suitable context, e.g. *She keeps on wishing, You can but hope, Stop pretending! Expect* and *hope* may, like some

THINKING verbs (§5.2), replace a post-predicate constituent by *so*, e.g. *Will John come tomorrow? I expect/hope so* (sc. that John will come tomorrow). Note the contrast between *hope so* and *hope*, with no following constituent in either case; the former is used for syntactic anaphoric reference to some definite constituent, e.g. *that John will come tomorrow* in the last example quoted, while the latter refers semantically to some general propensity of the Principal, e.g. *You'll never get rich quick—win the lottery or receive a huge bequest. Well, I can hope, can't I?*

We will now discuss the meanings of verbs in each group (returning in Chapter 7 to explain their occurrences with complement types in terms of these meanings). *Want*—taking a Modal (FOR) TO complement—is directly pragmatic, referring to something which could be achieved, e.g. *I want to talk to my boss this afternoon. Wish*, in contrast, may have wistful overtones, relating —through a THAT complement—to something that could not possibly be realised, e.g. *I wish (that) I could ask a few questions of Winston Churchill about how he fought the war.* (Note that we can have *make a wish* but not *make a want.) *Wish* can be used with a Modal (FOR) TO complement and is then marked as particularly definite—compare the cold, forced demand *I wish you to leave*, with the more comradely (and possibly more emotional) *I want you to leave. Desire* is not used much as a verb in present-day English; when it is there may be an overtone of hauteur (*I desire to be informed of any change*). Both *want* and *desire* are likely to have sexual implications when used with a human NP as surface object; compare the urgent and lustful *I want you* with the more polite and measured *Oh, how I desire you!* (which does invite a verbal response from the person desired). *Crave* describes an intense desire, often for some special foodstuff or other indulgence, which will be referred to by the O NP, e.g. *I crave fresh strawberries. Long (for)* has a similarly intense meaning, but covers a wider semantic range of 'things wanted', e.g. *I long for Mary to write. Pine (for)* carries the additional overtone that the well-being of the Principal is being adversely affected by his unrequited longing.

Whereas verbs of set (i) simply describe the Principal's eagerness that something acceptable (to him) will happen, *hope (for)* focuses on the Principal's thought that something acceptable may happen in the future. *Demand* involves the intersection of 'say' and 'want'; an Addressee can be included, introduced by *of*, e.g. *I demanded (of Mary) that she/John should clean my car*.

Set (iv) have similar meaning to necessity and obligation modals, *must, should*, etc. But whereas the modals tend to be used when the subject should/needs to do something, *need* and *require* are often used, with a passive complement clause, when something should/needs to be done to the subject, e.g. *You should encourage Mary; Mary needs to be encouraged*. Set (iv), unlike other WANTING verbs, may have an inanimate Principal, e.g. *The car needs to be cleaned*. (As already mentioned, there is one sense of *want*—more frequent in colloquial than in literary speech—that is close in meaning to *need*, e.g. *The car wants cleaning*.)

Need is similar to *want* (in its central sense) in often conveying a sense of emotional urgency, e.g. *I need my daughter to come home and look after me*, whereas *require* has a colder, more matter-of-fact sense, e.g. *I require three nurses, working in shifts, to look after me*. *Need* often relates to the Principal's physical and emotional state, and complement clause subject is most often the same as main clause subject, e.g. *I need to be loved* (compare with *?I require to be loved*, which sounds most odd). *Require* only rather seldom has complement clause subject coinciding with main clause subject, and is often used to specify the necessities of social interaction and employment obligations, e.g. *We require all our executives to join the superannuation fund* or the notice in a doctor's surgery *We require payment at time of consultation*. Both semantically and syntactically, *require* shows similarities to the MAKING type and to the ORDER subtype of SPEAKING, e.g. *The Sultan required/ordered/forced John to wash his feet*. (Note that *need* can modify *require*, but not vice versa, e.g. *Do you require the chancellor to call on you, sire? No, I don't need to require him to call, for the simple reason that he is already here*.) *Deserve* relates to something that should be done to someone as a payback for their (often, but not always, meritorious) behaviour; 'same subject' is normal, e.g. *Mary deserves to win the prize*, although 'different subject' is also possible, e.g. *Mary deserves for her dog to win the prize*.

Whereas *hope* refers to something acceptable that the Principal thinks may happen in the future, *expect* refers to something the

Principal thinks will probably happen, and it needn't be acceptable to him. If the Principal thinks that this future happening is something he would greatly dislike then the appropriate verb to use is *dread*, which involves the intersection of 'expect' and 'hate' (and is a cross-member of the LIKING type).

Set (vi) describes the Principal's thought that he will do a certain thing in the future; the most general and neutral verb here is *intend*. *Aim (for)* implies a single-mindedness of purpose; it most often has the same subject as the complement clause (e.g. *I aim to win*). *Mean* is often used in the past tense, referring to an intention that was not in fact fulfilled, e.g. *I had meant (for John) to clean the bathroom, but then forgot about it*. *Plan* involves a set of intentions, plus detailed thought and scheming. (It also belongs to the DECIDING type and, as a member of that type, can take a WH-complement, e.g. *I planned who would fire the shot*.) The transitive verb *prepare* has the meaning 'do what needs to be done in advance for some expected future happening'; it only takes a Modal (FOR) TO, not a THAT, complement clause. The past participle of this verb has a rather different meaning, 'get oneself in the right frame of mind to accept some expected (and probably unpleasant) event or news', and should perhaps be regarded as a separate lexeme. *Be prepared* does take a THAT complement— compare *I am prepared for a long meeting*, and *I am prepared that the meeting will be a long one*, with *I have prepared for a long meeting* but not **I have prepared that the meeting will be a long one*. (In §3.2 we categorised *prepared* as a member of the EAGER subtype of HUMAN PROPENSITY adjectives.)

Pretend has all the syntactic properties of a WANTING verb—it can take a THAT complement (*I pretended that Mary/I was president*) or a Modal (FOR) TO complement (*I pretended (for) Mary to be president*). If the complement clause subject is the same as main clause subject then it is omitted (*I pretended to be president*). The main difference from other WANTING verbs is that *pretend* generally refers to present or past, not to the future (its THAT complement is not expected to include a modal, as it is for other verbs from the type). But it is semantically like other WANTING verbs in referring to something that is not (yet) real.

6.2.2. POSTPONING

This type again requires one role additional to those of the complement clause verb—a Timer, who adjusts the time at which it is planned to do something. Members of the type are *postpone*, *defer*, *put* NP *off*, *delay* and—standing a little apart semantically—*avoid*.

All five verbs take ING complement clauses. The subject may be different from the subject of the main clause but if it is the same it is normally omitted, e.g. *She postponed (John's) going on fieldwork until the wet season was over*, *We delayed starting dinner until you arrived*, *I avoided helping with the painting (by going out all afternoon)*.

Avoid often omits the complement clause verb if it has a meaning similar to 'seeing' or 'attending/taking part in', e.g. *I walked home the long way round to avoid (seeing) the graveyard*, *He always manages to avoid (attending) formal dinners*.

The object of any of these verbs may be an ACTIVITY or SPEECH ACT noun, which is often put into subject slot by passivisation, e.g. *The meeting was postponed*, *The question was avoided*.

Postpone, *defer* and *put off* have very similar meanings; they generally refer to a conscious decision, made in advance, e.g. *They postponed the wedding until August*. In contrast, *delay* often describes an ad hoc change of time, perhaps to accommodate some unforeseen circumstances, e.g. *They delayed the start of the meeting since the bus bringing delegates from the north had not arrived*. *Avoid* refers to evasive action taken so as not to be involved in some unwanted activity, often, not being in a certain place at a certain time, e.g. *I avoid visiting Mum on days Grandpa is likely to call*.

6.3. Secondary-C types

Secondary-C verbs are like Secondary-B in introducing just one role (the subject of the Secondary verb) in addition to the roles of the verb in the complement clause. They differ semantically in that Secondary-B verbs simply describe the subject's attitude towards some event or state (*John wants/expects Mary to propose the toast*) whereas the subject of a Secondary-C verb plays a role in bringing about the event or state (*John forced/permitted/helped Mary to propose the toast*).

A Secondary-B verb often has complement clause subject identical to main clause subject and it is then normally omitted (*John wants (himself) to propose the toast*). A Secondary-C verb, in contrast, seldom has the two subjects identical, and if they do happen to be, then neither can be omitted (*John forced himself to propose the toast*, not **John forced to propose the toast*).

Another difference is that certain verbs may be omitted from the complement clause of a Secondary-B verb, e.g. *I want (to get) a new car*, *She expects John (to come) today*. This is possible after a Secondary-C verb only very occasionally, when the omitted verb could be inferred from the preceding discourse, e.g. *Why did Mary resign? Jane forced her to* (sc. resign). Some Secondary-B verbs, but no Secondary-C items, can be used with nothing following the predicate, e.g. *I'm just wishing/hoping*, but not **I'm just forcing/ allowing*.

The POSTPONING type has some semantic similarity with MAKING verbs, in that the subject has a role in controlling what happens, e.g. *I put off John's being examined by the doctor until tomorrow*, and *I forced John to be examined by the doctor*. However, the subject of a POSTPONING verb only organises the time of an event, he does not make or help it happen. POSTPONING is a Secondary-B type, with similar syntactic properties to WANTING, e.g. omission of complement clause subject (*I put off (my) being examined by the doctor until tomorrow*) and occasional omission of all post-predicate constituents (*She's always delaying*).

6.3.1. MAKING

This type has one independent role, the Causer, who does something to bring about an event or state, referred to by a complement clause. The subject of the main clause (the Causer) and the subject of the complement clause are most often human, but neither has to be, e.g. *These new shoes make my feet ache (by being too tight)*, *She caused/allowed the flowers to die (by not watering them when we were away)*. It is also possible, if not too common, for the Causer to be an ING complement clause, e.g.

Having been a failure in his first job made John try much harder in the second one. There may also be an optional constituent stating how the Causer brought things about; it is often introduced with *by*, e.g. *John made Fred open the safe by threatening to tell about his indiscretions*.

Unlike other types, each MAKING verb takes just one variety of complement clause. There are four semantically defined sets; their more important members are:

(i) *make*, *force*, *cause*, one sense of *drive*, causative senses of *get* and *have*; *tempt*—Modal (FOR) TO complement, with the *for* always omitted and the *to* sometimes omitted;

(ii) *let*, *permit*, *allow*—Modal (FOR) TO complement, again with the *for* always and the *to* sometimes omitted;

(iii) *prevent*, *stop*, *spare*, *save*, specific senses of *check* (*oneself*), *rescue*, *release*—FROM ING complement, with the *from* sometimes omitted;

(iv) *ensure*—THAT complement.

We first look briefly at the meanings of verbs in sets (i) and (ii). *Force* can imply coercion, e.g. *I forced the old lady to change her will in my favour by holding a gun at her head*. *Cause* is used of indirect action, often premeditated, e.g. *He caused Mary to crash by almost cutting through the brake cable and then sending her down the mountain road*; it may also be used of natural phenomena, e.g. *I believe that the underground nuclear tests caused that volcano to erupt/that earthquake*. *Make* has a wider meaning, referring to anything the Causer does to bring something about directly (including when the subject of the complement clause is not acting volitionally), e.g. *You made me burn the toast by distracting my attention, Lucy made Sandy wash up by saying he wouldn't get any pocket money unless he did*. (Note that *force* and *cause* are hyponyms of *make*, i.e. *make* could almost always be substituted for an occurrence of one of these verbs.) *Drive*, in its causative sense, implies continual pressure leading to some result, e.g. *Mary's nagging finally drove John to commit suicide*. *Tempt* combines 'make' and 'want', e.g. *The fact that gold bars were often left around the office tempted John to steal one* is a near paraphrase of *The fact that gold bars were often left around the office made John want to steal one*.

The causative senses of *get* and *have* refer to the Causer bringing something about, usually by indirect means, e.g. *She got Mary to wash up by saying how impressed John would be*, *She had Mary washing up when John arrived*. *Get* refers to arranging for something to happen and *have* for arranging that it be happening, e.g. *She had John and Mary talk about the crisis and then got Fred to join in*. This semantic difference parallels the contrast between *have* and *get* as members of the own subtype (§4.3), e.g. *She had two cars and then got a third*.

Turning now to set (ii), *permit* and *allow* may both be used impersonally; *permit* is often preferred where an official sanction is involved, e.g. *The law doesn't permit you to smoke on domestic flights in Australia*. The meaning range of *allow* includes reference to some concession, e.g. *I was only allowed to drive the Mercedes on my birthday*, or oversight, e.g. *Those tenants allowed the garden to run to weed*. In contrast, *let* focuses on the identity of the Causer (which is why *let* is seldom found in the passive), e.g. *Mother doesn't let me stay out late*. *Let* also has a broad meaning, including 'didn't prevent/forbid from doing', e.g. *She lets me do what I want*, *We let the cat go out at night if it wants to* (contrast with *We put the cat out at night*). *Permit* and *allow*—but not *let*—may omit a complement clause verb with the meaning 'get/receive/have', e.g. *Prisoners are only permitted (to receive) one visitor each month*; *She allowed John/herself (to have) just one chocolate*.

All verbs in sets (i) and (ii) take a Modal (FOR) TO complement clause. However, the *to* must be omitted after *make*, *let* and *have* when these verbs are used in the active. Compare:

(1a) *Mary forced/allowed/got John to mow the lawn*
(1b) *Mary made/had/let John mow the lawn*

Make may freely be used in the passive and then *to* is generally included, e.g. *John was made to mow the lawn*. *Let* is seldom used in the passive (except as part of the idiom *let go*, and there is then no *to*, e.g. *The rope was let go*). The causative sense of *have* can never be passivised. Note that *mow* in (1b) is in base form (not a tense form, which would be *mows* or *mowed*), which is what it would be in a TO complement. It is because of this that we describe (1b) as an instance of a TO clause with the *to* omitted; this omission does have semantic explanation and semantic consequences (see §§6.3.2 and 7.2.5).

A TO complement clause can have its predicate beginning with copula, progressive or passive *be*. This *be* (and the preceding *to*, for verbs that take *to*) may optionally be omitted after *get* and *make* and must be omitted after *have*, e.g.

> (2a) *I got John to be interested in the puzzle*
> (2b) *I got John interested in the puzzle*
> (3a) *I made/*had John be interested in the puzzle*
> (3b) *I made/had John interested in the puzzle*

There is a semantic difference. The (a) sentences, with *be*, imply that I exerted some influence over John so that he exercised his mind to be interested, whereas the (b) sentences imply that I did something as a result of which John became interested, quite spontaneously. That is why *have*, which refers just to 'something happening', is restricted to the (b) construction.

The three varieties of *be* show different possibilities for omission with these verbs. Both passive and progressive *be* must be omitted after *have*, may be after *get*, but are seldom or never omitted after *make*. With passive *be* we can have *I got John to be examined by the doctor/I made John be examined by the doctor* (did something so that he agreed to undergo the examination) and *I got/had John examined by the doctor* (arranged for it to happen) but not **I made John examined by the doctor* since, when the predicate refers to an event, there would be a conflict between the meaning of *make* 'I did something so that John did something' and the semantic implication of *be* omission 'something happens fairly spontaneously'.

A similar argument applies for progressive *be*. There are *I got John and Mary to be talking when Fred entered/I made John and Mary be talking when Fred entered* (did something so that they agreed to talk) and *I got/had John and Mary talking when Fred entered* (arranged for it to happen, without them really intending it), but not **I made John and Mary talking when Fred entered*, because of the same semantic conflict (when the predicate refers to an event).

With copula *be*—and a predicate referring to a state—all three verbs make the omission, e.g. *He made/got/had Mary angry* (*before Fred arrived*). The *be* can be retained, although it seldom is, with *make* and *get*. *He got Mary to be angry/He made Mary be angry* sound as if he persuaded her to pretend to be angry, whereas

He got/made Mary angry implies that she entered that state quite spontaneously, as a natural reaction to whatever he did. A copula can of course also be followed by an NP. We get *The Board made John President of the Company* (it elected him), where *be* would not be appropriate since John is not exercising any volition; and *Mary got him to be President*, which does include *to be* since it describes Mary using some stratagem so that he would agree to accept the position.

Force—but not *cause*, *make*, *let*, etc.—occurs in another construction type, perhaps another kind of complement clause, with an -*ing* predicate preceded by *into*, e.g. *I forced John into resigning*. This implies a lengthy process before the result is achieved, as compared to *I forced John to resign*, which may describe a result achieved rather quickly. (The other verbs to take INTO ING all refer to some drawn-out activity, e.g. *bully*, *coax*, *pester*.)

Verbs in set (iii) have meanings almost opposite to those of set (i). *Spare* and *save* indicate that the Causer obviates the need for someone to do a task that they should otherwise do, e.g. *John saved Mary from* (*having*) *to paint the porch by doing it himself*. *Prevent* and *stop* refer to the Causer making sure that someone does not do something that they may have wanted to do or tried to do; *prevent* often refers to indirect and *stop* to direct means, e.g. *He prevented her* (*from*) *going by hiding her passport*, and *He stopped her from going by standing in the doorway and barring the way*. (There is, however, a good deal of semantic overlap, and the two verbs are often used interchangeably.) There are also special senses of *check* (*oneself*), *rescue* and *release* that belong in set (iii), e.g. *John checked himself from correcting Mary, Jane rescued Tony from having to give the speech by offering to do it herself*.

All of these verbs take a FROM ING complement, like *discourage*, *dissuade* and *forbid* from the ORDER subtype of SPEAKING (§5.4). Unlike the *discourage* group, *prevent*, *spare* and *save* may optionally omit the *from* in an active clause (it would seldom be omitted from a passive); there is a meaning difference, which is discussed in §7.2.9.

There is another, related, sense of *stop* which belongs to the BEGINNING type, e.g. *She stopped swimming* (i.e. she was swimming and then decided not to any more). As mentioned in §6.1.2, this verb can be used causatively, and then shows some semantic and syntactic similarities to the Secondary-C verb *stop*. There are, however, crucial differences at both levels; compare

> (4a) *John stopped Mary swimming* (causative of Secondary-A verb *stop*)
>
> (4b) *John stopped Mary from swimming* (Secondary-C verb *stop*)

Sentence (4a) is the causative of *Mary stopped swimming*. This sentence implies that Mary was swimming and that John made her desist; note that *from* cannot be included in (4a). Sentence (4b) implies that John did not allow her to swim, i.e. she didn't enter the water. The *from*—which is optional after *prevent*, *spare* and *save*—would generally not be omitted from (4b), in order to distinguish the two constructions.

Set (iv), consisting just of *ensure*—which takes a THAT complement—may not refer to the Causer doing anything so that a certain state or event comes into being; the Causer might merely ascertain that something has been done (it does not matter by whom), e.g. *John ensured that all the doors were locked before going away on holiday*.

6.3.2. HELPING

This type has one independent role, the Helper (main clause subject), who joins in with someone (complement clause subject) to bring about some event. The main member of the type is *help*; there are also a number of hyponyms of *help* with specialised meanings, e.g. *aid*, *assist*.

Like MAKING verbs, *help* takes a Modal (FOR) TO complement. The subject of the complement clause must be different from the subject of the main clause. (There is an idiomatic usage, e.g. *He helped himself to the chocolates*, but the reflexive pronoun after *help* cannot here be followed by a verb.) *Help* differs from MAKING verbs in that either the subject or the post-subject portion of the complement clause can be omitted. One may say *John helped Mary* if one's listeners could be expected to know what he helped her do. And *John helped to paint the wall* is acceptable if one does not wish to specify who the other people painting were.

We noted that *force*, *allow*, etc. require the inclusion of *to* but that *make*, *have* and *let* require it to be omitted, at least in the active. With *help* the *to* may be either included or omitted, in both active and passive. There is a semantic difference. Compare:

(1a) *John helped Mary to eat the pudding* (by guiding the spoon to her mouth, since she was still an invalid)

(1b) *John helped Mary eat the pudding* (he ate half)

When *to* is omitted, as in (1b), the sentence is likely to mean that the Helper did part of the activity; when *to* is included, as in (1a), it is more likely to mean that the Helper made things easy for the complement clause subject so that she could do what needed to be done (see also §7.2.5).

The Helper is generally HUMAN, but can be a non-human noun or even a complement clause, e.g. *John's success helped him gain confidence*, *Believing in God helped me to get through that crisis*.

An alternative syntactic construction for *help* is for the 'person helped' to be followed by a preposition (usually *with*) and an *-ing* clause, e.g. *He helped Mary with writing the letter* (this is then more likely to have the sense of (1b) than that of (1a)).

Of the more specialised HELPING verbs, *aid* usually refers to help given by some official body, rather than by an individual (*America aided South Vietnam in fighting the communist terror*), while *assist* implies that the Helper fulfils a secondary role (*Fred assisted John in building the wall by handing him bricks*). There are also the inherently reciprocal verbs *cooperate* (*with*) and *collaborate* (*with*). All of these verbs can take a Modal (FOR) TO clause—the *to* may not be omitted—but are more frequently found with a preposition (often, *in*) plus an *-ing* clause, or else with an ACTIVITY noun in O slot, e.g. *America aided South Vietnam in its war against the communist terror*.

Hinder is opposite in meaning to one sense of *help*, but does not freely occur with a complement clause; the preferred construction is with a simple NP in O slot (referring to the person who was hindered) and then a relative clause or an adverbal clause describing the activity that was affected, e.g. *John hindered the workman who was/while he was installing a new telephone* (*by continually hiding his tools*). *Support* has some semantic similarity with *help*. This verb, and its opposite, *oppose*, take ING complements, e.g.

She supported/opposed John's being nominated for president of the company.

6.4. Secondary-D types

Secondary-D verbs are all intransitive and take a complement clause in subject slot. They may take one role additional to those of the complement clause; this is the Arbiter, which is marked by the preposition *to*, e.g. *That John should be promoted ahead of Dick seemed wrong (to Mary), That John should be promoted ahead of Dick didn't matter (to Mary).*

Statement of the Arbiter is often omitted and a Secondary-D construction then appears to have no roles beyond those of the complement clause verb. But some Arbiter is always implied and will be understood by listeners—according to pragmatic context—as being the speaker(s)—i.e. *to me, to us*—or else all rational or like-minded people—e.g. *to everyone*.

6.4.1. SEEM

Verbs from this type (*seem, appear, look, sound, feel* and *happen*) have two distinct modes of syntactic use. In the first they occur with an adjective—or adjectival phrase—as a kind of copula. In the second they may be used without any adjective.

When a SEEM verb is followed by an adjective this indicates that the Arbiter thinks—in a certain way (specified by the SEEM verb)—that the adjective is applicable to the event or state described by the complement clause, in subject slot.

SEEM verbs occur with just those adjectives that may take a complement clause in subject slot, i.e. VALUE, DIFFICULTY, QUALI-FICATION and the CLEVER subtype of HUMAN PROPENSITY (§3.2). Instead of the copula *be* we can have either *seem to be* or else just *seem*. Thus, with the VALUE type, *John's having resigned was/ seemed to be/seemed most odd, That John hit his grandmother is/ seems to be/seems out of character*; with a DIFFICULTY adjective, *It is/seems to be/seems hard for Mary to operate our mower, Our mower is/seems to be/seems hard to operate*; with QUALIFICATION adjectives, *It is/seems to be/seems definite that the King will visit, It is/seems to be/seems normal for no one to work on Christmas Day*, *John is/seems to be/seems likely to win*; with a CLEVER adjective, *It was/seemed to be/seemed very stupid of John (for him) to enter without knocking*.

Seem (to be) can replace the copula in every construction open to an adjective that takes a complement clause in subject slot (except in frame (iii) with the CORRECT subtype of QUALIFICATION, in which the subject of an extraposed complement clause is raised to fill main clause subject slot, e.g. *John was correct to stand when the bishop entered*, but not **John seemed (to be) correct to stand when the bishop entered*).

The second syntactic usage of SEEM verbs is in what has the appearance of an extraposed THAT complement, and what could be a special variety of Judgement TO construction:

(1a) *It seems that Mary found the body*
(1b) *Mary seems to have found the body*

Sentence (1a) has a very similar meaning to a *seem*-plus-adjective construction like:

(2) *It seems (to be) true/(to be) correct/to be the case that Mary found the body*

Sentence (2) is a genuine example of a THAT complement clause extraposed from subject position—we can have, with no extra-position, *That Mary found the body seems (to be) true/(to be) correct/to be the case*.

The fact that (1a) is a construction distinct from (2) is shown by the non-acceptability of the THAT clause in subject slot, i.e. **That Mary found the body seems*.

The syntactic and semantic relations between (1a) and (1b) are parallel to those between the THAT complement construction in (3a) and the Judgement TO construction in (3b):

(3a) *John knew that Mary was the murderer*
(3b) *John knew Mary to be the murderer*

Sentence (1a) simply involves a THAT complement clause and the verb *seem*. A THAT clause must include a subject, and so *Mary* could not be moved out of the complement clause to replace the im-personal subject *it*. But a TO clause does not have to include an overt subject, and in (1b) we do, effectively, get *Mary* replacing the *it*.

After verbs like *think*, *consider* and *imagine*, the *to be* of a Judgement TO complement may be omitted, e.g. *John thought her (to be) stupid* (see §7.2.6). Exactly the same omission is possible after *seem*, e.g. *Mary seemed (to be) stupid*. It appears that, following *seem*, *to be* can be omitted before an adjective or NP which makes a judgement, e.g. *He seems (to be) good, He seems (to be) a good doctor, He seems (to be) an idiot*; but *to be* cannot be omitted before an NP that does not involve a judgement—*He seems to be a doctor*, but not **He seems a doctor*.

There are two alternative constructions, one with *as if* and the other—occurring only in colloquial varieties of English—with *like* in place of *to be*, together with pronominal repetition of the main clause subject and a following copula, e.g. *John seems like/as if he's hitting Mary/hated by all his staff/stupid*.

Seem is used when the Arbiter is not fully certain whether the adjectival description is appropriate, or whether the statement of the complement clause in a construction like (1a) or (1b) is correct —perhaps when there is not quite enough evidence. *Appear* has the same syntactic possibilities and a very similar meaning, but may imply 'can be observed by me' in contrast to *seem* 'can be inferred by me'.

Look, *sound* and *feel* have similar grammar and meaning to *seem* and *appear*. *Look* is, like *appear*, often used when the Arbiter's evidence is visual observation, but it may also be employed whatever the nature of the evidence. *Feel* is most often used when the Arbiter has an intuition or other mental impression about something, and *sound* when the evidence is aural. Thus we get *It seems/sounds strange that John gave his car away, John looks/ seems likely to be sacked, It feels/seems strange that we may never see him again*. These three verbs are seldom followed by *to be*; they are used a lot in *like/as if* constructions, e.g. *John looks/ sounds like/as if he's seen a ghost*.

At the end of §5.1 we mentioned the intransitive use of some transitive ATTENTION verbs, e.g. *It sounds good, She looks pretty, It feels soft*. These could be treated as instances of the SEEM sense of the verbs, e.g. *That she is pretty looks (to be) true* is a fair if awkward paraphrase of *She looks pretty*. But note that *taste* and *smell* may also be used intransitively, and these are only very marginally found with meaning and syntax similar to *seem*.

Happen has a meaning something like 'it is, in fact, the case', and may carry the implication of it being somewhat surprising that this is so. It has a similar syntax to *seem* except that there must always be a following *to be*, and *happen* is not found in *as if/like* constructions. Thus, *That John is stupid happens to be true, John happens to be stupid*. *Happen* has a further sense, for which an ACTIVITY noun is subject, e.g. *The fight happened because John hit Mary*, or *The fight just happened* (no one started it). (*Come about* has a similar meaning to this sense of *happen*, e.g. *The fight came about because John hit Mary*.)

6.4.2. MATTER

The main member of this type is *matter*, which is often used in the negative, *doesn't matter*. It carries the meaning that the event or state referred to by a complement clause (in subject relation to *matter*) is important to the Arbiter, e.g. *That John won doesn't matter* (*one little bit*) (*to Fred*). Note that, unlike SEEM verbs, *matter* does not take a following adjective, but may be followed by something like *at all*, *one little bit* or *tuppence*.

Matter takes THAT and WH- complement clauses, which are frequently extraposed, e.g. *It doesn't matter* (*to John*) *who won the prize, Whether or not we are to be allowed to compete matters a hell of a lot to me*. It may also take an indefinite NP as subject and then the Arbiter may be introduced by *to* or by *for*, e.g. *Nothing/lots of things matter to/for John*.

One sense of *count* may also belong to this type (and may have *to* or *for* before the Arbiter). It appears to be restricted to a THAT complement in subject slot, e.g. *That John was a church-goer counted for a lot, That John was a church-goer didn't count for anything* (*for Mary*) (he had still killed a man).

It is worth noting that very few languages have ideas such as 'happen' and 'matter' expressed through verbs. This kind of qualification is more often achieved by adverbs, verbal clitics or some other grammatical means.

Notes to Chapter 6

§6.1.1. Coates (1983) is an insightful study of the syntax and semantics of Modals in English; earlier useful books on Modals include Leech (1971) and Palmer (1979). The contrast between *will* and *be going to* is revealingly discussed by Binnick (1971, 1972), Hall (1970) and McIntosh (1966).

§6.1.2. *Begin* and related verbs are discussed by Perlmutter (1970), Newmeyer (1970, 1975) and Freed (1979) among others.

§6.2.1. McCawley (1979) has a useful account of what can be omitted from a complement clause after *want* (see also §3.4). Bolinger (1942) provides an illuminating account of *need*.

Part C

Some Grammatical Topics

7

*I know that it seems that he'll make me
want to describe her starting to say that she
knows that it seems that . . .*
Complement clauses

There are, as outlined in §2.7, seven kinds of complement clause,
which can fill the object or subject (or, sometimes, a post-object)
slot in a main clause. All Secondary and Primary-B verbs take
complement clauses—but each one allows only some of the full
range of complement clause possibilities. Which complement
clauses a given verb may accept is determined by the meaning of
the verb and the meanings of the complement clause constructions.

In §7.2 we outline the meanings of the different kinds of
complement clause. §§7.3–4 then deal with Secondary and
Primary-B types, one at a time, looking at the overall meaning of
each type and the specific meanings of individual verbs within the
type, thus providing a semantic explanation for the complement
clauses that occur. §7.1 deals briefly with 'parentheticals', which
are related to THAT complement constructions.

We can recapitulate here the kinds of complement clause (from
the account in §2.7):

(i) THAT. The initial *that* may often be omitted when it
immediately follows the main clause predicate.

(ii) WH-. This is introduced by *whether/if*, or by any other *wh-*
word, e.g. *who*, *what*, *where*, *how*, *why*; this *wh-* introducer may
not be omitted.

(iii) ING. The complement clause subject, if included, may in
some circumstances be marked by *'s*.

(iv) Modal (FOR) TO. If the complement clause subject is
omitted, then *for* is also dropped. *For* may (with some verbs) or
must (with others) be omitted when the complement clause

subject is retained, and this then becomes surface structure object of the main verb.

(v) Judgement TO. Cannot undergo any NP omission. Complement clause predicate most often begins with *be*.

(vi) WH- TO. Similar to a Modal (FOR) TO construction where the complement clause subject is omitted under coreferentiality with main clause subject or object, and the complement clause is introduced by *whether* (not *if*) or by any other *wh-* word except *why*.

(vii) FROM ING. An ING clause with the subject (which is also surface object of the main clause) followed by *from*, the *from* being optionally omissible after one set of main verbs.

THAT and WH- complements have the full structure of a clause— they involve tense inflection, and may include a Modal. The other five kinds of complement clause cannot include either tense or a Modal. A subject must be stated for THAT, WH-, Judgement TO and FROM ING clauses, but can be omitted from ING and Modal (FOR) TO complements, and must be omitted from WH- TO clauses.

Some verbs that take an ING or Modal (FOR) TO complement must omit the complement clause subject (e.g. *begin*); others can optionally omit it (e.g. *like*); a further set must retain it (e.g. *see*, *allow*). A complement clause in object function, with no stated subject, is taken to have underlying subject coreferential with main clause subject; if the complement clause is in subject function its underlying subject is taken to be coreferential with main clause object. Thus, *Mary didn't know where to put the box*, and *Where to put the box perplexed Mary*.

A THAT, WH- or Modal (FOR) TO (but, generally, not an ING) complement clause in subject function may be extraposed to the end of the main clause, provided there is not also a complement clause in object or other post-predicate position.

It is important to repeat here one of the most important rules of English grammar: a preposition must be omitted before complementisers *that*, *for* and *to*. (It may optionally be omitted before a *wh-* word introducing a complement clause.)

The theoretical stance of this study involves investigating how semantic categories are mapped onto syntactic categories. The mapping is generally many-to-one. Thus, a number of semantic types are associated with each single grammatical word class. A number of semantic roles correspond to each syntactic relation e.g. Perceiver (with ATTENTION verbs), Speaker (with SPEAKING verbs), Experiencer (with LIKING verbs), Agent (with AFFECT verbs) all relate to the A (transitive subject) syntactic relation.

In a similar way, semantically diverse expressions may be mapped onto the same syntactic construction. Compare *They began eating the chicken* with *They discussed eating the chicken*; these are syntactically identical, with main verbs *began* and *discussed*, and complement clause *eating the chicken*. But *They began eating the chicken* describes an activity of 'eating', with *begin* being a Secondary verb that provides aspectual-type modification (and would in some languages be realised through a derivational affix to 'eat'). In contrast, *They discussed eating the chicken* describes a discussion, and the topic of the discussion is eating the chicken.

The seven kinds of complement clause cover a wide semantic range. Consider:

   all BEGINNING verbs take ING complements, most also take a reduced Modal (FOR) TO;

   all WANTING verbs take Modal (FOR) TO complement, most also take THAT;

   all THINKING verbs take THAT or WH- complements, most also take Judgement TO, some ING, and a few Modal (FOR) TO;

   all LIKING verbs take ING, most also THAT, and some Modal (FOR) TO.

A given kind of complement clause may be applicable to all members of a certain type (because of the meaning of the type, and of the complement construction), but to just some members of another type (depending on the specific meanings of certain verbs within that type).

There are many examples in this chapter of a single syntactic construction being used to code a variety of diverse semantic configurations.

7.1. Parentheticals

There will usually be some SPEAKING verb introducing any segment of direct speech. This can come at the end of the direct speech, or it can interrupt it, at any of the positions at which adverbs may occur (see §2.5); or, less usually, it could come at the beginning. Thus:

(1a) *'John has been drinking absinthe again', Mary remarked*

(1b) *'John', Mary remarked, 'has been drinking absinthe again'*

(1c) *'John has', Mary remarked, 'been drinking absinthe again'*

(1d) *Mary remarked: 'John has been drinking absinthe again'*

Direct speech can always be encoded as indirect speech, using a THAT complement clause, as in (2). And there are many THAT complement constructions which do not have any direct speech correspondents, as in (3).

(2) *Mary remarked (that) John had been drinking absinthe again*

(3) *I suspect (that) John has been visiting the fortune teller*

(The *that* complementiser may optionally be omitted when it immediately follows a transitive verb, as in (2) and (3).)

Now there is another construction type which shows some similarities to—but also important differences from—the THAT complement construction:

(4a) *John, I suspect, has been visiting the fortune teller*

(4b) *John has, I suspect, been visiting the fortune teller*

(4c) *John has been visiting the fortune teller, I suspect*

There are exactly parallel sentences relating to (2): *Mary remarked* could be inserted after *John*, or after *John had*, or after the whole of *John had been drinking absinthe again*.

In (4a–c) the complement clause, from (3), has become the main clause and the original subject-plus-main-verb, *I suspect*, becomes a parenthetical insert which can come at any of the positions normally open to adverbs (or to a clause introducing direct speech, as in (1a–c)): after the subject, or after the first auxiliary verb (or perhaps after a later auxiliary verb, or after the entire auxiliary constituent and before the main verb), or at the end of the sentence. The parenthetical insertion must be set off from the rest of the sentence—by commas in writing, or by appositional intonation when speaking.

A parenthetical may not normally come at the beginning of the sentence and remain parenthetical. If it occurs initially then it becomes the main clause and what is the main clause in (4a–c) becomes a complement clause, as in (3); the whole sentence is now a single intonation unit. (The verb *reckon*—in the sense 'think', not the sense 'calculate'—may for many speakers only occur in a parenthetical. In this case the parenthetical can occur sentence-intitially, e.g. *I reckon he's crazy*; note that *that* may not be included before *he's crazy* here.)

A parenthetical construction can parallel any kind of sentence which includes a THAT complement clause coming after the verb. One in object function, as in (4a–c), or one in post-object function,
as in:

(5a) *He promised me (that) the building will be ready on time*
(5b) *The building will, he promised me, be ready on time*

Or a THAT complement clause which has been extraposed from subject function, as in (6a–b), or even from derived passive subject function, as in (7b–c) (a corresponding active is given in (7a)):

(6a) *It is correct that Mary is a genius*
(6b) *Mary is, it is correct, a genius*
(7a) *People suspect (that) John has visited the fortune teller*
(7b) *It is suspected (that) John has visited the fortune teller*
(7c) *John has, it is suspected, visited the fortune teller*

There is a difference in meaning between pairs like (3) and (4a–c). Sentence (3) asserts a suspicion and details what it is (through a complement clause). Sentences (4a–c) assert that John has been visiting the fortune teller and then qualify the assertion by *I suspect*, which has a similar function to an adverb such as *allegedly*, *presumably* or *probably*.

The difference in meaning can be shown by a specific example. Suppose that a lady customer storms into the manager's outer office and tells his secretary that she has been short-changed. The secretary listens, and forms her own judgement. Then she takes the customer into the manager, and might say either (8a) or (8b):

(8a) *This lady complains (that) she has been short-changed*
(8b) *This lady has, she complains, been short-changed*

By uttering (8b) the secretary would be asserting that the customer had been short-changed, i.e. the manager would gather that the secretary was convinced that the complaint was a valid one. But if (8a) were uttered the secretary would be making no judgement at all, merely reporting the complaint.

A parenthetical is most often short, consisting of subject and verb or, just occasionally, of subject, verb and object (as in (5b) and in *The last person to leave must, she has instructed us, turn out the lights*). Subject and object are likely to be short—consisting just of a pronoun, or proper name, or article plus common noun. This is simply because a long parenthetical would be likely to provide too severe a disruption of the main clause, and make the listener lose track of what is happening. (Thus, one is most unlikely to encounter a parenthetical of the length of *The apartment will, our absentee landlord who lives in Florida and usually only communicates with us through his agent told my absent-minded but well-meaning room-mate, be sold after Christmas*.)

A parenthetical generally provides a simple statement, and is very unlikely to have a negative predicate; in (4a–c) *I suspect* could not be replaced by *I didn't suspect*. The most common situation is for the verb in a parenthetical to be in what is generally called 'present tense', with generic reference. But past tense is also possible (as in the parenthetical versions of (2), with *Mary remarked*), or perfect and/or progressive (as in *She is, we have been assuming, available on those dates*). We also find imperative parentheticals, e.g. *Tomorrow is, don't forget, a public holiday*, corresponding to the THAT complement construction *Don't forget (that) tomorrow is a public holiday!*; and interrogative parentheticals, e.g. *Has he, I wonder, enough stamina for the task?*

Every verb that occurs in parentheticals takes a THAT complement clause, but not vice versa. Thus, a syntactic analysis that derived parentheticals, like (4a–c), from complement clause constructions, such as (3), would be perfectly valid so long as due account was taken of the semantic differences involved.

We can now turn to the question of which verbs occur in parentheticals, dealing first with Primary and then with Secondary types. It appears that almost every verb in a Primary type—other than LIKING and ANNOYING—which takes a THAT complement clause can be used parenthetically. There is one qualification—the verb must have a positive meaning. Thus, just as we cannot have an overt negative in a parenthetical (**I didn't suspect*) so we cannot have a verb that is inherently negative, such as *forget* or *doubt*. We can, however, get a 'double negative', in the form of *not* plus a negative verb, e.g. *don't forget*, exemplified in the last paragraph but one, and *don't doubt*, in *Mary is, I don't doubt, a good doctor*.

Primary verbs that are used in parentheticals include all those from ATTENTION which take a THAT complement (except *watch* and *listen*, which have a special sense of that THAT construction—see §7.4.1), e.g. *see, hear, notice, discover, witness*; from THINKING, e.g. *think, imagine, suppose, speculate, dream, remember, know, learn, understand, conclude, argue, believe*; from DECIDING, e.g. *decide, resolve, choose*; and from SPEAKING, e.g. *shout, read, say, joke, report, regret, explain, suggest, undertake, promise, instruct, warn*.

It appears that very few verbs from the ANNOYING type may felicitously be used in parentheticals, e.g. not **He is, it annoys/ delights me, going to France on vacation* corresponding to *It annoys/delights me that he is going to France on vacation*; however, we do get *He is, it might interest you to know, going to France on vacation*. LIKING verbs which take a THAT complement generally include the impersonal pronoun *it* before this constituent. Two verbs that do not are *fear* and *rejoice*, and they appear to be the only members of the type to occur in parentheticals.

Turning now to the Secondary type WANTING, parentheticals are possible with *hope, expect, pretend* and perhaps with *plan* and *intend* (and with *wish* only when there is an impersonal subject, e.g. *one might wish*) but not with other members of this type such as *desire* and *require*. Consider:

> (9a) *I hope (that) he will come today*
> (9b) *He will, I hope, come today*

Sentence (9a) simply conveys a hope, and the addressee has no way of knowing what chance there is of it becoming realised. But on hearing (9b) one would infer that there is a very good chance of his coming—this is an assertion that he will come, quantified by the parenthetical *I hope*.

Now compare (9a) with sentences that show no corresponding parenthetical construction:

> (10) *I desire (that) he should come today*
> (11) *I require that they (should) report at the office on arrival*

Hope describes the Principal's thought that something may happen, and he may also have a good idea that it is likely to happen (as in (9b)). In contrast, *desire* simply comments on the Principal's eagerness that something should happen, and *require* on his opinion that something should be done—in neither case is there likely to be any degree of expectation that the something will eventuate. It is this expectation which is necessary for a WANTING verb to be used in a parenthetical, as in (9b).

Only *ensure* from the MAKING type accepts a THAT complement clause and this may be used as a parenthetical, e.g. *The property will, the contract ensures, revert to its original owner*. The Secondary-D verb *matter* can never be in a parenthetical.

Of the adjectives that may take a THAT complement, the VALUE and HUMAN PROPENSITY types (many of whose members have a similar meaning to LIKING and ANNOYING verbs) are not found in parentheticals. Most QUALIFICATION adjectives that take THAT complements may be used in parentheticals, e.g. *The King will, it is definite/probable/true/likely/certain/correct/right, visit this province in the spring*. (As before, negative forms such as *improbable*, *untrue* and *wrong* are excluded from parentheticals.)

Both *probable* and *possible* may occur in a parenthetical, e.g. *He will, it is probable, announce an election for next month* and *He may, it is possible, announce an election for next month*. Note that *probable*, implying a high chance, is compatible with modal *will* in the main clause, whereas *possible*, implying a much smaller chance, is more compatible with *may*.

Verbs of the SEEM type may appear in a parenthetical with an appropriate adjective (those exemplified in the last paragraph but one), e.g. *The King will, it seems definite/likely/etc., visit this province in the spring*. *Seem*, *happen* and *appear* may also appear alone in a parenthetical, e.g. *John is, it seems/appears/happens, a very polite person*.

Parentheticals may occur at the same syntactic positions as adverbs and often have a similar semantic effect. Thus, *definitely* may be substituted for *it is definite* with very little change in meaning, and also *probably*, *certainly*, *hopefully*. Some adverbs are roughly equivalent to parentheticals with first person subject, or with subject coreferential with main clause subject, e.g. *She will, regrettably, have to sell her car* could relate to *She will, I regret, have to sell her car* or to *She will, she regrets, have to sell her car* but scarcely to *She will, Fred regrets, have to sell her car*. Some are roughly equivalent to parentheticals with third person subject, e.g. *reportedly* to *he/she reports* but not to *I report* or *You report*.

Many verbs and adjectives used in parentheticals do not have a corresponding adverb. And for some which do have, the adverb has a quite different meaning. Compare *The King will, it is correct, enter by the front door* (i.e. this is a correct statement of what he will do) with *The King will, correctly, enter by the front door* (he will act in a correct manner).

7.2. Meanings of complement clauses

Each of the seven varieties of complement clause has a meaning—and range of use—relative to the other choices from the system. It is thus especially profitable to contrast their meanings, taking them two or three at a time.

7.2.1. THAT and WH-

A THAT complement refers to some definite event or state. Thus:

(12) *I know that John is on duty today*

WH- complements involve either (i) *whether* or *if*, which enquires about a complement event or state; or (ii) another *wh-* word (*who, what, which, why*, etc.) which enquires about some aspect of an event or state. They may be the indirect speech correspondents of questions, e.g. *They asked whether he is sick*, *She enquired who was sick*. WH- complements also occur with many verbs not concerned with speaking, then referring to something about which clarification is needed, e.g.

(13) *I (don't) know whether/if John is on duty today*
(14) *I (don't) know who is on duty today/when John is on duty*

The most typical pattern—with verbs like *know, hear, understand, remember, decide* and *remark*—is for a THAT complement to occur in a positive sentence and a WH- one in a negative one. Thus *I know that John is on duty today* and *I don't know whether John is on duty today*. But all WH- complements can be used without a negative, e.g. *I know whether John is on duty today*. And THAT clauses may be used with a negative, as in

(15a) *I don't know that John is on duty today*
(15b) *I didn't know that John was on duty today*

Both (15a) and (15b) would be likely to be used when someone else had made an assertion that John is on duty today. By using (15a), in present tense, the speaker declines to agree with the assertion—(15a) has a meaning not too different from *I don't believe that John is on duty today*. Sentence (15b), in past tense, indicates not so much disagreement as surprise—the speaker thought that he knew John's duty days, and hadn't realised today was one of them.

Verbs like *ponder, speculate, wonder* and *guess* tend to relate to some matter that requires clarification, and typically take a WH-complement without also including *not* (although they can also accept *not*), e.g. *I wondered whether/when I would get released, She guessed what he would be wearing/who would come*.

Doubt has an inherently negative meaning and commonly takes a *whether* complement in a positive clause; it also takes a THAT complement. There is a subtle difference in meaning—*I doubt that he is sick* is more likely to imply disagreement with an assertion which has been made that he is sick, whereas *I doubt whether he is sick* could be used when no one has seriously suggested that he was sick, but the idea has just been floated as one possible explanation for his absence. A negative sentence with *doubt* may take a THAT complement, e.g. *I don't doubt that he is sick*, and is very close in meaning to the positive assertion *I believe that he is sick*. A negative statement with *doubt* does not permit a *whether* complement, **I don't doubt whether he is sick* (it is as if a double negation does not make sense in connection with an appeal for clarification); but note that a negative question with *doubt* may take a *whether* complement, e.g. *Don't you doubt whether he ever intended to do it?*

Verbs *ask*, *request*, and *enquire* can refer to an act of questioning and are then restricted to a WH- complement clause. *Ask*—but not *enquire*—has a second sense of 'ordering' and then takes a THAT complement, which will generally include a modal, e.g. *I asked that he (should) clean the stables*.

Almost all verbs that take WH- complements also take THAT clauses. The few exceptions include *enquire* (mentioned in the last paragraph) and *discuss*, which must refer to some ongoing activity (through an ING complement) or to something about which clarification is sought (through a WH- clause). There are a fair number of verbs that take a THAT but not a WH- complement, e.g. *believe, assume, suppose*, which make unequivocal assertions, and *order, urge*, which issue instructions.

The LIKING and ANNOYING types describe an Experiencer's feelings about a Stimulus, something which is not compatible with a clause that indicates a need for clarification; most verbs from these types take THAT clauses but none accept WH- complements. A number of Secondary verbs take THAT complements but these are essentially providing semantic qualification of the verb of the complement clause, and again it would not be appropriate to have a WH- clause in this function. We can thus say both *I didn't know (that) it was you* (sc. coming) and *I hoped (that) it was you* (sc. coming) but only *I didn't know who it was*, with the Primary verb *know*, not **I hoped who it was*, since *hope* is a Secondary verb. (A WH- clause is possible with the Secondary-D verb *matter*, e.g. *Whether he wins matters to me*.)

Of the adjectives that take complement clauses, WH- complements are found in subject function with a handful that have negative meanings, e.g. *be unsure, be uncertain*, and with others when there is a negative in the sentence, e.g. *not be certain*, as in *It is not certain whether he will come*. WH- complements may also occur after some HUMAN PROPENSITY adjectives, e.g. *He is curious (about) where we'll sleep tonight, She is interested (in) whether we'll be allowed in*.

(In any investigation of WH- complement clauses one must take special care to distinguish these from fused relatives, such as *I like who my daughter married*, i.e. I like the person who my daughter married, and *I like what you have*, i.e. I like that which you have. See §§2.6, 2.7.)

In §2.7 we mentioned a group of verbs which commonly take *should* in a THAT complement (in fact, the meanings of the verbs imply 'should') and may freely omit it, e.g. *He suggests that we (should) go tomorrow*. They include *order, urge, recommend* and others from the ORDER subtype of SPEAKING; *propose, suggest* and *insist*; and a very limited sense of *want* (as in *I want that you (should) be satisfied*).

7.2.2. THAT and ING

A THAT complement essentially refers to some activity or state as a single unit, without any reference to its inherent constitution or time duration. In contrast, an ING complement refers to an activity or state as extended in time, perhaps noting the way in which it unfolds. Compare:

(16a) *I heard that John had slapped his sister*
(16b) *I heard John('s) slapping his sister*
(17a) *He thought that Mary would apply for the job*
(17b) *He thought of Mary('s) applying for the job*

Sentence (16a) states that I heard a piece of news, whereas (16b) implies that I overheard what actually happened—the noise of palm hitting arm, the girl's screams, etc. And (17a) states an opinion that the application would be made, where (17b) may be taken to relate to how she would go about it—searching for pencil and paper, wondering how to frame the letter, then buying a stamp.

Some verbs are, by virtue of their meaning, restricted to only one of these complement constructions. *Suppose*, which relates to whether or not something might happen or have happened, may only take THAT. The meaning of *describe* implies reference to the unfolding of an activity, and this verb is restricted to an ING complement.

For many verbs THAT and ING complements show considerable overlap in meaning and use. But there is always an implicit—or potential—semantic contrast, along the lines we have described. Consider *propose*, in

(18a) *I propose (our) walking from John o'Groats to Land's End to raise money for charity*

(18b) *I propose that we (should) do the walk in the spring*
(18c) *I propose that we (should) forget the whole thing*

Each of (18a–c) could have a THAT or an ING complement. The ING alternative sounds fine in (18a), since it introduces the idea of a continuous activity. For (18b) a THAT construction is preferred—the walk is now being referred to as an 'event' and a time suggested for it. Sentence (18c) again refers to the walk as a 'unit'; the ING alternative to (18c), *I propose (our) forgetting the whole idea*, sounds particularly infelicitous.

There is another factor which motivates the choice between THAT and ING complement clauses: only an ING construction allows the complement clause subject to be omitted when it is coreferential with an appropriate main clause constituent. There is, in most styles of English, a preference to omit a repeated constituent and —all else being equal, or nearly equal—an ING complement may be preferred to a THAT one for this reason. Thus, if I were the only person planning to walk the length of Britain, then *I propose doing the walk in the spring* might be preferred to *I propose that I (should) do the walk in the spring*. Or, consider *regret*, which can take a THAT or ING complement as in:

(19a) *I regret that they didn't walk out of that film when the violence started*

(19b) *I regret their not walking out of that film when the violence started*

Native speakers find (19a) and (19b) about equally acceptable. However, when the complement clause subject is coreferential with main clause subject they exhibit a preference for the ING construction, *I regret not walking out . . .*, over the THAT one, *I regret that I didn't walk out . . .* (although the latter is still considered grammatical).

The predicate of a THAT complement clause must involve a tense inflection, and can include any of: a Modal, perfect *have*, progressive *be*. An ING clause may not include tense or a Modal. The time reference of an ING clause can often be inferred from the lexical meaning of the main verb, e.g. in (18a) it is taken to refer to something projected for the future because *propose* has an inherently future meaning, and in (19b) to something which took place in the past, because of the meaning of *regret*. Note that past time can be shown in an ING or TO complement clause by the *have* auxiliary (see §2.7). An alternative to (19b) is *I regret their not having walked out* . . . But to include *have* here would be a little pedantic, since the past tense reference of the ING clause in (19b) can adequately be inferred from the meaning of the main verb *regret*.

7.2.3. Modal (FOR) TO, Judgement TO, and THAT

There is, at first blush, syntactic similarity between constructions like (20)–(21) and those like (22)–(23).

(20) *I want Mary to be a doctor*
(21) *She forced him to recite a poem*
(22) *I discovered him to be quite stupid*
(23) *We had assumed Mary to be a doctor*

In fact (20)–(21) are examples of Modal (FOR) TO complement constructions, while (22)–(23) are Judgement TO constructions. There are considerable semantic and syntactic differences, which fully justify the recognition of two varieties of complement clause both involving *to*.

Modal (FOR) TO complements relate to the subject of the complement clause becoming involved in the activity or state referred to by that clause, or to the potentiality of such involvement. Thus: *I am hoping for John to go tomorrow*, *I wish (for) Mary to accompany me*. The *for* may optionally be omitted after certain main verbs (with a semantic effect), the complement clause subject then becoming surface object to the main verb; this is discussed in §7.2.4. Note that some verbs must retain *for*, e.g. *hope*, whereas some must omit it, e.g. *force*.

It is always possible—and often obligatory—for the subject to be omitted from a Modal (FOR) TO clause when it is coreferential with an NP in the main clause; *for* is then also omitted. If the complement clause is in subject function then its subject is omitted under coreferentiality with main clause object, e.g. (*For Mary*) *to have to travel so much annoys John*. If the complement clause is in object function then its subject may be omitted under coreferentiality with main clause subject, e.g. *I don't want* (*Mary*) *to travel so much*. If the complement clause is in post-object slot with verbs of the ORDER subtype then its subject is omitted under coreferentiality with main clause object, e.g. *I asked (the matron for) Mary to nurse me.*

Many verbs that take a Modal (FOR) TO complement also accept a THAT complement clause. The meaning of the (FOR) TO construction is often similar to the meaning of the THAT construction when a Modal is included. Compare:

(24a) *I wish that John would go*
(24b) *I wish (for) John to go*
(25a) *I decided that Mary should give the vote of thanks*
(25b) *I decided for Mary to give the vote of thanks*
(26a) *I decided that I would give the vote of thanks*
(26b) *I decided to give the vote of thanks*
(27a) *I expect that Mary will be appointed*
(27b) *I expect Mary to be appointed*
(28a) *I ordered that the flag should be raised*
(28b) *I ordered the flag to be raised*

It seems here as if the complementiser *to* carries the same sort of semantic load as a Modal does in a THAT clause; this is why we refer to this variety of complement as 'Modal' (FOR) TO.

Some verbs which take both Modal (FOR) TO and THAT complements are seldom found without a Modal in the THAT clause. But others may freely include or omit a Modal. Alongside (25a) and (26a) we get:

(29) *I decided that I was sick*

There is no (FOR) TO correspondent of (29). We do get *I decided to be sick*, but this is most similar in meaning to *I decided that I would be sick*, which does include a Modal.

Although a Modal (FOR) TO construction will frequently have a similar meaning to a THAT construction with a Modal, they will never be exactly synonymous. Compare:

(30a) *I remembered that I should lock the door (but then decided not to, as a way of asserting my distaste for authority)*
(30b) *I remembered to lock the door (but then Mary took the key and pushed it down a grating, so I couldn't)*

The THAT clause in (30a) simply records a fact, what my obligation was; it says nothing about my attitude to that obligation. A (FOR) TO complement, as in (30b), refers to the involvement in an activity of the subject of the complement clause (which is here coreferential with the subject of the main clause). The unmarked situation is that he would if at all possible become so involved, i.e. on hearing just *I remembered to lock the door* one would infer that the speaker did lock it. The subject would only not become involved if something outside his control intervened, as in the parenthesis added onto (30b).

A further pair of sentences exhibiting the delicate semantic contrast between THAT (with a Modal) and Modal (FOR) TO is:

(31a) *John and Mary have decided that they will get married* (e.g. when both have completed their professional qualifications)

(31b) *John and Mary have decided to get married* (e.g. next month)

Sentence (31a) announces an intention to get married; no date need yet have been mooted. But (31b) carries an implication that they have definite plans to marry in the foreseeable future.

Judgement TO complements have a rather different meaning. The subject of the main clause verb ventures a judgement or opinion about the subject of the complement clause predicate (this semantic characterisation will be expanded in §7.4.3). Most often the judgement is about some state or property which is either transitory, e.g. *I noticed John to be asleep*, or else a matter of opinion, e.g. *They declared Fred to be insane*. A Judgement TO construction is unlikely to be used to describe some permanent, objective property; thus, one would be unlikely to hear ?*He noticed her to be Chinese* (only *He noticed that she was Chinese*). And most often the subject of the Judgement TO clause is human—?*I believe that glass to be unbreakable* sounds rather odd.

Whereas a Modal (FOR) TO complement can fill subject, object or post-object slot, a Judgement TO clause must immediately follow a transitive verb, effectively in object function. There is never any *for*, and the underlying complement clause subject is surface syntactic object of the main verb. This constituent is seldom coreferential with main clause subject (since it is relatively unusual to make judgements about oneself); when it is it can never be omitted. Compare the Modal (FOR) TO construction *I want Mary to win* and, with optional coreferential omission, *I want (myself) to win*, with the Judgement TO constructions *I consider Mary (to be) cleverer than Fred* and *I consider myself to be cleverer than Fred*. *Myself* cannot be omitted from the last example.

A Judgement TO construction is frequently found with the main clause passivised, often so as to avoid specifying who is responsible for the judgement, e.g. *He was declared to be insane*. In fact the verb *say* only takes a Judgement TO complement in the passive, e.g. *Mary is said to be a good cook* (but not **They say Mary to be a good cook*).

The predicate of a Judgement TO clause most often begins with *be*. This can be the copula *be*, as in *I reported John to be absent today*; or passive *be*, as in *I believed John to be beaten*; or progressive *be*, as in *I suspect him to be hiding in the shrubbery, eavesdropping on what we are saying*. Past tense can be shown—as in ING and Modal (FOR) TO complements—by the inclusion of *have*, e.g. *I believed John to have been beaten*. It is possible to have Judgement TO complements without *be*, as in (33b), but they are relatively rare. (There is a special kind of Judgement TO construction with the SEEM type, and here complements without *be* are commoner—see §§6.4.1, 7.3.5.)

All verbs which take Judgement TO also accept a THAT complement clause, sometimes with a very similar meaning. Compare:

(32a) *I know that Mary is clever*
(32b) *I know Mary to be clever*
(33a) *I know that Mary raced giraffes in Kenya*
(33b) *I know Mary to have raced giraffes in Kenya*

Note that a Judgement TO complement corresponds semantically to a THAT clause without a Modal. It is of course possible to include a Modal in a THAT clause after *know*:

(34) *I know that Mary may/must/should be clever*

But there is then no corresponding Judgement TO construction. A TO clause cannot include a Modal and there is no means of coding the information shown by the Modal in (34) into a Judgement TO construction. (It is also relevant to note that a Judgement TO clause puts forward a specific assertion, and the inclusion of a Modal would be semantically incompatible with this.)

This is a major difference between the two varieties of TO complement. A Modal (FOR) TO clause frequently corresponds semantically to a THAT clause with a Modal, as in (24)–(28). If a Modal is not included in the THAT clause, as in (29), then there is no corresponding Modal (FOR) TO construction. In contrast, a Judgement TO clause corresponds to a THAT clause without a Modal, as in (32)–(33). Once a Modal is included in the THAT clause, as in (34), there is no corresponding Judgement TO construction.

Many verbs take a Modal (FOR) TO complement in object slot and a fair number take a Judgement TO clause, but only a handful may occur with both. Those which do—*remember*, *know* and *learn* —never omit the *for* from a Modal (FOR) TO clause when the complement clause subject is included, so that there could be no difficulty in the listener spotting which type of complement is being used. In fact these verbs most often have the subject of a Modal (FOR) TO clause coreferential with main clause subject and then omitted, as in (37b).

(35a) *I remembered that Mary was very smart*
(35b) *I remembered Mary to be very smart* (Judgement TO)
(36a) *I remembered that Mary should sign the visitors' book*
(36b) *I remembered for Mary to sign the visitors' book* (Modal (FOR) TO)
(37a) *I remembered that I should sign the visitors' book*
(37b) *I remembered to sign the visitors' book* (Reduced Modal (FOR) TO)

There is a further, rather special, kind of Modal (FOR) TO construction. For some, but not all, verbs that take a (FOR) TO clause in object or post-object slot there is a noun derived from the verb that can be head of the subject NP, with the original subject becoming the possessor within this NP; the main clause then has as its predicate head the copula *be*. Compare:

(38a) *I had intended (for) us to have lunch on top of the mountain*
(38b) *My intention was for us to have lunch on top of the mountain*

Such a post-copula Modal (FOR) TO clause cannot omit the *for* if the complement clause subject is retained. However, the complement clause subject frequently is coreferential with the original main clause subject (now possessor within the subject NP) and is then omitted, together with *for*. Thus

(39a) *I hope to be chosen as captain*
(39b) *My hope is to be chosen as captain*
(40a) *She prefers to go in the evening*
(40b) *Her preference is to go in the evening*

This construction is available to some verbs from the WANTING type—*wish, desire, crave/craving, long/longing, hope, need, intend/intention, plan, aim* (but not *want, mean, prepare*)—and with at least *prefer/preference* from the LIKING type. Note that some of these verbs are unchanged in form when used as a noun, while others have a derived form.

Warn and *instruct* from the ORDER subtype take a post-object Modal (FOR) TO complement. They enter into a similar construction (with nouns *warning* and *instruction*) and here the original direct object is marked by preposition *to*, within the subject NP, e.g.

(41a) *I instructed the hired hands to keep out of the paddock*
(41b) *My instruction to the hired hands was to keep out of the paddock*

There are in English wider possibilities for adjectival modification of a noun than there are for adverbial modification of a verb. The (b) alternatives in (38)–(41) are likely to be used when such modification is desired. We might find *my unwavering intention* in (38b), *my fondest hope* in (39b), *her firm preference* in (40b) and *my strict instruction* in (41b). The corresponding adverbs either seem a little clumsy (*strictly*) or else have a different meaning (*fondly, firmly*), or are not really acceptable at all (**unwaveringly*).

The next sections continue this discussion of kinds of TO complement, dealing with the omission of *for*, the omission of *to* from Modal (FOR) TO, and the omission of *to be* from both Judgement TO and Modal (FOR) TO.

7.2.4 The role of *for* in Modal (FOR) TO complements

A Modal (FOR) TO complement clause can be in subject, object or post-object function in the main clause. When in object function it is open to passivisation (although in fact Modal (FOR) TO complements seldom are passivised, for semantic reasons—see Chapter 9). A Modal (FOR) TO clause in subject—including derived passive subject—function is most often extraposed, as in (42b).

(42a) *They had intended for Mary to lead the parade*
(42b) *It had been intended for Mary to lead the parade*

A Modal complement clause can include *for* before its subject. Or it can omit the *for* while still retaining this underlying subject NP, which then becomes surface direct object of the main verb, as in (43a). It is this NP which is then subject to passivisation, as in (43b).

(43a) *They had intended Mary to lead the parade*
(43b) *Mary had been intended to lead the parade*

In §2.7 we stated that *for* can only be omitted when the complement clause immediately follows a transitive main verb (and gave a list of the other possible positions for a Modal (FOR) TO clause, when *for* must be retained). This is because the complement clause subject then becomes main clause object, and an object NP must immediately follow its verb.

In §2.5 we mentioned that an adverb cannot intrude between a verb and an NP object, but it may come between verb and complement clause object. An adverbial phrase like *quite seriously* could in (42a) be placed after *had* or after *intended*; in (43a) it could only come after *had*, since here *intended* has an NP object.

What is the semantic consequence of omitting *for*? This can best be inferred from study of those verbs which do allow it to be either included or omitted. A pair of sentences with *choose* was given at (44)–(45) in §2.7. Consider also:

(44a) *I had wished for Mary to win the prize*
(44b) *I wish Mary to stand up*
(45a) *I'd like it for you to kiss Auntie Daphne every time she calls*
(45b) *I'd like you to kiss Auntie Daphne now (she's just arrived)*

(With LIKING an *it* is generally included before a Modal (FOR) TO clause; *it* drops when the *for* drops.)

A construction without *for* and with the underlying subject of the Modal (FOR) TO clause as main clause object is used when the sentence relates directly to the referent of that NP: (44b) might be used in addressing a class of children that included Mary; (45b) is an instruction to the addressee to kiss Auntie Daphne at once. In contrast, a construction with the *for* retained is likely to be used for a more general statement, without the same pragmatic pressure directed towards the complement clause subject. Sentence (44a) could be a wistful thought, which Mary wasn't even aware of; (45a) is a general request concerning what the addressee should do whenever an appropriate occasion arises, i.e. when Auntie Daphne calls. (Note that *it for* could be omitted from (45a), giving this sentence more pragmatic force; but *it for* could not be included in (45b).)

Similar semantic considerations apply to complement clauses— with and without *for*—following *intend*. Little difference may be discernible between (42a) and (43a) but when different NPs are chosen the contrast becomes plainer. Suppose I had understood that I was to lead the parade and then saw someone else in position. I would be more likely to say to the organiser *You said (that) you intended me to lead the parade*, rather than *You said (that) you intended for me to lead the parade*. Omitting *for* and making *me* (rather than the whole clause *for me to lead the parade*) the object of *intended* adds force to my complaint about how the organiser had wronged me in this instance.

In summary, when the activity referred to by the main clause relates directly to the subject of a Modal (FOR) TO complement clause, in object function, then the *for* will be omitted and the complement clause subject becomes surface direct object of the main verb.

Some verbs that take a Modal (FOR) TO complement never omit the *for* when the complement clause subject is retained, e.g. *hope, long, decide, undertake, remember*. The meanings of these verbs are incompatible with the pragmatic implications of having complement clause subject become main clause object. There is a second set of verbs that may either retain or omit the *for*—besides *intend, choose, wish, like* (and other LIKING verbs), this set includes *desire, propose, recommend, urge*.

A third class of verbs—including *want, need, require, order*— may have the verb followed by an adverb and then a complement beginning with *for*, but when there is no adverb the *for* will be omitted. Thus *I need most urgently for Mary to give me an injection* but only *I need Mary to give me an injection*, not (in most dialects) **I need for Mary to give me an injection*. It seems that the pragmatic force of these verbs is such that the complement clause subject should normally also be main clause object. But verbs of this class do not readily take an adverb between subject and verb (*?I most urgently need . . .* sounds odd, although not totally impossible). Because of this there is a preference for the adverb to follow the verb and in such circumstances a *for* must be included.

A final class comprises Secondary-C verbs of the MAKING and HELPING types. The meanings of these verbs require complement clause subject to become main clause object, and *for* must be omitted. It is not permissible to include an adverb after a verb from these types, e.g. we can only say *He stupidly forced her to sign the paper*, not **He forced stupidly for her to sign the paper*.

The question as to whether *for* can be, or may be, or may not be included in a Modal (FOR) TO clause is largely determined by the semantic nature of the main verb. The meaning of the Modal (FOR) TO complement—relating to its subject getting involved in the activity referred to—is basically the same in each instance. Consider:

(46a) *The boss decided for Dr Jane Smith to examine Mary Brown* (*but she refused*)

(46b) *The boss decided for Mary Brown to be examined by Dr Jane Smith* (*but she refused*)

(47a) *The boss expected Dr Jane Smith to examine Mary Brown* (*but she refused*)

(47b) *The boss expected Mary Brown to be examined by Dr Jane Smith* (*but she refused*)

(48a) *The boss tried to force Dr Jane Smith to examine Mary Brown* (*but she refused*)

(48b) *The boss tried to force Mary Brown to be examined by Dr Jane Smith* (*but she refused*)

It has been suggested that *force* differs syntactically from verbs like *decide* and *expect*. The reason given is that active and passive complement constructions with *force*—as in (48a/b)—show a striking difference in meaning, which is not the case for active and passive constructions for verbs like *expect* and *decide* (as in (47a/b), (46a/b)).

In fact (46a/b), (47a/b) and (48a/b) are syntactically parallel. They involve the same syntactic and also semantic differences; it is just that the semantic differences are more evident with *force*, because of the meaning of that verb. The semantic congruence of (46a/b), (47a/b) and (48a/b) can be seen with the addition of *but she refused*. In each of the six sentences the *she* is taken to refer to the complement clause subject—to *Dr Jane Smith* in (46a), (47a) and (48a), and to *Mary Brown* in (46b), (47b) and (48b). Active and passive versions of a Modal (FOR) TO clause show the same basic semantic difference for every main verb, because a different NP is in the crucial complement clause subject slot in the two alternatives; the meaning of the Modal (FOR) TO construction relates to this complement clause subject becoming involved in the activity (or state) referred to by that clause.

This provides a further point of difference from Judgement TO complements, where the substitution of passive for active in the complement clause provides no more overall difference in meaning than this substitution produces in a main clause, e.g. *I believed Dr Jane Smith to have examined Mary Brown* and *I believed Mary Brown to have been examined by Dr Jane Smith*. One could add *but she denied it* to these two sentences and in each case the reference of *she* is unclear—it could relate to *Dr Jane Smith* or to *Mary Brown*. A Judgement TO construction does not provide the semantic means to resolve this ambiguity, as a Modal (FOR) TO construction does.

7.2.5 Omitting *to* from Modal (FOR) TO complements

As already mentioned, verbs from the MAKING and HELPING subtypes must omit *for* from a Modal (FOR) TO complement. Most of them do retain *to*, e.g. *force*, *cause*, *get*, *tempt*, *permit*, *allow*, *assist*. However, *make*, *have* and *let* must omit the *to* in an active sentence:

(49) *Mary made/had/let John drive the car*

Make may be used in the passive and *to* is then retained, e.g. *John was made to drive the car*. *Let* is only used in the passive in a few idiomatic combinations and no *to* is included, e.g. *The balloons/ pigeons/prisoners were let go*. The causative sense of *have* is not used in the passive.

We were able to focus on the semantic role of *for* by considering those verbs that allow it optionally to be omitted and seeing what semantic effect this has. There is one verb for which *to* may be either included or omitted; this is *help*. The pair of sentences *John helped Mary eat the pudding* and *John helped Mary to eat the pudding* were mentioned in §6.3.2 (see also Erades 1950*a* and Bolinger 1975*b*: 75). Now consider:

(50a) *John helped me to write the letter*
(50b) *John helped me write the letter*

Sentence (50a) might be used to describe John facilitating my writing the letter—suppose that he provided pen and ink, suggested some appropriate phrases and told me how one should address a bishop. But, in this scenario, I actually wrote the letter myself. Sentence (50b), on the other hand, might be used to describe a cooperative effort where John and I did the letter together, perhaps writing alternate paragraphs.

Sentence (50b)—without *to*—is likely to imply that John gave direct help; there is here a direct link between the referents of main and complement clause verbs. In contrast, (50a) is more likely to be used if he gave indirect assistance. This semantic principle explains, at least in part, the inclusion or omission of *to* with MAKING verbs. As outlined in §6.3.1, *cause* can be used of indirect action which brings about a certain result; it naturally takes *to*. *Make*, in contrast, relates to something done—on purpose or accidentally—to bring something about directly. *Let* focuses on the main clause subject, and the effect it has on the subject of the complement clause. These two verbs naturally exclude *to*. (This does not, however, explain why *force*, which often relates to coercion, takes *to*; and why the causative sense of *have*, which may involve some indirect means, omits *to*.)

There is a small group of ATTENTION verbs which (together with *know*) take what appears to be a variety of Modal (FOR) TO complement; *to* is omitted in the active but included in the passive:

(51a) *They saw/heard/noticed John kick Mary*
(51b) *John was seen/heard/noticed to kick Mary*

These do demonstrate the semantic characteristics of a Modal (FOR) TO complement—they describe John becoming involved in the activity of kicking Mary. (Note that if the complement clause is passivised we get an unacceptable sentence *They saw/heard/noticed Mary (to) be kicked by John*, simply because Mary—who is now complement clause subject—is not the participant who initiates the activity.) *See*, *hear* and *notice* do, in this construction, imply direct and often spontaneous perception of some activity (without the additional semantic overtones carried by verbs such as *recognise*, *discover* and *witness*, which do not occur in the construction). It may be because of this that the *to* is omitted.

But why is it that *to* must be included when *make*, *see*, *hear* and *notice* are used in the passive? Putting (49) (with *make*) or (51a) in the passive, in the context of a Modal (FOR) TO complement clause, loses the pragmatic immediacy of (49) and (51a). The passive verges towards being the description of a state, and that is why *to* is included. (*Help* may include or omit *to* in the passive, as in the active, but—for the same reason—it does seem more likely to include it in the passive.) Interestingly, *watch* and *listen to* occur in a construction like (51a) (*They watched John kick Mary, I listened to him sing*), but there is no corresponding passive, either with or without *to* (**John was watched (to) kick Mary*, **John was listened (to) sing*). One must instead employ what could be analysed as a reduced relative clause with progressive aspect (*John was watched kicking Mary*). The meanings of *watch* and *listen to* imply perception over a period of time, which is highly compatible with a reduced relative in progressive aspect. A Modal (FOR) TO construction is allowed in the active, but its passive equivalent ('in a state of being watched/listened to') is rejected in favour of a construction more in keeping with the meanings of *watch* and *listen to*.

7.2.6 Omitting *to be* from TO complements

The sequence *to be* can be omitted from some Judgement TO and from some Modal (FOR) TO complements. The conditions for this omission are quite different in the two cases.

For Judgement TO, a limited number of verbs may omit both the *to* and a *be* which begins the predicate when the predicate is a typical semantic accompaniment for the verb.

Most ATTENTION and SPEAKING verbs must retain the *to be*, e.g. nothing can be dropped from *She saw/reported/acknowledged him to be stupid/wrong/the decision-maker*. *Declare* and *proclaim* may omit *to be* when they are used in a performative sense, with a predicate that is prototypical for that verb, e.g. *The Council of Barons proclaimed Alfred (to be) King, The doctor declared him (to be) dead on arrival, The judge declared Mary (to be) the winner*. Note, though, that *to be* could scarcely be omitted from non-prototypical sentences involving these verbs, e.g. not from *They proclaimed/declared him to be clever*.

The verbs *think*, *consider* and *imagine*, from the THINKING type, may omit *to be* from a Judgement TO complement that makes a straightforward assertion concerning a quality or state, where this is shown by an adjective or by the passive form of a verb, e.g. *I thought him (to be) stupid/wrong/healthy/dead/vanquished*. *To be* may not be omitted from other kinds of Judgement TO complement with these verbs, e.g. not from *I thought him to be getting healthier each day*.

Find and *prove* may omit *to be* when the Judgement TO complement relates to some official or objective judgement, e.g. *find guilty*, *prove wrong*; but *to be* would be likely to be retained in a sentence like *We found him to be very unsure of himself*. (See also §6.4.1.) *To be* can be omitted after *believe* with the adjective *dead* (e.g. *He was believed (to be) dead*), a semi-idiomatic usage; nothing is likely to be omitted from *He is believed to be clever/the fastest gun in the West*. Verbs like *know* and *assume* appear never to omit *to be* from a Judgement TO complement, perhaps because there is no particular kind of predicate that could be considered prototypical for these verbs.

Turning now to Modal (FOR) TO complements, in §6.3.1 we discussed how *make* and *get* can omit *be* or *to be*, and the causative sense of *have* must omit *be*. A sentence with no *(to) be*, such as *I made John interested in the puzzle*, implies that I did something as a result of which he became spontaneously interested. In contrast, *I made John be interested in the puzzle* carries a more direct meaning—I influenced John to force himself to be interested in it.

To be may also be omitted from a Modal (FOR) TO complement after a small group of verbs which includes *order*, *wish*, *want*, *need* and *require*. This happens when the complement clause subject is not the controller of the activity (and so it would not be appropriate for *to* to be included). Typically, the complement clause will be in the passive, with an inanimate NP as derived passive subject, e.g. *He ordered the floors (to be) cleaned, I want this picture (to be) restored, I need my bandages (to be) changed.* Note that *to be* must be included when the main clause is passivised, e.g. *The floors were ordered to be cleaned.*

There is surface similarity to a construction where an object NP is followed by a 'resulting state' adjective, e.g. *She shot him dead, I swept it clean* (see §4.2). The two constructions are, in fact, quite different. *Shoot dead* is simply verb-plus-adjective—no *to be* enters in the passive, for instance (*He was shot dead*, not **He was shot to be dead*), whereas *cleaned* in *I ordered it cleaned* is a reduced clause—other clause constituents can be included with it (e.g. *I ordered it (to be) cleaned by an expert*).

In summary, *to be* can be omitted from a Judgement TO clause when the main clause verb and the adjective from the predicate of the complement clause typically belong together (e.g. *declare X dead, proclaim X King, find X guilty*). With Modal (FOR) TO clauses a (*to*) *be* can be omitted if the main clause subject does not directly 'control' the complement clause subject in doing something.

7.2.7. ING and Modal (FOR) TO

An ING construction describes the complement clause subject taking part in some activity which is extended in time. A Modal (FOR) TO clause refers to (the potentiality of) the subject's getting involved in some activity. Compare:

(52a) *John tried to drive the Datsun*
(52b) *John tried driving the Datsun*

Sentence (52b) states that he did drive the Datsun for a while, perhaps for long enough to know whether he liked the car; (52a) suggests that he wasn't able actually to drive it (perhaps he is only used to automatics and this is a manual, or perhaps the owner of the car wouldn't let him drive it).

ING, Modal (FOR) TO and THAT complements all occur after *remember*, with significant semantic differences:

(53a) *The doctor remembered that he had examined Mary Brown*

233

(53b) *The doctor remembered examining Mary Brown*
(53c) *The doctor remembered to examine Mary Brown*

Sentence (53a) might be used when he remembered that the consultation had taken place but couldn't recall any of the details —he just remembers the 'fact' of the examination; (53b) implies that he had a clear recollection of what happened—Mary Brown's giggles when he asked her to put out her tongue, the high blood pressure reading, and so on. Both (53a) and (53b) refer to some actual event, in the past. In contrast, (53c) has a prospective meaning, stating that he knew he had to involve himself in an activity. Unless something is stated to the contrary we would infer from (53c) that he did examine her. However, the sentence could be continued: *but when he looked in the waiting room he found she'd grown tired of waiting and gone off home.*

Another contrastive illustration of the three complement types is given in §7.4.5, with the verb *like*.

7.2.8. WH- TO

A WH- TO complement is like a Modal (FOR) TO clause with a *wh-* word (as in a WH- complement) at the beginning, in place of *for*. The complement clause subject must be coreferential with either main clause subject or object, and omitted. The *wh-* word refers to any constituent of the main clause except its subject.

A WH- TO clause combines the meanings of Modal (FOR) TO and of WH- complements. It refers to some activity in which the subject has the potential for getting involved, and it is an activity about which some clarification is required. Compare the THAT construction in (54a), the Modal (FOR) TO one in (54b), the plain WH- in (54c), and the WH- TO complement in (54d).

(54a) *He knew (that) he should stand up when the judge entered*
(54b) *He knew to stand up when the judge entered*
(54c) *He didn't know whether he should stand up when the judge entered*
(54d) *He didn't know whether to stand up when the judge entered*

Any verb which permits both a WH- and a Modal (FOR) TO clause will also take a WH- TO complement. Besides *know*, these include *remember* and *decide*, e.g. *He couldn't remember whether to close the window or leave it open*, and *I'll decide tomorrow who to fire, when to fire them, and how to appease the union*. It appears that no verb which does not take a plain WH- complement may take WH- TO. But there are verbs which take WH- and not Modal (FOR) TO and do accept WH- TO, e.g. *report, think (about)* and *understand*, as in *She's thinking about whether to accept the offer*, and *I don't understand how to behave*.

A plain WH- complement, such as (54c), may include *whether* or *if*, with a subtle difference in meaning (see Bolinger 1978); only *whether* is allowed in a WH- TO clause such as (54d). All other *wh-* words may begin a WH- TO complement excepting *why*. There appears to be a semantic reason for this. Consider first

(55) *I don't know why I should go*

This sentence is acceptable, with a meaning something like 'I don't know what my obligation is supposed to be that would make me go.' Now recall that there is always a semantic difference between a THAT construction including *should* and a Modal (FOR) TO construction; this was exemplifed at (30a/b) in §7.2.3 with *remember*. Whereas a THAT-plus-*should* clause refers to some extraneous obligation, a Modal (FOR) TO construction refers to the potentiality of the subject's getting involved in the activity. *I don't know why to go* is ungrammatical since *why*, demanding clarification of the reason for entering into an activity, is semantically incompatible with Modal (FOR) TO, stating that the subject does volitionally become involved in the activity. But Modal (FOR) TO is perfectly compatible with all other *wh-* words, e.g. *I don't know how to open the door/when to arrive/who to blame*.

7.2.9. (FROM) ING

The (FROM) ING variety of complement clause occurs with negative verbs from the ORDER subtype of SPEAKING and with negative verbs from the MAKING type. It relates to the subject of the main clause doing something so that the subject of the complement clause does not become involved in the activity described by that clause.

We can first compare *persuade* and *dissuade*, positive and negative members of ORDER:

(56a) *I persuaded John that Mary/he should go*
(56b) *I persuaded Mary to go*
(57) *I dissuaded Mary from going*

Sentence (56a) has a THAT complement in post-object slot. Example (56b) has an underlying Modal (FOR) TO clause in post-object function; the complement clause subject must be coreferential with main clause object, and then omitted (together with *for*). Sentence (57) is exactly parallel to (56b); the difference is that with *dissuade* there is no corresponding THAT construction. The object NP may be passivised in (57) as in (56b), e.g. *Mary was persuaded to go*, *Mary was dissuaded from going*. The other ORDER verbs that occur in a (FROM) ING construction include *discourage* and *prohibit*. *Forbid* was originally used with a Modal (FOR) TO complement but nowadays an increasing number of speakers prefer a (FROM) ING complement, which accords better with the negative meaning of this verb. One hears both *She forbade him to go* and *She forbade him from going*, with no difference in meaning.

Looking now at positive and negative members of the MAKING type:

(58) *I made her go*
(59) *I forced her to go*
(60) *I prevented her (from) going*

Sentences (58)–(59) involve a Modal (FOR) TO complement clause in object function; the *for* must be omitted with verbs of this type, and complement clause subject becomes surface object of the main clause. Sentence (60) is a construction exactly parallel to (58)–(59), in the same way that (57) parallels (56b). The other MAKING verbs which take a (FROM) ING construction include *stop*, *save*, *spare* and special senses of *check* (*oneself*), *rescue* and *release*.

The interesting point here is that *from* can be omitted from a (FROM) ING complement following some negative MAKING verbs, and its omission carries a semantic difference. *I prevented her going* would be likely to be used when I employed some direct means, e.g. I blocked her path. In contrast, *I prevented her from going* would be the appropriate thing to say if I used indirect means, e.g. *I used my influence to make sure she didn't get her passport renewed.* ORDER verbs, such as *dissuade*, must include *from*, and this is at least partly because such verbs refer to the use of speech to bring about some result, which is necessarily an indirect means. (The other part of the reason may be syntactic— the fact that (57) relates to a post-object complement clause, and (60) to a complement clause in object function.)

The semantic effect of omitting *from* is very similar to that of omitting *to* from Modal (FOR) TO clauses, discussed in §7.2.5. In each case the loss of a preposition implies a direct link between the referents of main clause and complement clause verbs. Note that, like *to*, *from* may be omitted from an active clause but is always likely to be retained in the passive, e.g. *She was prevented from going*, but scarcely **She was prevented going*.

7.2.10. Summary

The main points from our discussion of the meanings of kinds of complement clauses are:

THAT complements refer to some assertable activity or state as a single unit, without any reference to its inherent constitution or time duration.

WH- complements relate to some aspect of an assertable activity or state (again, treated as a single unit), about which clarification is needed.

ING complements refer to some activity or state as extended in time, perhaps noting the way in which it unfolds.

Modal (FOR) TO complements relate to (the potentiality of) the subject of the complement clause becoming involved in the state or activity referred to by that clause.

Judgement TO complements refer to a judgement or opinion which the main clause subject makes, through the complement clause, generally relating to a state or property of the subject of that clause.

WH- TO complements effectively combine the meanings of WH- and Modal (FOR) TO, referring to some activity in which the subject will get involved, and about some aspect of which clarification is required. (All verbs that take WH- TO also take WH- complements.)

(FROM) ING complements relate to the subject of the main clause doing something so that the subject of the complement clause does not become involved in the activity or state referred to by that clause.

THAT or WH- complements must show tense inflection and may include a Modal. The other five varieties of complement clause do not take tense inflection, although past can be coded through the *have* auxiliary. With certain verbs the time reference of an ING complement is not stated, but can often be inferred from the meaning of the verb (e.g. future with *propose*, past with *regret*). Many verbs which take a Modal (FOR) TO complement also accept a THAT clause, and then the meaning of the Modal (FOR) TO construction is generally similar—though not identical—to a THAT construction where the complement clause includes a Modal. All verbs that take Judgement TO also accept a THAT complement, and the meaning of the Judgement TO construction is similar to the meaning of a THAT construction which does not include a Modal.

THAT and WH- complements must contain an overt subject. For Judgement TO and (FROM) ING the underlying complement clause subject must be included, but is coded as surface object of the main verb. A WH- TO complement must have its subject coreferential with main clause subject or object, and then omitted. ING and Modal (FOR) TO complements may omit their subject NP when it is coreferential with an NP in appropriate function in the main clause (*for* then also drops). With some main verbs this omission is obligatory, with some it is optional, and with others it is not allowed.

A Modal (FOR) TO complement may, when it directly follows a transitive main verb, drop the *for*; complement clause subject then becomes surface direct object of the main verb. *For* is omitted when the subject of the complement clause is directly affected by the activity referred to by the main verb. *To* from a Modal (FOR) TO and *from* from a (FROM) ING complement may be omitted after some verbs (and *to* must be after others) when there is a direct link between the activity referred to by the main verb and that referred to by the complement clause verb.

7.3 Complement clauses with Secondary verbs

Leaving aside Modals, Secondary verb constructions in English show a non-alignment between syntax and semantics. The Secondary verb is syntactically the main verb but from a semantic point of view it modifies the verb of the complement clause, which is the semantic focus of the sentence.

The kinds of semantic relation between a Secondary verb and the verb in the subordinate clause can be coded—in semantically appropriate ways—by THAT, ING, Modal (FOR) TO and (FROM) ING complement constructions. Secondary verbs of types A, B and C do not show WH- or WH- TO complements since they provide semantic qualification of another verb, which is incompatible with seeking clarification; and they do not occur in Judgement TO constructions since they do not delineate opinion or judgement. The Secondary-D types have somewhat different properties—SEEM may occur in a special kind of Judgement TO construction, and MATTER may occur with a WH- complement.

7.3.1. MODALS and SEMI-MODALS

The SEMI-MODALS—*be going to, have to, have got to, be able to, be about to, get to* and *be bound to*—could on syntactic grounds be regarded as main verbs taking a Modal (FOR) TO complement clause (with subject that is coreferential with the main clause subject and thus omitted), similar to *attempt* or *fail*. The main reason for our linking them with MODALS lies in the semantic parallels between *will* and *be going to, must* and *have (got) to, can* and *be able to*.

But we did demonstrate a recurrent semantic difference, in examples (1a/b), (2a/b) and (3a/b) of §6.1.1. MODALS tend to indicate prediction, ability, necessity, etc. under specific circumstances, while SEMI-MODALS are more likely to have an 'unconditional' sense and relate to the subject's involvement in an activity. Compare (61a), with MODAL *must*, and (61b), with SEMI-MODAL *have to*:

(61a) *You mustn't mind what he says when he's drunk*
(61b) *You have to watch out for muggers after dark in the midtown area*

It is thus entirely appropriate for all SEMI-MODALS to include *to*, in terms of the meaning of the Modal (FOR) TO complement discussed in the last section.

In §§6.1.5 and 6.2.1 we illustrated the two uses of *dare* and of *need*. When used to refer to some general circumstance (almost always in questions and negatives) they may behave syntactically like MODALS, e.g.

(62) *No one dare question my credentials*

But when *need* and *dare* refer to a definite subject becoming involved in some activity, then they behave like a non-MODAL and take complementiser *to* (although this may sometimes be omitted), e.g.

(63) *That man dared (to) question my credentials*

Just three of the fifteen MODALS include *to*. This is semantically appropriate with *be to*, a verb which most often has a human subject who is scheduled to become involved in an activity, e.g. *I am to call on the Vice-Chancellor tomorrow*. However, it is hard to discern any semantic reason for the *to* of *ought to* and *used to*; we should perhaps search for a historical explanation in these instances.

7.3.2. BEGINNING, TRYING, HURRYING and DARING

A Secondary-A verb shares all the semantic roles of the verb it modifies. It is thus, on a priori syntactic grounds, restricted to a choice from ING and Modal (FOR) TO, the only complement types that may omit the complement clause subject when it is coreferential with main clause subject. In fact, these two complement constructions reflect the semantic possibilities of a Secondary-A verb: an ING clause is used when the Secondary verb construction refers to an activity taking place over a period of time, and a reduced Modal (FOR) TO complement is used in a construction that refers to the subject's getting involved in an activity.

The semantic contrast between ING and Modal (FOR) TO complements with Secondary-A verbs is illustrated at (52a/b) of §7.2.7, (1a/b), (2a/b) of §6.1.3 and in:

(64a) *Mary tried telling that joke about nuns (but no one laughed)*

(64b) *Mary tried to tell that joke about nuns (but forgot how it went)*

(65a) *Fred started hitting Mary (but she cried so much he stopped)*

(65b) *Fred started to hit Mary (but checked himself before actually delivering the blow)*

(66a) *John continued painting the wall (despite all distractions)*

(66b) *John continued to paint the wall (after that interruption)*

Sentence (64a) implies that Mary did tell the joke (or a good part of it); hearing (64b) one might infer that, despite her best efforts, Mary wasn't able properly to become involved in telling it. Sentence (65a) implies that Fred hit Mary for a period; (65b) could be used if he raised his stick, ready to bring it down on her head— if nothing else were said one would assume that he did hit her at least once, but the sentence could be continued as in the parenthesis of (65b). Sentence (66a) states that John carried on with an established activity, rather than stopping it, whereas (66b) might be used when he become involved again after having stopped.

All BEGINNING verbs can take an ING complement. Members of this type refer to the inception, continuation or ending of some continuous activity referred to by the verb of the complement clause. *Begin, start, continue, go on* and *cease* also occur with TO complements, whereas *commence, keep (on), finish, stop, complete* and *discontinue* do not. For most (perhaps all) of these verbs there is a semantic explanation as to why they do not take TO.

As discussed in §6.1.2, *finish* has 'object orientation'; in *John has finished peeling the potatoes* the activity terminates because the potatoes are all peeled. It would not be appropriate to use a Modal (FOR) TO construction, since this must relate to the subject's involvement in (here, finishing) an activity. *Cease*, in contrast, relates to an activity terminating because of something to do with the subject—he withdraws involvement; so we could, conceivably, say *He ceased to shell the peas*.

Commence and *complete* are also object-oriented, referring to some definite and significant piece of work, and must take an ING clause referring to the durative activity needed to achieve the work. *Keep (on (with))* implies uninterrupted pursuit of some task, and is restricted to ING. *Continue (with)* and *go on (with)* can refer to an activity continuing without a break and then take ING, as in (66a). Or they can—unlike *keep* (*on* (*with*))—refer to something being re-started, and may then take Modal (FOR) TO, as in (66b).

Cease, *stop* and *discontinue* have rather similar meanings, but there are also crucial differences. As discussed in §6.1.2, *cease* can imply 'gradually falling away', e.g. *My faith gradually faded during those adolescent years and I finally ceased to believe in God on my sixteenth birthday. Stop* tends to refer to something terminating rather abruptly, e.g. *I stopped believing anything Reagan said after the Iran–Contra business became public.* But this does not explain why *stop* should not take a TO complement. The crucial factor here may be syntactic interference from the intransitive REST verb *stop*, which typically takes an (*in order*) *to* construction; thus *stop* in *I stopped to eat* is always identified as the REST verb, not the BEGINNING one.

Discontinue has subject orientation, like *cease* and *continue*, and on these grounds would be expected to take a Modal (FOR) TO complement. Interestingly, most verbs commencing with the negative prefix *dis-* may not take any kind of TO complement clause, even though the corresponding positive verb does—compare *agree/disagree*, *believe/disbelieve*, *claim/disclaim*, *like/dislike*, *prove/disprove*, *allow/disallow* and *persuade/dissuade*, *encourage/discourage*. This lack may be in some way connected with the meanings of *dis-* and of TO complement constructions.

Turning now to the TRYING type, we mentioned in §6.1.3 that *try* itself has two different senses. The first, which correlates with a Modal (FOR) TO complement, relates to the subject making efforts to get involved in some activity (but not necessarily being able to). The second, which takes an ING complement, relates to him engaging in it for a sample period.

As their meanings were described in §6.1.3, *attempt*, *manage*—and *fail*, in many contexts—all imply considerable effort on the part of the subject, which is why they are found most often with a Modal (FOR) TO complement (although *attempt* and *manage* are, occasionally, used in an ING construction). *Succeed* and *miss* have a wider, more general meaning—it is possible to succeed with scarcely any effort, and one can miss (e.g. seeing someone) entirely by chance; only the ING complement is compatible with these meanings. The semantic difference between *fail* and *miss* is brought out in *He just failed to run her over* (i.e. he tried to kill her, but didn't manage it), where a Modal (FOR) TO clause indicates volition, and *He just missed running her over* (he didn't intend to hit her, but she seemed just to step in front of the car and he had to swerve), where the choice of an ING clause shows that the subject did not attempt to get involved in the deed.

Practise refers to a continuous activity, which must be described by an ING clause. *Repeat* refers to a complete activity being done again; once more ING is, on semantic grounds, the appropriate choice.

Looking now at the HURRYING type, *hurry* (*over/with*) takes both ING and Modal (FOR) TO complement clauses:

(67a) *Tom hurried over eating his dinner*
(67b) *Tom hurried to eat up his dinner*

Sentence (67a) would be used appropriately to describe Tom eating quickly right through the meal, whereas (67b) might describe him hurrying only towards the end, perhaps when he realised that it would be taken away if he didn't eat everything before the bell sounded. (The inclusion of *up* adds a perfective sense; (67b) has a very similar meaning to *Tom hurried to finish eating his dinner*.) An ING clause is likely to describe the subject doing something fast over the whole duration of an activity, whereas a Modal (FOR) TO clause is likely to describe the subject doing something fast to reach a particular goal. *Hasten* (*over/with*) has a similar meaning to *hurry* (*over/with*) (see §6.1.4) but is more often used to describe an action directed towards a goal, and is thus more often found with a Modal (FOR) TO complement (although ING is also possible). *Dawdle* (*over*) refers to doing something slowly over the whole duration of the activity, and is restricted to an ING construction.

Hesitate (*over/with*) relates to uncertainty on the part of the subject over whether to engage in some activity, referred to by the complement clause. When an ING complement is used the unmarked implication is that the subject did undertake the activity, e.g. *She hesitated over writing the letter* (*but eventually she did write it*). When a Modal (FOR) TO complement is used a listener might understand—if nothing else were said—that the subject did not in the end get involved in the activity, e.g. *She hesitated to write the letter herself* (*and finally prevailed upon her mother to write it for her*).

Dare, and *venture*, from the DARING type, indicate that the subject has sufficient courage to become involved in some activity; they are thus naturally restricted to a Modal (FOR) TO complement construction. (And *dare* can also be used like a Modal, with no *to*, to describe some general circumstance—see §7.3.1.)

7.3.3. WANTING and POSTPONING

These two Secondary-B types both introduce one role (the subject of the Secondary verb) in addition to the roles of the verb in the complement clause: this is the Principal role for WANTING, and the Timer role for POSTPONING.

A WANTING verb describes the Principal's attitude towards the event or state described by the complement clause. This can be expressed through a THAT complement clause (usually including a Modal), or through a Modal (FOR) TO clause. Compare:

(68a) *I'm hoping* (*that*) *John won't fight the bully*
(68b) *I'm hoping for John to beat up the bully*

The Modal (FOR) TO construction, in (68b), is appropriate when the Principal would like to see the subject of the complement clause get involved in the activity described by that clause. The THAT construction, in (68a), is more neutral, and might be preferred when the Principal just wished for a certain result.

A WANTING verb frequently deals with the Principal's attitude towards something that he is involved in. The complement subject can be omitted (together with *for*) from a Modal (FOR) TO clause when it is coreferential with main clause subject. A THAT clause, of course, can never omit the subject. Thus:

(69a) *I'm hoping that I will be allowed to visit him in jail*
(69b) *I'm hoping to be allowed to visit him in jail*

The Modal (FOR) TO alternative is frequently preferred, in such circumstances, simply because it does allow subject omission. Indeed, if a verb like *hope* or *wish* has coreferential subjects and the subject controls the activity referred to by the complement clause (which it does not in (69a/b)), then only a Modal (FOR) TO complement may be allowed—(70a), but not (70b):

(70a) *I hope to visit him in jail*
(70b) **I hope that I will visit him in jail*

Note that although a coreferential complement clause subject is generally omitted after a WANTING verb, it can be included, usually in a situation of special emphasis, e.g. *I didn't want John to be chosen, I wanted MYSELF (or ME) to be chosen.*

Some WANTING verbs allow *for* to be retained; the complement clause subject then does not become surface object of the Secondary verb. We mentioned in §7.2.4 that *for* tends to be omitted when the Principal is communicating his attitude directly to the complement clause subject, and to be retained when the attitude is expressed more indirectly. Compare (42a/43a), (44a/b) in §7.2.4, and also:

(71a) *I hadn't intended for you to find out about the party until your actual birthday*
(71b) *I had intended you to overhear what we were saying*

Sentences (72a–c) contrast three constructions with *wish*: (72a), a Modal (FOR) TO with the *for* retained, relates to the Principal's (lack of need for any) desire that John should make an effort to behave better; (72b), with the *for* omitted after *wish*, is used to describe the Principal telling John this, quite directly; (72c), with a THAT clause, expresses a general wish concerning John's behaviour.

(72a) *I couldn't have wished for John to behave any better*
(72b) *I told John that I wished him to improve his manners*
(72c) *I wish that John would improve his manners*

The meanings of some verbs from the WANTING type are such that they can only be used in an indirect manner (as in (68b)). These verbs—*hope, long, pine, wait, plan, aim, prepare, crave, deserve, dread*—always include *for* before the subject of a Modal (FOR) TO clause. *Demand* behaves in a similar way—we can say *I demand that you (should) resign*, but only *I demand for you to resign*; for a direct, pragmatic communication to the complement clause subject a verb like *order* is preferred, e.g. *I order you to resign*, rather than **I demand you to resign*.

A second set of verbs from this type can either include or omit *for*; it includes *wish, desire, intend, mean, pretend*. A final set have meanings which imply a direct communication of the attitude, and these verbs—*want, need, require, expect*—omit *for* from a Modal (FOR) TO complement when it immediately follows the main verb. They can, however, retain the *for* when an adverb intervenes, e.g. *I want very much for Mary to win* (but only *I want Mary to win*, not —in most dialects—**I want for Mary to win*). And when the complement clause is syntactically 'dislocated' from its main verb, the *for* may optionally be included, e.g. *I need Mary to help me, not (for) John to help me*.

We can now discuss the meanings of some of the individual verbs in the type, as they relate to the choice of complementiser. *Want* is directly pragmatic, relating to the Principal's attitude towards the complement clause subject getting involved in some activity regarded as achievable, e.g. *I want Mary to sing*. Because of this *want* is restricted to a Modal (FOR) TO construction; it is one of the few WANTING verbs not to take a THAT clause. *Wish* may have a wistful sense, relating to something that is not possible, and then takes a THAT complement (usually with past tense, perfect aspect or a 'subjunctive' modal such as *would* or *could*), e.g. *I wish (that) Mary could sing (but I know that she can't, after the throat operation)*. Interestingly, when *wish* is used with a Modal (FOR) TO clause it takes on a quite different sense, becoming more peremptory and authoritarian than *want*, e.g. *The Queen wishes you to sing*. This may be because Modal (FOR) TO is the 'marked' complement choice for *wish*, and thus has a 'marked' meaning. *Long (for)* and *crave (for)* describe emotional attitudes of great intensity, and in view of this they are almost restricted to Modal (FOR) TO complements.

Need also has a strongly pragmatic meaning, being typically used to say what should be done, to a person who could be expected to do it; like *want*, it cannot take a THAT complement but is restricted to Modal (FOR) TO, e.g. *I need you to wash up for me (since I've got a rash on my hands)*. *Require* tends to be used for an impersonal or institutional obligation on the subject of the complement clause to become involved in an activity, and is often used in the passive with a Modal (FOR) TO complement, e.g. *You are required to sign here*. It may also refer to some general instruction, through a THAT clause, e.g. *The duchess requires that her sheets be changed each day*.

Aim (*for*) differs semantically from *intend* in implying a single-mindedness of purpose—this is why it is typically used in a Modal (FOR) TO construction with coreferential subjects (and thus omission of complement clause subject), e.g. *I aim to win*, as against *I intended Mary to win*. *Prepare* relates to the complement clause subject becoming involved in an activity and is—like *want* and *need*—restricted to a Modal (FOR) TO construction, e.g. *I am preparing for John to bring his new bride home to meet me*.

All WANTING verbs take a Modal (FOR) TO complement. All save *want*, *need* and *prepare* take a THAT complement. An ING complement clause (whose subject must be coreferential with main clause subject, and then omitted) is possible with those verbs which relate to the Principal's thought that he will do a certain thing in the future—*intend*, *plan*, and also *prepare for*, *aim at*. Compare:

(73a) *He is planning to build a rockery*
(73b) *He is planning building a rockery*

Sentence (73a), with a Modal (FOR) TO complement, just states that he has the idea of 'getting involved' in putting in a rockery; (73b), with an ING complement, suggests that he is thinking of the details of the activity—where it will go, how to build the stones up, and so on.

Verbs in the POSTPONING type generally refer to some activity with temporal extent, and thus naturally take ING complements, e.g. *I delayed writing the letter, The Prime Minister put off meeting the union leaders*. Alternatively, an ACTIVITY or SPEECH ACT noun may fill the O slot, e.g. *He put off the meeting*. Verbs from this type do not take a THAT complement, simply because they refer to a projected event, not to the fact of an event, i.e. not **He delayed that he would write the letter*.

7.3.4. MAKING and HELPING

Positive verbs from the MAKING type refer to the Causer (main clause subject) doing something so that the complement clause subject becomes involved in the activity referred to by that clause. For verbs from the HELPING type the Helper (again, main clause subject) joins in with the complement clause subject to bring about some event. Both of these semantic specifications are compatible only with a Modal (FOR) TO construction, and one where the *for* is omitted.

Both main and complement clause subjects are typically human, although either can be inanimate, e.g. *The flooded river forced/ caused me to change my plans*, and *He made/let the marble roll into the hole*. The Causer or Helper is unlikely to be coreferential with complement clause subject; when it is, the latter cannot be omitted, e.g. *I made/let myself eat the chocolates*, not **I made/let eat the chocolates*.

Help may omit *to*, implying a direct link between the referents of main and complement clause verbs, or retain it, in the case of an indirect link (§§7.2.5, 6.3.2). *Make* and *let* imply a direct link and must omit *to* in an active sentence. As an illustration, compare *let* with *permit* and *allow* which do take *to* since they can both refer to indirect sanction, e.g. *Standing orders don't allow/permit you to enter the hangars*. One could scarcely say **Standing orders don't let you enter the hangars*, although *The Squadron Leader won't let you enter the hangars* is fine since it relates to direct interaction between Causer and complement clause subject.

As mentioned in §7.2.5 we would—on semantic grounds— expect *force* to omit the *to*, whereas it always retains it; and we would expect the causative sense of *have* to retain the *to*, whereas it always omits it.

Negative verbs from the MAKING type take a (FROM) ING complement, in keeping with their meaning. As described in §7.2.9, the *from* can be omitted—in much the same way that *to* can be omitted after *help*—when direct means of coercion are employed.

Ensure stands out from other MAKING verbs in that it can simply refer to the 'Causer' checking the fact of something being in a certain state; it may not matter who put it in that state. This meaning of *ensure* demands a THAT complement, referring to an 'assertable event or state', e.g. *She ensured that all the windows were open*.

7.3.5. SEEM and MATTER

A verb from the SEEM type may function like a copula, being followed by an adjective and with a complement clause in subject

function. As mentioned in §6.4.1, the complement clause possibilities are determined by the adjective. The semantic profiles of
complement clauses described in this chapter still apply. Thus, a
Modal (FOR) TO clause is appropriate when the complement clause
subject is to get involved in some activity, e.g. *It appears to be*
normal for the captain to lead his team onto the field. A THAT clause
is likely for describing some state of affairs, e.g. *It seems curious*
that Mary went. And an ING clause may be chosen to describe a
durational activity, e.g. *John's walking to work this morning seems*
strangely out of character.

SEEM verbs can also occur without an adjective, followed by a
THAT clause and with impersonal *it* in subject slot, as in (74a),
(75a). There is a corresponding Judgement TO construction in
which the complement clause subject replaces *it* as surface subject
of the SEEM verb, as in (74b), (75b).

(74a) *It seems that Fred wants to go*
(74b) *Fred seems to want to go*
(75a) *It seems that Tom is stupid*
(75b) *Tom seems (to be) stupid*

Note that, as is normal with Judgement TO constructions, (74b)
and (75b) correspond to THAT constructions with no Modals, in
(74a), (75a). If a Modal were inserted in a sentence like (75a), e.g.
It seems that Tom may/must/could be stupid, then there is no
corresponding TO construction.

There is an important difference between a Judgement TO
construction with a SEEM verb, as in (74b), (75b), and a Modal
(FOR) TO clause in subject relation (and extraposable) before a
SEEM verb, acting as copula, and an adjective, e.g. *It seems unusual*
for him to come home so late. If such a Modal (FOR) TO clause could
be replaced by a THAT complement—with similar meaning—then
the latter would often include a Modal, e.g. *It seems unusual that*
he should come home so late.

Matter, and *count*, from the MATTER type, relate to the fact of
some event, not to any potentiality of involvement, or to the
durational detail of an activity. They are in view of this restricted
to a THAT or WH- complement clause, e.g. *That John cheated*
matters a lot to his mother, and *It matters to me who gets to deliver*
that speech.

7.4. Complement clauses with Primary-B verbs, and with adjectives

Complement clauses can function as subject for verbs from the ANNOYING type, as object for LIKING, ATTENTION, THINKING and DECIDING, and in either object or post-object slot for SPEAKING. Some adjectives can take a complement clause in subject and others in post-predicate position. Only some verbs from the COMPARING and RELATING types may (like some verbs from MAKING and HELPING) have complement clauses in both subject and object relations.

7.4.1. ATTENTION

Verbs in the ATTENTION type have a number of special properties that set them off—semantically and syntactically—from other types. Firstly, they are generally used to describe the Perceiver seeing or hearing something outside himself. The subject of a complement clause will normally be different from the main clause subject. And in the rare instances when it is the same it must still be stated; that is, ATTENTION verbs do not permit omission of a coreferential subject from ING or Modal (FOR) TO complement clauses, e.g. *I heard myself telling a story on the radio*, not **I heard telling a story on the radio*.

Secondly, one may become aware of some activity—using sight or hearing—either directly or indirectly. With ATTENTION verbs, THAT complements are used to refer to indirect knowledge. Compare *I heard that John let off the fireworks* (i.e. I heard someone recounting this piece of news) with *I heard John letting off the fireworks* (i.e. I heard it happening). And also *I noticed that Mary had hit Jane* (I may have seen Mary grasping a blood-stained stick, and Jane holding her head and weeping, and thus drawn this conclusion) with *I noticed Mary hitting Jane* (I saw the actual blows).

Some ATTENTION verbs take a Modal (FOR) TO complement, which of course relates to direct perception of the complement clause subject becoming involved in the activity. Since, for this type, THAT clauses refer only to indirect perception we do not get the meaning similarity between a Modal (FOR) TO and a THAT-including-Modal complement, which was noted in §7.2.3 for verbs from other types.

Modal (FOR) TO complements with ATTENTION verbs must omit the *for* and also—in an active sentence—the *to*. Compare the Modal (FOR) TO construction in (76a), with the ING construction in (76b):

(76a) *I saw John jump across the stream*
(76b) *I saw John('s) jumping across the stream*

(The *'s* on the subject of an ING complement clause after an ATTENTION verb is often omitted; it cannot generally be included after an inanimate subject e.g. *I saw it (*s) raining.* See §2.7 (and §5.1).

An ING complement refers to some durative activity; (76b) might be used when John was seen crossing the stream by jumping from one stepping-stone to the next. Sentence (76a) states that I saw John get involved in the act of jumping across the stream; the details are immaterial—(76a) could relate to a single jump that took him clear across, or to a series of jumps.

We described (in §7.2.4) how, when the activity referred to by the main clause relates directly to the subject of a Modal (FOR) TO complement clause in object function, then *for* should drop, with the complement clause subject becoming surface object of the main verb. This semantic condition plainly prevails with ATTENTION verbs; hence, *for* cannot be included. In §7.2.5 we saw that the *to* is omitted when there is a direct connection between the referents of main clause and complement clause verbs. This connection holds in (76a)—which describes direct perception—and so *to* must be omitted. Note though that *to* has to be included in the passive version of (76a), i.e. *John was seen to jump across the stream.* A passive provides an adjective-like description which lacks the pragmatic immediacy of the active (it is almost 'John was in a state of being seen . . .') so that *to* is not omitted.

In §5.1 we distinguished seven subtypes of ATTENTION . The LOOK class—with *look (at), stare (at), hunt (for)* and so on—refers to the Perceiver directing his attention onto some Impression, which will be an NP, not a complement clause; some verbs in this subtype (*investigate, examine, check, explore*) may relate to the Perceiver directing his attention to uncovering some information, that can be realised through a WH- clause, e.g. *He investigated whether she was dead/who had killed her.*

The SEE subtype involves straightforward description of an act of perception. SHOW describes how one person assists another to see or hear something. RECOGNISE relates to perceiving something and knowing what it is, and DISCOVER to perceiving something that was not apparent before. Verbs from these four subtypes take THAT and WH- complements, and also Judgement TO clauses, e.g.

(77a) *I saw/recognised/discovered that he was their leader*
(77b) *I saw/recognised/discovered him to be their leader*

Only SEE and SHOW may relate to a durative activity and thus only verbs from these subtypes accept ING clauses. The Modal (FOR) TO complement construction (with both *for* and *to* omitted in the active) occurs most commonly with the SEE subtype, dealing with a straightforward act of perception.

Witness, making up a subtype on its own, must describe some activity, rather than a state. It takes THAT, WH- and ING clauses, but not Judgement TO. *Watch* refers to deliberate perception over a period of time. It is generally found with an ING clause (e.g. *I watched John building the wall*), although a Modal (FOR) TO is also possible in the active (*I watched John build the wall*) but not in the passive (**John was watched (to) build the wall*).

Watch, and the sense of *listen* (*to*) that belongs to the WATCH subtype, may also take a THAT (or WH-) complement, but with a quite different meaning from the 'indirect knowledge' sense of THAT with SEE, SHOW, RECOGNISE and DISCOVER . A THAT clause with *watch* or *listen* (*to*) simply relates to the fact of some event, with an instruction to ensure that it does or doesn't take place; compare the THAT complement in *You watch that the soup doesn't boil*, with the ING clause in *You watch the soup boiling*. (Significantly, *watch* and *listen* are perhaps the only verbs from the ATTENTION, THINKING and DECIDING types which take a THAT construction but may not be used in a parenthetical—see §7.1.)

7.4.2. THINKING

This type includes verbs of thinking, knowing, believing and the like. They typically refer to some unit of information, which can be realised as a THAT, WH-, WH- TO or Judgement TO complement. Thus, *I thought that it would rain today*, *She forgot whether she had turned the stove off*, *We pondered over who to appoint*, *She believed him to be handsome*.

The ASSUME subtype and positive members of the BELIEVE class must refer to something quite definite, and thus cannot take WH- or WH- TO complements. Compare with verbs from CONCLUDE, which can indicate that a conclusion has been reached without necessarily revealing what it is; thus *We believe that John did it*, but not **We believe who did it*, as against *We have inferred that John did it* and *We have inferred who did it*. *Doubt*, a negative member of BELIEVE, takes *whether* (and also THAT) clauses—see §7.2.1.

Verbs from the PONDER subtype refer to modes of thinking; they typically take WH- complements, e.g. *We speculated over who might have killed him*, *They brooded over whether to go or not*. Most of these verbs will seldom (or never) occur with THAT complements—referring to some definite fact—or with Judgement TO clauses. *Forget* and *doubt*, because of their inherently negative meanings, are seldom found with Judgement TO—thus *I remembered/believed her to be polite* but not **I forgot/doubted her to be polite* (although some speakers can say *I'd forgotten him to be so tall*).

Verbs in the THINK, PONDER and REMEMBER subtypes, and *understand* from KNOW—but not ASSUME, CONCLUDE, SOLVE, BELIEVE and the remainder of KNOW—may relate to some continuous activity, by means of an ING complement, e.g. *I thought of/pondered over/remembered her building that wall all by herself*. If the complement clause subject is coreferential with main clause subject it will be omitted, e.g. *I thought of/remembered building that wall all by myself*. The potential semantic contrast between THAT (referring to some specific event or state) and ING (referring to something extended in time) is brought out in:

(78a) *I can understand that Mary was upset* (*when her spectacles broke*)

(78b) *I can understand Mary('s) being upset* (*all this year, because of the legal fuss over her divorce*)

Remember, *forget*, *know* and *learn* may relate to the complement clause subject getting involved in some activity, described by a Modal (FOR) TO complement, e.g. *I remembered/knew for Mary to take a pill after breakfast yesterday*. One most commonly remembers etc.

something that one should do oneself; complement clause subject will then be coreferential with main clause subject and will be omitted (together with *for*), in the same way that the coreferential subject of an ING clause is omitted—thus *I remembered/knew to take a pill after breakfast yesterday*. For *teach*, a lexical causative related to *know* (see §5.2), the subject of the complement clause—which is in post-object slot—is omitted when coreferential with main clause object, e.g. *I taught Mary to take a pill after breakfast each day*. *Think* can also be used with a Modal (FOR) TO complement in marked circumstances (typically, in a question or a negative clause), e.g. *Did you think to lock the door?* or *I didn't think to lock the door* (but scarcely **I thought to lock the door*).

7.4.3. DECIDING

Decide (on) and related verbs have two senses: (*a*) a reasoned judgement about the present or past, e.g. *I decided that it was too cold to cycle to work today*; and (*b*) an intention regarding the future, e.g. *I decided that I would drive instead*. They may take THAT or WH- complement clauses in both senses. Corresponding to sense (*b*) there can be a Modal (FOR) TO or a WH- TO construction, e.g. *I decided to drive today*, *I'll decide when to drive*. The Decision-Maker most frequently thinks about something that concerns himself; complement clause subject (plus *for*) is omitted when it is coreferential with the main clause subject, as in the example just given. But it is possible for the subjects to differ, e.g. *I decided for Mary to make the sandwiches and John the scones*. The *for* may not then be omitted, after *decide*, *determine* or *resolve*, since the main verb relates to the complete activity referred to by the complement clause, not specifically to its subject. *Choose* can, however, be used to address the complement clause subject, as when addressing a class of children: *I choose Mary to carry the banner*; the *for* is then omitted (see also (44)–(45) in §2.7).

   Decide (on) and *determine (on)*—but not *resolve* or *choose*—can relate to some durational activity, and may then take an ING complement, e.g. *I decided/determined on re-laying the lawn while Mary is away on vacation in Florida*.

As mentioned in §7.4.2, most THINKING verbs may take a Judgement TO complement—compare *I think/know/believe that John is stupid* with *I think/know/believe John to be stupid*. The Judgement TO construction is only marginally acceptable with verbs from the CONCLUDE subtype of THINKING, e.g. *?I concluded/ inferred/argued John to be stupid*. It is quite unacceptable with DECIDING verbs, e.g. *I decided that John is stupid*, but not **I decided John to be stupid*. It seems that Judgement TO can only be related to some straightforward impression or opinion, not to the result of a process of reasoning.

7.4.4. SPEAKING

Verbs of this type cover a wide semantic spectrum, and take a corresponding diversity of complement clauses. It will be useful to deal with the subtypes one at a time. Note that all those verbs which may introduce direct speech can also show reported speech (in the Message role) through a THAT and/or a WH- complement clause.

TALK verbs—such as *talk*, *speak*, *chat*, *joke*—refer to the activity of social communication. They can introduce an ING or WH- clause by a preposition and this omits its subject when coreferential with main clause subject, e.g. *John spoke about (Mary('s)) leaving home*.

Verbs from the DISCUSS subtype are transitive, with the Message in O function. They report some activity (which is likely to be extended in time), or something about which clarification is required—coded by an ING or WH- or WH- TO clause, e.g. *They described the police rescuing the trapped child, We discussed whether to invite Mary*.

The SHOUT subtype refers to manner of vocal production. These verbs may be used intransitively, without any mention of the Message (or Addressee or Medium). But they can also introduce direct speech, or a THAT clause, or a Message consisting of Label NP plus preposition plus Content, which may be an ING or WH- complement clause. The Label can be omitted but the preposition must then be retained; this contrasts with verbs from the DISCUSS subtype where the preposition will drop with the Message-Label. Thus:

(79a) *They discussed/referred to (the news about) John('s) being arrested*

(79b) *He shouted/read (the news) about John ('s) being arrested*

The meanings of DISCUSS verbs relate to a specific Message (which must be stated); it can be a complement clause in O function. But the Message is an optional accompaniment of a SHOUT verb, and it is thus appropriate that any complement clause (as Message-Content) be introduced by a preposition. There is an important difference between *refer to* (in (79a)), which is a strictly transitive verb including an inherent preposition, and *shout* (in (79b)) which can optionally take an appropriate preposition plus complement clause or NP.

The REPORT subtype contains a fair number of verbs, which in §5.4 we divided into eight sets. Leaving aside for the time being set (viii) (with *promise* and *threaten*), REPORT verbs are transitive with the Message in O slot. This may always be a THAT or WH- clause, corresponding to direct speech.

Verbs *say, declare, state, affirm* (in sets (i) and (ii)) necessarily make an assertion, and are restricted to THAT or WH- complements. Other REPORT verbs may relate to some fact, or to a durational activity, and then accept an ING complement, e.g. *She reported/ commented on/boasted about/admitted (John's) having spent the past year in jail*. (With *confess (to)* the complement clause subject must be coreferential with main clause subject and thus omitted, simply because one can only confess to something one has done oneself, e.g. *He confessed to taking the gold*.)

A Judgement TO construction is possible with *declare, state, report, announce, claim, admit* and other verbs that can provide straightforward introduction to an opinion about someone's state, e.g. *They declared/admitted him to be insane*. (*Say*, from this subtype, may only take a Judgement TO construction in the passive, e.g. *He is said to be insane*.) The Judgement TO construction is not possible with verbs that include an inherent preposition, such as *remark (on), boast (about/of), complain (about/of)*—one must say *She boasted that he was clever* or *She boasted about him/his being clever*, not **She boasted (about) him to be clever*. (The prohibition may essentially relate to the meanings of verbs like *boast* and *complain*, which include an emotional component that would not accord well with the 'judgement' meaning of this TO construction.) *Explain* is another verb which is not allowed in a Judgement TO sentence (*She explained that he was ill*, not **She explained him to be ill*); the meaning of *explain* 'give reasons for something' is incompatible with the meaning of the Judgement TO complement 'give a judgement about something'.

Promise and *threaten* have the Addressee in O slot; this can be followed by *with* plus Message-Content, or a THAT clause, or direct speech. These verbs, plus *undertake*, *offer* and *propose* (which have the Message in O slot), may relate to the subject of the complement clause getting involved in the activity referred to by that clause, and this can be expressed through a Modal (FOR) TO complement. Since one generally promises/threatens/offers to do something oneself, the complement clause subject is most often coreferential with main clause subject and is then omitted, together with *for*, e.g. *I offered to clean the house.* All dialects allow a similar construction with *promise* and *threaten* when the Addressee NP is not stated, e.g. *I promised to clean the house.* Only some dialects permit this construction with *promise* when the Addressee is stated, e.g. *I promised John to clean the house* (dialects which exclude this are here restricted to a THAT construction, e.g. *I promised John that I would clean the house*). *Promise* is perhaps the only verb which—in some dialects—can freely omit the subject of a post-object Modal (FOR) TO clause when it is coreferential with main clause subject, i.e. in *I promised John to clean the house* it is I who will do the cleaning. All other verbs—e.g. *order, persuade, urge*—omit this NP when it is coreferential with main clause object, i.e. in *I ordered John to clean the house* it is John who should do the cleaning. It may be this surface similarity with *I ordered John to clean the house*—and the danger of semantic confusion—which has unconsciously motivated speakers of some dialects to consider *I promised John to clean the house* an ungrammatical sentence. (There are a couple of verbs which can omit the subject NP from a post-object Modal (FOR) TO complement when it is coreferential with the main clause subject, only if the complement clause is passive, e.g. *I asked/ begged John to be allowed to clean his house.*)

Undertake and *offer* may, exceptionally, have a Modal (FOR) TO clause with subject different from that of the main clause; *for* must then be retained—e.g. *I offered for my charwoman to clean the house.* Such a construction is infelicitous with *promise* and *threaten*, a THAT clause being used instead—thus *I promised (John)*

that my charwoman would clean the house, not **I promised (John)
for my charwoman to clean the house*.

The INFORM subtype has Addressee in O slot. The Message is
introduced by *of* or *on* or *about* (the preposition must drop before
a THAT and may drop before a WH- complement). These verbs may
relate to some fact (THAT), clarification (WH- or WH- TO), or
durational activity (ING complement), e.g. *Remind me that I have
to set the alarm*, *She'll inform us (about) whether (we have) to dress
for dinner*, *Fred informed Mary about John's having been waiting
outside her door all afternoon*. The basic construction for verbs
from the TELL type is with Addressee as O, followed by preposition
or or *about* plus Message, which can be a THAT, WH- or ING
complement, very much as for INFORM.

Verbs from the ORDER subtype relate to a Message directed at
the Addressee. The Addressee is in O slot, and is followed by the
Message which can be a THAT clause (generally including a Modal)
or a Modal (FOR) TO or WH- TO complement. Alternatively, the
Message may be direct speech. The Addressee may be omitted in
the presence of direct speech or a THAT clause. The complement
clause subject is sometimes not coreferential with main clause
object. If this is so then *for* must be retained in a Modal (FOR) TO
clause (recall that it may only be omitted when the complement
clause immediately follows the main clause verb), e.g. *The general
ordered all officers for their men to parade at dawn*. (A fair number
of speakers find this ungrammatical, and might instead use a THAT
construction, i.e. *The general ordered all officers that their men
should parade at dawn*.) Typically, someone is ordered or
instructed or recommended to do something himself (rather than
for someone else to do something); the expectation with ORDER
verbs is for the subject of a Modal (FOR) TO complement clause to
be coreferential with main clause object and then the complement
clause subject (and *for*) are omitted, e.g. *The general ordered all
officers to parade at dawn*. *Recommend*, from this subtype, offers
advice rather than instructions, and may then take an ING
complement (see §5.4).

There is a certain parallel between the Secondary verb type
MAKING and the ORDER subtype of SPEAKING, with Causer cor-
responding to Speaker and the complement clause with the
MAKING verb to the Message of the ORDER verb. Thus, *I forced John*

to go and *I ordered/persuaded John to go*. There are, however, significant differences. MAKING verbs involve action to bring about some event and are restricted to Modal (FOR) TO complements; ORDER verbs merely use speech to influence the Addressee and may also take THAT complements. Note also that there is an additional role with ORDER, the Addressee, which may be included before the complement clause, e.g. *I ordered/persuaded John that his wife should sign the declaration herself.*

Some ORDER verbs may have a passive complement clause with inanimate subject, e.g. *General Vasey ordered the barracks to be cleaned.* In fact he must have ordered the appropriate people to perform the task; the use of this construction focuses on what was done to the barracks, ignoring the insignificant matter of which particular minions did it. (From the MAKING type only *cause* behaves in this way, e.g. *He caused it to be destroyed.*)

Just like negative MAKING verbs, so negative ORDER verbs such as *prohibit, dissuade, discourage* (and, nowadays, *forbid*) take a (FROM) ING complement. Here the main clause object must be identical to complement clause subject—thus *John dissuaded Mary from going* is a close syntactic analogue of *John prevented Mary (from) going.*

The FORGIVE type conveys the speaker's emotional attitude towards the Addressee, which is often realised through speech. As discussed in §5.4, some verbs from this type may have an ING clause, introduced by a preposition, giving additional information about the attitude or the reason for it. Like TALK and DISCUSS, this subtype does not usually introduce direct speech (some minor exceptions were mentioned in §5.4), and cannot take a THAT or WH- complement clause.

7.4.5. LIKING, ANNOYING and adjectives

Verbs from the LIKING and ANNOYING types describe the feelings an Experiencer (who must be human) has about a Stimulus. For LIKING the Experiencer may control the activity, and is mapped onto subject function (e.g. *John tried to like Mary*). For ANNOYING the Experiencer has no possibility of control but in some circumstances control may lie with the Stimulus if it is human, and Stimulus is thus in subject relation (e.g. *Mary tried to please/annoy John*).

The Stimulus may be some object, referred to by an NP (e.g. *Mary hates horses*), or some habitual or durative activity, shown by an ING clause (*Mary hates riding horses*). Or it can involve Label-plus-preposition-plus-Content. The Label can be an NP with an abstract noun as head, or else just *it*; the Content can be an NP or a THAT, ING or Modal (FOR) TO complement clause.

A LIKING verb can relate just to the Experiencer's feelings about the fact of a certain thing happening (he may not be at all interested in the internal details of the event). A THAT complement is then appropriate, as in:

> (80a) *I like it that Mary sings the blues each Friday evening (because she goes out, and I get peace to work out a betting system for Saturday's races)*

Or the LIKING verb may relate to the Experiencer's feelings about some activity as it unfolds; ING is then the appropriate complement choice:

> (80b) *I like Mary('s) singing the blues (and could listen to her all night)*

Or, the Experiencer might have good (or bad) feelings about the complement clause subject's getting involved in an activity (without necessarily enjoying the activity per se); a Modal (FOR) TO complement would then be used:

> (80c) *I like (it for) Mary to sing the blues (because she makes a lot of money doing it)*
>
> (80d) *I would like Mary to sing the blues (because I think her voice is just right for that style—although in fact my own preference is for opera)*

In §7.2.4 we described how the *for* should be omitted when the emotional feeling described by the LIKING verb is directed particularly at the complement clause subject, rather than at the whole clause; *it* must then also drop, and the complement clause subject becomes surface object of the main verb. See examples (45a/b) in §7.2.4.

It is perfectly normal for the complement clause subject to be different from the main clause subject, or equally for them to be coreferential. In the latter case the complement clause subject drops from an ING or Modal (FOR) TO clause (and then *for* and *it* also drop), e.g. *I like singing the blues, I like to sing the blues*.

Only some LIKING verbs have the width of meaning that allows all three complement choices; they include *like, love, hate, prefer*. Other verbs—such as *loathe, admire, value, regret, (don't) care about*—can relate to feelings about the fact of some event or about a durational activity, but less readily to a potentiality of involvement; these are unlikely to be found with Modal (FOR) TO complements. A third set of LIKING verbs are pretty well restricted by their meanings to reference to durational activity and thus to an ING complement, e.g. *enjoy* 'get pleasure from something happening', *object to* 'take exception to something happening' (see the fuller list in §5.5). Finally, there are *worship* and *fall for*, which must have an entity (i.e. an NP, and not a complement clause) as Stimulus, e.g. *He worships Allah/money, She fell for him*.

Subject and object possibilities are effectively reversed between the LIKING and ANNOYING types. THAT, ING and Modal (FOR) TO complements may, as Stimulus, fill the subject slot for ANNOYING verbs. Complement clause subject can be omitted when it is coreferential with main clause subject, from an ING or a Modal (FOR) TO clause (the *for* also drops). THAT and Modal (FOR) TO complements can be extraposed to the end of the main clause with *it* then filling subject slot. Note that *for* can never be omitted when complement clause subject is retained (even under extraposition) —see the discussion of syntactic and semantic conditions on *for* omission in §§2.7 and 7.2.4.

The same semantic principles apply as with LIKING. An ANNOYING verb can relate to the Experiencer's feelings about the fact of some event, referred to by a THAT clause:

(81a) *That Phil is now dating Sue surprises me/It surprises me that Phil is now dating Sue*

Or it can refer to an ongoing activity, referred to by an ING clause:

(81b) *Fred('s) telling jokes all evening entertained us greatly*

Or to the potentiality of someone's getting involved in some activity,

(81c) *It would please me for John to marry Mary*
(81d) *It might confuse you to try to learn three new languages all at the same time*

When there is a Modal (FOR) TO clause as Stimulus—with an

ANNOYING or a LIKING verb—the main clause predicate often includes a Modal, as in (80d), (81c), (81d). Indeed, there is often also a Semi-Modal in the Modal (FOR) TO clause (which, of course, cannot include a Modal), as in:

(82) *To have to carry a fifty-kilo pack on my back would exhaust me*

The ANNOYING type carries a wide semantic range (far broader than LIKING), e.g. *scare, surprise, offend, delight, amuse, worry, annoy, anger, puzzle, interest, disgust, tire*. It seems that all these verbs have the potential for taking all three kinds of subject complement; but most do have preferences that are determined by their individual meanings, e.g. *surprise* is perhaps most used with a THAT clause, *satisfy* with an ING complement.

Turning now to Adjectives, we find that the VALUE type and a number of subtypes of HUMAN PROPENSITY have similar meanings and complement possibilities to ANNOYING and LIKING verbs (see §3.2). *Fond of*). from HUMAN PROPENSITY, refers to a durational activity and thus takes an ING clause, similar to *enjoy*, e.g. *She's fond of listening to Bach, She enjoys listening to Bach*.

Adjectives from the ANGRY, HAPPY and UNSURE subtypes have similar meanings to the past participles of ANNOYING verbs. The UNSURE set involve the speaker's assessment about some potential event and are confined to THAT or WH- complements, e.g. *I'm certain that a crime was committed but I'm unsure (about) who to blame*. The ANGRY subtype—including *angry (about), jealous (of), mad (about)*—describe an emotional reaction to some definite happening (either the fact of an event, or some durational activity), and may take a THAT or ING complement, e.g. *Fred was angry that Mary resigned, I'm sad about John's digging up the flower garden*. Verbs from the HAPPY subtype—including *anxious (about), happy (about), afraid (of)*—deal with an emotional response to some actual or potential happening; besides THAT and ING they may also take a Modal (FOR) TO complement, relating to the potentiality of complement clause subject becoming involved in an event, e.g. *I'd be happy/afraid (for Mary) to cross the desert alone*.

VALUE adjectives provide a judgement about some unit event or durational activity and may take a THAT or ING clause in subject function, e.g. *It is good that Mary plays hockey*, *Flying kites is amusing*; subset (*b*) (see §3.2) may also have a Modal (FOR) TO subject complement, e.g. *It was strange for Mary to resign like that*. Some VALUE adjectives are similar in meaning and syntax to ANNOYING verbs, except that the latter relate the emotional judgement to a specific Experiencer (in object slot), whereas VALUE adjectives purport to give an objective, impersonal judgement—compare the examples just given with *It pleases her uncle that Mary plays hockey*, *Flying kites amuses some people*, *It puzzled me for Mary to resign like that*. Compare also *That John likes Bach is curious/surprising* with *That John likes Bach interests/ surprises me*.

Adjectives from the EAGER subtype of HUMAN PROPENSITY are similar in meaning and syntax to WANTING verbs, expressing the Principal's attitude towards some event or state that is not (yet) real. Like WANTING verbs, EAGER adjectives can take a THAT or a Modal (FOR) TO complement, e.g. *I'm eager (for Mary) to enter the race*, *I want (Mary) to enter the race*. *Ready* focuses on the subject's involvement in some activity and is restricted to a Modal (FOR) TO complement; it is thus like *want*, *need* and *prepare* from the WANTING type—see the discussion in §7.3.3.

Those adjectives which are most different in meaning from verbs are the DIFFICULTY and QUANTIFICATION types, and the CLEVER subtype of HUMAN PROPENSITY. Some QUANTIFICATION adjectives— such as *definite*, *probable*, *true*—provide a factual qualification regarding a definite event, and are restricted to THAT subject complements, e.g. *It is true that John forged Mary's signature*. Others describe the speaker's opinion about some actual or potential happening and may take THAT or Modal (FOR) TO subject complements, e.g. *It is normal/sensible for a policeman to carry a gun*. One group of QUANTIFICATION adjectives relate to the potentiality of the complement subject behaving in a certain way; this subject may then be raised from an extraposed Modal (FOR) TO complement to replace *it* in main clause subject slot—compare *It is likely that Reagan will bomb Tripoli* (the event is likely) with *Reagan is likely to bomb Tripoli* (it is likely that Reagan will act in this way).

Adjectives in the CLEVER subtype of HUMAN PROPENSITY have similar properties. They can relate to a unit event, through THAT, or to someone's involvement in an activity, through Modal (FOR)

TO, e.g. *It was stupid that no one answered the door*, *It would be stupid for John to ignore those rumours* (see §3.2). These adjectives may also directly describe some person, who is in subject slot, with a preposition introducing a clause that gives the reason for this description, e.g. *John is stupid in the way that he is always trying to buck authority*.

Adjectives from the DIFFICULTY class may relate to some specific involvement in an event, through a Modal (FOR) TO subject complement, e.g. *It is hard for young children to sit still during a long sermon*. Or they can refer to some very general mode of behaviour, then taking as subject an ING complement with subject omitted, e.g. *Cooking scones is easy (for some people)*.

The difficulty or value of an activity may be a function of the object of the complement clause, and there is an alternative construction with this NP as subject of the adjective, e.g. *Scones are easy to cook*.

7.4.6. Other Primary-B types

Verbs from the COMPARING type—e.g. *resemble*, *differ from*—and Adjectives from the SIMILARITY type—e.g. *like*, *unlike*, *similar (to)*, *different (from)*—must have subject and post-predicate (direct object or prepositional object) constituents with comparable meanings. Both may refer to people, things or places, e.g. *Harare resembles Auckland in some ways*. Or both may relate to kinds of activity, which can be referred to through subjectless ING complements, e.g. *Trying to get John to smile is like getting blood out of a stone*.

Verbs from the RELATING type refer to some natural or logical relationship. The possibilities for both subject and object slots are: (i) an NP, often with a SPEECH ACT noun as head; (ii) an NP of this kind followed by a THAT clause which is referred to by the head noun of the NP, e.g. *the report that John is lost* or *the verdict that he is guilty*; (iii) a plain THAT clause; (iv) an ING complement; or (v) a WH- complement clause. A THAT complement in subject slot with a verb from this type is most unlikely to be extraposed to the end of the main clause, e.g. *That John was found innocent indicates that the jury was made up of fools,* not **It indicates that the jury was made up of fools that John was found innocent*.

Indicate, *show*, *demonstrate* and *suggest* (in their meanings that fall within the RELATING type) take any of (i)–(iv) as subject. They may describe how the situation referred to by a THAT clause in object slot follows from that referred to by the subject, e.g. *The fact that John didn't turn up suggests that he may be sick, Mary's having slept through the concert shows that she doesn't care for Mozart.* Or the referent of the subject may help resolve some point of clarification posed by a WH- clause as object, e.g. *The fact that John had flecks of cream in his beard suggests (to me) who it was that stole the trifle. Imply* is limited to the first sense, with a THAT object clause; it does not take a WH- clause in object slot.

Relate (and *is related to*) simply state that two things are connected. The subject may be any of (i)–(v) and the object any of these save a plain THAT clause, e.g. *Mrs Smith's being so rude to you relates to the fact that she was friendly with my first wife. Depend on* will typically link two hypotheticals, both expressed by WH- clauses, e.g. *How we climb the mountain depends on what equipment John brings. Result from* deals with a connection between two actual states or activities; it must take NP or NP-plus-THAT-clause or ING clause in subject and object slots, e.g. *The fact that John was found innocent results from the jury('s) being totally incompetent.* None of *relate to*, *depend on* and *result from* may take a plain THAT clause in object slot; this may be at least in part because the preposition would then have to drop before *that*, and it is an important component of each verb. Compare *That Arwon won the Melbourne Cup demonstrates (the fact) that he is a horse of quality*, with *That Arwon won the Melbourne Cup relates to the fact that he is a horse of quality*, where *the fact* could not be omitted.

Some verbs from the ACTING type may relate either to an entity (shown by an NP), e.g. *She copied the poem on the board*, or to some activity (shown by an ING complement clause), e.g. *She copied John's eating his cake with a fork*.

Verbs such as *experience* and *undergo*, from the HAPPENING type, have in O slot a description of something that happened to the subject. This can be expressed through an ACTIVITY or STATE noun or through an ING complement clause (often in the passive, as is appropriate for something that befalls the subject), e.g. *She underwent an operation for appendicitis, She underwent having her belly cut open and the appendix taken out*.

Notes to Chapter 7

§7.1. The classic paper on parentheticals is Urmson (1952). He gives an example which is similar to my (8a/b): suppose John knows that the trains are on strike and sees Mary rush to the station. John could then use a THAT complement construction *Mary believes that the trains are running*. But he could not, in these circumstances, use the parenthetical construction *The trains, Mary believes, are running* since by so doing he would be implying that the trains are running. Another paper dealing with parentheticals is Hooper (1975).

§7.2–4. A large number of books and papers have been published in recent years on the syntax (and sometimes also the semantics) of complement clauses in English, all of them containing useful information and ideas but none making the full set of distinctions revealed in this chapter. These include Akmajian (1977); Bolinger (1968, 1972, 1977a); Bresnan (1979); Duffley (forthcoming); Huddleston (1984); Kiparsky and Kiparsky (1970); Menzel (1975); Ney (1981); Noonan (1985); Ransom (1986); Riddle (1975); Stockwell, Schachter and Partee (1973); Thompson (1973); Vendler, (1967, 1972); Wierzbicka (1988).

§7.2.2. The omission or inclusion of *'s* in an ING complement clause is not an automatic matter, and may sometimes carry a meaning difference. This is a topic that will repay further research.

§7.2.3–4. Rosenbaum (1967) drew a distinction between 'noun phrase complements' and 'verb phrase complements'. Verbs like *force*, *help* and *order* were said to take VP complements while *believe*, *expect*, *remember* and others were said to take NP complements. This categorisation has been repeated in many works since, e.g. Perlmutter and Soames (1979). As shown in §7.2.4 there is no essential syntactic or semantic difference between the Modal (FOR) TO complements with *force*, *help*, *order*, *expect* and *remember*. *Believe* takes a quite different variety of complement construction, Judgement TO. Other differences that have been quoted in the literature between verbs like *force* and *help*, on the one hand, and verbs like *believe* and *expect*, on the other, are a consequence of differences in meaning, and carry no syntactic implications. The Rosenbaum distinction is simply incorrect. (For a line of argument similar to that followed here, see Schmerling 1978.)

§7.2.6. Borkin (1973, 1984) discuss conditions for the omission of *to be*.

8

I kicked at the bomb, which exploded, and wakened you up.
Transitivity and causatives

Some languages have a strict division of verbs into transitive—those that take A (transitive subject) and O (transitive object) core syntactic relations—and intransitive—those that have just one core syntactic relation, S (intransitive subject). A few languages even employ morphological marking so that there can never be any doubt as to whether a verb is transitive or intransitive, e.g. if a verb in Fijian shows a transitive suffix then it must have an object; if it lacks this suffix there will be no direct object.

Transitivity is a much more fluid matter in English. There are, it is true, a number of verbs that are strictly transitive, e.g. *like*, *promote*, *recognise*, *inform*, and a few that are strictly intransitive, e.g. *arrive*, *chat*, *matter*. But many verbs in English may be used either transitively or intransitively.

There are two kinds of correspondence between the syntactic relations of intransitive and transitive constructions:

(i) those for which S = A, e.g. *She's following (us), Have you eaten (lunch)?, He's knitting (a jumper), I won (the game)*;

(ii) those for which S = O, e.g. *The ice melted/Ivan melted the ice, Mary's arm hurts/John hurt Mary's arm, Fred tripped up/Jane tripped up Fred, Tim is working hard/Tim's boss is working him hard*.

If the transitive version is taken as prior for (i), then we can say that the intransitive version is obtained by omitting the object, and that this is possible for some—but not all—transitive verbs in English. If the intransitive construction is taken as prior for (ii), then we can say that the transitive is a causative version of the intransitive, with the original S becoming O and a 'Causer' brought in as A. A full discussion of dual transitivity is in §8.3.

There is also the matter of prepositions. Some transitive verbs may optionally insert a preposition before the direct object, e.g. *He kicked* (*at*) *the door*, *She bit* (*on*) *the strap*. Is the original object NP still an object, when it is now preceded by a preposition? Some verbs may omit the preposition before a peripheral constituent, either before a 'measure phrase', e.g. *run* (*for*) *a mile*, *stand* (*for*) *two hours in the rain*, or before a non-measure phrase, e.g. *jump* (*over*) *the ravine*, *speak* (*in*) *French*. Are measure phrases like *a mile* and *two hours*, or non-measure phrases like *the ravine* and *French*, now in direct object function? (Note that in each instance the inclusion or omission of a preposition has a definite semantic effect.)

There are a number of verbs that must take a preposition, and this behaves in some ways as if it were an 'inherent' part of the verb; a following NP will have many of the characteristics of a direct object, e.g. *rely on*, *hope for*. Related to this are 'phrasal verbs', combinations of verb and preposition that have meaning (and syntax) not inferable from those of the two components, e.g. *take after*, *put off*. §8.2 discusses the question of prepositions and transitivity.

8.1. The semantic basis of syntactic relations

A verb has—according to its semantic type—one or two or three semantic roles; each of these must be mapped onto a core or peripheral syntactic relation.

If there is only one role then it is mapped onto S. As mentioned in §3.3.1, S has a wide semantic range, relating both to roles that control an activity (e.g. *He ran*, *They chatted*, *She winked*) and those that cannot—or are unlikely to—exercise control (e.g. *The stone rolled down the hill*, *The old man died*, *My bubble burst*).

If there are two or more core roles then one will be mapped onto A and the other onto O syntactic relation. That role which is most likely to be relevant to the success of the activity will be A, e.g. *the wind* in *The wind blew down my house*, and *the thunder* in *The thunder frightened the child*. Most often, the role mapped onto A will be human and 'most relevant to the success of the activity' then equates with 'could initiate or control the activity'.

For most semantic types one particular role will always be mapped onto A (i.e. there is no choice involved)—this is the Perceiver for ATTENTION, the Cogitator for THINKING, the Speaker for SPEAKING, the Human for CORPOREAL, the Causer for MAKING, the Principal for WANTING, and so on. The GIVING type uses different lexemes depending on whether Donor or Recipient is exercising control, and is thus in A relation, e.g. *Mary* (Donor: A) *tried to lend the blue hat* (Gift: O) *to me* (Recipient) and *I* (Recipient: A) *tried to borrow the blue hat* (Gift: O) *from Mary* (Donor). The LIKING and ANNOYING types involve the same two roles; for LIKING the Experiencer may be in a position to exercise control, and so is in A relation, whereas for ANNOYING the success of the activity may be due to the Stimulus, and this is A—compare John (Experiencer: A) *tried to like/dislike Mary* (Stimulus: O) and *Mary* (Stimulus: A) *tried to please/annoy John* (Experiencer: O).

The only verbs that may allow either of two roles to be mapped onto A relation are some from AFFECT. Normally the agent is A, e.g. *John* (Agent: A) *hit Mary* (Target: O) *with his stick* (Manip), but there is another construction in which Manip is A, e.g. *The stick* (Manip: A) *hit Mary* (Target: O) (e.g. as John swung it). Use of this construction may effectively deny that the Agent was responsible for the action, suggesting that it was, perhaps, an accident.

If a verb has just two core roles then that which is not coded into A is placed in O syntactic relation—the Impression for ATTENTION, the Thought for THINKING, the Substance for CORPOREAL, the Stimulus for LIKING, the Experiencer for ANNOYING.

But verbs from some types have three core roles. There is no question about which role should be in A syntactic relation—that which is most relevant to the success of the activity. Of the remaining roles, that which is most salient to the activity (often, that which is affected by the activity) is mapped onto O; the roles which do not correspond to A or to O are marked by an appropriate preposition. For instance, some subtypes of SPEAKING focus on the Addressee (which goes into O relation) while others focus on the Message (which is then O)—compare *He* (Speaker: A) *informed Mary* (Addressee: O) *of the floods in Queensland*

(Message) and *He* (Speaker: A) *mentioned the floods in Queensland* (Message: O) *to Mary* (Addressee).

The O relation does in fact show much more variation than A in connection with which roles may be mapped onto it. There are a number of verbs from types that involve three roles—AFFECT, GIVING and SPEAKING—which allow two construction types, with different roles in O relation (that is, with different roles being focused on, as particularly salient in that instance of the activity). One would be likely to use *John* (Agent: A) *hit the vase* (Target: O) *with his stick* (Manip) if the vase broke, but to use *John* (Agent: A) *hit his stick* (Manip: O) *against the concrete post* (Target) if the stick broke.

8.2. Prepositions and transitivity

The primary use of prepositions in English is to introduce a peripheral noun phrase, providing locational or temporal specification (e.g. *in the house, at three o'clock*) or marking an instrument (*with a stone*), a beneficiary (*for Mary*), a recipient (*to John*), etc. Each type of prepositional NP can occur with a wide variety of verbs.

Prepositions have two further uses—within 'inherent preposition' verbs and within phrasal verbs. It is important to distinguish these two kinds of verb. The root of an inherent preposition verb is not normally used alone—*refer* only occurs in *refer to*, with an object NP, e.g. *She referred to my book*. *Refer to* is syntactically parallel to *mention*, as in *She mentioned my book*, suggesting that *refer to* should be treated as a single, transitive verb, lexeme.

The root of a phrasal verb is used alone, but its meaning in a phrasal verb is quite different from its meaning when used alone. Thus we have the simple transitive root *take*, and also phrasal verbs such as *take after* 'resemble (e.g. one's mother)', *take up* 'practise (e.g. medicine)', *take on* 'accept (e.g. new responsibilities)'. The meaning of a phrasal verb cannot be inferred from the meanings of its constituent root and preposition; it must be regarded as a separate lexeme.

We thus distinguish (i) verbs that consist just of a root, e.g. *take*, *mention*; (ii) those that consist of root plus preposition, where the root cannot be used alone, e.g. *refer to*; and (iii) those that consist of root plus preposition, where the root can be used alone, but with a different meaning, e.g. *take after, take up, take on*. §8.2.1 deals with type (ii), with an inherent preposition. We show that the inclusion of a preposition, and the choice of which preposition, is semantically motivated. §8.2.2 deals with type (iii), phrasal verbs; there are six syntactic types, exemplified by *set in, take after* NP, *put* NP *off*, *see* NP *through* NP, *take up with* NP and *put* NP *down to* NP. §§8.2.3–5 then consider the semantic and syntactic effects of the insertion of a preposition, e.g. *kick* (*at*) *the door*, and of the omission of a preposition, e.g. *swim* (*across*) *the river*.

8.2.1. Verbs with an inherent preposition

There are two ways of treating verbs like *refer* and *rely* within a grammar of English: either (i) as part of two-word lexemes *refer to* and *rely on*, which behave as transitive verbs; or (ii) as intransitive verbs, which must obligatorily be followed by a prepositional NP. Under (ii) they would be treated as similar to verbs like *travel* and *float*, which may optionally take prepositional NPs, e.g. *refer to Jespersen, travel* (*to Japan*), *rely on his sense of propriety, float* (*on the pool*).

There are two difficulties with alternative (ii). One is that an NP which follows *refer to* or *rely on* behaves like a transitive object in that it can freely become passive subject, quite unlike an NP which follows *travel to* or *float on*. Thus, *Jespersen was referred to by everyone attending the symposium*, but not **Japan was travelled to by everyone attending the symposium*, and *John's sense of propriety can be relied on*, but not **That pool has been floated on*. The second point to note is that *travel, float* and other intransitive verbs can be followed by any one of a number of prepositions (e.g. *travel to/towards/around/in Japan, float* (*in/on/across the pool*)) whereas *refer* must take *to* and *rely* is confined to *on*.

We thus opt for (i), treating *refer to, rely on, decide on, wish for, approve of* and other 'inherent preposition' combinations each as a single, transitive verb. There is often semantic and syntactic similarity to a simple transitive verb, e.g. *approve of* and *like, wish for* and *want, decide on* and *choose, refer to* and *mention, rely on* and *trust*.

As already mentioned, some inherent preposition verbs can take a complement clause in object relation; following a general rule of English syntax (§2.11B), the preposition drops before complementisers *that, for* and *to*. Compare:

(1) *We decided on/chose Spain for a holiday this year*
(2) *We decided/chose that we would go to Spain*
(3) *We decided/chose to go to Spain*

Many transitive verbs in English may omit the object NP in appropriate circumstances (see §8.3.1 and the discussion throughout Chapters 4-6). Not surprisingly, some inherent preposition verbs fall into this category; and when the object NP is omitted the preposition also drops—thus, *listen (to), confess (to), approve (of)*. Note that, as with *refer to* and *rely on,* the prepositional choice is fixed, and the object is readily passivisable, e.g. *That recording which I handed in with my essay last week hasn't been listened to yet.*

Having suggested that *decide on, refer to* and similar combinations should be treated as a type of transitive verb, we must now hasten to add that it is not an arbitrary matter that some verbal lexemes consist of just a root, while others involve root plus preposition. The inclusion of a preposition—and which preposition is included—is, without doubt, semantically motivated. Inherent preposition verbs have a meaning which is subtly but significantly different from corresponding simple verbs.

Each preposition in English has a fair semantic range. There is generally a fairly concrete sense—for *at* this is demonstrated by *stay at the seaside*—but in addition a set of more abstract senses—as in *at a rough estimate, jump at the chance, laugh at John, be dismayed at the news*. It is intended that a second volume of this grammar should examine prepositional meanings in some detail; we will then be in a position to explain the semantic rationale for the inclusion of *on* with *rely, of* with *approve*, and so on. Meanwhile, just a few informal remarks can be offered on why certain verbs include a preposition, but related verbs do not.

(i) *Wish for* and *want*. With *wish* the preposition *for* introduces an object that may not be attainable, e.g. *For twenty-five years Nelson Mandela wished for his freedom*, whereas *want* most often relates to something that can readily be achieved, e.g. *I want my dinner now*. (One can say *John often wants the unobtainable*, and this implies that John is unrealistic, treating the unobtainable as if it were something that he could get.)

(ii) *Confess to* and *admit*. One is likely to confess after a lengthy inner struggle (or after extended questioning by the police); the details of the crime may already be known. The verb *confess* thus focuses on the fact that the subject now says that he did do it, with preposition *to* marking the event that the confession is orientated towards. With *admit* the main interest is likely to be on the object constituent (what the subject did), which may be new information. (*Admit* may, for some speakers, optionally include *to* before the object; it is likely to include *to* when the possibility of the subject's having committed the crime etc. has already been mooted, i.e. in similar circumstances to that in which *confess to* is used.)

(iii) *Refer to* and *mention*. The verb *mention* has casual overtones—in conversation I might just 'mention' Huddleston's grammar. But in writing a paper I would be likely to 'refer to' it; *refer to* carries a sense of purpose and directionality, which is brought out by the inclusion of *to*.

(iv) *Decide on* and *choose*. The verb *choose* can be employed where there was little mental effort involved, and it may be used in a way that relates pragmatically to the object role, e.g. *'I'd have chosen you', he told her, 'if it had been up to me'*. *Decide* is likely to refer to an act that involved considerable thought, and focuses on the mental act; preposition *on* introduces the object that the decision finally rested on. (Cf. the remarks in §7.4.3 on the possible omission of *for* from a Modal (FOR) TO complement clause after *choose*, but not after *decide*.)

There is one limited context in which *decide* can be used without *on* preceding an object NP. Compare:

(4) *The President decided on the order of precedence*
(5) *The President decided the order of precedence*

Sentence (4) could be used when the President sat down, thought out the order of precedence, and announced it (no one else need be involved). But (5) might be used when there was a dispute over the order of precedence and he settled it; this sentence focuses on the matter of the order. (Note that *on* could not be omitted after *decide* before other kinds of NPs, referring to things that are not crucially affected by the act of deciding, e.g. not from (1) above or from *The Duke decided on Eton for his son's education*.)

(v) *Look at* and *see*, *listen to* and *hear*. *See* and *hear* refer to acts of attention that need not be volitional but must have a positive result; it is in view of this that they are simple transitive verbs, e.g. *I saw the car go by*. *Look* and *listen* refer to the Perceiver directing his attention in a certain way; he may not necessarily achieve a desired goal. These verbs can be used intransitively, e.g. with an adverb (*He looked up*, *She listened carefully*); or else an object can be included after a preposition. But why should *look* take *at* and *listen* take *to*? Well, one directs one's gaze 'at' a thing, and may see nothing else. But our ears pick up every sound around; it is necessary to concentrate one's mind and direct it towards one particular type of sound. (It is possible to use *listen* with *at*, e.g. *He listened at the door*, when he put his ear against the door, but here *at the door* is a locative expression, whereas in *He looked at the door*, the *at* is part of the verbal expression *look at*.)

8.2.2. Phrasal verbs

English has some hundreds of phrasal verbs, each a combination of verb plus preposition(s) that has a meaning not inferable from the individual meanings of verb and preposition(s), so that it must be regarded as an independent lexical item, and accorded a dictionary entry of its own.

There are six varieties of phrasal verb. Their structures can be abbreviated, using 'p' for preposition and 'N' for a noun phrase or functionally equivalent constituent:

(i) verb-plus-p, e.g. *set in, come to, pass out*
(ii) verb-plus-pN, e.g. *set about X, come by X, pick on X*
(iii) verb-plus-Np, e.g. *put X off, take X on, bring X down*
(iv) verb-plus-NpN, e.g. *see X through Y, hold X against Y*
(v) verb-plus-ppN, e.g. *take up with X, go in for X, scrape by on X*
(vi) verb-plus-NppN, e.g. *put X down to Y, let X in for Y, take X up on Y*

The difference between (ii) and (iii) is particularly important. A p can move to the left over a noun (but not over an unstressed personal pronoun) in (iii), e.g. *put the meeting off, put off the meeting*; the p cannot move in (ii) e.g. *pick on Mary*, not **pick Mary on*. Some verbs of set (vi) may also move the first p to the left over a preceding noun (but not over a pronoun), e.g. *He played John off against Mary, He played off John against Mary*.

The vast majority of phrasal verbs are based on monosyllabic roots of Germanic origin, almost all belonging to the types MOTION (e.g. *bring, carry*), REST (*sit, stand*), AFFECT (*cut, kick, scrape*), GIVE (*give, get, have*), MAKING (*make, let*), or the grammatical verbs *be* and *do*. The resulting phrasal verbs are distributed over a wider range of types; some of them have quite abstract and specialised meanings, for which there is no monomorphemic synonym, e.g. *let X in for Y, see X through Y, take up with X*. Nevertheless, only a small proportion of them allow a complement clause in one of the slots designated 'N' in the formulas above.

The transitivity of phrasal verbs is a fascinating and not altogether easy question. Firstly, an N which immediately follows the verbal element, as in (iii), (iv) and (vi), is clearly a direct object; it may become passive subject, e.g. *The meeting was put off, His political opinions were held against John, Her failure was put down to nerves*. In these phrasal verb types the lexical unit is effectively discontinuous—we should write *put — off, hold — against*, and *put — down to*, the dash showing that a direct object intervenes between the elements of what is in each case a single semantic unit.

It would be reasonable to expect the N in a phrasal verb of type (ii) to behave like the NP following an inherent preposition verb such as *refer to* or *decide on*. In fact, it does not do so. Whereas the object constituent after *refer to, decide on* and similar verbs may freely passivise, the N in a phrasal verb of type (ii) may only occasionally become subject of a passive construction—it may for *pick on* (e.g. *Mary is always being picked on by the new teacher*), but it does not for *set about* and it does not very easily for *come by*, for instance. The N in type (ii) behaves syntactically like a prepositional object (as in *He sat on the river bank*), although it follows verb-plus-preposition that make up a single semantic unit. The N in type (v) shows even less tendency to passivise—a passive is barely possible with just a few phrasal verbs from this set, e.g.

put up with, *look down on*, *make up for* (but not with *rub off on*,
come round to, *pull out of* or many others).

We noted that the 'inherent preposition' from a verb like *hope
for*, *decide on* or *think about* is dropped before a *that*, *for* or *to*
complementiser. How do prepositions from phrasal verbs behave
in these circumstances? In answering this question it will be useful
to discuss the varieties one or two at a time:

Structure (ii), *verb-plus-pN*. Out of a sample of about a hundred
phrasal verbs of this kind I have found none that may take a THAT
clause in the N slot. There are a few that allow ING clauses (e.g. *He
set about picking the grapes*, *She couldn't deal with her husband's
making passes at all the maids*) and one or two that may take an NP
which includes a THAT clause, but not a THAT complement alone
(e.g. *She played upon the fact that he was frightened of the dark*, *He
fell for the suggestion that he should nominate Mary*). It seems as if
a THAT clause is never used with a phrasal verb of this type because
that cannot normally follow a preposition with which its clause has
a close syntactic connection, and to omit the preposition would
destroy the phrasal verb (either changing the meaning of the
sentence, or rendering it unintelligible).

The same argument should apply in the case of (FOR) TO
complements; the preposition of a phrasal verb would have to
drop before *for* or *to*, destroying the lexical form of the phrasal
verb. In fact, (FOR) TO complements do not generally occur with
phrasal verbs of type (ii). But there is an exception: *press for*, as
in *She pressed for a re-count*. Since this verb ends in *for* it
can perfectly well be followed by a Modal (FOR) TO complement
clause, e.g. *She pressed for the returning officer to re-count the
votes* or *She pressed for the votes to be re-counted*. (There are in
underlying structure two occurrences of *for*, and one is omitted.) If
the complement clause subject is coreferential with main
clause subject then it should be omitted, together with complementiser *for*. Here the *for* of the phrasal verb would immediately
precede complementiser *to* and must be omitted; this is why a
sentence like ?*She pressed to re-count the votes* is at best dubiously
acceptable.

Structure (iii), *Verb-plus-Np* (where the p may be moved to the
left over a preceding non-pronominal constituent). There are a

small number of phrasal verbs of this type where the N may be (i) an NP, or (ii) an NP in apposition with a THAT clause:

    (6a) *He put the news about*
    (6b) *He put about the news*
    (7a) *He put the news that I had resigned about*
    (7b) *He put about the news that I had resigned*

There are further possibilities:

    (7c) *He put the news about that I had resigned*
    (7d) *He put it about that I had resigned*

We could say that in (7c) the THAT clause from the complex appositional constituent *the news that I had resigned* has been extraposed to the end of the sentence (parallel to the extraposition in *The news angered me that we are to have a new secretary*). In (7d) there must be—for most speakers—an *it* between *put* and *about*, effectively marking the fact that this is a phrasal verb of type 'verb-plus-Np'. (We cannot have **He put that I had resigned about*, and scarcely ?*He put about that I had resigned*, where *the news* has been omitted without trace.)

It appears that a THAT clause can follow the 'p' element of a phrasal verb of type 'verb-plus-Np' only when there is some constituent filling the N slot.

Other phrasal verbs of type (iii) which occur in constructions (6)–(7d) include *bring — about, give — out, put — across*. There are also just a few for which—at least in some dialects—the *it* may be omitted from a construction like (7d), e.g. *let — out* 'disclose', *work — out* 'deduce', *lay — down* 'assert'.

Since a preposition does not drop before an ING complement, it is possible to have an ING clause in the N slot for phrasal verbs of type (iii), e.g. *She'll never live down her husband's being sent to jail*. Note that here leftward movement of the preposition is almost obligatory, both to put the 'heavy constituent' at the end of its clause (§2.11A) and to ensure that the two words making up the phrasal verb are not too far apart.

Structures (iv), verb-plus-NpN, and (vi), verb-plus-NppN. There are relatively few phrasal verbs with these structures. A handful of them may take a complex NP including a THAT clause in the first N slot (i.e. as direct object) and then behave exactly like type (iii), with an *it* following the verbal root, and the THAT clause coming at the end of the main clause, e.g. *He held it against me that I didn't vote for him, I took it up with Mary that she didn't vote at all* and *I put it down to laziness that he never writes*.

The second N slot in structure (vi) may take NP-including-THAT-clause, e.g. *I played the fact that he can't cook off against the fact that I hate washing up*, but not a complement clause alone.

Structure (v), verb-plus-ppN. Here, the first preposition is like that in a phrasal verb of type (i)–(iv) and the second resembles an 'inherent preposition' (as in *decide on, hope for*). That is, the second NP is omitted before a THAT clause in N slot—compare *He didn't let on about the accident* and *He didn't let on about Mary's being injured* with *He didn't let on (*about) that Mary had been injured*. Another phrasal verb that omits the second preposition before *that* is *catch on to*.

In conclusion, we can state firstly that an N which comes immediately after the verbal part of a phrasal verb (syntactically intruding into the middle of a single semantic unit) in types (iii), (iv) and (vi) is clearly a direct object, and those phrasal verbs are transitive. The final N in types (iv) and (vi) is a core semantic role, but it is not in object syntactic relation.

The N in type (ii) has weak object status, since it may occasionally become passive subject; this object status is weaker than that of an NP which follows an inherent preposition, as in *hope for, refer to*. The N in type (v) has similar syntactic status—there are limited passivisation possibilities, and when N is a THAT complement clause the second of the two prepositions will drop before it.

Only phrasal verbs of structure (i) are fully intransitive.

8.2.3. Inserting a preposition

In §8.1 we said that a role may be assigned to O syntactic relation if it is saliently affected by the activity. Recall also the discussion in §3.3.1 showing that an O NP will generally have specific reference (which explains the unacceptability of **John gave good causes all his money*). Related to this, we can note that a prototypical transitive sentence will refer to a complete unit of activity, involving a specific O (e.g. *She baked a cake, He broke the plate*).

If the activity referred to by a transitive verb does not achieve a definite result, or does not relate to some specific object, then a preposition may be inserted between verb and O NP, to mark the deviation from an 'ideal' transitive event.

A semantically canonical sentence with *kick* is something like *He kicked the ball*; one assumes that he aimed his foot at the ball, it made contact, and the ball flew off. On hearing *He kicked at the ball* one might infer that the aim was not achieved, i.e. he missed making contact. Similarly, *He kicked the door* implies that he intended to deliver a kick to the door, and did so, with the required result. One also hears *He kicked at the door*; here— unlike in the case of *He kicked at the ball*—contact is likely to have been made between foot and door. Inclusion of *at* could imply that an aim was not achieved—he might have tried to open the door with a kick or two, but it didn't budge. (Suppose that eventually he did succeed. One might say, *He kicked at the door for twenty minutes and eventually he did kick it down*, where use of the phrasal verb *kick down* here signals success.) Or, *He kicked at the door* could be used to focus on the fact that he was angry and just kicking out in fury, and what the kicks made contact with is of secondary importance.

When *bite* has a non-animate object it generally refers to separating a portion of something with one's teeth, and eating it. On hearing *She bit the apple* one would infer that a piece was bitten out of the fruit, and then chewed and swallowed. But someone can also bite to relieve tension, e.g. if being operated on without an anaesthetic. In this instance a preposition would be inserted, e.g. *She bit on the leather strap*. Nothing really happens to the strap (a piece wasn't taken out of it) and this is marked by *on* since it is peripheral to the main focus of the sentence—the fact that she is biting.

Hold behaves in a similar way. The canonical sense focuses on the affect the activity has on an object, e.g. *John held the pig (then it couldn't run away)*. If the subject clutches something so as to affect himself—e.g. *John held onto the post (so that he wouldn't be blown off his feet by the gale)*—then a preposition is inserted, marking the fact that the actual identity of the object is of peripheral interest, and that it is not affected by the action.

The verb *pull* implies that a Causer exerts pressure on an object so that it moves. If it does move then a plain transitive construction is appropriate, e.g. *John pulled the rope*. If he cannot get it to move then *pull* may still be used but with a preposition inserted, to signal this non-achievement, e.g. *John pulled on the rope*.

A quite different kind of example involves *win*. When there is a specific object NP the plain transitive verb will be used, e.g. *Vladimir won that game of chess last night*. But if the object is generic and non-specific the preposition *at* must be inserted, e.g. *Vladimir usually wins at chess*.

In fact only a handful of transitive verbs may insert a preposition before an object to mark that it lacks some of the salient properties associated with the syntactic relation 'object'. They include a number of AFFECT items such as *hit, strike, hammer, cut, saw, punch, kick, scrape, rub, tear* (all taking *at*), a few MOTION and REST verbs such as *pull* (*on*) and *hold* (*onto*), a number of CORPOREAL verbs such as *bite, chew, nibble, suck* (taking *on* or *at*), *smell, sniff* (taking *at*) (but not *eat* or *drink*), perhaps just *win* (*at*) from COMPETITION, and some from the TELL subtype of SPEAKING (§5.4(*f*)).

Many of these verbs may not (except in some marked context) be used intransitively—we cannot say just *He hit* or *She cut*. Some object must be specified, but the fact that it is not an 'ideal' object in this instance of the activity can be shown by the insertion of a preposition.

Hunt is particularly interesting. There is a semantic link between *hunt* and *hunt for*—both being associated with killing game—but the plain transitive is most similar to AFFECT verbs, whereas *hunt for* is more like *look for* and *search for* from the ATTENTION type. The sentence *He is hunting lions* suggests that there may be a known group of lions that the hunter is attempting to kill. But *He is hunting for lions* implies only that he is directing his attention towards finding lions (which he would then kill). The NP *lions* refers to something that may not be attainable, and it is naturally introduced by *for* (cf. the *for* in *wish for*).

In summary, a preposition can be inserted before the object NP of a transitive verb to indicate that the emphasis is not on the effect of the activity on some specific object (the normal situation) but rather on the subject's engaging in the activity.

8.2.4. Omitting a preposition, before non-measure phrases

In the last subsection we described how a preposition can be inserted before an O NP which is not saliently affected by the activity, or when it does not have specific reference.

There are also instances of what could be called the opposite kind of circumstance. If the referent of a peripheral NP, marked by a preposition, is particularly salient in some instance of an activity, then it may drop its preposition and move to a position immediately after the verb, becoming direct object. As we shall show, this can happen with both intransitive and transitive verbs.

A Locus description can—but need not—be included with a verb from the RUN subtype of MOTION, e.g. *jump* (*over the log*), *climb* (*up the mountain*), *swim* (*across the stream*). If the activity could be considered a significant achievement, with regard to the nature of the Locus, then the preposition can be omitted and the Locus NP moved to a position immediately after the (now, transitive) verb, as its direct object. *They climbed up the mountain* leaves open whether they got to the top, but *They climbed the mountain* indicates that the pinnacle was reached. The prepositionless construction would be likely to be used when it was a difficult mountain to climb—one would surely always say *They climbed Everest*, with no *up*, but *We climbed up the little hill in the south-east corner of Regent's Park*, with *up* included. Similar considerations apply to *swim*—*She swam the English Channel*, a considerable achievement which is marked by having *the English Channel* as direct object, as opposed to *She swam across the millstream*, which anyone who can swim at all can do, and here the Locus is marked by preposition *across*.

Jump may be used for motion up (*jump up onto the ledge*) or down (*jump down off/from the ledge*) or over some vertical obstacle (*jump over the fence*) or over a discontinuity in the ground (*jump over the brook*) or it can just refer to a mode of locomotion (*jump around the garden*). Only the preposition *over* can be omitted, and then just when the vertical obstruction or the discontinuity in the ground poses a definite challenge (which not everyone could meet). Thus, *She jumped the six-foot fence/the wide ravine* but not, because of the piffling nature of the obstruction, **She jumped the snail/the ten-inch gap in the path* (these sentences require *over*). A best-selling Australian auto-biography was called *I can jump puddles*; the author, Alan Marshall, had been crippled by polio and for him jumping a puddle represented a significant achievement, thus he omitted the preposition before *puddles*.

Any verb from the RUN subtype may have the Locus promoted from a prepositional NP to be direct object, if that Locus is in some way significant for the activity; for many verbs there is no such Locus, e.g. *crawl, stroll, roll*. With other RUN verbs a degree of contextualisation is necessary. A professional golfer, on the day before a big tournament at an unfamiliar location, is likely to *walk (over) the course*. Here the preposition may be dropped, not because this is any sort of achievement (in the way that swimming the Channel is) but because the salient fact here is not just his walking, but his walking-the-course, looking at the lie of the land from every angle.

Intransitive verbs from other subtypes may occasionally drop a preposition in appropriate circumstances. The CORPOREAL verb *pee* can take a prepositional NP indicating where the stream of urine was directed, e.g. *He peed into the potty*. But in *He peed (into) his pants* the preposition can be omitted, since the pants are saliently affected by the activity. (This construction is similar to *He wet his pants*.)

In §5.4 we described how *speak* and *talk* may omit the preposition before a Medium NP, e.g. *speak (in) French*. This is likely to happen when the Medium itself is being focused on—compare *The President spoke some harsh words in French to his secretary* (the harsh words are the focus of this sentence) with *They speak French in that bank*, or *French is spoken in that bank* (the fact of that language being spoken there is focused upon). Another example is *Can you really speak Fijian?*, where being able to converse in that language is being highlighted, as an unusual feat.

The basic syntactic frame for GIVING verbs is with the Gift as O and with the Recipient marked by preposition *to*. But when the Recipient is the most salient non-A role it can drop its preposition and move into direct object slot, immediately after the verb. Compare:

(8) *I've lent all my phonetics books to different people*
(9) *I've lent my favourite student a bunch of different sorts of books*

Sentence (8) focuses on the specific NP *all my phonetics books* whereas (9) directs attention onto *my favourite student*. In a construction like (9) the original O NP (the Gift) is still retained, as a sort of 'second object'. (There are similar syntactic possibilities with verbs from the TELL subtype of SPEAKING—§5.4(*f*).)

As mentioned in §4.3, *borrow* is the converse of *lend*. But here the Gift must be O, i.e. *John borrowed a book from Mary*. *Borrow* and related verbs (e.g. *buy*, *purchase*) focus on what is given, and this cannot be displaced from the object slot by the Donor.

In §4.6 we mentioned the construction *That free kick won/lost the match for us*, with *win* and *lose* from the COMPETITION type. Here the NP marked by *for* can be focused on, and moved into direct object slot, e.g. *That free kick won/lost us the match*.

Search for can be considered an inherent preposition verb, similar to *refer to*. A location can be specified, by a prepositional NP, e.g. *He searched for his wallet in the field*. This verb allows a location NP to drop its preposition and move into direct object slot if the location is somehow significant and worth focusing on, e.g. *He searched (in) forty-three different places for his wallet (before eventually finding it)*.

We have thus far examined instances of 'prepositional omission' with intransitive verbs (*jump*, *climb*, *swim*, *walk*, *pee*, *speak*), with transitive verbs (GIVING, the TELL subtype of SPEAKING, *win* and *lose* from COMPETITION), and with an inherent preposition transitive verb (*search for* from ATTENTION). In each case the omission takes place in circumstances particular to the type or subtype.

There is one general circumstance in which a preposition can be omitted (with the NP it governed becoming direct object). This involves *for* + NP (or, sometimes, *to* + NP) with the benefactive sense 'for NP to get'. Thus (cf. (7a/b) and (8a/b) in §3.3.1):

(10a) *I cut a slice of bread for Mary*
(10b) *I cut Mary a slice of bread*
(11a) *I brought an apple for Mary*
(11b) *I brought Mary an apple*
(12a) *I knitted a jumper for Mary*
(12b) *I knitted Mary a jumper*
(13a) *I threw an apple to Mary*
(13b) *I threw Mary an apple*
(14a) *I chose a book for Mary*

(14b) *I chose Mary a book*
(15a) *I recommended a good thriller to Mary*
(15b) *I recommended Mary a good thriller*

A benefactive NP of this kind may omit the *for* or *to* and become direct object (displacing the original direct object to become 'second object'), with a variety of verbs from at least MOTION, AFFECT, DECIDING and SPEAKING. The 'beneficiary' can, in appropriate circumstances, be regarded as the most salient non-A role with these verbs.

Note that each of the (a) sentences quoted has two senses: (i) for Mary to get the slice of bread/apple/jumper/etc.; and (ii) the activity being done on behalf of Mary—suppose Mary was meant to slice the bread but I did it instead. The NP governed by *for* can be promoted to direct object only in sense (i), not (ii).

Now consider verbs of GIVING. We can have

(16a) *John* (Donor) *sold a book* (Gift) *to Fred* (Recipient) *for Mary* (Beneficiary) (i.e. for Fred to give it to Mary)
(16b) *John* (Donor) *sold Fred* (Recipient) *a book* (Gift) *for Mary* (Beneficiary)
(17a) *Fred* (Recipient) *bought a book* (Gift) (*from John* (Donor)) *for Mary* (Beneficiary)

As described above, we have the possibility in (16a) of promoting the Recipient to O slot, if it is sufficiently salient—as in (16b). It is perhaps in view of this that with verbs like *sell*, *lend* and *give*, the Beneficiary may not become object. (On hearing **John sold Mary a book to Fred*—derived from (16a) by promotion of *Mary*—one would interpret the first five words as implying that Mary was the Recipient, and then be confused by the final *to Fred*.) But, as noted above, the Donor cannot be promoted to object in (17). Here the beneficiary may be promoted, in the same way that it can be with *cut*, *bring*, *knit*, etc., i.e.

(17b) *Fred* (Recipient) *bought Mary* (Beneficiary) *a book* (Gift) (*from John* (Donor))

But note that while construction (17b) is fully acceptable with *buy*, it is more marginal with the syntactically and semantically related verb *borrow*, *?Fred borrowed Mary a book* (*from John*). This may be because people often buy things to give them to someone else, whereas it is rare to borrow something from someone and then pass it on to a third person.

In summary, a non-measure NP that is normally marked by a preposition (and is a peripheral part of the activity) may lose its preposition and be moved into object slot if it is being focused on, as a particularly salient element, in some instance of the activity.

8.2.5. Omitting a preposition, before measure phrases

Any verb of MOTION, and some from other types such as ATTENTION, can take a peripheral NP that contains a numeral (or *a*) and a noun that refers to a unit of spatial measure. This NP is normally marked by a preposition (generally, *for*) but this can be omitted, e.g. *He runs (for) three miles before breakfast every day, She carried the parcel (for) twenty-five miles, From the top of that mountain you can see (for) thirty miles on a clear day.*

Analogously, an NP referring to temporal measure can occur with a wider range of verbs, including MOTION, REST, AFFECT, CORPOREAL and TALK. The preposition may again be omitted, e.g. *I like to run (for) an hour and then walk (for) an hour, She stood (for) twenty minutes in the pouring rain, He whipped the dog (for) two hours yesterday, You've been talking (for) twenty minutes without stopping.*

In the last subsection we explained how non-measure phrases that lose a preposition move into direct object slot, immediately after the verb. As always, an adverb may not intervene between verb and object—compare *He walked (purposefully) over the course (purposefully)* with *He walked (*purposefully) the course (purposefully)*.

A prepositionless measure phrase behaves quite differently. It is not in direct object slot and does not have to come immediately after the verb, e.g. *She stood in the pouring rain twenty minutes.* Even if a prepositionless measure phrase does occur next to the verb, an adverb can still come between them, e.g. *She stood (pathetically) twenty minutes in the pouring rain.* A non-measure phrase promoted into direct object slot can often be passivised, e.g. *That mountain has not yet been climbed*, but a prepositionless measure phrase can only very exceptionally become passive subject, e.g. we cannot have **Three miles is run by John before* *breakfast every day*. (It should be noted that *the mile*, as in *The mile was first run in four minutes by Roger Bannister*, is effectively functioning here as a non-measure phrase; it would normally be *the mile*, rather than *a mile*.)

Although omitting the preposition from a measure phrase does not make it an object NP there is still a semantic effect that bears some relation to the omission of a preposition from a non-measure phrase: attention is directed towards the measure, as a particularly significant aspect of the activity—the *length* of time or distance will often be significant. Thus, I might offer the accusation *You whipped the dog two hours solid* (with no preposition, emphasising the enormity of doing it for so long) and you could reply *I only whipped it for about three seconds* (including the preposition).

A measure phrase may be used without a preposition when that particular measure carries implications about the completion of the activity. *She followed the thief seven miles into the forest* might be used when he travelled seven miles to his hide-out and she followed him all the way, whereas *She followed the thief for seven miles into the forest* could be appropriate when he travelled further, but she only followed him for the first seven miles.

There is not always a choice involved. If a distance phrase is included with *throw* it is normally a significant result of the activity and a preposition is seldom or never included, e.g. *He threw the javelin (?for) eighty yards*. With *fall* a preposition is likely to be omitted in a sentence that refers to a 'completed' event, e.g. *She fell (*through) thirty feet to her death*. However, a preposition may be included when there is an incompletive overtone, e.g. *She fell (through) thirty feet until her fall was arrested by the branches of a tree*.

In summary, a non-measure phrase may omit its preposition if the temporal or spatial distance is particularly significant; but this NP does not have to come immediately after the verb, and it does not become a direct object.

8.3. Dual transitivity

Many verbs in English may be used either with an object (transitively) or without any object (intransitively). They divide

into two classes according as the intransitive subject is identical
with the transitive subject (S = A) or with transitive object (S = O).

8.3.1. S = A, transitive verbs that can omit an object

For almost all verbs that are used both transitively and intransitively with the same subject, the transitive form can be taken as
basic; we simply have to say that the object can be omitted, under
certain circumstances.

First, a note about two kinds of exception. There are some
basically intransitive verbs such as *climb, jump, swim, speak*
(discussed in §8.2.4) which may omit the preposition before a non-
measure NP and make this into a direct object. Occurrence in a
transitive frame is a secondary property for such verbs.

Then there are a number of CORPOREAL and WEATHER verbs that
are basically intransitive but may be followed by a cognate NP,
e.g. *He laughed a really dirty laugh, It thundered the most ear-
splitting crack of thunder*. A cognate NP is always likely to include
some modifiers (**He laughed a laugh* sounds infelicitous) and is
likely to be used because there are much greater possibilities for
adjectival etc. modification of a noun than there are for adverbial
modification of a verb. We suggested in §§4.4 and 4.5 that these
cognate NPs have at best very weak object properties, e.g. they do
not readily become passive subject. Other CORPOREAL verbs are
clearly transitive. Thus, alongside *yawn, laugh, sleep, wink* that
can only be followed by a cognate NP (not by a full direct object)
there are verbs like *swallow, bite, taste* and *pee* which can take a
direct object or a cognate NP.

It was suggested, in §§4.4 and 5.2, that *think* and *dream* belong
to both the CORPOREAL and THINKING types. In the former sense
they can be followed by a cognate NP (with no preposition), which
cannot normally become passive subject, e.g. *I thought the most
horrid evil thoughts* (*which I'm now ashamed of*). And in the latter
sense they take an inherent preposition plus a direct object, which
can passivise, e.g. *People have been thinking about your idea an
awful lot, Your idea has been thought about an awful lot*.

Verbs in the SHOUT subtype of SPEAKING may have a Message
NP —with a speech act noun as head—in object relation, e.g.
recite a poem, narrate a story. There are speech act nouns cognate

with some of the verbs from this subtype (e.g. *recitation*, *narration*) but —as with CORPOREAL and WEATHER items—there is a tendency not to use verb and noun together unless there is some significant modification of the noun, e.g. *He prayed a really beautiful prayer*, *She prayed a prayer about redemption*. (There is the commonly used *sing a song*, with no modifier, but this has the status of an idiom.) A SPEECH ACT NP can become passive subject (although it may be less likely to be if it has as head a noun cognate with the verb, e.g. *The sermon should be preached before the benediction is given*, but scarcely *?A really beautiful prayer was prayed at this morning's service*). It thus seems that such a speech act NP should be accorded full object status, unlike the cognate NPs that can follow CORPOREAL and WEATHER verbs, whose object status is at best weak. In summary, verbs from the SHOUT subtype appear to be basically transitive, but the Message role in O slot can be omitted.

Turning now to the main body of transitive verbs, we can enquire in what circumstances an object may be omitted. How is it, for instance, that an object need not be stated after *saw*, *knit*, *notice*, *remember*, *know*, *choose*, but should be (save in exceptional circumstances) after *hit*, *wrap*, *discover*, *realise*, *take*? It appears that the conditions for object omission vary across different semantic types.

An AFFECT verb will generally describe some unit of activity that involves a specific Target or Product, e.g. *He sawed the log*, *She knitted a jumper*. But an Agent may pursue a certain type of activity for a longish period, and/or on a variety of Targets or Products. It is then possible to use the appropriate verb without a stated object. The fact that the activity was extended is then generally marked by progressive aspect *be . . . ing*, or by a time phrase like *all day*, or a time adverb such as *always*, e.g. *She is knitting*, *He has been sawing all morning*. If past tense were used, with no time adverbal, then **She knitted*, **He has sawn* would be incomplete—an object should be added to obtain a grammatical sentence. (But note that an object may be omitted from such verbs when they are linked together, e.g. *First she knitted, then she sewed*; or where a reason clause is included, e.g. *She knitted to pass away the time*.)

Verbs like *saw*, *knit*—and others such as *sweep*, *rake*, *polish*—

refer to activities that often are done over an extended period. Other AFFECT verbs—*hit* and *wrap*, for instance—generally refer to discrete actions. These may (unusually) be done over an extended period or habitually, but an object NP can never be omitted (although it may have a very general noun as head, e.g. *He's always hitting people, She's been wrapping things all morning*).

Some transitive CORPOREAL verbs omit an object under similar conditions to AFFECT verbs like *saw* and *knit*; that is, in the presence of progressive *be . . . ing* or an appropriate adverbial—*He's eating/drinking, He's always eating/drinking! Eat* may also omit an object NP in quite different circumstances—where the identity of the object could be inferred from social context. If a guest calls at 1 p.m. you might politely ask *Have you eaten?*; this would be understood as an abbreviation of *Have you eaten lunch yet?* But if a friend knocks on the door at 1 a.m. it would be distinctly odd just to enquire *Have you eaten?* Suppose that he did look thin and hungry and you thought of offering food, the appropriate thing to say would be something like: *Have you eaten anything recently?*, including an object NP.

Transitive verbs of MOTION, REST and GIVING must generally specify an object—one could say *He often throws things*, but scarcely **He often throws*. In §4.1 we mentioned an exception: *follow* and *lead* have converse meanings and if they are used together either or both objects may be omitted, e.g. *I'll lead* (sc. you) *and you follow* (sc. me). There are other instances of a pair of semantically related verbs being used together and both omitting the object (which would, in normal circumstances, have to be stated). Thus, in chapter 7 of *Through the Looking Glass* the White King explains to Alice about his messengers: 'I must have *two*—to fetch and carry. One to fetch, and one to carry.' And people say *It is better to give than to take*.

A number of basically intransitive verbs from MOTION, AFFECT and CORPOREAL may be used in causative form, e.g. *The officer marched the soliders, The nurse sat the patient up, John wakened Mary*. The object NP could never be omitted from any transitive sentence for which there was a corresponding intransitive with S = O. If the O NP were omitted from *John wakened Mary*, then *John wakened* would be understood to imply that it was John who came out of a sleep, not that he caused someone else to. (We noted in §4.1 that *ride* and *drive* appear to belong to the RUN subtype of MOTION, but may only be used transitively, e.g. *He drove his car here*. Since there is no corresponding S = O intransitive (**The car drove here*) these verbs do allow the O NP to be omitted, e.g. *He drove here*.)

Quite different circumstances attend the omission of an object constituent after some of the most common verbs from Primary-B and Secondary types. If the identity of the object could be inferred by a listener from what has gone before in the discourse, or from what can be observed of the situation, or from shared knowledge, then it may be omitted. This applies to *see*, *hear* and *notice* from ATTENTION (§5.1); *remember*, *forget*, *know*, *realise* and *understand* from THINKING (§5.2); *decide* and *choose* from DECIDING (§5.3) but not to other verbs—which have a more specialised meaning—from these types. It also applies to a few Secondary verbs such as *help* and *try*. Suppose I see that John is attempting, without success, to unscrew a bottle top. I might say *Can I help?* (sc. to unscrew it), and he might reply *OK, you try!* (sc. to unscrew it).

Some verbs from these types may—like some from MOTION and GIVING—omit an object when used contrastively, e.g. *He theorises* (sc. about languages) *but I just describe* (sc. languages).

There are many transitive verbs which can never be used without a specified object (which may be an NP or a complement clause). They include all those in the LIKING type, all in ANNOYING (save *worry*, *grieve* and *delight*, §8.3.2), as well as many from other types, e.g. *want*, *attempt*, *force*, *let*, *recognise*, *inform*, *mention*, *put*, *appoint*, *imply* and *resemble*.

In summary, an object NP may be omitted in varying circumstances: when an activity is extended in time and/or may relate to a variety of objects, rather than one specific object; when the identity of the object can be inferred, from the situation; and when two verbs are used contrastively, with the same implied object, e.g. *You should think* (sc. about the question) *before you answer* (sc. the question). Object omission is more likely with frequently used verbs, which have a wide, general meaning.

8.3.2. S = O pairs, which is basic?

For verbs that show dual transitivity on the S = A pattern, native speakers have a clear intuition that the transitive use is prior, i.e. they consider *knit*, *saw*, *eat*, *remember*, *know* and *help* to be basically transitive verbs, which may also be used intransitively.

For most verbs with dual transitivity on the S = O pattern, native speakers consider the intransitive sense to be prior (e.g. *The horse trotted around the park, My leg hurt*) and the transitive to be a secondary, causative sense (e.g. *I trotted the horse around the park, John hurt my leg*). This applies to:

- (i) *march, run, walk, fly, swim, shake* from the RUN subtype, and *return* from the ARRIVE subtype, of MOTION;
- (ii) *sit, stand, lie, float, lean* from the SIT subtype, and *settle* from the STAY subtype, of REST;
- (iii) *wake(n), grow, hurt, bleed* from CORPOREAL;
- (iv) *work* from SOCIAL CONTRACT;
- (v) *race* from COMPETITION.

(It appears that the only true transitive verbs which may be used causatively are the Secondary-A forms *start, stop, keep, begin, hurry* and *hasten*, e.g. *The workmen started laying the tiles this morning, I started the workmen laying the tiles this morning*. Native speakers regard the non-causative use of these verbs as basic.)

There are a number of verbs from the DROP subtype of MOTION and from the BREAK and STRETCH subtypes of AFFECT which have dual transitivity on the S = O pattern:

DROP	BREAK	STRETCH
(a) *drop, spill, upset, overturn*	(a) *break, crush, smash*	(a) *extend, stretch, coil*
(b) *trip*	(a-b) *tear, chip*	(b) *bend, curl; freeze, cool, melt, dissolve, burn*
	(b) *burst, explode*	

Native speakers consider certain of these verbs to be basically intransitive, and certain of them to be basically transitive; for others it is difficult to assign priority to either transitivity value.

Thus, from the BREAK subtype, *break*, *crush* and *smash* are considered basically transitive, *burst* and *explode* basically intransitive, with *tear* and *chip* some way in between. Similarly, *drop*, *spill*, *upset* and *overturn* are considered basically transitive but *trip* basically intransitive; and *extend, stretch, coil* basically transitive but *bend, curl* and *freeze, cool, melt, dissolve* and *burn* basically intransitive. (Note that native speaker intuitions vary a little from person to person, and some are stronger than others. The opinions quoted here are based on two samples of about fifteen people each.)

The principle in operation here appears to be: if the S/O role often gets into the state described by the activity on its own, without outside assistance, then the verb is thought to be basically intransitive. But if one would normally expect there to be a Causer (even if one might not know who or what it is) then the verb is thought to be basically transitive. A person can trip without anyone else being around—so *trip* is regarded as an intransitive verb, with derived causative form. But if a liquid spills it is normally someone's fault—the basic construction for this verb is transitive, although it may also be used intransitively. (*The liquid spilled* is normally used to disclaim responsibility, in a rather disingenuous way, cf. construction type III for AFFECT verbs, e.g. *Oh, did my stick hit you?* in §4.2. In each case the Causer/Agent is omitted.) Similarly, things may readily burst (a bubble or a balloon) or explode (a nut that falls into the fire) without any human intervention. Something *may* break by itself (e.g. the bough of a tree, as it becomes old and dry) but for most instances of breaking a human agent is involved.

Some verbs pose additional problems due to special syntactic or semantic features. *Open* and *close* are used as transitive verbs, but in intransitive constructions one most frequently finds the related adjectives *open* and *closed* (e.g. *The door is open*), although intransitive use of the verbs is also possible (*The door opened silently*). The verb *return* is regarded as basically intransitive, and the S NP is likely to be a human (e.g. *The librarian returned to work today*); when it is used transitively the O NP is likely to be inanimate (e.g. *John returned the book to the library*). *Settle* is another verb described as basically intransitive; the S NP can be any human or animal. But it may also be used transitively, and then the A NP is likely to be someone in a position of authority, e.g. *The nurse settled all the sick children down for the night*, and *The Israeli government has now settled Jewish farmers in the Gaza strip*.

Worry, *grieve* and *delight* are transitive verbs in the ANNOYING type, e.g. *Mary's staying out late every night worries Granny*. They can be used in the passive, e.g. *Granny is/gets worried by Mary's staying out late every night*. But they may also—unlike most other ANNOYING verbs—be used intransitively, e.g. *Granny worries a lot* (*over/about Mary's staying out late every night*). When asked about *worry*, native speakers did not have any strong intuition that either of the transitive and intransitive senses is more basic than the other.

Finally, we can note that the set of verbs which have dual transitivity of type S = A and the set which have dual transitivity of type S = O are not mutually exclusive. At least some verbs from the RUN subtype of MOTION enter into pairs of both kinds, e.g. *That horse* (S) *jumped over the gate*, *That horse* (A) *jumped the gate* (O), and *John* (A) *jumped the horse* (O) *over the gate* (but notice that the preposition *over* cannot be omitted from the causative, even if it is a significant piece of jumping—one can say *John jumped the gate*, but not **John jumped the horse the gate*). A sentence like *M jumped the N* is potentially ambiguous between (i) M being the Causer and N the Moving role; and (ii) M being the Moving and N the Locus role. In fact the choice of NPs is likely to provide disambiguation, e.g. the Causer is generally HUMAN and an inanimate NP can only be Locus, so that *The horse jumped the gate* must be (ii) and *John jumped the horse* is most likely to be (i).

8.3.3. Causatives

All verbs with dual transitivity on the S = O pattern can be considered to be underlyingly intransitive, with a causative version that involves S becoming O and a new role, the Causer (which is most frequently human), entering as A. (For some AFFECT verbs the Causer coincides with Agent.) This applies both to (i) those verbs that native speakers think of as basically intransitive, e.g. *walk*, *bleed*, *work*, *trip*, *burst*, *curl*, *burn*, and to (ii) those that native speakers think of as basically transitive, e.g. *drop*, *spill*, *break*, *extend*, *coil*. The difference lies in the fact that verbs of set (ii) are thought of as generally involving a Causer, and those of set (i) as just occasionally involving a Causer.

Only a limited number of intransitive verbs can be used in a simple causative (i.e. S = O transitive) construction. But virtually all verbs—both intransitive and transitive—can occur in a periphrastic causative construction with Secondary verbs from the MAKING type, i.e. *make, force, cause, get, have*. Although 'causative' is the traditional label for these constructions (which I retain here), in fact a periphrastic construction with the verb *cause* —often referring to action which brings about a result by indirect means—is far removed in meaning from a simple causative. The verb *cause* in English has a limited range of use—one could scarcely say *He caused the dog to walk in the park*, and if one could it would mean something quite different from *He walked the dog in the park*.

It is instructive to compare *make* (the most commonly used verb from the MAKING type) with a simple causative:

(18a) *John walked the dog in the park*
(18b) *John made the dog walk in the park*
(19a) *Mary opened the door*
(19b) *Mary made the door open*
(20a) *Fred dissolved the sugar in the liquid*
(20b) *Fred made the sugar dissolve in the liquid*

There is considerable semantic difference between sentences in each pair. The (b) alternatives imply that some difficulty was encountered, that the event did not happen naturally. Hearing (18b) one might infer that the dog did not want to walk in the park, (19b) that the door could have been stuck and needed a hard shove, (20b) that Fred had perhaps to heat the liquid to get the sugar to dissolve. In contrast, the (a) sentences imply a natural activity—the dog was eager to walk, the door opened easily, and the sugar began to dissolve as soon as it was put in the liquid.

The differences between the (a/b) pairs relate to the fact that in (b) *the dog/door/sugar* is subject of the complement clause verb (it is also coded as surface direct object of *make*, but this is a secondary matter). It has the semantic properties of a subject, the role which is most relevant to the success of the activity. It is generally only appropriate to use a *make* construction when the subject of the complement clause is—by its character or nature— impeding the success of the activity; *make* refers to overcoming this impedance. In contrast, *the dog/door/sugar* is in the (a) sentences simply the object of the complement clause verb; it has the semantic characteristics of an object, i.e. the role which is most saliently affected by the activity described by the verb (there is here no hint of an impedance which has to be overcome).

Other MAKING verbs enter into constructions with a meaning similar to the (b) sentences. *He got the dog to walk in the park* and *He forced the dog to walk in the park* also imply that there was an element of impedance which had to be overcome.

Verbs from the MAKING type also occur freely with HUMAN PROPENSITY adjectives, e.g. *She made me (be) angry, She got me (to be) angry*. Adjectives from other types can also be used with *make*, in appropriate circumstances. We mentioned, in §3.2, that many adjectives from the DIMENSION, PHYSICAL PROPERTY, SPEED, AGE and COLOUR types may be used as both intransitive and transitive verbs, either in root form (e.g. *narrow, warm*) or by the addition of a derivational suffix *-en* (e.g. *deepen, sweeten*). There is a semantic contrast between a lexical causative such as *deepen, sweeten*, and a periphrastic one such as *make deep, make sweet*. The lexical form is most often used when the quality referred to by the adjective was already present to some extent and has now been intensified, i.e. *deepen*, 'make deeper', *sweeten* 'make sweeter'. The periphrastic causative states that the quality has been engendered (it may or may not have been present to some degree before), e.g. *Mary made the tea very sweet (in my opinion) but John complained and she had to sweeten it some more*. (See also the discussion, in §5.6, of periphrastic causatives involving the past participles of ANNOYING verbs, e.g. *make frightened*, and the meaning contrast between this and *frighten*.)

The simple causative construction (as in (18a), (19a), (20a)) is available for those intransitive verbs for which it is plausible that a Causer could be responsible for the event happening in a natural manner.

Almost all transitive verbs in English lack a simple causative use. This appears to be due to a syntactic constraint. Transitive verbs already have a direct object and any putative causative construction would be likely to be confused with the straightforward transitive. If corresponding to the periphrastic causative *Mary made John cut the cake* we were to have a simple causative, then *Mary*—as Causer—would become subject of *cut*. We could get either *Mary cut John PREPOSITION the cake* or else *Mary cut the cake PREPOSITION John*. Each of these would be understood to imply that Mary did the cutting, whereas what we are trying to describe is John doing the cutting and Mary making him do it. (There is an 'inherent preposition' transitive verb that does form a causative, *refer to*, e.g. *Noam referred me to McCawley's new book*, alongside *I referred to McCawley's new book*. Here the presence of the preposition avoids any possibility of confusion.)

However, Secondary-A verbs involve no roles beyond those of the complement clause verb—nothing comes between the two verbs in *John started running* or *Nanny started washing the baby*. *Start*—and also *stop, keep, begin, hurry, hasten*—can be used causatively (see §6.1.2). The new Causer comes in before *start* with the original subject now moving to a position between the two verbs, e.g. *The official started John running* (i.e. gave the signal for him to start) or *Mother started Nanny washing the baby* (told her it was now bath-time). Note the difference in meaning from *The official made John start running*, which carries the implication that he didn't want to run.

There are two points to note about simple causatives of Secondary-A verbs. The first is that only an ING complement clause may be involved, not a Modal (FOR) TO complement—we can say *John started to run*, but not **The official started John to run*. This is because Modal (FOR) TO relates to the subject getting involved in the activity normally on his own volition, not at a signal from someone else. The second is that there is no simple causative construction with *finish*; that is, there is no causative corresponding to *John finished making the beds*. A putative causative **Mother finished John making the beds* would imply that she gave a signal for the activity to terminate, and this would be incompatible with the 'object orientation' meaning of *finish*—the activity terminates when all the beds are made. (But note that we can have *Mother made John finish making the beds*, demonstrating once again the considerable semantic difference between simple causatives and periphrastic causatives in English.)

The verb *marry* has wide syntactic possibilities. In §2.9.6 we classed it as an 'inherent reciprocal' verb that may omit an O NP if it is *each other*, e.g. *John and Mary married (each other)*, corresponding to *John married Mary* and *Mary married John*.

There is a causative corresponding to this, e.g. *Father O'Leary married John and Mary*. There is also a causative corresponding to the simple transitive (non-reciprocal) use of *marry*, e.g. *Father O'Leary married John and Bill to Mary and Jane respectively*— here *to* introduces what is direct object in the non-causative *John and Bill married Mary and Jane respectively*.

In summary, a periphrastic causative construction, with a verb from the MAKING type, can, potentially, involve any transitive or intransitive verb or any adjective. It most often involves getting someone to do something that they did not want to do, or getting something into a new state. Simple causatives are available for some Secondary-A verbs, for some intransitive Primary-A verbs (the verb is used in a transitive frame, with the original S becoming O) and for adjectives from certain types (either the adjectival root is used as a transitive verb, or *-en* is added). A simple causative implies that the Causer is responsible for an event happening in a natural manner, or for a property being intensified.

Notes to Chapter 8

There are some minor exceptions to the general statement about transitivity in Fijian, in the first paragraph of this chapter—for full details see §18.1 of Dixon (1988).

§8.2.2. See Dixon (1982a) for a fuller discussion of phrasal verbs in English, and further references therein (including Bolinger 1971). Note that other terms are sometimes used for what are here called 'phrasal verbs', e.g. 'verb-particle combination' (Lipka 1972; Fraser 1974). Quirk and Greenbaum (1973: 347 ff.) use 'phrasal verb' for my p and Np varieties and 'prepositional verb' for my pN; ppN is then called a 'phrasal-prepositional verb'.

§8.2.3. The criteria given by Hopper and Thompson (1980) for transitivity correlate well with the evidence presented here, e.g. if an O NP is not fully affected this 'lowering of transitivity' may be marked by inserting a preposition before it.

§8.2.4. See also Green (1974) for discussion of benefactive constructions.

§8.2.5. See also McCawley (1988) for discussion of prepositionless measure phrases.

9

The plate, which had been eaten off, was owned by my aunt.
Passives

A passive sentence in English is not an automatic transformation of an active one. It is an alternative realisation of the relation between a transitive verb and its object, and involves an intransitive construction with a subject (corresponding to the transitive object), a copula-like verb *be* or *get*, and a participial form of the verb. Thus, corresponding to *A man took away the mad dog* we get the passive *The mad dog was taken away*. A passive clause may include an NP, introduced with *by*, corresponding to the transitive subject (e.g. *by a man*), but it does so only relatively seldom (in formal, written English, more than 80 per cent of passives are agentless, and the figure is undoubtedly higher for colloquial, spoken styles).

There is always a meaning difference between active and passive constructions. There are some transitive verbs which—for semantic or other reasons—never occur in the passive (§§9.2, 9.3) and, for many verbs, ability to passivise depends on the nature of the object. As Bolinger (1977*a*: 10) puts it: 'We can say *George turned the pages* or *The pages were turned by George*; something happens to the pages in the process. But when we say *George turned the corner* we cannot say **The corner was turned by George* —the corner is not affected, it is only where George was at the time. On the other hand, if one were speaking of some kind of marathon or race or game in which a particular corner is thought of as an objective to be taken, then one might say *That corner hasn't been turned yet*. I can say *The stranger approached me* or *I was approached by the stranger* because I am thinking of how his approach may affect me—perhaps he is a panhandler. But if a train approaches me I do not say **I was approached by the train*, because all I am talking about is the geometry of two positions.'

The passive is a marked construction, used according to one or more of a number of factors that are mentioned in §9.1. A passive should ideally be quoted together with its discourse and socio-cultural context; sometimes, a putative passive which sounds odd when spoken in isolation is immediately acceptable when placed in an appropriate context. When judging the examples quoted in this chapter, the reader is asked to keep his or her imagination on a loose rein, adding a bit of prior discourse and attributing to the speaker a motive for using a passive construction.

9.1. The nature of passive

Everything else being equal, a speaker of English will prefer to use a verb with two or more core roles (a transitive verb) in an active construction, with subject and object stated. A passive construction may be employed in one of the following circum-stances:

1. To avoid mentioning the subject
A surface subject is obligatory in each non-imperative English sentence. It is always possible to put *someone* or *something* in the subject slot, but such an indefinite form serves to draw attention to the fact that the subject is not being specified as fully as it might be. The passive may be used (*a*) if the speaker does not know who the subject was, e.g. *Mary was attacked last night;* or (*b*) if the speaker does not wish to reveal the identity of the subject, e.g. *It has been reported to me that some students have been collaborating on their assignments*; or (*c*) the identity of the subject is obvious to the addressees and does not need to be expressed, e.g. *I've been promoted;* or (*d*) the identity of the subject is not considered important.

Heavy use of the passive is a feature of certain styles; in scientific English it avoids bringing in the first person pronoun, e.g. *An experiment was devised to investigate . . .* rather than *I devised an experiment to investigate . . .* This is presumably to give an illusion of total objectivity, whereas in fact the particular personal skills and ideas of a scientist do play a role in his work, which would be honestly acknowledged by using active constructions with first person subject.

2. To focus on the transitive object, rather than on the subject
In §3.3 we enunciated the semantic principles that underlie the assignment of semantic roles to syntactic relations, and stated that the role which is likely to be most relevant to the success of the activity will be placed in A (transitive subject) relation.

We can construct a referential hierarchy, going from first person pronoun, through second person, proper names of people, human common nouns with determiner or modifier indicating specific reference (e.g. *that old man*, *my friend*), human common nouns with indefinite reference, to inanimate nouns. It is certainly the case that a transitive subject is likely to be nearer the beginning of the hierarchy than its co-occurring object, e.g. *I chose the blue cardigan, You should promote John, My teacher often canes boys, The fat girl is eating an ice cream.*

However, the object can—in some particular instance of the activity—be nearer the beginning of the hierarchy than the subject. In such a circumstance the passive construction may be used, putting the role which is in underlying O relation into the surface S slot. Thus, in place of *A boy kicked Mary at the picnic*, the passive *Mary was kicked (by a boy) at the picnic* might be preferred. Similar examples are: *Guess what, you have been chosen (by the team) as captain, I got promoted, My best friend often gets caned.* Compare these with prototypical transitive sentences (subject above object on the hierarchy), for which a passive sounds most odd, e.g. *The blue cardigan was chosen by me, An ice cream is being eaten by the fat girl.*

We mentioned in §3.3 that if there are several non-A roles, any of which could potentially be coded onto O relation, then one which has specific reference is likely to be preferred over others which have non-specific reference (e.g. *John told the good news* (O: Message) *to everyone he met*, but *John told Mary* (O: Addressee) *something or other*). In the same spirit, an O NP which has specific reference is more likely to be amenable to passivisation than one which is non-specific. For example, *Our pet dog was shot by that new policeman* sounds much more felicitous than *A dog was shot by that new policeman* (here the active would surely be preferred—*That new policeman shot a dog*).

3. To place a topic in subject relation
A discourse is normally organised around a 'topic', which is likely to recur in most sentences of the discourse, in a variety of semantic roles. There is always a preference for a topic to be subject, the one obligatory syntactic relation in an English sentence (and the pivot for various syntactic operations—see (4)). If a topic occurs in underlying O relation then a passive construction may be employed, to put it in surface S slot, e.g. *The hold-up man hid in the woods for five days, living on berries, and then he* (deep O, passive S) *was caught and put in jail*. (A topic NP is of course likely to have specific reference, demonstrating a correlation between criteria (2) and (3).)

4. To satisfy syntactic constraints
Every language has some syntactic mechanism for cohering together consecutive sentences in an utterance, identifying common elements and eliminating repetitions. English has a straightforward syntactic rule whereby, if two consecutive clauses have the same subject, this may be omitted from the second clause, e.g. *John took off his coat and then (John) scolded Mary*. However, if two coordinated clauses share an NP which is in subject relation in one and in object relation in another, then omission is not possible —from *John took off his coat and then Mary scolded John* the final *John* cannot be omitted. In such circumstances a passive construction may be used; the NP which would be in O relation in an active transitive becomes subject of the passive and, in terms of the syntactic convention, can now be omitted, e.g. *John took off his coat and was then scolded by Mary*. (A pronoun may in English substitute for a repeated noun between coordinated clauses whatever the syntactic relations involved, and pronominalisation would of course be used when omission of the NP is not permissible.)

Conditions (4) and (3) for using a passive interrelate. If an object NP in one clause has been subject in a previous clause then it is functioning as topic for at least a small segment of the discourse, and will almost certainly have specific and individuated reference. On these grounds, quite apart from wanting to meet the syntactic condition on omission, it would be a prime target for passivisation.

A reflexive clause—one in which subject and object are identical—is very unlikely to be cast into passive form, since none of the conditions just listed for using a passive can be satisfied: (1) it is impossible to avoid mentioning the subject, since it is identical with the object; (2) it is not meaningful to focus on object rather than on subject, since they are identical; and (3)–(4) there is no advantage in moving O into surface subject slot, since it is already identical with the subject. If a reflexive passive is ever used it is likely to be an 'echo' of a preceding sentence in the discourse that was in passive form, e.g. *My brother was taught linguistics by Kenneth Pike*, followed by *Oh really! Well my brother's a better linguist than yours and he was taught by himself.*

5. To focus on the result of the activity
The passive construction involves a participial form of the verb which functions very much like an adjective; it forms a predicate together with copula *be* or *get*. This participle is also used to describe the result of the activity (if it does have a definite result). A passive construction may be used in order to focus on this result, e.g. *My neighbour was appointed to the board* (*by the managing director*), *The goalkeeper is being rested from next week's game, That cup was chipped by Mary when she washed the dishes.*

There are two possibilities for the first element in a passive VP—*be* and *get. Be* is the unmarked form and—as discussed in §9.2–3—may be used with a wider range of verbs than *get*. It seems that *get* is often used when the speaker wishes to imply that the state which the passive subject (deep O) is in, is not due just to the transitive subject, or to the result of chance, but may in some way be due to the behaviour of this passive subject. Consider *John was fired*—this could be used if there was a general redundancy in the firm. But *John got fired* implies that he did something foolish, such as being rude to his supervisor, which would be expected to lead to this result.

The verb *get* has a wide range of senses: (1) it is a member of the OWN subtype of GIVING, e.g. *Mary got a new coat*; (2) *get to* has an achievement sense, as a member of the SEMI-MODAL type, e.g. *John got to know how to operate the machine*; (3) it is a member of the MAKING type, e.g. *I got John to write that letter to you*; (4) it can be a copula before an adjective or it can begin a passive VP, in both cases generally implying that the surface subject was at least partly responsible for being in a certain state, e.g. *Johnny got dirty, Mary got promoted*.

In fact the copula/passive sense, (4), can plausibly be related to the causative sense, (3). We can recall that, as a member of the MAKING type, *get* takes a Modal (FOR) TO complement clause, and the *for* must be omitted (§7.3.4), e.g. *The boss got Mary to fire John*. The complement clause can be passive and *to be* may then be omitted under certain semantic conditions (discussed in relation to (2a/b) in §6.3.1)—thus, *The boss got John fired*.

Now the object of a MAKING verb (which is underlying subject of the complement clause) is not normally coreferential with the main clause subject; if it is it cannot, as a rule, be omitted (§7.3.4); that is, we may say *John forced himself to be examined by a specialist*, but not **John forced to be examined by a specialist*.

Thus, a normal MAKING complement construction would be *John got himself fired*. I suggest that the *get* passive is related to this, through the omission of *himself*. The point is that this omission— of main clause object (= complement clause subject) when it is coreferential with main clause subject—is not allowed for other MAKING verbs, but is put forward as a special syntactic rule which effectively derives a *get* passive from a MAKING construction involving *get*. This formulation states that an underlying *get* (MAKING verb) plus reflexive pronoun plus *to* (complementiser) plus *be* (unmarked passive introducer) plus passive verb can omit both the *to be* and the reflexive pronoun, and *get* then appears to be the marker of a variety of passive, parallel to *be*.

This analysis explains the distinctive meaning of *get* passives. Syntactic support is provided by the possible positionings of an adverb such as *immediately*. This can occur at the places marked by '(A)' in:

(1) *John was (A) fired (A)*
(2) *John (A) got (A?) fired (A)*

Some speakers will accept *John got A fired* but it is much less acceptable than *John A got fired*. **John A was fired* is judged as ungrammatical.

With an active predicate an adverb can come between subject and predicate or after the first (or a later) word of the predicate (§2.5). With a canonical passive, involving *be*, an adverb may come between *be* and the passive verb (as in (1)) but not between the subject and *be*. In a causative construction with a passive complement clause the adverb placement is as shown in: *Mary (A) caused John to be (A) fired (A)*. When the *to be* is omitted, with causative *get*, the adverb position which immediately followed *to be* becomes less acceptable, e.g. *Mary (A) got John (A?) fired (A)*. We suggested that the *get* passive is essentially a reflexive version of this construction, i.e. *John (A) got (himself) (A?) fired (A)*. This does precisely explain the adverb possibilities in (2). (Note that when the *himself* is dropped, the adverb position immediately before *fired* becomes even more marginal than it was before.)

Although the *get* passive thus appears to be syntactically related to the MAKING verb *get*, it has now taken on a wider range of meaning, and does not always imply that the passive subject is partly responsible for being in the described state. *That meeting got postponed*, for instance, could not felicitously be expanded to *That meeting got itself postponed*, although it does carry a certain overtone that the meeting seems fated never to be held. The *get* passive is certainly more used in colloquial than in formal styles. I have the feeling that a *by* phrase is less likely to be included with a *get* passive than with a *be* passive (even in the same, colloquial, style); this is something that would need to be confirmed by a text count. *Get* passives may also carry an implication that something happened rather recently—one might hear *He got run over* concerning something that occurred last week, but for something that took place ten years ago *He was run over* would be a more likely description.

Returning now to our discussion of the nature of the passive, we can conclude that almost anything can be stated through an active construction but that only rather special things are suitable for description through a passive construction. For instance, there may be some special significance to the object NP, as it is used with a particular verb, or with a particular verb and a certain subject.

Consider *John's mother saw a brick in the bar*. The passive correspondent of this, *A brick was seen by John's mother in the bar*, sounds ridiculous, something that is most unlikely to be said. But if the event reported were *John's mother saw him in the bar*, then the passive, *John was seen (by his mother) in the bar*, is perfectly feasible. If the passive were used one might guess that he shouldn't have been there, and may now get into trouble. 'John' is a definite, individual human, a prime candidate to be in the subject relation. Casting the sentence into passive form implies that the concatenation of John's being in the bar and his mother's seeing him there has a particular significance.

9.2. Which verbs from Primary types may passivise

For the great majority of transitive verbs it is possible to find some O NP (or some particular combination of O and A NPs) which has the right sort of semantic significance—in conjunction with the meaning of the verb—for a passive construction to be a felicitous alternative to the unmarked active. But very few (if any) verbs may passivise with equal facility on *any* kind of O. Consider *leave*, for instance. This verb can have as object a person, place or thing. A person or thing can be affected or potentially affected by being left—a person may refuse to be left, may run after the person who is trying to leave them somewhere; a thing might become liable to be stolen if left in a certain place. Corresponding to *Fred left Mary at the station* and *Fred left your bicycle at the station* we can have passives *Mary was left at the station (by Fred)* and *Your bicycle was left at the station (by Fred)*. However, if *leave* has a place description as object there is not likely to be a corresponding passive, simply because the place is not affected in any way by someone departing from it—one could say *Fred left the office at five o'clock*, but scarcely *The office was left (by Fred) at five o'clock*.

Verbs which are particularly open to passivisation are those whose object is likely to be human, or else something with specific reference that is being particularly focused on. ANNOYING verbs, for instance, have the Experiencer in O relation and this is generally human. Verbs from this type are very frequently used in passive form, e.g. *John was pleased (by that concert)*. (See §5.6 for the semantic and syntactic contrast between passive and past participle (derived adjective) use of ANNOYING verbs.) Most ANNOYING verbs may take either *be* or *get*, e.g. *He was annoyed* (*by her behaviour*), or *He got annoyed*, which could be used when he worked himself up into a state of being annoyed. Those which would seldom be used with *get* include *delight, please, satisfy, amuse* and *astonish*, verbs referring to feelings that tend to be experienced naturally, with the Experiencer having little or no role in bringing them about.

In §8.2.4 we described how, with certain verbs, if the referent of a peripheral NP marked by a preposition is particularly salient in that instance of the activity, it may drop its preposition and move into direct object slot, e.g. *They climbed up a little hill* (preposition included) but *I climbed a high mountain* (preposition omitted). Such an NP, by virtue of its salience, is a good candidate for passivisation, and this is particularly likely when it is nearer the beginning of the referential hierarchy described under condition (2) in §9.1 than is the A NP, e.g. *That tall mountain hasn't yet been climbed* (*by anyone*) alongside the active *No one has yet climbed that tall mountain* (note how the negation appears in the predicate for the passive but in the A NP of the active).

When there is already an object NP, as in example (3), this remains when a peripheral NP is promoted into the first object slot, as in (4):

(3) *John gave a single red rose to Mary*
(4) *John gave Mary a single red rose*

Only the object NP *a single red rose* may be passivised from (3), but—for most speakers—either of the objects from (4) can become passive subject:

(3a) *A single red rose was given to Mary* (*by John*)
(3b) **Mary was given a single red rose to* (*by John*)
(4a) *Mary was given a single red rose* (*by John*)
(4b) *A single red rose was given Mary* (*by John*)

(As mentioned in §8.2.5, when the preposition is omitted from a measure phrase this does not become direct object and is not open to passivisation. In §§4.4, 4.5 and 8.3.1 we discussed cognate NPs which can follow CORPOREAL and WEATHER verbs and decided that these have only weak object properties, largely because they can only become passive subject in rather special circumstances.)

We can now consider those transitive verbs from Primary types in English which do not allow a passive, or else have one in very limited circumstances. There appear to be three main reasons for this: a verb may be symmetrical, it may refer to a static relation, or it may inherently focus on the subject. Taking these one at a time:

(*a*) Symmetric verbs
These are verbs referring to a state or activity that relates equally to two entities—either could be subject and the other will then be object. Thus, if it is the case that *Mary resembles John* it must also be the case that *John resembles Mary*. Alternatively, we can use a reciprocal construction *John and Mary resemble each other* or *Mary and John resemble each other*. Either of the roles may be placed in subject slot, and so there is no possible need for a passive construction.

Some verbs, such as *resemble* and *look like*, must be symmetrical. Others have two senses, one with a symmetrical meaning and one without. *John met Mary at the station* is, for instance, ambiguous between (i) he went to the station to meet her off a train, and (ii) they just happened to meet each other there. Sense (ii), but not (i), could be paraphrased *Mary met John at the station*. The passive *Mary was met* (*by John*) *at the station* is not ambiguous; it can only relate to the non-symmetrical sense, (i). Similarly, *fight* may be symmetrical, with a human as O, e.g. *John fought Tom in 1979/Tom fought John in 1979*, or non-symmetrical with an activity noun as O, e.g. *Tom fought a fierce battle*. Only the second sense is open to passivisation (and even this would need considerable contextualisation, since *a fierce battle* is below *John* on the referential hierarchy).

(*b*) Verbs that refer to a static relationship
Verbs such as *contain, cost, weigh* and *last*—as in *The carton contains milk, This book costs ten dollars, My son weighs a hundred and fifty pounds, The meeting lasted all morning*—indicate a static relationship between two things. Nothing 'happens' and so a passive construction, which normally describes the result of an activity, could not be used. (Note also that in a passive construction the *by* phrase is always omittable, and for these verbs both poles of the relationship must be stated.) Other

verbs of this kind include *fit, suit, comprise, depend on, result from, relate to*. Some symmetric verbs, like *resemble*, specify a relationship, and their lack of passive is due to (*b*) as well as to (*a*).

Verbs in the OWN subtype of GIVING refer to the relationship between Owner and Possession roles. The verb *own* can form a passive, e.g. *John owns that car, That car is owned by John*. Why is it that *have* does not form a corresponding passive, **That car is had by John?* In fact the corresponding active is inadmissible, at least in the present tense—we would not say *John has that car* (where *have* has a meaning similar to *own*; there is another sense of have, 'be using', and in this sense we can say *John has that car today*). *Have* refers to a general property of the Owner, e.g. *John has a car. Own*, in contrast, focuses on the Possession and implies that the Owner has legal or some other official right to it; the Possession can be foregrounded as passive subject (but note that the Owner is invariably included, through a *by* phrase). *Belong to* is effectively the converse of *own* and *have*, with Owner in object slot, after *to*; if a speaker wishes to focus on the Owner, putting it in subject slot, he will use *own* or *have*, rather than a passive of *belong to. Lack* is never used as a passive participle since it does not refer to the result of an activity (contrast with *is owned by*, which could be used to describe the result of a purchase or bequest, say); the present participle is used instead, e.g. *Brains are sorely lacking in that family*, alongside the active *That family sorely lack brains*.

The verb *equal* generally describes a static relationship, e.g. *Two and two equals four*, and cannot then be used in a passive construction. But it can also be used with a more dynamic sense, to describe something getting into a relationship of equality with something else. Suppose Tom runs a mile in three and a half-minutes and then Fred repeats the feat the following month; we can say *Fred equalled Tom's time*—Tom's time existed first, and then Fred came along and clocked a time that was equal to it. In this circumstance it is permissible to use a passive, especially if the O of equal is an established topic: *Tom set up a new world record, but it was equalled by Fred the next month*.

(*c*) Verbs that inherently focus on the subject
The LIKING type is the converse of ANNOYING in terms of role–

relation correspondence. LIKING verbs have the Experiencer (which is normally human) in A relation and the Stimulus as O; they express a feeling that the Experiencer has about a Stimulus. It is thus scarcely plausible to avoid stating A, or to focus more on the identity of O than of A. The object of a LIKING verb will seldom be passivised—it is most likely to be when continuing an established topic, e.g. *That concert, which was put on by the sixth-grade pupils, was thoroughly enjoyed.*

Possess, from the OWN subtype, differs from *own* in that it implies a strong emotional or mental connection between Owner and Possession, e.g. *She possesses a fine sense of loyalty/a good brain.* It is because of this focus on the Owner that *possess*—unlike *own*—is seldom used in the passive. (The verb *be possessed by* (e.g. *the devil*) is best considered a separate lexeme.)

Know and *believe* are further verbs that focus on the subject and are only occasionally found in the passive—generally, when the original A NP has non-individual or indefinite reference, e.g. *His testimony was believed by every person in court that day*. For *know*, the past participle is used, with an NP introduced by *to*, and this is often preferred over a passive construction, especially when the underlying A is human, e.g. *John is known to (?*by) everyone in the room.*

The verb *join*, in the sense 'become a member of', has as subject an NP referring to a person (or perhaps a few people) and as object the name of an organisation, e.g. *John joined the Catholic Church, Mary joined our film society.* The object refers to a group of people; the important point is not that the group became slightly enlarged (what does it matter if the film society has fifty members or fifty-one?), but that Mary joined it. The subject must be more important than the object, for this activity, and that is why a passive construction would not be appropriate.

In summary, those Primary verbs which are seldom or never found in the passive fall into three classes, (*a*)–(*c*), which can be accounted for in terms of conditions (1)–(5) from §9.1.

9.3. How verbs from Secondary types passivise

Overall, Secondary verbs passivise much less readily than do

Primary verbs. There are a number which occur in a *be* passive construction, but rather few that take a *get* passive.

Secondary-D verbs, the SEEM and MATTER types, are essentially intransitive and thus not open to passivisation. Secondary-C verbs, from the MAKING and HELPING types, can take a direct object (which is underlying complement clause subject). Some of these may passivise on this object NP, e.g. *John was made/permitted/ allowed/helped to fill in the form, Mary was prevented from seeing the doctor.* A passive is scarcely possible, however, with *let* (save of the idiomatic *let X go*), since this verb focuses on the main clause subject (§6.3.1), or with the causative sense of *get*, and quite impossible with the causative sense of *have*. *Force* may have a normal passive, e.g. *The guerrillas forced John to walk home* (*by holding a gun to his back*) and *John was forced to walk home* (*by the guerrillas, holding a gun to his back*). There is also a special passive of *force* that cannot have a *by* phrase but which may include a subordinate clause stating a reason, e.g. *John was forced to walk home, because his car has broken down* (the corresponding active, something like *John's car breaking down forced him to walk home*, feels somewhat strained).

With the Secondary type WANTING, the subject of a Modal (FOR) TO complement clause is often identical with the subject of the WANTING verb, and is then omitted. But they can be different, and with some WANTING verbs *for* may be or must be omitted, so that the complement clause subject becomes surface object of the main verb. It should then theoretically be available for passivisation. A passive construction is used with some verbs from this type, e.g. *expect* and *intend*—we can say *Mary was expected/intended to drive the bus today.* Passive is much less plausible with *want, wish* and *deserve* simply because the meanings of these verbs inherently focus on the subject, expressing the subject's attitude towards something—this is (*c*) from §9.2.

Some WANTING verbs, and a few Primary-B verbs such as *choose* and *order*, may have both main and complement clauses in passive form, the original complement clause object first becoming derived passive subject of that clause, simultaneously—in the absence of *for*—surface object of the main clause, and then derived passive subject of the main clause, e.g. from *They intended someone to murder Hitler* we can get *They intended Hitler to be murdered* and finally *Hitler was intended to be murdered*. Such a double-passive construction becomes rather less acceptable if any *by* phrase is included, e.g. ?*Hitler was intended by the Russians to be murdered by their crack marksman*.

The BEGINNING type of Secondary-A verbs is particularly interesting from the point of view of passivisation. We can recall that these verbs have no independent role, sharing with the verb for which they provide semantic modification its subject (and, if it is transitive, its object), e.g.

(5) *The warders began to count the prisoners*
(6) *The warders began counting the prisoners*

Now (5) and (6) each contain two verbs, *begin* and *count*. We can enquire whether it is possible (*a*) to have a passive form of *begin*, but not of *count*; (*b*) to have a passive form of *count*, but not of *begin*; (*c*) to have both verbs in passive form. Consider:

(5a) **The prisoners were begun to count*
(6a) **The prisoners were begun counting*
(5b) *The prisoners began to be counted*
(6b) *The prisoners began being counted*
(5c) *The prisoners were begun to be counted*
(6c) *The prisoners were begun being counted*

Sentences (5a) and (6a), where just *begin* is in passive form, are totally ungrammatical. However, (5b) and (6b), where just *count* is in passive form, are quite acceptable, to all native speakers. Sentences (5c) and (6c), with both verbs in passive form, are rejected by perhaps the majority of native speakers, but judged as perfectly acceptable by a significant minority.

There appears to be a potential difference in meaning between the (b) and (c) alternatives for those speakers who can accept either. Suppose that the prisoners began to file past the head warder in order to be counted—(5b) or (6b) might be an appropriate description for this. But (5c) or (6c) could just refer to a much-postponed counting of the prisoners finally being undertaken by the warders, and maybe the prisoners themselves weren't even aware of it, e.g. *The prisoners were finally begun to be counted at four o'clock*.

These passive possibilities support our proposal that a BEGINN-ING verb forms a single semantic unit with the verb it modifies. We can suggest that in (5b) and (6b) *begin* modifies a passive verb, whereas in (5c) and (6c) the whole complex of *begin*-plus-active-transitive-verb is passivised. A sentence like *The warders began to count the prisoners*, with a secondary verb in the main clause, is syntactically similar to *John likes/decided/remembered to kiss Aunt Mary*, with a primary verb in the main clause (and both clauses having the same subject, this being omitted from the complement clause). Note that we can here get a construction that looks like (5b), e.g. *Aunt Mary likes/decided/remembered to be kissed*, but nothing at all that resembles (5c) (i.e. not **Aunt Mary is liked/was decided/was remembered to be kissed*). This again emphasises the secondary nature of verbs from the BEGINNING type, that they effectively form a semantic unit with the following verb (although this is syntactically in a complement clause).

Finish, start and *continue* have basically the same passive possibilities as *begin*. Of the other verbs in the type, *cease, stop* and *keep on* are restricted to the (b) passive, while *commence, complete* and *discontinue* are scarcely plausible in any variety of passive.

When a complement clause verb is omitted (§6.1.2), BEGINNING verbs passivise like any other transitive verb, e.g. *They finished the house on Tuesday, The house was finished on Tuesday*.

In §6.1.2 we mentioned intransitive uses of BEGINNING verbs, with an activity noun as subject. Corresponding to *They began (fighting) the battle on Tuesday* there is *The battle began on Tuesday*. There is a contrast between the intransitive and the passive of the transitive, i.e. *The battle was begun on Tuesday*. The passive implies a deliberate decision to begin fighting on that day, whereas the plain intransitive could be used if it just happened—if fighting broke out spontaneously.

TRYING is another Secondary-A type. Most TRYING verbs are similar to *want, wish, possess* and the LIKING type in that they focus semantically on the subject, and are thus not appropriate in a passive construction; there are no *try* sentences parallel to (5c) and (6c). TRYING verbs can, of course, modify either an active or a passive verb in the complement clause, e.g. *John failed to invite Mary, Mary failed to get invited*. HURRYING verbs also occur in constructions parallel to (5b), (6b) but not (5c), (6c). MODALS and SEMI-MODALS have no passive form, although they can of course modify a passive verb, e.g. *Mary ought to be punished*.

All the examples we have given of the passive of secondary verbs have involved *be*. The *get* variety is far rarer—*get allowed* or *get needed* or *get intended* or *get expected* are at best marginal, while *get begun* is almost impossible. *Get* passives may be used with some members of the Secondary-B type POSTPONING and also, to a limited extent, with Secondary-C verbs such as *force* and *prevent*.

9.4. Complement clauses as passive subjects

An ING complement clause in O relation can almost always become passive subject. This applies whether the verb of the main clause is primary—*Mary's having been passed over was mentioned at the party*—or secondary—*Counting the prisoners was begun/ tried on Tuesday*. It also applies to ING clauses that are the object of a verb with an inherent preposition, e.g. *Jane's having been promoted was pondered over*. As mentioned in §9.2, the NP object of a LIKING verb is not very frequently passivised, and this applies also to an ING clause, although it is just possible to say, for instance, *Mary's singing the blues was preferred to John's warbling Verdi*.

A THAT or WH- clause in O relation passivises much like an ING clause, except that here the complement clause is most often extraposed to the end of the main clause, with *it* filling the subject slot, e.g. with primary verbs, *It was reported that war had broken out, It was recognised that we would all die*, and with secondary verbs, *It was expected/hoped that it would all be over quickly*. Exceptions include *ensure*, the only verb from the MAKING type to take a THAT complement, which is scarcely acceptable in the passive; and LIKING verbs, which must include *it* before a THAT complement (*They like it that Mary plays the fiddle*) do not allow the THAT clause to become passive subject (**It is liked that Mary plays the fiddle*).

Verbs from the ORDER subtype of SPEAKING have an Addressee NP in O slot, and this can be followed by a THAT clause. Most ORDER verbs may omit the Addressee, and the THAT clause may then be passivised, e.g. *It is requested that empty cans be placed in the litter bin, It has been ordered that all prisoners should be shot at dawn*. However, if an Addressee NP is included only this may become passive subject, not the THAT clause, e.g. *The firing squad have been ordered that all prisoners should be shot at dawn*, not **It has been ordered the firing squad that all prisoners should be shot at dawn*.

A Modal (FOR) TO complement clause has three variant forms: (i) the full form with *for* retained, e.g. *I chose for Mary to go*— here *for Mary to go* fills the O slot; (ii) a reduced form in which *for* is omitted but the complement clause subject retained, e.g. *I chose Mary to go*—here *Mary* is surface object of the main verb, with *to go* being a post-object constituent; (iii) a further reduced form where the complement clause subject is omitted under coreferentiality with the subject NP in the main clause, e.g. *I chose to go*— here *to go* fills object slot. As discussed above, the only possible passive of type (ii) is on the surface object NP (which is also underlying subject of the complement clause), e.g. *Mary was chosen to go*. We can now enquire whether the *for* clause in (i) and the *to* clause in (iii) may become passive subject.

They may be in principle, but seldom are in practice. A Modal (FOR) TO complement describes the complement clause subject getting involved in an activity, but also carries a sense that the subject of the main clause wanted it to happen; in view of this, the transitive subject is seldom open to demotion, in a passive. It is just possible for a full Modal (FOR) TO clause to be passivised with some verbs from DECIDING, WANTING and LIKING, e.g. *For John to receive the house and Mary the money was finally decided on* or *It was finally decided for John to receive the house and Mary the money*; *It had been intended for Mary to go*; and *It was preferred for the sermon to come last*. A reduced form of Modal (FOR) TO, as in (iii) of the last paragraph, may also become passive subject with some verbs from DECIDING and WANTING (but not, it seems, from LIKING), e.g. *It was decided to eliminate wastage; It is hoped/planned/intended to complete these tasks today*.

For a Judgement TO complement the complement clause subject is always the surface object of the main verb. This kind of complement construction is very frequently passivised, often so as to avoid specifying who is responsible for the judgement, e.g. *They know John to be stupid, John is known to be stupid*. The verb *say* only takes a Judgement TO complement in the passive, e.g. *He is said to be stupid* but not **They say him to be stupid*. The verb *rumour* may take a THAT or a Judgement TO complement clause but is seldom (or never) found in anything but the passive, e.g. *It was rumoured that John had died, John was rumoured to be dead* (but scarcely **They rumoured that John had died, *They rumoured John to be dead*). Similar remarks apply to *repute*, which is generally used in the passive, with a Judgement TO complement, e.g. *Mary is reputed to be a secret drinker*, but not **They repute Mary to be a secret drinker*.

The subject of a FROM ING complement clause is always also identified as surface object of the main verb, and may be passivised, e.g. *John was stopped from going* (see §7.2.9). WH- TO complements seldom or never passivise, partly because, as with Modal (FOR) TO, the semantic orientation of the main clause subject demands that it be kept in that syntactic slot (e.g. *They didn't understand how to behave*, but not **How to behave was not understood*).

In summary, the possibilities of a complement clause, in underlying object function, becoming passive subject are again determined by conditions (1)–(5) from §9.1.

9.5. Prepositional NPs becoming passive subjects

In §8.2.1 we discussed verbs that must take an inherent preposition before an NP. This NP has many of the characteristics of a direct object, and can almost always passivise. Quite a range of prepositions are involved and the verbs come from a fair array of types, e.g. *deal with, rely on, decide on, think about, listen to, look at, wonder at, dawdle over, search for*. The object of the inherent preposition verb *confess to* does not readily become a passive subject but this is because *confess to* focuses semantically on the subject, similar to LIKING verbs, and *want* and *possess*—see (c) in §9.2—and it is not appropriate to demote this subject. (Similar remarks apply to *boast of/about* and *brag of/about*, but to a lesser extent—a passive here, although not common, is possible.)

Phrasal verbs, discussed in §8.2.2, are combinations of verb plus preposition(s) which have an independent meaning, not predictable from the meanings of the component elements. An NP which immediately follows the verbal element has direct object status and may always passivise, e.g.

Np type: *They put the wedding off until next week, The wedding was put off until next week*

NpN type: *They took me for a preacher, I was taken for a preacher*

NppN type: *They tied the conference in with the school holidays, The conference was tied in with the school holidays*

An NP which follows the preposition(s) of a phrasal verb (with no other NP preceding it) has weak object status, and shows limited passivisation possibilities, e.g.

pN type: *The teachers are always picking on John, John is always being picked on (by the teachers)*

ppN type: *They did away with the position of Assistant Secretary, The position of Assistant Secretary was done away with*

If there is a direct object NP, coming immediately after the verbal component, and a second NP following the preposition(s), as in NpN and NppN types of phrasal verb, then the later NP can never be passivised. For example, *a preacher* and *the school holidays* from the examples above could not become passive subject.

Leaving aside the special cases of inherent preposition verbs and phrasal verbs, we can now consider the question of passivisation of an NP that is straightforwardly governed by a preposition. This is plainly possible in English—as in *Oh dear, my new hat has been sat on* and *This bed was slept in by Queen Elizabeth*—but in quite limited circumstances. What are these circumstances?

Recall that a direct object NP may only become passive subject when it is sufficiently special—in that semantic-syntactic context— to merit being focused on, perhaps in contrast to something else. At a party, someone could wander into another room and exclaim: *Hey, whiskey is being drunk in here*; one would infer that something less strong was being consumed in the room he has just left. A peripheral NP, marked by a preposition, may also be passivised when it refers to something that is the most significant element in an activity. If you were handed a glass and noticed someone else's dregs at the bottom, or lipstick on the rim, you could use a construction with an adjectival predicate—*This glass is dirty*; or a construction with the underlying direct object passivised

—*This glass has been used*; or a sentence that involves passivisation on a peripheral NP to the verb *drink* (which is the activity being alluded to)—*This glass has been drunk out of.*

There are two syntactic restrictions on a peripheral NP becoming passive subject:

(*a*) There must be no direct object present. If there is, it is only the direct object that can be passivised, not the prepositional object. Consider *Someone has drunk whiskey out of this glass*; it is quite unacceptable to say **This glass has been drunk whiskey out of*. It is only when the object NP is omitted that passivisation on a prepositional NP becomes possible. As further examples we can quote *This spoon has been eaten with* but not **This spoon has been eaten beans with*, and *My new cushion has been sat on by a dog* but not **My new cushion has been sat a dog on* (corresponding to the causative *Someone has sat a dog on my new cushion*).

This restriction relates to our earlier observation that an NP which follows the preposition(s) of a phrasal verb may sometimes be passivised but only if there is no preceding direct object NP which comes between verbal and prepositional components, i.e. N_2 may sometimes be passivised from pN_2 and ppN_2 but never from N_1pN_2 or N_1ppN_2.

It is not the case that a passive verb may not be followed by a direct object. Where a prepositional NP with a transitive verb is promoted into object slot (§8.2.4) the original object remains, e.g. *give Mary a book, tell Mary a story*. Either of the two objects may be passivised, with the other remaining after the verb in the passive clause, e.g. *Mary was told a story, A story was told Mary*. The rule appears to be that if there are two objects then either may passivise, but if there is an object and a prepositional NP then passivisation is restricted to the object. Only when there is no object present may the prepositional NP become passive subject.

(Quasi-exceptions to this rule involve idioms such as *shake hands with, find fault with, make an honest woman of*. It is possible to say things like *Have you been shaken hands with yet?*)

(*b*) The prepositional NP must not be alternatively codable as direct object. We often have available two possible syntactic frames for a given concatenation of verb and semantic roles; a certain role may be mapped onto O relation in one frame and marked by a preposition in another frame. In such a case, it will generally be passivisable only from the frame in which it is object, and not from that in which it appears with a preposition. There are several kinds of instance of this restriction:

(i) In §8.2.3 we discussed a group of transitive verbs that may insert a preposition before a direct object NP, e.g. *He kicked the box, He kicked at the box*. This NP may be passivised from simple direct object position, but not as a rule when there is a preceding preposition. We could say *That box was kicked* (*and dented*), *This sheet has been torn* but scarcely **That box has been kicked at* (*and dented*), **This sheet has been torn at*. Inserting the preposition indicates that the activity did not relate to some specific object, or did not achieve a specific result, and in such semantic circumstances we would not expect passivisation to be possible.

There is one notable exception: one can say *Mary was shot* (implying that the bullet or arrow hit her) or *Mary was shot at* (suggesting that the projectile missed her). In the second sentence the Target is not physically affected but she is likely to be mentally disturbed by the incident—she will have had a scare, and may realise that she is at risk of a further attack. It is here possible to passivise on an NP governed by a preposition (even though there is an alternative construction in which it is direct object); but this appears only to be possible when the NP has animate reference since only animates are affected by being shot at.

(ii) In §8.2.4 we discussed verbs that may promote a peripheral NP—normally marked by a preposition—into direct object slot, if it is particularly significant in this instance of the activity. It was remarked, in §9.2, that the salience of such an NP is such that it may readily be passivised (especially if the transitive subject is non-specific), e.g. *The English Channel was first swum in 1875, That peak has never been climbed, French is spoken throughout my chain of boutiques*. Such an NP—which can be promoted to object and passivised from that slot—may never be passivised from its original post-prepositional position. That is, we could not say **The English Channel was first swum across in 1875, *That peak has never been climbed up*, or **French is spoken in throughout my chain of boutiques*.

Promotion to object is also possible in transitive sentences, e.g. *John gave an apple to Mary, John gave Mary an apple; Granny knitted a jumper for Mary; Granny knitted Mary a jumper*. The NP

Mary may only be passivised from the second sentence of each pair
—*Mary was given an apple* (*by John*), *Mary was knitted a jumper*
(*by Granny*). Passivisation of *Mary* from the first sentence of each
pair, where this NP is marked by a preposition, is blocked on two
grounds: (i) it is preceded by a direct object, and (ii) there is an
alternative construction available in which it is direct object. Thus,
we do not get **Mary was given an apple to*, or **Mary was knitted a
jumper for*.

In §4.2 we described, for AFFECT verbs, frame I which has Target
role as O and Manip role marked by a preposition, e.g. *John hit
the vase with that stick*, and frame II which has Manip as O and
Target marked by a preposition, e.g. *John hit that stick on the vase*.
The Target may only be passivised from frame I, in which it is
object (*The vase was hit with that stick*), and the Manip may only
be passivised from frame II, in which it is object (*That stick was hit
on the vase*). There are again two reasons why we cannot passivise
the Manip when it is preceded by *with*, in frame I, or the Target
when it is preceded by a preposition like *on*, in frame II: (i) they
are preceded by a direct object NP; and (ii) there is an alternative
construction in which this role is in direct object relation. This
explains the unacceptability of **That stick was hit the vase with* and
*The vase was hit that stick on.

In summary, English may allow a prepositional NP to become
passive subject (the preposition remaining after the verb) only if
there is no direct object and if there is no alternative construction
type in which the NP could be coded as direct object.

Passivisation of a peripheral NP seldom happens in English. We
can mention three of the kinds of circumstance in which it is
permitted:

(*a*) When the referent of the NP has been (or may be) affected,
to its detriment, by the activity; a *by* phrase, marking passive
agent, is unlikely to be included, e.g. *That window shouldn't be
leaned against* (it might break); *My new hat has been sat on*.

(*b*) Where it is a particular feature of some object that it was
involved in a certain activity with a particularly important subject.
Here the significant factor is concatenation of object and verb with
that subject, which must be included, in a *by* phrase. Imagine an

auctioneer describing a four-poster: *The next item is an antique bed which is reputed to have been slept in by Queen Elizabeth I.*

(*c*) Where the NP is discourse topic and is brought into passive subject slot for this reason, e.g. (cf. Bolinger 1977*b*: 69) *Those stairs were built by John, then they were run up by Mary and promptly collapsed.* (On its own *Those stairs were run up by Mary* is much less acceptable.)

Note the contrast between (*a*) and (*b*). If you are shown to an hotel room and notice that the sheets on the bed are all mussed up you might exclaim in annoyance: *This bed has been slept in!* (It doesn't matter who by; the fact you are drawing attention to is that it's not clean.) But in a higher-quality establishment the manager might conduct you to his finest suite and announce with pride: *This bed was slept in by Winston Churchill.* In the first utterance a *by* phrase would not normally be included; in the second it must be.

Circumstance (*a*) invariably deals with something that is regarded as undesirable. It does in fact shed interesting light on our cultural norms—the acceptability of *This plate has been eaten off, This spoon has been eaten with, This cup has been drunk out of, This bed has been slept in* illustrates the phobia English-speakers have about certain kinds of cleanliness. *This knife has been cut with* should be just as natural a sentence, on syntactic grounds, but in fact we don't usually care so much whether a knife has been used previously. For that reason—and that reason alone —this sentence sounds less felicitous than the others.

A wide range of prepositions may be involved in this kind of passivisation, similar to those which occur as 'inherent preposi-tions'—*in, on, against, with, to* (*I've never been written to by Maria*), *at* (*That hat is always getting laughed at*), *over* (*The bewitched diamond is being fought over again*), *for* (*John was sent for*), *about* (*The accident is being talked about a lot*), and *from* (*Comrie's book on aspect is always being quoted from*).

Notes to Chapter 9

Useful general discussions of passives—in English and other languages—include Jespersen (1909–49: Part iii, pp. 299–319), Hasegawa (1968), Huddleston (1971: 93–108), R. Lakoff (1971), Sinha (1974), Bolinger

(1975*a*), Barker (1975), Davison (1980), Keenan (1981, 1985), Chappell (1980), Rice (1987), Thompson (1987). Langacker and Munro (1975) discuss passives in Uto-Aztecan and Mojave, and treat them in a way similar to that followed here for English. Figures on the percentages of passives for which no agent is given are quoted in Svartvik (1966), Givón (1979) and Thompson (1987).

§9.2. Kruisinga (1927) has an interesting discussion of the passivisability of both objects with verbs such as *ask*. Lists of verbs that do not passivise are included in Quirk and Greenbaum (1973: 359), G. Lakoff (1970: 19), Svartvik (1966: 115).

§9.4. The passivisation of prepositional NPs is discussed in Bolinger (1977*b*), Van Der Gaaf (1930) and Givón (1984).

10

What sells slowly, but wears well?
Promotion to subject

10.1. General characteristics

We have said, several times, that the semantic role which is most likely to be relevant for the success of an activity is placed in syntactic subject relation; this is *Mary* in *Mary sells sports cars, Mary cut the veal with the new knife, Mary poured the custard* (*onto the pie*) *with the new jug*. If an adverb like *quickly, easily, properly* or *well* is added to these sentences it will be taken to describe the way in which the subject performed the activity—*Mary certainly sells sports cars quickly, Mary cut the veal easily with the new knife, Mary didn't pour the custard properly* (*onto the pie*) *with the new jug* (*but spilt some on the cloth*).

It is possible, in some particular instance of an activity, for the success or lack of success to be due not to the subject (which is usually the responsible role) but to some role in non-subject relation. If this is so, then that role may be promoted into subject slot (and the original subject is omitted from the sentence). For example, *Sports cars sell quickly* (this implies that it is inherent in the nature of the vehicle that people want to buy them), *The veal cuts easily* (it isn't tough or sinewy), *The new knife cuts veal easily* (it is nice and sharp), *The custard doesn't pour properly* (it has too many lumps in it), *The new jug doesn't pour properly* (it may have a crooked spout), *The new jug doesn't pour custard properly* (but it might be all right for water or milk, which have a thinner consistency).

Some linguists have labelled constructions like *Sports cars sell*

322

quickly as 'ergative'. They say that a transitive object (O) becomes intransitive subject (S) and point out that 'ergative' is the term used to demonstrate a link between O and S. This terminology is misconceived, for at least three reasons. Firstly, promotion to subject is available for some O NPs (as with *Sports cars sell quickly, The veal cuts easily, The custard won't pour properly*) but it is also possible from a peripheral NP (as with *The new knife cuts the veal easily, The new jug doesn't pour the custard properly*). Secondly, promotion to subject does not alter the transitivity of a sentence; if an NP other than object is promoted to subject then the object may be retained (as *the veal* and *the custard* are in examples just given). An O NP or a peripheral NP from a transitive clause is promoted into A relation, not S. Thirdly, even if it were only O that could be promoted, and even if it were promoted to S, ergative would still not be an appropriate label. 'Ergative' is normally used of a linguistic system where A is marked in a distinctive way (by ergative case), differently from S and O which are marked in the same way (by absolutive case). It is not an apt label for describing an S derived from O. (In fact, passive S does correspond to transitive O. People who label *Sports cars sell quickly* as ergative should, if they were consistent, apply the same label to a passive like *Sports cars are sold quickly*, where there is a definite link between O and S.)

It is possible to find sentences describing some complex activity where any one of four roles may be held to be responsible for the success of the activity—see the examples given in §2.9.4 and:

(1) *Mary washed the woollens* (*with Softly*) (*in the Hoovermatic*)

Mary, in subject slot, refers to the person who does the washing. She may do it well:

(1a) *Mary washed the woollens well* (*with Softly*) (*in the Hoovermatic*)

But the garments may be manufactured in such a way that they respond well to washing (to any sort of washing, or to washing with that brand of soap mixture and/or washing in that make of washing machine):

(1b) *The woollens washed well* (*with Softly*) (*in the Hoovermatic*)

Washday success could alternatively be attributed to the type of soap used:

(1c) *Softly washed the woollens well* (*in the Hoovermatic*)

Or to the machine employed:

(1d) *The Hoovermatic washed the woollens well* (*with Softly*)

Note that when a non-subject role is promoted to subject the original subject is lost. It cannot be included as a peripheral constituent (in the way that a transitive subject can be included, as a *by* phrase, in a passive). Non-subject roles that are not promoted to subject may be retained in their original post-verbal position. And—also unlike passive, which has an explicit marker *be-* . . . *-en*—nothing is added to the verb in a promotion-to-subject construction.

The fact that the direct object may be retained (as *the woollens* is in (1c) and (1d)) when a non-object NP is promoted to subject shows that constructions (1b–d) are still transitive sentences. What we have in (1b–d) is a single semantic role effectively functioning in two syntactic relations simultaneously. *The Hoovermatic* in (1d) is still in locative relation to the verb, as it is in (1a–c), but it is also in subject relation, as a means of showing that the success of this particular instance of washing activity is due to the machine in which the clothes were placed. In (1b) *the woollens* is still understood to be in object relation to the verb (this NP refers to the things that are affected by the activity, i.e. they get washed) but it is also in surface subject slot, to mark that the success of the activity is due to the nature of this instance of the role. Subject relation takes precedence over other syntactic relations in determining where the NP comes in the sentence, but anyone who hears (1b) will understand that *the woollens*, although in surface subject slot, is also the object of the verb; and so on.

Most examples of promotion to subject involve transitive clauses, but there are some intransitive instances. Consider *John jumped with the pogo stick*. This could have a satisfactory outcome either because John is something of an expert, e.g. *John jumped well with the pogo stick*, or because the pogo stick has a good spring in it, e.g. *That pogo stick jumps well*. Potentially, any non-subject NP from a transitive or intransitive clause may be promoted into subject slot; the transitivity of the clause is not affected.

There is a clear difference between promotion-to-subject clauses and passives (which are intransitive). Recall that a prepositional object can only become passive subject if there is no direct object, that it leaves its preposition behind it, and that the original transitive subject can be retained in a *by* phrase, e.g. *This knife has been cut with by John*. A prepositional NP can be promoted to subject even if there is a direct object (which may be retained), its preposition is omitted, and the original subject is omitted, e.g. *This knife cuts (veal) easily*.

There is also a clear semantic difference between passive and promotion to subject. Passivisation does not change or add to the relation between object and verb—it merely focuses on the object, or on the effect the activity has on it. In *The woollens were washed well* the *well* is taken to refer to the skill of the transitive subject, even though this is not identified here, exactly as it is in (1a). Compare this with *The woollens washed well*, where *well* refers to the washable qualities of the clothes. We can also compare *The custard wasn't poured properly* (the person holding the jug didn't look to see what they were doing) with *The custard doesn't pour properly* (it is too thick, and will have to be spooned onto the pie).

Although an object can be retained when a peripheral NP is promoted to subject, it is not available for passivisation. If it were, confusion could arise. If corresponding to *The Hoovermatic washed the woollens well* we could have *The woollens were washed well (by the Hoovermatic)*, this could be confused with a passive corresponding to sentence (1a), *The woollens were washed well (by Mary) (in the Hoovermatic)*. Since a *by* phrase may always be omitted, *The woollens were washed well* would then be irretrievably ambiguous, and a listener would not know whether *well* referred to the Agent, the machine, the soap mixture, or what.

10.2. The circumstances in which promotion is possible

Promotion to subject is possible when there is some marker of the success of the activity. This marker can be an adverb, the negative particle, a modal, or emphatic *do*:

(*a*) Adverb. Only a small set of adverbs occur in promotion-to-subject constructions. They are based on adjectives from three semantic types: (i) SPEED—*slowly, fast, quickly, rapidly*, as in *The bucket rapidly filled*; (ii) VALUE—*well, badly, properly, oddly, strangely* (but not most other members of this type), e.g. *I am afraid that this scene does not photograph well*; (iii) DIFFICULTY—*easily* and the adverbial phrases *with/without difficulty* (there is no adverb *difficultly*), e.g. *These mandarins peel easily but those oranges peel only with great difficulty*. All of these adverbs may also be used as comparatives, e.g. *Datsuns sell quicker than Toyotas, Those tiles lay better if you wet them first*.

(**b**) Negation. This can be used when the lack of success of some activity is imputed to the qualities of the referent of a non-subject role, e.g. *That book didn't sell. Not* often co-occurs with the modal *will*, e.g. *The middle house won't let*.

(**c**) Modal. Most modals may be the marker in a promotion-to-subject construction, e.g. *Do you think this material will make up into a nice-looking dress? Yes, it must/should/ought to/might make up into a really stunning gown*.

(**d**) Emphatic *do*. The semantic effect of *do* can be similar to that of an adverb like *well*, e.g. *These red sports models do sell, don't they?*

The most common tense choice for promotion to subject is 'present', with generic time reference, e.g. *That type of garment wears well*. But past tense is also possible, as in (1b–d). Sometimes an adverb like *well* may be omitted when the construction is in 'present' tense, perhaps reinforced by an adverb such as *always*, e.g. *I find that Easter eggs always sell* (sc. well).

It must be emphasised that some marker from (*a*)–(*d*) is almost always obligatory if a non-subject role is to be promoted into subject slot, with the transitivity value of the sentence maintained. Sentences like *The new jug pours, Sports cars sell, The woollens washed* are ungrammatical; but if something like *well* or *don't* or *won't* is added they become acceptable English sentences. *Sell* is one of the verbs most frequently used in promotion to subject constructions, and one does hear, with a definite subject, a sentence like *Did those sports cars sell?* or *Those sports cars didn't sell*, with no marker; but most verbs always require a marker.

In §3.2 we mentioned that VALUE and DIFFICULTY adjectives—i.e. two of those types whose adverbs may assist promotion to subject

—are used in a special construction in which what would be object of a complement clause functions as subject of the adjective. Alongside a regular Modal (FOR) TO construction such as *It is easy (for anyone) to shock John* we can have:

(2) *John is easy to shock*

Recall that although we may say *That picture is good to look at*—a construction parallel to (2) but involving a VALUE adjective—there are no corresponding sentences, with a closely similar meaning, that have a Modal (FOR) TO clause in subject relation. We can say *It is good to look at that picture* but this has a different meaning from *That picture is good to look at*.

Now compare (2) with the promotion-to-subject construction:

(3) *John shocks easily*

The two sentences have similar, but not identical, meanings: (2) would be preferred when someone deliberately sets out to shock John, and succeeds without any real difficulty (the someone could be mentioned by using the related construction, *It was easy for Mary to shock John*); (3) would be preferred if John just gets shocked at the mildest swear-word without anyone meaning to shock him (an 'agent' NP could not be included in (3)). The contrast between these construction types is less clear when the subject is inanimate, e.g. *Porcelain sinks are easy to clean*, and *Porcelain sinks clean easily*, but still the first sentence implies that some effort is required (although not so much as with other kinds of sink) while the second sentence suggests that one just has to wipe a cloth over and the job is done. With other adjective/adverb pairs the difference between constructions like (2) and those like (3) is even more obvious; *These clothes are good to wash* seems to imply that it's fun washing them, a quite different meaning from *These clothes wash well*.

Promotion to subject is an even more marked construction than passive, and is used only when the nature of the referent of a non-subject NP is the major factor in the success of some instance of an activity. There has to be a contrast involved—some models of car sell quickly and others slowly, some types of woollens wash easily but others don't.

10.3. Which roles may be promoted

At the beginning of Chapter 9 we noted that a passive should really be quoted together with the full context in which it might be used. This applies at least as much in the case of promotion-to-subject constructions. Instead of doing this, we rely on the reader's imagination, on his being able to invest the referent of a non-subject NP with the particular properties that make or mar some instance of an activity, and justify its promotion into subject slot.

For those verbs which exist in both transitive and intransitive forms, with S = O, it can be hard to distinguish between promotion-to-subject of an O NP and a plain intransitive. Consider *waken*—this can be intransitive, as in *Mary wakened at seven o'clock*, or transitive, as in *John wakened Mary at seven o'clock*. A sentence such as *Mary wakens easily* is ambiguous between (i) a simple intransitive construction, in which the adverb *easily* implies that Mary is able to waken spontaneously, at any time she sets her mind to; and (ii) a promotion-to-subject construction from a transitive clause with the meaning that she is able to be wakened easily—one only has to whisper 'It's seven o'clock' and Mary is immediately wide awake and ready to get up. For some S = O verbs there is no ambiguity—*The dog walks slowly* would be taken to be a plain intransitive and not a promotion-to-subject version of a causative (such as *Mary walks the dog slowly*). But many verbs from the DROP, STRETCH and BREAK subtypes, and some such as *hurt*, *bleed* and *drown* from CORPOREAL, show the same sort of syntactic ambiguity as *waken*. Because of this, we will omit S = O verbs from the brief survey that follows.

It must be noted that promotion to subject is not a very common phenomenon. It applies only for certain kinds of NP filling non-subject relations, for just a handful of verbs from any one type. But it does occur with a fair spread of verbs, from quite a number of semantic types.

The discussion below deals mainly with the promotion to subject of core roles. But, as exemplified above and in §2.9.4, promotion is also possible for some peripheral roles—instruments like *with the Beyer microphone* and *with Softly* or, in very special circumstances, locational descriptions such as *in Studio B* and *in a Hoovermatic*.

We will first consider Primary-A types, i.e. those for which every role must be realised by an NP (not by a complement clause):

MOTION and REST. There are some examples of the Moving and Resting roles being promotable to subject, with verbs for which they are not the natural subject. Besides *The custard doesn't pour easily* we can have *This boomerang throws well, That box lifts easily, The new design of ball catches well, Your case carries easily, Evonne's racket handles well, That pram pushes easily*.

AFFECT. There are quite a number of examples of Manip and Target being promoted to subject (from frames I and II in §4.2). Examples involving Manip are *That knife cuts well, This string won't tie properly, My new steel-tipped boots kick well*. Those with Target promoted are *That cheese cuts easily, Stainless-steel pans clean easily, That shape of box doesn't wrap up very easily, Clothes iron better when damp*. We can also get *This dirt won't brush off my coat* and *That flour cooks well, This oven cooks well*.

GIVING. The Gift NP may be promoted to subject, as in *Those cars sell quickly, These Mills and Boon novels lend rather rapidly* (said by a librarian), *Top-floor apartments tend not to rent so easily as ground-floor ones*, and *Milk won't keep in hot weather (but it does keep if you put it in a fridge)*. The Recipient may also be promoted, as in *The Kingsland police bribe easily*.

CORPOREAL. The Substance role may be promoted to subject with just a few verbs, e.g. *These pills swallow easily, This meat chews rather easily, That wine drinks well*. An instrumental NP is promoted in *This straw sucks well*.

From the other Primary-A types, listed in §4.6, we may get *This new board game plays well* for a COMPETITION verb, *That machine operates easily* and *Those clothes wear well* from the USING type, and perhaps *That kingdom governs easily* from SOCIAL CONTRACT.

In summary, there are *some* examples of promotion to subject for every role (that is not canonically mapped onto subject) with Primary-A verbs.

We now turn to Primary-B, those types which have one role that may be realised either through a complement clause or through an NP. This role is in transitive subject relation for ANNOYING and in object or a post-object slot for the other Primary-B types.

ATTENTION. The Impression, in O slot, cannot be promoted to subject. Alongside *John watched that film* and *Mary heard thunder* it is not possible to say **That film watches well* or **Thunder hears easily*. (One could instead use the derived adjective *watchable*, as in *That film is very watchable*, and the alternative construction with *easy*, illustrated by example (2) above, i.e. *Thunder is easy to hear*.)

THINKING. Again the role (here, Thought) in O slot may not be promoted. Alongside *John learnt Swahili*, *Fred remembers the Kennedy years*, *I believe his story*, *I believe in God*, we cannot say **Swahili learns easily* (only *Swahili is easy to learn*), **The Kennedy years remember well* (here one could say *The Kennedy years were memorable*) or **His story/God believes well* (*His story is believable* is acceptable, but *God is believable* much less so).

DECIDING. The Course role, in O slot, may not be promoted to subject. Corresponding to *Mary chose the Persian kitten* we cannot have **The Persian kitten chose easily*. However, some verbs of the DECIDING type show a special kind of reflexive construction, with a meaning not dissimilar from promotion to subject with verbs from other types, e.g. *That cute little Persian kitten really chose/picked itself* (i.e. it was so appealing that I couldn't help but buy it). *That cute little Persian kitten* is properly the object of the DECIDING verb but also functions simultaneously as subject, in this unusual kind of reflexive construction. (There are several points of difference between this reflexive and promotion to subject; for instance, the reflexive does not require an adverb, modal or negation.)

SPEAKING. This type has four roles (one with two components). The Speaker is always underlying subject. There are just a few instances of an Addressee being promotable to subject, e.g. *She persuades easily* (as an alternative to *She is easy to persuade*) and *He insults easily*. The Medium role may just occasionally be promotable to subject slot, as in *Pica type reads more easily than Élite*. The Message role may have two components: Message-Label, which can only be an NP, and Message-Content, which can be an NP or a complement clause. There are some examples of Message-Label (but none of Message-Content) being promoted to subject, e.g. *That joke tells well, doesn't it?*, *Your new story/book/ poem reads well*, *That sermon, from the old book I found, preaches well*.

LIKING. The Stimulus role, which is mapped into O relation, can be a plain NP, or NP plus complement clause, or a complement clause. It may not be promoted to subject. That is, we cannot say **Ballet likes well*, **Insincerity hates easily*, or even **John pities easily* (meaning that people are always pitying him).

ANNOYING. Here the Experiencer, which is in O slot, must be an NP (normally with Human reference). This may be promoted to subject—in the presence of an appropriate marker—with a number of ANNOYING verbs, e.g. *Mary scares/excites/annoys/ angers/shocks easily, Granpa tires quickly these days*.

COMPARING. The object of *compare* may be an NP with plural reference, or several coordinated NPs, e.g. *The travel agent compared those two countries/Greece and Italy in terms of cuisine.* Such an O can be promoted to subject—when there is an adverb or negation etc. present—*Those two countries compare favourably in terms of cuisine, Greece and Italy don't compare in terms of cuisine.* Alternatively, we can have an NP as O and a post-object constituent introduced by *with*; the O NP can be promoted to subject and the *with* phrase remains in post-verbal position, e.g. *The travel agent compared Greece with Rome in terms of cuisine, Greece doesn't compare with Rome in terms of cuisine.* Less frequently, the O and the following *with* constituent for *compare* can be coordinated ING clauses, e.g. *John compared lying in the sun with going to a garden party at the Governor's.* Here the ING clause can be promoted to subject, in the right circumstances, e.g. *Lying in the sun compares quite favourably with going to a garden party at the Governor's.* (Other verbs from the COMPARING type, discussed in §5.7, appear not to occur in promotion-to-subject constructions.)

If we leave aside, for the moment, the single verb *compare*, this survey of which roles may be promoted to subject yields an intriguing generalisation:

> those non-subject roles that may be realised by an NP or a complement clause are not promotable to subject; but those which must be realised through an NP (not a complement clause) are potentially promotable.

We saw that all non-subject roles with Primary-A verbs may be promoted. For Primary-B types those roles that can be realised by a complement clause may not be promoted—Impression for ATTENTION, Thought for THINKING, Course for DECIDING, Message-Content for SPEAKING and Stimulus for LIKING. But those roles that can only be filled by NPs are promotable—Addressee, Medium and Message-Label for SPEAKING, Experiencer for ANNOYING.

The only serious counter-example is *compare*, where the 'object of comparison', in O relation, may be NPs or ING clauses, and either of these may be promoted to subject. Note that all other roles (mentioned in the last paragraph) which are not open to promotion may involve several different kinds of complement clause. It may be that *compare* is simply an exception—note that it is the only verb which allows a complement clause (rather than just an NP) to be promoted. Or the generalisation should perhaps be amended: roles which may be realised by a complement clause other than ING may not be promoted to subject. (We noted in §2.7 that ING clauses are the closest of all complements to an NP in their syntactic function.)

There is a single, quite minor, exception to the generalisation: we might expect that Stimulus-Label for LIKING should be promotable, parallel to Message-Label for SPEAKING, but in fact it appears not to be.

The force of this generalisation should be emphasised. If a certain role can be realised by a complement clause (other than ING) for *some* verbs from a type then that role may not be promoted to subject for *any* verb from the type. We related all ATTENTION verbs to the Perceiver and Impression roles. Impression may be either an NP or a complement clause for some subtypes, e.g. SEE and DISCOVER, but it may only be an NP for some verbs from the LOOK subtype such as *scrutinise*, *survey*, *explore* and *visit*. The Impression role may not be promoted to subject with LOOK verbs, any more than it can be for SEE and DISCOVER (that is, we cannot say **This document scrutinises easily*, or **That terrain explores easily*). This provides justification for the category 'role', which is a critical component of my semantically oriented approach to syntactic study. Each role has a certain semantic character, and only those roles which relate to entities, described by NPs (or activities, described by ING clauses)—not those which may relate to THAT or Modal (FOR) TO complements, etc.—can contribute to the success of an activity in such a way that they may be promoted into subject slot.

Secondary verbs take a syntactic complement clause, containing a verb which they modify semantically. The only possible promotion to subject is with BEGINNING, and then only where promotion is possible for an underlying complement clause verb. When this verb is omitted, the promotion may still be possible, now to the subject of the BEGINNING verb. Thus, *John read that novel*, *That novel reads well*; *John began (reading) that novel*, *That novel begins well* (but not **That novel begins reading well*). And *Mary told that joke about nuns*, *That joke about nuns tells well*; *Mary began (telling) that joke about nuns*, *That joke about nuns begins well* (but not **That joke about nuns begins telling well*). (We mentioned in §6.1.2 that some BEGINNING verbs may occur in an intransitive frame with an activity noun as subject, e.g. *The sale began at three o'clock*. Such sentences can involve an adverb, e.g. *That sale began slowly*, but this is not an instance of promotion to subject, parallel to those discussed above.)

There is one circumstance in which a promotion-to-subject construction might be ambiguous. Consider a transitive verb where the object may be omitted (a dual transitivity verb of type $S = A$, §8.3.1). If we get a construction consisting only of SUBJECT, TRANSITIVE VERB, ADVERB, how do we know whether this is the original subject, with the object omitted, or whether it involves promotion to subject of the transitive object, with the original subject having been omitted?

There will be no danger of ambiguity if the various roles have different referential possibilities. Only a human can pour, only a liquid can be poured, and only a container can be poured out of. We know that *John pours well* is a transitive clause with object omitted, but that *The custard pours well* and *The jug pours well* involve promotion to subject.

There are verbs for which subject and object can be human, and which do allow the object to be promoted to subject. But these are all strictly transitive, i.e. the object cannot be omitted. If such a verb occurs with just a subject and no stated object, we know that the subject must be a promoted object, e.g. *bribe*, *persuade*, and verbs from the ANNOYING type.

There is a verb which can involve ambiguity—*translate* (and *interpret* might provide similar examples). This can omit its object, and does also permit promotion of object into subject slot. *John translates well*, where the O NP is omitted, is an acceptable sentence (the speaker will probably assume that the listener already knows what sort of thing John translates, and between what languages). With a stated object NP we get *Many people have translated Shakespeare's works into Greek* and then, with the O promoted into A slot, *Shakespeare's works translate well into Greek*. The subject of *translate* will have human reference, with the object generally referring to some piece of written or spoken language. But a set of literary works is sometimes abbreviated to just the name of the author—instead of *Shakespeare's works* people will often say just *Shakespeare*. With this particular object NP there will be no ambiguity. *Shakespeare translates well into Greek* will be understood as a promotion-to-subject construction, not as a transitive clause with object omitted, simply because people know that Shakespeare is dead and that he didn't do any translating. However, if we were talking about some living author (call him Adam Dawkins) whose works do get translated and who also undertakes translation himself, then *Adam Dawkins translates well into Greek* would be ambiguous. If Dawkins were equally well known for his original works, which are translated into many languages, and for the translations he does, then the unmarked interpretation of this sentence would surely be that it was a transitive construction with the object omitted (that is, *Adam Dawkins* would be taken as underlying subject, not object, of *translate*).

This underlies the point we made earlier, that promotion-to-subject is a marked construction, and is only permitted where there is space left by the rest of the grammar.

Notes to Chapter 10

There are useful discussions of 'promotion to subject' in Jespersen (1909–49: part iii, pp. 347–52) and especially in Erades (1950*b*). They include examples gathered from written English texts and I have freely drawn on their examples in this chapter. Bradley and Bradley (forthcoming) mention that promotion to subject seems especially common in Australian

English, and quote examples such as *Unless you're a very skilful investor, the money whittles away quickly* and *Sydney's new dock, now building*.

§10.1. For a general account of the misuse of the term 'ergative' see Dixon (1987: 5–6, 13). Scholars who deal with what is here referred to as 'promotion to subject' within a discussion of 'ergative in English' include Halliday (1967) and J. M. Anderson (1968).

11

She gave him a look, they both had a laugh and then took a stroll.
GIVE A VERB, HAVE A VERB and TAKE A VERB
constructions

Parallel to *Mary walked in the garden* we can say *Mary had a walk in the garden*. Here the verb *have* substitutes for *walk*, and takes tense inflection. The original verb base *walk* now functions as head of an NP which follows *have*, with the singular indefinite article *a*. The locational phrase *in the garden* is carried over unaltered. These two sentences, *Mary walked in the garden* and *Mary had a walk in the garden*, have a similar meaning; there is, however, a definite and predictable semantic difference, which we discuss in §11.3.

There is also the TAKE A VERB construction, built on similar principles—compare *John kicked at the ball* and *John took a kick at the ball*. TAKE A VERB, like HAVE A VERB, is most frequently used with intransitive verbs (there are exceptions, discussed in §11.2). The GIVE A VERB construction differs in that it most often involves a transitive verb, e.g. *Mary punched John* and *Mary gave John a punch*. Here *give* substitutes for the original verb, which becomes (in base form) the head of a 'second object' NP, again preceded by the indefinite article *a*.

Many verbs occur with HAVE A, TAKE A and GIVE A, but there are many others which resist use in such constructions. Compare the following samples:

Possible	Impossible
have a walk in the garden	**have an arrive at the gate*
have a swim in the river	**have a cross over the bridge*
have a sit-down on the sofa	**have a settle-down in the country*

336

have a look at the baby	**have a see of the baby*
have a think about the solution	**have a know of the solution*
have a talk with Mary	**have a speak with Mary*

The verbs which occur with TAKE A, in British English, appear to be a subset of those which occur with HAVE A. One can *take a walk*, *take a swim* or *take a look* but not **take a sit-down*, **take a think* or **take a talk*. Parallel to *have a kick* and *have a bite* there are *take a kick* and *take a bite*; but although it is possible to say *have a shave* or *have a laugh*, it is not permissible to say **take a shave* or **take a laugh*.

Turning now to GIVE A, we can contrast:

Possible	Impossible
give the rope a pull	**give the rope a tie*
give the lamp a rub	**give the bottle a break*
give the child a carry	**give the child a take*
give the pudding a stir	**give the pudding a bake*
give Mary a smile	**give Mary a laugh*

I have examined about 700 of the most common English verbs and find that about one-quarter of them can occur in at least one of the constructions HAVE A VERB, TAKE A VERB and GIVE A VERB. Whether or not a verb can occur in one or more of these constructions is largely semantically based, as we shall show in this chapter.

Most grammars of English scarcely mention the HAVE A, GIVE A and TAKE A construction types. The linguist Edward Sapir did mention them, putting *give him a kick* alongside *kick him*, and *take a ride* with *ride*. He commented (Sapir 1949: 114): 'at first blush this looks like a most engaging rule but . . . anyone who takes the trouble to examine these examples carefully will soon see that behind a superficial appearance of simplicity there is concealed a perfect hornet's nest of bizarre and arbitrary usages . . . . We can "give a person a shove" or "a push," but we cannot "give him a move" nor "a drop" (in the sense of causing him to drop).' The aim of the discussion below will be to show that the occurrence of verbs with HAVE A, TAKE A and GIVE A is not at all arbitrary.

These constructions tend to carry an overtone of friendliness and intimacy, and are found far more frequently in colloquial than in formal styles of English. Some examples are found in the older literature, e.g. *give a cry* from 1300, *have a run* from 1450, but these are comparatively rare. Note, though, that very little of premodern literature reflected colloquial usage.

It does seem likely that the use of the constructions has increased over the past two hundred years, and that it has done so in different ways in different dialects. In British (and Australian) English HAVE A VERB has increased in popularity while TAKE A VERB may actually have dropped in frequency; in American English the TAKE A construction has become more common and HAVE A appears to have contracted. This would account for the fact that Americans prefer to say *take a run/kick/swim/look* where an Englishman would use *have a run/kick/swim/look* (although the TAKE A construction is also possible in British English and differs in meaning from HAVE A, as will be discussed below). GIVE A appears also to occur with a more limited range of verbs in American English, e.g. *give the child a carry* is generally accepted by speakers of British English but rejected by Americans.

There are also periphrastic constructions with *make*, *do* and *pay* that show some similarity to HAVE A/GIVE A/TAKE A VERB. *Pay* is very restricted—the main verbs it occurs with are *visit* and *compliment*, as in *visit Mary*, *pay Mary a visit*; *compliment Mary*, *pay Mary a compliment*. *Do* occurs with a slightly larger set of verbs, e.g. *do a dance/mime/dive/jump/pee* (and in 'The Stockbroker's Clerk', a client tells Sherlock Holmes that he was *sitting doing a smoke*). *Make* occurs with quite a number of verbs from the THINKING, DECIDING, SPEAKING, ATTENTION and COMPARING types. Sometimes the plain verb base becomes head of an NP following *make* (with the indefinite article *a*), e.g. *make a remark/claim/comment/report/ mention/request*, but in most cases it is a derived nominal, e.g. *make a statement/suggestion/complaint/confession/enquiry/ decision/assumption/inspection/comparison*. MAKE/DO/PAY A VERB constructions fall outside the scope of our discussion in this chapter.

The next section presents criteria for distinguishing between the HAVE A, GIVE A and TAKE A constructions which are the topic of this chapter, and other constructions involving these verbs. §11.2 deals with the syntax of the constructions, and then §11.3 discusses their meanings. Finally, §11.4 explains which verbs may occur in the constructions; this relates to the meaning of a given verb and the meanings of the construction types.

11.1. Criteria adopted

The large *Oxford English Dictionary* lists 27 senses of *have*, 64 of *give* and 94 of *take*. Each of these verbs shows a very varied set of syntactic usages. In view of this, it is important that I should give explicit criteria to define the constructions I am describing, which will serve to distinguish them from other constructions involving *have*, *give* and *take*.

The criteria I adopt relate to: (*a*) form; (*b*) meaning; (*c*) adverb/ adjective correspondence; and (*d*) preservation of peripheral constituents. In discussing these it will be useful to refer to a 'basic sentence' and then to a peripheral HAVE A, GIVE A or TAKE A correspondent of this, e.g. *Mary walked in the garden* is a basic sentence, and *Mary had a walk in the garden* is a periphrastic HAVE A version of it.

(*a*) Form
A periphrastic construction should show (i) the same subject as the basic sentence; (ii) *have*, *take* or *give* as the main verb; (iii) the base form of the verb of the basic sentence as head of a post-predicate NP, preceded by the indefinite article *a ~ an*.

I had a kick of the ball is a bona fide HAVE A construction, as can be seen by comparison with *I kicked the ball*. But *I had a kick from the horse* is not a HAVE A correspondent of *The horse kicked me* since the two sentences have different subjects.

I am here adopting the quite restrictive condition that a plain verb base (not a derived form) must occur, with *a*, in an NP following *have*, *give* or *take*. *John and Mary had a chat about the accident* is an instance of the HAVE A construction, since it relates to the basic sentence *John and Mary chatted about the accident*. But *John and Mary had a discussion about the accident* is not, since the NP involves a derived noun, *discussion*, and not the verb root *discuss*. Relating to *John regretted that he had to leave early* there is *John had regrets about leaving early*, but this does not satisfy the criterion since the post-verbal NP is *regrets* rather than *a regret*. (It also fails criterion (*d*) concerning peripheral constituents, since the basic sentence involves a THAT complement clause and the *have* construction shows preposition *about* plus an ING clause.)

The topic of nominals derived from verbs (e.g. *discussion, regrets, arrival, building, expectation, warning, hatred, liking, annoyance, reference, tendency, feeling*) is not dealt with in the present volume. It is a most important topic for future research and would include the role of deverbal nouns in periphrastic constructions with verbs like *have, give* and *take*. Such a study would, in important ways, interrelate with the discussion of this chapter.

(*b*) Meaning
We will show in §11.3 that each of HAVE A, GIVE A and TAKE A adds a special semantic element to the basic sentence. Leaving this aside, criterion (*b*) demands that the periphrastic sentence should have essentially the same meaning as the basic sentence. *I looked in the suitcase* and *I had/took a look in the suitcase* satisfy this criterion. But *I chanced to see Mary* and *I had a chance to see Mary* have quite different meanings—the first can mean 'I saw Mary accidentally' and the second 'I had the opportunity to see Mary but didn't avail myself of it'. By criterion (*b*), *I had a chance to see Mary* is not an instance of the HAVE A construction that is the topic of this chapter. (Note also that *the* can be used in place of *a*, e.g. *I had the chance to see Mary*. This is never possible in a HAVE A, TAKE A or GIVE A construction, e.g. not **I had/took the look in the suitcase*.)

Criteria (*a*) and (*b*) interrelate to give similar results. In *John had a talk with Mary* it is the base form of the verb that has become head of the NP, and this sentence does have a similar meaning to *John talked with Mary*. But in *John gave a speech to Mary* the NP involves a derived noun (not the verb base *speak*), and this sentence does have a quite different meaning from *John spoke to Mary*, confirming that *give a speech* is not an example of our GIVE A construction.

Corresponding to *Mary thought about the party* we get the HAVE A sentence *Mary had a think about the party*, where the NP does involve the base form of the verb. These two sentences have similar meanings—the thinking went on for a period of time (and need not necessarily have yielded any conclusive ideas). Contrast these with *Mary had a (sudden) thought about the party*, which has a quite different meaning (referring to a flash of inspiration) and also involves the derived noun *thought*; this sentence is thus not an instance of the HAVE A construction.

(*c*) Adverb/adjective correspondence
The way in which an adjective provides semantic modification to the head of an NP is similar to the way in which an adverb modifies a verb. Corresponding to an adverb in a basic sentence we would expect an adjective in a corresponding periphrastic HAVE A, TAKE A or GIVE A constructions, e.g.

> *John climbed easily up the rocks/John had an easy climb up the rocks*
> *Mary kissed him passionately/Mary gave him a passionate kiss*
> *Fred looked more closely at the hole in the fence/Fred took a closer look at the hole in the fence*

An adverbial phrase describing time or distance, in a basic sentence, may correspond to an adjective in a periphrastic construction.

> *I sat down briefly/I had a brief sit-down*
> *I sat down for a long while/I had a long sit-down*
> *I walked (for) a long distance* ⎤
> *I walked for a long while* ⎦ */I had a long walk*

And the adverb *again* may correspond to adjective *another*:

> *She looked again at the ring/She had another look at the ring.*

The condition that there should be adverb/adjective correspondence often helps to distinguish a true HAVE A, TAKE A or GIVE A construction from one of the verbs *have, take* or *give* used with an independent noun that has the same form as the verb. In

> (1a) *She scratched her mosquito bites savagely/for a long time*
> (1b) *She gave her mosquito bite a savage/long scratch*

the adverb/adjective condition is satisfied. But now consider:

> (2) *She gave him a long scratch on the leg*

This does not relate to *She scratched him on the leg for a long time*. It is not the action of scratching which is long; rather, a long wound has been inflicted on him by the scratching. This indicates that *scratch* is an independent noun in (2), and that this is not an instance of the GIVE A construction.

Drink, as an independent noun, may be the object of a verb like *consume*, or of *have*, e.g. *He consumed a* (or *the*) *drink/a* (or *the*) *drink of whiskey/a* (or *the*) *whiskey* and *He had a* (or *the*) *drink/a* (or *the*) *drink of whiskey/a* (or *the*) *whiskey*. Also, corresponding to a basic sentence such as *Go on, you drink my new Californian wine* we can get the HAVE A construction *Go on, you have a drink of my new Californian wine*.

The sentence *Have a drink* is thus ambiguous between these two readings. However, the inclusion of an adverb may help to resolve this ambiguity. Corresponding to *Have a sneaky/quick drink of the whiskey* there is *Drink the whiskey sneakily/quickly*, the adjective/adverb correspondence showing that this is a true HAVE A construction. On the other hand, corresponding to *Have an ice-cold drink* it is not possible to say **Drink ice-coldly*, showing that *drink* is here an independent noun.

The dividing lines between similar construction types are seldom watertight, in any language. People do say *Have a quick whiskey*, which is a blend of *Have a quick drink* (the HAVE A construction based on *Drink quickly*) and *Have a whiskey/drink of whiskey/drink*, which is a different *have* construction, involving an independent noun as NP head. Still, blends like this are unusual; in the vast majority of cases the adverb/adjective correspondence condition does enable us to distinguish between HAVE A, GIVE A, TAKE A and other constructions involving these verbs.

It will be seen that a number of roots, like *scratch* and *drink*, may be used (i) as a verb, extended to occurrence in HAVE A, TAKE A or GIVE A constructions; and (ii) as a noun. But there are other roots which may only be used as a verb, not as an independent noun. *Carry*, for instance, only occurs in an NP within a HAVE A or GIVE A construction, e.g. *John gave the baby a carry*.

(d) Preservation of peripheral constituents
In the next section we discuss the syntax of HAVE A, GIVE A and TAKE A constructions. To anticipate: if HAVE A or TAKE A relates to a basic sentence that is transitive, the preposition *of* is likely to be inserted before the erstwhile direct object, e.g. *I smelt the pudding*, and its

periphrastic correspondent *I had a smell of the pudding*. GIVE A may relate to an intransitive basic sentence including a prepositional NP, with the preposition being omitted in the GIVE A construction, e.g. *Mary winked at John, Mary gave John a wink*.

Leaving aside these differences, which involve core constituents, all peripheral constituents of the basic sentence should be exactly preserved in the periphrastic construction. Thus, *I always swim in the pool before breakfast on weekdays* and *I always have a swim in the pool before breakfast on weekdays*—here the correspondence of *in the pool*, *before breakfast* and *on weekdays* between the two sentences shows that we are dealing with a bona fide HAVE A construction.

Now consider:

(3a) *John painted the wall with Dulux*
(3b) *John gave the wall a paint with Dulux*
(4a) *Mary coated the table with wax*
(4b) *Mary gave the table a coat of wax*

Sentence (3b) is a GIVE A construction since the peripheral NP *with Dulux* has the same form as in the basic sentence. Sentence (4b), in contrast, is a different kind of construction, since it includes the NP *a coat of wax* where (4a) has *coat . . . with wax*.

It may be useful at this stage briefly to mention one of the many other constructions involving *give*, and one of those involving *have*, that we are excluding from consideration here:

(i) The 'Permissive' *give* construction, e.g. *I gave Mary a lick of my lollipop*, which is similar in meaning to *I let Mary lick my lollipop*. Compare this with the GIVE A construction *I gave my lollipop a lick*, corresponding to the basic sentence *I licked my lollipop*.

(ii) The 'Experiencer' *have* construction, e.g. *I had/experienced a heart attack/a stab in the back/the misfortune to be dropped from the side/a brainwave/a move to head office.*

A fair number of forms that function as verbs and enter into the HAVE A construction also function as an independent noun in the Experiencer *have* construction. A doctor might say: *Go on, cough gently* or else he could use the HAVE A sentence: *Go on, have a gentle cough*. But *cough* may also be used as a noun, as in *I had a bad cough* (parallel to *I had a headache*).

Other Experiencer *have* sentences are *I had/got/received a kick from Mary/a kiss from Mary*; these relate to sentences with a different subject, *Mary kicked/kissed me*. Notice the contrast with the HAVE A verb sentences *I had a kick at the ball* (basic sentence *I kicked at the ball*) and, with plural subject, *John and Mary had a kiss* (corresponding to *John and Mary kissed*).

Walk enters into HAVE A constructions (e.g. *Why don't we have a little walk before breakfast?*). But it is also an independent noun, as in *That walk tired me* and *I had a tiring walk*; the fact that the last sentence is Experiencer *have* and not the HAVE A construction is seen from the failure of the adverb/adjective criterion (**I walked tiringly* is scarcely felicitious). *He had a fall* is also an instance of Experiencer *have*; any one of an array of adjectives may be included in the NP (e.g. *nasty, awful, serious*), but for most of these there is no corresponding adverb that could be used with *I fell*.

Take also occurs in an 'Experiencer' construction, e.g. *He took a (bad) tumble, She took a punch in the stomach* (relating to *Someone punched her in the stomach*), *She took offence at John's behaviour* (relating to *John's behaviour offended her*).

11.2. Syntax

More than two-thirds of the verbs from my sample occurring in HAVE A or TAKE A constructions are intransitive. This is a very natural syntactic correlation. The verbs *have* and *take* involve two core NPs—the original subject remains as subject and an NP consisting of *a* plus the original verb base goes into post-verbal position, e.g. *I rode (on the elephant), I had/took a ride (on the elephant)*.

There are, however, a fair number of instances of HAVE A and TAKE A with transitive verbs. Here a new syntactic slot has to be created in the periphrastic construction for the original transitive object. It is generally introduced by the preposition *of*. Thus *John bit/smelt the cake* and *John had a bite/smell of the cake*. Similarly, *Can I borrow your ruler?* and *Can I have a borrow of your ruler?*; also *Can I ride your bike for a little while?* and *Can I have a little ride of your bike?*

About 90 per cent of the verbs occurring in the GIVE A construction are transitive. This is again a natural syntactic correlation—a transitive clause will have two core NPs and *give* has three, with *a*-plus-verb-base making up the third. Subject remains as is, the original object remains as first object of *give*, and *a* plus the original verb fills the second object slot, e.g. *John pushed Mary, John gave Mary a push*.

For the lexical verb *give*, referring to transfer of possession, the most basic syntactic frame is with Gift in O slot and Recipient introduced by preposition *to*, e.g. *John gave the book to someone*. In §8.2.4 we described how a prepositional NP—such as the Recipient here—can drop its preposition and move into direct object slot when it is particularly salient to some instance of an activity, e.g. *John gave Tom a book*. GIVE A constructions invariably employ the latter syntactic frame—one would say *give Mary a push*, scarcely **give a push to Mary*. In fact, GIVE A constructions tend only to be used when the original transitive object has a specific, individuated reference, and thus fits naturally into object slot; the NP consisting of *a* plus verb base does not have reference to an entity, and it is not plausible for an NP like *a push* to be first object, with an NP like *Mary* relegated to a prepositional phrase.

Note also that although the lexical verb *take* may passivise on its object, and *give* may potentially passivise on both first and second objects (§9.2), the *a*-plus-verb-base NP in a HAVE A, TAKE A or GIVE A construction may never become passive subject—we would never hear **A swim (in the pool) was had/taken* or **A push was given Mary*. The HAVE A, TAKE A and GIVE A constructions satisfy none of the criteria for passivisation that were presented in §9.1.

Some intransitive verbs—and also some inherent preposition verbs—do occur in the GIVE A construction. They divide into two sets. With one set *give* has a single NP following it, consisting of *a* plus the intransitive verb base, e.g. *John laughed, John gave a laugh*. With the other set there are two NPs following *give*, the second being *a* plus verb root while the first corresponds to a prepositional NP (generally marked by *at* or *to*) from the basic sentence, e.g. *John looked/smiled/winked at Mary, John gave Mary a look/smile/wink*; and *Mary waved to/at John, Mary gave John a wave*.

345

There are rare instances of the GIVE A construction occurring with a ditransitive verb, such as *lend* in *Will you give me a lend of your ruler?* This is most appropriately related to the basic sentence *Will you lend me your ruler?* (itself derived from *Will you lend your ruler to me?* by promotion of the prepositional NP into direct object slot). The original first object remains as first object, *a* plus verb base is the new second object, and the original second object becomes marked by *of* in the GIVE A construction (as a constituent within the NP *a lend of your ruler*). *Of* here plays a similar role to that described above for HAVE A and TAKE A constructions involving a transitive verb—compare with the basic sentence *Can I borrow your ruler?* and periphrastic *Can I have a borrow of your ruler?*

11.3. Meaning

(a) HAVE A VERB

We can say *I walked in the garden after lunch yesterday* or *I walked in the garden from dawn until dusk yesterday*. The periphrastic construction *have a walk* is possible in the first instance, *I had a walk in the garden after lunch yesterday*, but not in the second; one would not use *have a walk* with *from dawn until dusk*. Similarly, one can say *We ran around the oval until the rain began* but scarcely **We had a run around the oval until the rain began*.

Looking now at locational specification, we can say *walk in the park* or *walk from Oxford to Reading*. The first is fine for *have a walk* but not the second; *have a walk* would not be used with a definite statement of journey or destination, such as *from Oxford to Reading*. Similarly, one could say *have a swim in the river* but scarcely **have a swim across the river*.

It appears that there is no periphrastic HAVE A construction corresponding to a basic sentence describing some activity that is related to a time or space limitation, or that is being used to achieve some goal. The HAVE A construction emphasises the activity, and the fact that the subject indulges in it for a certain period. The subject is not trying to walk or swim to get anywhere, he is just 'having a walk' or 'having a swim'. One could say that an element of the meaning of the HAVE A construction is 'do it a bit'.

Indeed, it is common to insert *a bit of* between *a* and the verb, e.g. *We had a bit of a walk/talk/think*.

It is possible to *have a long walk* or *have a long laugh* or *have a short swim*. The adjective indicates that the subject indulged in the activity for a long or short time (or over a long or short distance)— but he is still just walking or whatever because he wants to, rather than to get anywhere or for any other purpose.

The verb *stroll* refers to 'slow, leisurely walking, with no desire to arrive somewhere'. This accords well with the meaning of HAVE A. In fact, *stroll* is one of the verbs most frequently used in the HAVE A construction.

HAVE A always describes some volitional act and the subject must be human (or perhaps a higher animal). We can say *That child had a roll down the grassy bank* (when he was doing it on purpose, for fun) but not **That stone had a roll down the grassy bank*. The volitional element is brought out by comparison between *slip*, which refers to an unwanted, uncontrolled activity, and *slide*, which can refer to something done voluntarily, for pleasure. One may say *She had a slide on the ice* but not **She had a slip on the ice* (or, if the latter is possible, it must be an instance of the Experiencer *have* construction—§11.1).

HAVE A describes something done 'a bit', done voluntarily. And we have said that it is an activity the subject indulges himself in—if not for pleasure, then for relief. Suppose someone is upset, and holding back tears. We might encourage them: *Go on, you have a cry*. That is: you indulge in the activity of crying, for a period, for the relief it will provide. Similarly, *have a grumble* (you'll feel better after it) or *have a sit-down* (after all, you've been standing up all morning).

It is interesting that one often hears *Have a sit-down* or *Have a lie-down* but seldom *Have a stand-up*. The last example is perfectly possible; it is just that the circumstances for its use do not readily arise. It can, however, easily be contextualised. Suppose a lot of people are sitting or squatting in a restricted space, some getting cramps, and there is room for just one person at a time to stand up. The leader might say: *Go on Tom, you have a stand-up now* (that is, indulge yourself for a while in the activity of standing up).

In summary, the HAVE A construction carries meaning elements: (i) something done voluntarily, by the subject; (ii) to indulge

347

himself in something he enjoys doing, or which provides relief; (iii) the activity being done 'for a bit', at the subject's whim (rather than to achieve any transcendental goal).

(*b*) GIVE A VERB

We can distinguish two subtypes of the GIVE A VERB construction: (I) involving an NP (with noun or pronoun as head) as first object, before the NP consisting of *a* plus verb base, e.g. *She gave me a punch/push/kiss/smile/look*; (II) where the only NP following *give* is *a* plus verb base—this occurs with some verbs from the CORPOREAL type and from the SHOUT subtype of SPEAKING, e.g. *He gave a laugh/cry/sob/sigh/cough/shout*.

Some of the restrictions on the GIVE A construction are similar to those on HAVE A. We can say *She looked at him all day* but not **She gave him a look all day*, and *I pushed the car all the way home* but not **I gave the car a push all the way home*. It is acceptable to say *I gave the child a carry while going up that hill on the way to town* but scarcely **I gave the child a carry to town*. From these and similar data we can infer that the GIVE A construction refers to the subject doing something at his own whim, for a certain period, and not to satisfy any external goal (as expressed by *all day*, *to town*, etc.).

There is a subtle difference between the HAVE A and GIVE A constructions. We have already said that HAVE A implies 'do it for a bit'. If a certain verb refers to some activity that can be done in incremental units, then GIVE A plus that verb is likely to refer to just one unit of the activity. *Give a laugh* most often relates to a single 'ha', whereas *have a laugh* could describe someone laughing for a minute or two at something he found excruciatingly funny. *Give a cry* (or *sob*) is likely to be a single sob, whereas *have a cry* could be someone crying their heart out, for as long as it took to relieve some condition of distress. A trainer might say to a boxer: *Go on, you have a punch of the punchball now*; this invites him to rain punches on it for a reasonable period of time. But if he said: *Go on, you give it a punch*, just a single hit might be expected. The difference is apparent even with *pull* and *push*, which describe activities that are most often continuous. *You have a pull of the rope* could be realised by the addressee pulling for a few minutes, whereas *You give the rope a pull* might relate to a single tug. The verb *jerk* generally refers to a single unit of pulling; note that we can say *Give it a jerk* but not **Have a jerk of it.* (It is sometimes possible to use *a bit of* with *give*, if the underlying verb can refer to a continuous activity—*Give it a bit of a pull* has a meaning very similar to *Have a bit of a pull of it*. The important point is that when *a bit of* is not included, the GIVE A construction is likely to refer to a single unit of activity.)

Like HAVE A, the GIVE A construction of type (I) is limited to human subjects acting with volition. If Mary were walking past John then *He bumped her* could describe either a purposeful or an accidental bump but *He gave her a bump* must refer to something done on purpose.

Let us turn now to a critical semantic difference between HAVE A and GIVE A constructions. Consider:

(5a)   *Mary looked at John* (*through the window*)
(5b)   *Mary had a look at John* (*through the window*)
(5c)   *Mary gave John a look* (*through the window*)

Sentence (5b) describes Mary indulging herself in looking at John, for a period; it is immaterial whether or not John realises that he is being observed. Sentence (5c), in contrast, describes Mary communicating with John—she gives him a look and he notices it. It could be a look of warning, of invitation, of loathing, or of love.

The GIVE A construction of type (I) describes something being 'transferred' from subject to object (a metaphorical extension of the 'transfer of possession' in lexical use of *give*)—that is, the object must be affected by the activity.

Give a carry can have a human object as in *I gave the child a carry*; the child is affected by this beneficial gesture (it does not now have the effort of walking on its own). But it would be quite infelicitous to say **I gave the suitcase a carry*, since the suitcase would not be affected by being carried. The GIVE A construction can involve a verb with an inanimate object, but there is always an implication that the object is affected in some way, e.g. *give the table a wipe* (it was dirty before and is now clean), *give the door a kick* (say, to break it down), *give the pudding a warm* (to make it more palatable), *give the car a push* (to get it to start), *give the rope a pull* (to try to dislodge the end from where it is trapped).

The verb *smile* has two senses: (i) showing amusement at something, e.g. *smile at Zelig's antics*; (ii) using the gesture to communicate with someone, e.g. *smile at Mary*. The first sense is similar to *laugh* in *laugh at Zelig's antics*, the second to *wink* in *wink at Mary*. Now *smile* can occur in both HAVE A and GIVE A constructions. But it is the first sense that is involved with HAVE A, e.g. *Tom had a smile at Zelig's antics*, where Tom is indulging himself in smiling, for a period, at something he finds funny (whether Zelig knows that his antics have evinced a smile is immaterial). And it is the second sense of *smile* that is involved in a GIVE A construction of type (I), e.g. *Tom gave Mary a smile*; use of this sentence implies that Mary did notice the smile. *Laugh*, parallel to the first sense of *smile*, occurs just with HAVE A but not with the GIVE A construction of type (I), e.g. *Tom had a laugh at Zelig's antics* but not **Tom gave Mary a laugh*. And *wink*, parallel to the second sense of *smile*, takes just GIVE A, e.g. *Tom gave Mary a wink* but not **Tom had a wink at Zelig's antics*. The two senses of *smile* are, in fact, parallel to the two senses of *look* (one contemplative, one communicative) illustrated in (5b) and (5c).

It may be useful to give one further example of the semantic difference between HAVE A and GIVE A. The verb *stroke* can occur in

(6a) *Go on, you have a stroke of it!*
(6b) *Go on, you give it a stroke!*

Now consider two scenarios. In the first a friend has bought a new fur coat, which you admire. She invites you to stroke it. Would she be more likely to use sentence (6a) or (6b)? In the second scenario a friend's cat brushes against you. The friend knows that you like cats and encourages you to stroke it. Again, would she use (6a) or (6b)?

Native speakers prefer sentence (6b) for stroking a cat and (6a) for stroking a fur coat. The GIVE A construction is used when the object is likely to be affected by the action—the cat will probably enjoy being stroked, and may purr in response. The HAVE A construction is appropriate for stroking a coat; the garment is unaffected and in this instance it is simply the stroker who is indulging himself.

In summary, the GIVE A construction, type (I), carries the following meaning elements: (i) something done voluntarily by the subject; (ii) to 'transfer' something to an object, either affecting the object in some physical way, or communicating with another person; (iii) the activity being 'done a bit', at the subject's whim—and often, if the verb refers to an activity that can be incremental, just one unit of the activity is performed. (Note that the 'one unit' interpretation does not always apply, e.g. *give the cat a stroke* could refer to as long or longer a period of stroking as *have a stroke of the fur coat*.)

We can now look at GIVE A construction type (II), where there is no object NP of the underlying verb. Semantic characteristic (iii) certainly applies: *give a laugh/cry/cough/shout*, is likely to refer to a single corporeal gesture in contrast to *have a laugh/cry/cough/ shout*, which is likely to refer to someone indulging in the activity for as long as they need.

Semantic characteristic (ii) applies in an indirect way in that an act of communication may be involved (as it never could be with HAVE A). Someone may *give a cough* to warn a friend to be careful in what he says, or *give a hollow laugh* to show that he doesn't think much of what has just been said; and similarly with *give a sigh*, *give a whistle*. In these circumstances the activity is voluntary, according with (i). It is, however, possible for someone to *give a cough* (or *a laugh*) spontaneously, without planning to do so; and we can also have a non-human subject, as in *The machine gave a long hiss/a loud bang and suddenly stopped*. It appears that the second type of GIVE A construction does not necessarily carry meaning element (i), that the subject acts in a volitional manner.

(*c*) TAKE A VERB

The lexical verb 'take' refers to a unit of activity that is volitional and premeditated; it involves physical effort, e.g. *She took the bottle out of the fridge*, *He took his shirt off*.

The periphrastic TAKE A VERB construction has relatively limited use in British English, being restricted to a subset of those verbs that occur in the HAVE A construction. We will show that there are definite semantic differences between TAKE A and the HAVE A and GIVE A constructions. We will also show that the meaning of TAKE A shows some similarities to the lexical meaning of *take*.

Like HAVE A and type (I) of GIVE A, TAKE A refers to some volitional activity, done for its own sake (rather than to meet some external goal). Like HAVE A there is no overtone of a 'transfer', with the object being affected by the activity, which we identified for GIVE A.

TAKE A is like GIVE A—and contrasts with HAVE A—in often referring to a 'single unit' of activity. Both HAVE A and TAKE A can be used with *smell* and *sniff* but *take a sniff of it* seems a little more felicitous than *have a sniff of it* (because the verb *sniff* generally refers to a single inhalation) whereas *have a smell of it* is preferred over *take a smell of it* (since *smell* is likely to refer to an action extended in time, with many inhalations). TAKE A is particularly at home with *bite* and *swallow*—activities that have to be performed incrementally—and generally refers to a single unit of activity. But with verbs like *taste* and *suck*—referring to non-segmented activities—TAKE A sounds odd; *have a taste* and *have a suck* would be preferred. The 'unit' interpretation of TAKE A is most noticeable with CORPOREAL verbs but can also appear with verbs from other types. One may *take a walk around the lake*—the perimeter of the lake is a 'unit' walking course—in contrast to *have a walk in the park*—where the subject just walks 'for a bit'.

One important aspect of the meaning of TAKE A is that there is often physical effort involved on the part of the subject. Suppose Maggie is a small child playing off to one side; all you have to do is turn your head to look at her. I might suggest *Have a look at Maggie!*, if she is doing something cute. But if Maggie were asleep in her cot in another room and I wanted you to make sure she was all right, I would be likely to use the TAKE A construction (since you will have to move in order to check up on her), e.g. *Could you go and take a look at Maggie?* Indeed, it is normal to say *Have a look at this* but *Take a look at that*, since more exertion is likely to be involved in looking at 'that' than at 'this'.

The 'physical effort' component explains why one can use TAKE A with *walk* or *swim* but not with *sit down*; with *kick* or *bite* but not with *think*, *talk*, *laugh*, *cry* or *cough* (HAVE A can be used with all these verbs).

TAKE A often refers to a premeditated action, whereas HAVE A may be used for something done on the spur of the moment. One is likely to plan to *take a stroll* (e.g. *We always take a stroll after lunch on Sundays*) but one could just *have a stroll* at whim (e.g. *We had a stroll around the garden while we were waiting for you to get ready*).

In summary, the TAKE A VERB construction carries the meaning elements: (i) something done voluntarily, by the subject; (ii) often a definite premeditated activity; (iii) generally involving some physical effort on the part of the subject; (iv) just one unit of the activity being completed.

It was noted in §11.2 that there is a strong correlation (but not a coincidence) between transitivity and the use of HAVE A/TAKE A versus GIVE A. This has a semantic basis.

Type (I) of the GIVE A VERB construction refers to something being 'transferred' to an object. Plainly, transitive verbs, which refer to activities that link subject and object, are prototypical fillers of the 'VERB' slot. We also find that GIVE A occurs with a few inherent preposition verbs like *look at*, and with a few others like *smile* and *wink* where there is an 'addressee' marked with a preposition.

HAVE A and TAKE A just refer to the subject indulging in or taking part in some activity, for his or her own sake. It is natural that they should occur mostly with intransitive verbs. There are also a fair number of occurrences with transitive verbs, describing the subject indulging in doing something with respect to a particular object. With some of these verbs a preposition can intrude before the O NP in the basic sentence, and carries over into the periphrastic construction (e.g. *kick at the door*, *have a kick at the door*). With others *of* is inserted before the transitive object just in the HAVE A or TAKE A construction (e.g. *have a lick of the ice-cream*).

In §§2.9.5–6 we mentioned transitive verbs that may omit a reflexive or reciprocal pronoun, e.g. transitive *shave* (*someone*) and the inherently reflexive intransitive *shave* (sc. oneself); transitive *kiss* (*someone*) and the inherently reciprocal intransitive *kiss* (sc. each other). As might be predicted, the transitives occur with GIVE A and the intransitives with HAVE A. Thus, *John gave Fred/himself a shave* and *John had a shave* (this is in fact ambiguous between the HAVE A construction, where John does the shaving, and the Experiencer *have* construction, when it is related to *The barber shaved John*, *John had a shave at the barber's*). With *Mary gave John a kiss* we see that John is affected by the activity, which would be expected to be a single kiss. This contrasts with *John and Mary had a kiss*—they are indulging themselves in the activity of kissing, for a period of time.

353

In final summary, the semantic conditions for the GIVE A construction, involving 'transfer' from one participant to another, are similar to the characterisation of a transitive verb (i.e. that there be two core semantic roles). This is why the great majority of verbs taking GIVE A are transitive. The semantic conditions for HAVE A and TAKE A are that the activity be focused on, not its effect on any object; this is why most verbs occurring in these construction types are intransitive.

11.4. Occurrence

The semantic characteristics of the HAVE A, GIVE A and TAKE A constructions determine the verbs that occur in these syntactic frames. They are only compatible with verbs that describe volitional activities, and where the subject can just do it for a short period, without necessarily reaching any final result. GIVE A normally involves 'transfer' to some object which must be concrete (preferably human), never abstract.

It will be useful quickly to run through the semantic types, examining those verbs which have a semantic characterisation compatible with one or more of the HAVE A, GIVE A and TAKE A constructions.

MOTION and REST. Verbs in the RUN subtype describe a mode of motion (but no end-point) and may take HAVE A and TAKE A if it is plausible that the subject should want to indulge in that sort of activity, e.g. *run, walk, crawl, slide, roll, climb, dive, stroll, jump, swim*. Note that these verbs only occur in periphrastic constructions when they describe the activity done for its own sake, not when it has some definite goal—we can say *He had a jump down the path* parallel to *He jumped down the path*, but not **He had a jump over the fence* alongside *He jumped over the fence*.

Similar comments apply to the SIT subtype, which includes *sit (down), stand (up), lie (down), crouch (down), lean, float*; here HAVE A is possible but not TAKE A (possibly because there is no physical effort involved). If some SIT verbs seem uneasy with HAVE A this is simply because people do not often indulge themselves in that activity, e.g. *?Have a crouch*. But such usages can be contextualised, as we demonstrated in §11.3 for *have a stand-up*.

Some RUN verbs can be used as causatives. These may occur with GIVE A, parallel to the corresponding intransitive with HAVE A, e.g. *I walked for a while after lunch, I walked the dog for a while after lunch, I had a bit of a walk after lunch, I gave the dog a bit of a walk after lunch.*

SIT verbs may also be used causatively, e.g. *I sat down after lunch, I sat the child down after lunch.* Yet we can say *I had a bit of a sit-down after lunch* but not **I gave the child a bit of a sit-down after lunch.* There is a straightforward explanation. The intransitive verb *sit* (*down*) has two senses: (i) get into a sitting position, e.g. *He sat down rather suddenly*, and (ii) be in a sitting position, e.g. *He sat* (*down*) *on the sofa all afternoon.* HAVE A can only apply to sense (ii), a continuous activity with no end-point, whereas the causative is based on sense (i), 'put into a sitting position' (this cannot be 'done a bit' and so is incompatible with the GIVE A construction).

Verbs in the ARRIVE, TAKE, STAY and PUT subtypes describe motion or rest with respect to a definite Locus, e.g. *arrive, return, go, cross, take, send, move, stay, put.* One either arrives at a place or one doesn't, crosses a bridge or one doesn't, puts a thing in a place or one doesn't—it is not possible to indulge in arriving or crossing or putting for a short while. Because of their meanings, these verbs cannot be used with HAVE A, TAKE A and GIVE A.

Sapir's example *move* is particularly interesting. The way this verb is generally used—both intransitively and transitively—it implies shifting position from one definite Locus to another, e.g. *They've moved* (*from London to Bristol*) or *She moved it* (*from the mantelpiece to the coffee table*). There is an end-point implied, which is why *move* is not used with HAVE A, GIVE A or TAKE A. Note that HAVE A is quite acceptable with a verb such as *wriggle*—from the RUN subtype—which does just refer to a mode of motion, with no end-points.

The FOLLOW subtype refers to motion with respect to something that is moving, e.g. *follow, lead, track*, and the CONTAIN subtype to position with respect to something that is at rest, e.g. *surround.* The meanings of these types are incompatible with the HAVE A, TAKE A and GIVE A constructions.

The CARRY subtype refers to motion in juxtaposition with some moving object. Here HAVE A is possible when the subject just wants to indulge in the activity for a little while, e.g. *Let me have a carry of that new suitcase you designed*, and GIVE A when the thing carried is affected (it may be saved from exertion by the carrying), e.g. *Give the sick dog a carry. Handle* and *catch*, from the HOLD subtype, may also be used to refer to the subject indulging himself in something for a bit and may occur with HAVE A, e.g. *Let me have a handle of that new racket/catch of that new ball.*

Verbs from the THROW subtype describe causing something to be in motion. Such an activity can be done 'a bit', at the subject's whim, and these verbs may occur with HAVE A and GIVE A, e.g. *Can I have a throw of that new Frisbee?* and *Give the bed a push, will you, then I can sweep around this side*. Once again, the activity must be potentially continuous—we can *pull the rope* or *give the rope a pull* but, parallel to *pull/draw the sword from the scabbard* it is not possible to say **give the sword a pull/draw from the scabbard*, since this activity does have an end-point.

Open, close and *shut*, from the OPEN subtype, refer to an end-point and are not semantically compatible with HAVE A, TAKE A or GIVE A. Most verbs in the DROP subtype describe involuntary motion, e.g. *fall, spill*. There is *drop*, referring to something that may be done deliberately, but it is instantaneous—one either drops a vase or one doesn't; it would not be plausible to indulge in 'having a drop of the vase' or 'giving the vase a drop'.

AFFECT. Many verbs of straightforward affect, from the HIT, STAB, RUB and TOUCH subtypes, may occur with HAVE A or GIVE A. There is a tendency to use GIVE A with a basic sentence in straightforward transitive form, but HAVE A with a basic sentence that has a preposition inserted before the object (§8.2.3), e.g. *give the door a kick* (here the kick affects the door) and *have a kick at the door* (here the subject indulges in kicking, with where the kick is aimed being quite secondary). Similarly with *stroke, punch, rub, wipe, brush*. Note that one can *have a shoot at* (e.g. *the rabbits*) but not **give the rabbits a shoot* (this could only be interpreted as the Permissive *give* construction, §11.1). Shooting something implies a definite result, and it cannot be 'done a bit'.

Whether a periphrastic construction is possible may depend on the semantic nature not only of the verb but also of the object NP.

For instance, one could say *have a kick of the ball* (with a meaning difference from *have a kick at the ball*), but scarcely **have a kick of the door*.

A number of nouns describing weapons or implements may also be used as AFFECT verbs, e.g. *stone*, *spear*, *knife*, *whip*, *belt*, *brush*. They would generally not be used with GIVE A if the object is human because of the possibility of confusion with the lexical verb *give*, e.g. we can say *They stoned the Christians* but scarcely, with similar meaning, *They gave the Christians a stone*—this would imply handing them a stone, rather than throwing stones at them. (Note that the lexical verb is likely to be accorded precedence, if there is a conflict between lexical use of *give* and the periphrastic GIVE A construction.) However, GIVE A constructions with such verbs are acceptable if the object is inanimate, and could not be Recipient of the lexical verb give, e.g. *give the overcoat a brush* (note that GIVE A is allowed here since the overcoat is affected by the activity, being made clean).

HAVE A and GIVE A are most common in colloquial styles and often refer to something done quite casually, for fun. A professional painter, for instance, would scarcely be likely to say that he was *having a paint*—he just paints, because that's his job. But if a group of friends had organised a painting party, doing up someone's house, then someone could well extend an invitation: *Come on, John, you have a paint now!* or *Why don't you give the banisters a paint, Mary?*

Verbs from the AFFECT type that refer to an end-product are unlikely to be found with HAVE A or GIVE A, e.g. *clothe*, *cover*, *bake*, *melt*, *break*, *chip*, *crash*. However, a verb like *tear* refers to an activity that may be done to varying degrees—one can *tear it a little bit*, or *give it a little tear* (whereas one cannot, because of the meaning of *smash*, **smash it a little bit* or **give it a little smash*).

TAKE A is found with only a handful of AFFECT verbs—*take a kick at the ball*, *take a punch at Tom*, and very few others.

GIVING. Some verbs from this type refer to temporary transfer of possession, which can be for a short while; these verbs may occur with HAVE A or GIVE A. The interesting point is that the focus appears always to be on the Recipient. Thus *lend* has Recipient as object and here GIVE A is used (e.g. *I'll give you a lend of my boat for the weekend if you like*) whereas *borrow* has Recipient as subject and this verb occurs with HAVE A (e.g. *Can I have a borrow of your boat for the weekend, please?*). *Rent* can be used in either syntactic frame and so we get both *I'll give you a rent of my boat* and *Can I have a rent of your boat?* (*Can I have the/a loan of your boat for the weekend?* involves the derived form *loan*, plus either definite or indefinite article. There appears to be little meaning difference between this and the HAVE A construction, *Can I have a lend of your boat for the weekend?* The latter may just be more colloquial.)

Other GIVING verbs refer to some definite action which could not be done 'for a bit'; i.e. something is either given, sold, bought, bequeathed, presented, exchanged or not, with no half-measures possible. These verbs are thus not found in HAVE A, GIVE A or TAKE A constructions.

CORPOREAL. HAVE A is possible with many verbs of this type, whether describing something that is taken into or expelled from the body, or just referring to a bodily gesture or state, e.g. *drink*, *chew*, *suck*, *smoke*, *bite*, *taste*, *sniff*, *fart*, *pee*, *yawn*, *sneeze*, *sleep*, *hug*, *kiss*, *fuck*. HAVE A is plainly not possible with an end-point verb like *die*, nor with something that describes an inevitable process and could not normally be indulged in just a bit, such as *breathe* (although one might conceivably say to a sick person: *Have a breathe of this oxygen*). TAKE A is possible with verbs describing things being taken into the body, particularly if this is likely to be performed incrementally, e.g. *bite*, *swallow*, *sniff*.

It is interesting to consider why we can *have a drink/bite/chew/nibble/taste* but not **have an eat*. There may in fact be a number of contributory reasons. One could be that there is an independent noun *drink*, cognate with the verb *drink*, but corresponding to *eat* there are only the non-cognate nouns *feed* and *meal*. It may be because we can say *Have a* (e.g. *ice-cold*) *drink*, where *drink* is a noun, that the HAVE A construction is also used with *drink*, e.g. *Have a sneaky drink*, where *drink* is a verb. I must confess to being slightly mystified as to why **have an eat* is unacceptable; we are not, however, unduly impoverished by this lack since the activity of consuming food 'just a bit' may be expressed by *have a bite/*

nibble/taste (e.g. *of this pie*), parallel with *have a drink/sip/taste* for the consumption of a liquid.

Transitive verbs from the CORPOREAL type that refer to something which affects another person may take the GIVE A construction type (I), e.g. *smile, wink, kiss, hug, fuck, wake*. And a number of verbs describing bodily gestures take GIVE A sense (II), where there is no independent object, e.g. *laugh, cry, sob, cough*.

The other Primary-A types do not occur with HAVE A, GIVE A or TAKE A. WEATHER verbs lack a human subject. And verbs in COMPETITION, SOCIAL CONTRACT, USING, and OBEYING are not amenable to a 'do it a bit' interpretation. The verb *use*, for instance, implies using something for a purpose, and not just indulging in using it for the sake of doing so.

Turning now to Primary-B verbs, the LOOK and WATCH subtypes of ATTENTION refer to the Perceiver directing his attention, and this may be done 'just a bit'. Thus, HAVE A may be used with *look (at)*, *listen (to), search, hunt* and *watch*, e.g. *Have a look at this photo, Have a listen to my new record, if you like. Look* may also occur with TAKE A, when the subject has to move to see, and with GIVE A, referring to a mode of communication. The other subtypes of ATTENTION—with verbs such as *see, hear, notice, show, recognise, discover, witness*—refer to some definite act of perception, which could not be done 'a bit'; they are not found in HAVE A, TAKE A or GIVE A constructions.

HAVE A can be used with those verbs from the THINKING type that can refer to a general, undifferentiated chain of thought—*think, ponder* and perhaps also *meditate*. Verbs like *remember, assume, suppose, know, believe* (as well as all in the DECIDING type) refer to some definite act, while *consider* implies that all aspects of some topic are carefully thought over; for none of these is an 'indulge' or 'do a bit' meaning possible. *Guess* can also refer to a definite act but *have a guess* is said, often with strongly jocular overtones— *How old am I? Oh, I don't know. Go on, have a guess!*

Many SPEAKING verbs have a derived nominal which may be used with *make a*, and sometimes with *have a* or *give a*, e.g. *suggestion, declaration, explanation, proposal*. Some occur in their base form, e.g. *make a promise/offer, give a promise*. None of these satisfy the criteria set out in §11.1 (peripheral constituents in the basic sentence may not all be retained when *give* or *have* is added). HAVE A VERB constructions of the kind dealt with in this chapter occur just with some verbs from the TALK subtype, referring to the activity of vocal communication (e.g. *have a talk/chat/joke*), and with some from the SHOUT subtype, referring to the manner of vocal production (e.g. *have a shout/swear/pray/whistle*). *Shout* itself also occurs with GIVE A. The occurrence of *shout* in peripheral constructions is very similar to that of *laugh*—compare *give a shout* (a single cry, which may be involuntary) and *have a shout* (the subject indulges in the activity, perhaps to let off steam).

Speak just refers to the fact that someone uses a language; *talk*, in contrast, describes the use they make of it (recall the discussion in §5.4). The activity referred to by *talk* can be done 'for a bit'— alongside *John and Mary talked in the lounge* there is *John and Mary had a talk in the lounge*. With *speak*, on the other hand, one either does it or one doesn't; this is why it is not felicitous to say **John and Mary had a speak in the corridor*, corresponding to *John and Mary spoke in the corridor*. Note that *give a talk* is not an instance of GIVE A, since it fails the semantic criterion—*John talked to the children* can be quite casual but *John gave the children a talk* (or *John gave a talk to the children*) implies a formal address. *Talk* is here an independent noun, just like *speech* in *John gave a speech*.

Argue is an interesting verb. There is the derived noun *argument* —one can *have an argument*. But there is also the HAVE A construction *have (a bit of) an argue*. This would only be said in colloquial speech, and it could only refer to a mild, friendly altercation, in contrast to *have an argument*, which implies a more deeply felt disagreement. (If two people were having an argument about something then it might lead to blows, but if they were having (a bit of) an argue it never would.)

Some verbs in the ANNOYING type can occur with *give* and *a*, e.g. *He gave me a shock/scare/surprise*, but this is not the GIVE A construction. It fails criterion (*a*) in §11.1 since the subject of an ANNOYING verb can be an NP or a complement clause but the subject of *give a* plus ANNOYING verb can only be an NP—we can say *That John has been released from prison scares me* but not

*That John has been released from prison gives me a scare (only *John gave me a scare*). Note that the verb *frighten*, with similar meaning to *shock*, *scare* and *surprise*, takes on a different form after *give*, i.e. *give a fright*. LIKING verbs also have derived nominals (e.g. *take a liking to*) but they do not occur with HAVE A, TAKE A or GIVE A. The ACTING, HAPPENING, COMPARING and RELATING types are not amenable to a 'do it a bit' interpretation and so are not used with HAVE A, TAKE A or GIVE A.

No secondary verbs are found in HAVE A, TAKE A or GIVE A constructions. There are collocations *have a try* (*at*), *have a* (*further*) *attempt* (*at*), *give it a try*, (*don't*) *have a hope* (*of*) but these do not satisfy the criteria set out in §11.1. HAVE A and GIVE A constructions may not productively be based on sentences with *try*, *attempt* or *hope*—that is, corresponding to *Try to eat the spinach*, *Try eating the breadfruit*, *I don't hope to win*, we cannot say **Have a try to eat the spinach*, **Have a try eating the breadfruit*, **I don't have a hope to win*. There are of course many idioms involving *have*, *give* and *take*—e.g. *have a go*, *give* (*someone*) *a hand* (*with*), *take hold* (*of*)—which must be carefully distinguished from the constructions discussed in this chapter.

We have seen, in this section, that the occurrence of a verb in the HAVE A, GIVE A and TAKE A construction is determined by whether the meaning of the verb is compatible with the meaning components of the constructions, as they were described in §11.3.

The fact that HAVE A, GIVE A and TAKE A are most used in colloquial speech may impose another restriction—only colloquial-sounding verbs are likely to be found in this construction. One may talk about *having a pee* but not **having a urinate*, and *having a think* but not **having a contemplate*.

It would surely be instructive to study the occurrence of HAVE A, TAKE A and GIVE A across a variety of speech styles. Indeed, these constructions might well prove to be an indexical feature for the sociolinguistic classification of different formal and informal speech styles.

Notes to Chapter 11

My criterion (*c*) in §11.1, concerning adverb/adjective correspondence, is based on Cattell (1969: 278 ff). Other useful discussions of these constructions include Strang (1970: 101), Vissler (1963: 138–41), Curme (1931: 22–3), Poutsma (1926–9: part II, sec. iii, pp. 397–400), Olsson (1961), Green (1974), Prince (1972, 1974), Nickel (1968), Cattell (1984) and especially Wierzbicka (1982).

Research on this topic was assisted by consulting materials in the Survey of English Usage, at University College London. In 1980 Professor Randolph Quirk allowed me to riff through drawers of slips, and in 1987 Professor Sidney Greenbaum let me search the computerised corpus. Calvert Watkins and Steve Johnson provided most insightful comments during seminar presentations of an earlier version of this chapter, in 1980, at Harvard and at University College London respectively.

Appendix
List of adjective and verb types, with sample members

The lists below recapitulate the adjective types given in §3.2 and the verb types from Chapters 4–6, and their semantic roles and subtypes, with the sample members quoted there.

Adjective types

DIMENSION type, e.g. *big, great, short, thin, round, narrow, deep*

PHYSICAL PROPERTY type, e.g. *hard, strong, clean, cool, heavy, sweet, fresh, cheap*
   CORPOREAL subtype, e.g. *well, sick, ill, dead*; *absent*

SPEED type—*quick, fast, rapid, slow, sudden*

AGE type—*new, old, young, modern*

COLOUR type, e.g. *white, black, red, crimson, mottled, golden*

VALUE type, e.g. (*a*) *good, bad, lovely, atrocious*; (*b*) *odd, strange, curious*; *necessary, crucial*; *important*; *lucky*

DIFFICULTY type, e.g. *easy, difficult, tough, hard, simple*

QUALIFICATION type
   DEFINITE subtype, e.g. *definite, probable, true*
   POSSIBLE subtype, e.g. *possible, impossible*
   USUAL subtype, e.g. *usual, normal, common*
   LIKELY subtype, e.g. *likely, certain*
   SURE subtype, e.g. *sure*
   CORRECT subtype, e.g. *correct, right, wrong, appropriate, sensible*

HUMAN PROPENSITY type
   FOND subtype, e.g. *fond* (*of*)
   ANGRY subtype, e.g. *angry* (*about*), *jealous* (*of*), *mad* (*about*), *sad* (*about*)
   HAPPY subtype, e.g. *anxious, keen, happy, thankful, careful, sorry, glad* (all taking *about*); *proud, ashamed, afraid* (all taking *of*)
   UNSURE subtype, e.g. *certain, sure, unsure* (all taking *of* or *about*), *curious* (*about*)

EAGER subtype, e.g. *eager, ready, prepared* (all taking *for*), *willing*
CLEVER subtype, e.g. *clever, stupid; lucky; kind, cruel; generous*

SIMILARITY type, e.g. *like, unlike, similar* (*to*), *different* (*from*)

Primary-A verb types

MOTION type (Roles: Moving, Locus)
　　MOTION-a, the RUN subtype, e.g. *run, walk, crawl, slide, spin, roll, turn, wriggle, swing, wave, rock, shake, climb, dive, stroll, trot, gallop, jog, dance, march, jump, bounce, swim, fly, play; ride, drive*
　　MOTION-b, the ARRIVE subtype, e.g. (i) *arrive, return, go, come;* (ii) *enter, cross, depart, travel, pass, escape; come in, go out;* (iii) *reach, approach, visit*
　　MOTION-c, the TAKE subtype, e.g. (i) *take, bring, fetch;* (ii) *send;* (iii) *move, raise, lift, steal*
　　MOTION-d, the FOLLOW subtype, e.g. (i) *follow, track, lead, guide, precede, accompany;* (ii) *meet*
　　MOTION-e, the CARRY subtype, e.g. *carry, bear, transport, cart*
　　MOTION-f, the THROW subtype, e.g. *throw, chuck, fling, pour, spray, water; push, press; pull, jerk, drag, tug, draw*
　　MOTION-g, the DROP subtype, e.g. *fall, drop, spill, tip* (*over*), *upset, overturn, capsize, trip, slip*

REST type (Roles: Resting, Locus)
　　REST-a, the SIT subtype, e.g. *sit* (*down*), *stand* (*up*), *lie* (*down*), *kneel, crouch, squat, lean, hang* (*down*), *float*
　　REST-b, the STAY subtype, e.g. *stay, settle* (*down*), *live, stop, remain, reside; attend*
　　REST-c, the PUT subtype, e.g. (i) *put, place, set, arrange, install, put* NP *on, sow, plant, fill, load, pack; hide; beach, land, shelve;* (ii) *leave, desert, abandon, take* NP *off*
　　REST-d, the CONTAIN subtype, e.g. *contain, enclose, encircle, adjoin; surround*
　　REST-e, the HOLD subtype, e.g. (i) *hold, handle;* (ii) *grab; grasp, clutch, catch, gather, pick up; capture, trap*
　　REST-f, the OPEN subtype, e.g. *open, close, shut; lock*

AFFECT type (Roles: Agent, Target, Manip)
　　AFFECT-a, the TOUCH subtype, e.g. *touch, stroke*
　　AFFECT-b, the HIT subtype, e.g. *hit, strike, punch, bump, kick, knock, tap, bash, slap, spank; whip, belt, stone, cane, hammer; shoot*
　　AFFECT-c, the STAB subtype, e.g. *pierce, prick, stab, dig, sting, knife, spear; cut, prune, mow, saw, slice, chop, hack*

AFFECT-d, the RUB subtype, e.g. *rub, wipe, scrape, scratch, mark; sweep, brush, shave, rake; polish, lick; wash*

AFFECT-e, the WRAP subtype, e.g. *wrap; cover; butter, roof, veil, clothe, dress, grease; plaster, paint, coat; surround, frame; put NP on; unwrap, uncover, unroof, undress; take NP off, peel, shell*

AFFECT-f, the STRETCH subtype, e.g. *stretch, extend, compress, bend, curl, fold, coil; twist, pinch, squeeze; fade; vaporise, liquefy, solidify, melt; dissolve; freeze, cool (down), warm (up), heat (up), burn, singe*

AFFECT-g, the BUILD subtype (Product role), e.g. *build, knit, tie, weave, sew, shape, form, stir, mix, knead; fry, bake, cook; mend, repair; draw, write, sign, forge*

AFFECT-h, the BREAK subtype (Breaking role), e.g. *break, crush, squash, destroy, damage, wreck, collapse; tear, split, chip, crack, smash, crash; burst, explode, blow NP up, let NP off, erupt*

GIVING type (Roles: Donor, Gift, Recipient), e.g. *give, hand (over), lend, sell, rent, hire, pay, owe, bequeath; serve, feed, supply; present; donate, contribute, deliver, let; tip; reward, bribe; market; exchange, trade; borrow, buy, purchase, accept, receive*

OWN subtype (Roles: Owner, Possession), e.g. *have, lack, get, obtain, come by, gain, own, possess; belong to; lose*

CORPOREAL type (Roles: Human, Substance), e.g. *eat, chew, suck, drink, smoke; bite, nibble, sip; smell, feel, taste, sniff, swallow, breathe, smile, fart, burp, cough, spit, shit, pee, vomit; live; yawn, sneeze, laugh, leer, wink, blink, sob, sleep, dream, think, die; weep, cry, shiver, faint, pass out, wheeze, sweat, rest, ache, suffer, come to, recover, be born; wake, waken, grow, swell, hurt, bleed, heal, drown; bring to, comfort, console, cure, soothe, ease, nurse, doctor; kill, murder, assassinate, beat up, injure, wound, poison, give birth to; kiss, embrace, hug, cuddle, fuck*

WEATHER type (no roles), e.g. *rain, snow, hail, thunder*

COMPETITION type (Competitor role), e.g. *conquer, beat, overcome, race (against); resist, fight, play; win, lose; attack, guard, shield, surrender; defend; compete (with), struggle (against)*

SOCIAL CONTRACT type, e.g. *appoint, employ, dismiss, sack, fire; promote, nominate, convert, arrest, prosecute, impeach, punish; govern, rule, civilise, missionise, join; manage; apply for; qualify for, resign from; withdraw (from), work (at); marry*

USING type, e.g. *use, operate, manipulate, work, employ, wear, waste, fiddle with*

OBEYING type, e.g. *obey, execute, process, deal with, grant, refuse; perform*

Appendix

Primary-B verb types

ATTENTION type (Roles: Perceiver, Impression)

ATTENTION-a, the SEE subtype, e.g. *see, hear, smell, taste, feel; observe, notice, perceive*

ATTENTION-b, the SHOW subtype, e.g. *show; demonstrate*

ATTENTION-c, the RECOGNISE subtype, e.g. *recognise, spot*

ATTENTION-d, the DISCOVER subtype, e.g. *discover, find*

ATTENTION-e, the WITNESS subtype—*witness*

ATTENTION-f, the LOOK subtype, e.g. *look (at), listen (to); stare (at), glare (at), peep (at), peer (at), squint (at), eavesdrop (on); search (for), look (for), hunt (for); inspect, study, investigate, scan, scrutinise, examine, check, view; explore, survey; visit*

ATTENTION-g, the WATCH subtype, e.g. *watch, listen (to)*

Also: (i) *ignore, disregard, overlook, pass — over*; (ii) *appear, disappear*; (iii) *look, sound; smell, taste, feel*

THINKING type (Roles: Cogitator, Thought)

THINKING-a, the THINK subtype, e.g *think (of/about/over), consider, imagine*

THINKING-b, the ASSUME subtype, e.g. *assume, suppose*

THINKING-c, the PONDER subtype, e.g. *ponder (on/over), meditate (on/about), brood (on/over), speculate (on/about), wonder (at/about), reflect (on/about), dream (of/about), contemplate*

THINKING-d, the REMEMBER subtype, e.g. *remember, forget*

THINKING-e, the KNOW subtype, e.g. *know, sense, feel, realise, learn, understand; teach*

THINKING-f, the CONCLUDE subtype, e.g. *conclude, infer, reason, argue, prove, demonstrate, show, guess*

THINKING-g, the SOLVE subtype, e.g. *solve, work — out, devise, make — up; analyse*

THINKING-h, the BELIEVE subtype, e.g. *believe, suspect, doubt*

DECIDING type (Roles: Decision-maker, Course)

DECIDING-a, the RESOLVE subtype, e.g. *decide (on), determine (on), resolve, plan, settle*

DECIDING-b, the CHOOSE subtype, e.g. *choose, select, pick (out), appoint, elect, vote (for/on)*

SPEAKING type (Roles: Speaker, Addressee(s), Medium, Message—with components Message-Label and Message-Content)

SPEAKING-a, the TALK subtype, e.g. *speak, talk, chat, gossip, converse, communicate, quarrel, argue, joke; write*

SPEAKING-b, the DISCUSS subtype, e.g. *discuss, refer to, describe*

SPEAKING-c, the SHOUT subtype, e.g. *shout, call, cry, roar, swear, pray, preach, narrate, recite, intone, read, sing; whistle, warble; translate, pronounce, mispronounce, utter; name*

SPEAKING-d, the REPORT subtype

set (i), e.g. *say, declare, assert, observe, joke, put — about, give — out,let — out, put — across, let on about*

set (ii), e.g. *state, affirm, rumour*

set (iii), e.g. *announce, proclaim, mention, note, report, regret*

set (iv), e.g. *remark (on), comment (on); explain*

set (v), e.g. *boast (about/of), brag (about/of), complain (about/of), grumble (about)*

set (vi), e.g. *suggest, claim, acknowledge, admit, confess (to), repute*

set (vii), e.g. *undertake, offer, propose, agree (with)*

set (viii), e.g. *promise, threaten*

SPEAKING-e, the INFORM subtype, e.g. *inform, lecture, agree (with); remind*

SPEAKING-f, the TELL subtype, e.g. *tell, ask, request, beg, enquire, demand; answer, reply (to)*

SPEAKING-g, the ORDER subtype, e.g. (i) *order, command, urge, instruct, encourage; warn, caution, persuade, invite, recommend (to); tell, remind, ask, request, beg;* (ii) *forbid, discourage, dissuade, prohibit*

SPEAKING-h, the FORGIVE subtype, e.g. (i) *insult, slander, curse, abuse, scold, blame, rebuke, forgive, pardon, praise, thank, congratulate, compliment, tell — off, pick on;* (ii) *accuse, excuse;* (iii) *greet, welcome, introduce;* (iv) *cheer, applaud, apologise*

LIKING type (Roles: Experiencer, Stimulus—with components Stimulus-Label and Stimulus-Content), e.g. (i) *like, love, hate, prefer, fear; dread;* (ii) *dislike, loathe, abhor, admire, value; regret; rejoice at; (don't) mind (about), (don't) care (about);* (iii) *enjoy, favour, object to, approve of;* (iv) *worship, fall for;* also: *envy, pity*

ANNOYING type (same roles as LIKING), e.g. *frighten, terrify, scare, shock, upset, surprise; offend; delight, please, satisfy, entertain, amuse, excite, inspire; impress, concern, trouble, worry, grieve, dismay, depress, sadden; madden, infuriate, annoy, anger, disappoint; confuse, bewilder, perplex, puzzle; interest, distract, bore; attract; embarrass, disgust; tire, exhaust, bother*

ACTING type, e.g. *act, behave; adopt, copy, imitate, mimic, mime, reproduce*

HAPPENING type, e.g. *happen, take place; organise, arrange, bring — about; commit, attend to, neglect, put NP on, take NP on, do, tie — in with, change, devise; experience, undergo*

COMPARING type, e.g. *resemble, differ (from); take after; distinguish (between), compare; class, group, cost, grade; match, balance, measure, weigh, time, count; fit, suit; equal; include, comprise, consist of, be made up of*

RELATING type, e.g. *depend (on), result (from), indicate; relate (to), imply, be due (to); show, demonstrate, suggest*

Secondary-A verb types (no independent roles)

MODAL type—*will, would, shall, should, ought to, must, can, could, be to, may, might; used to; had better; need, dare*

SEMI-MODAL type—*be going to, have to, have got to, be able to, be about to, get to, be bound to*

BEGINNING type, e.g. (i) *begin, start, commence;* (ii) *continue (with), keep (on (with)), go on (with);* (iii) *finish, cease, stop, complete, discontinue;* also: *set in, break out*

TRYING type, e.g. (i) *try; attempt;* (ii) *succeed (in/at), manage;* (iii) *miss, fail;* (iv) *practise, repeat.*

HURRYING type, e.g. *hurry (over/with), hasten (over/with); dawdle (over); hesitate (over/with)*

DARING type, e.g. *dare, venture*

Secondary-B verb types

WANTING type (Role: Principal), e.g. (i) *want, wish (for), desire, crave, long (for), pine (for);* (ii) *hope (for);* (iii) *demand;* (iv) *need, require, deserve;* (v) *expect, wait (for), dread;* (vi) *intend, plan (for), aim (for), mean, prepare (for);* (vii) *pretend*

POSTPONING type (Role: Timer), e.g. *postpone, defer, put off, delay; avoid*

Secondary-C verb types

MAKING type (Role: Causer), e.g. (i) *make, force, cause, drive, get, have; tempt;* (ii) *let, permit, allow;* (iii) *prevent, stop, spare, save, check (oneself), rescue, release;* (iv) *ensure*

List of adjective and verb types

HELPING type (Role: Helper), e.g. *help*, *aid*, *assist*; *cooperate* (*with*), *collaborate* (*with*); *hinder*; *support*, *oppose*

Secondary-D verb types (Role: Arbiter)

SEEM type, e.g. *seem*, *appear*, *look*, *sound*, *feel*; *happen*, *come about*

MATTER TYPE, e.g. *matter*, *count*

References

Adams, V. (1973), *An Introduction to Modern English Word-Formation* (London: Longman).

Akmaijan, A. (1977), 'The complement structure of perception verbs in an autonomous syntax framework', in P. Culicover *et al.* (eds.), *Formal Syntax* (New York: Academic Press), 427–81.

Anderson, J. M. (1968), 'Ergative and nominative in English', *Journal of Linguistics*, 4: 1–32.

Anderson, S. R. (1971), 'On the role of deep structure in semantic interpretation', *Foundations of Language*, 7: 387–96.

Barker, E. J. W. (1975), 'Voice—beyond the passive', *Proceedings of the Annual Meeting of the Berkeley Linguistics Society*, 1: 16–24.

Binnick, R. I. (1971), '*Will* and *be going to*', *Papers from the Regional Meeting of the Chicago Linguistic Society*, 7: 40–51.

—— (1972), '*Will* and *be going to* II', *Papers from the Regional Meeting of the Chicago Linguistic Society*, 8: 3–9.

Bolinger, D. L. (1942), '*Need*, auxiliary', *College English*, 4: 62–5.

—— (1968), 'Entailment and the meaning of structures', *Glossa*, 2: 119–27.

—— (1971), *The Phrasal Verb in English* (Cambridge, Mass.: Harvard University Press).

—— (1972), *That's That* (The Hague: Mouton).

—— (1975*a*), 'On the passive in English', in A. Makkai and V. B. Makkai (eds.), *The First LACUS Forum, 1974* (Columbia, SC: Hornbeam Press), 57–80.

—— (1975*b*), 'Concept and percept: two infinitive constructions and their vicissitudes', in *World Papers in Phonetics: Festschrift for Dr Onishi's Kiju* (Tokyo: Phonetic Society of Japan), 65–91.

—— (1977*a*), *Meaning and Form* (London: Longman).

—— (1977*b*), 'Transitivity and spatiality: the passive of prepositional verbs', in A. Makkai *et al.* (eds.), *Linguistics at the Crossroads* (Padua: Liviana Editrice; and Lake Bluffs, Ill.: Jupiter Press), 57–78.

—— (1978), 'Yes-no questions are not alternative questions', in H. Hiż (ed.), *Questions* (Dordrecht: Reidel), 87–105.

—— (1979), 'The jingle theory of double *-ing*', in D. J. Allerton *et al.* (eds.), *Function and Context in Linguistic Analysis, a Festschrift for William Haas* (Cambridge: Cambridge University Press), 41–56.

Borkin, A. (1973), '*To be* and not *to be*', *Papers from the Regional Meeting of the Chicago Linguistic Society*, 9: 44–56.

—— (1984), *Problems in Form and Function* (Norwood, NJ: Ablex).

Bradley, D., and Bradley, M. (forthcoming), *Australian English* (Melbourne: Oxford University Press).

Bresnan, J. W. (1979), *Theory of Complementation in English Syntax* (New York: Garland).

Cattell, N. R. (1969), 'The role of give and some related verbs in English Syntax' (Ph.D. thesis, University of Newcastle, NSW).

—— (1984), *Composite Predicates in English* (Syntax and Semantics, 17) (Sydney: Academic Press).

Chappell, H. M. (1980), 'Is the *get*-passive adversative?', *Papers in Linguistics*, 13: 411–52.

Coates, J. (1983), *The Semantics of the Modal Auxiliaries* (London: Croom Helm).

Curme, G. O. (1931), *A Grammar of the English Language,* iii. *Syntax* (Boston: Heath).

—— (1935), *Parts of Speech and Accidence* (Boston: Heath).

—— (1947), *English Grammar* (New York: Barnes and Noble).

Davison, A. (1980), 'Peculiar passives', *Language*, 56:42–66.

Dixon, R. M. W. (1970), 'Syntactic orientation as a semantic property', in *Mathematical Linguistics and Automatic Translation, Report NSF–24* (Harvard University Computation Laboratory), 1–22. Reprinted in J. D. McCawley (ed.), *Notes from the Linguistic Underground* (Syntax and Semantics, 7) (New York: Academic Press, 1976), 347–62. Reprinted in Dixon 1982*b*; 141–55.

—— (1972), *The Dyirbal language of North Queensland* (Cambridge: Cambridge University Press).

—— (1977), 'Where have all the adjectives gone?', *Studies in Language*, 1: 19–80. Reprinted in Dixon 1982*b*, 1–62.

—— (1980), *The Languages of Australia* (Cambridge: Cambridge University Press).

—— (1982*a*), 'The grammar of English phrasal verbs', *Australian Journal of Linguistics*, 2: 1–42.

—— (1982*b*), *Where have all the Adjectives gone? And Other Essays in Semantics and Syntax* (Berlin: Mouton).

—— (1987), 'Studies in ergativity: introduction', *Lingua*, 71: 1–16. This volume of *Lingua* was also issued as a monograph: R. M. W. Dixon (ed.), *Studies in Ergativity* (Amsterdam: North-Holland, 1987).

—— (1988), *A Grammar of Boumaa Fijian* (Chicago: University of Chicago Press).

Duffley, P. (forthcoming), *The Infinitive in Contemporary English: To or Not To.*

Erades, P. A. (1950*a*), 'Points of Modern English syntax, X', *English Studies*, 31: 121–4.

References

—— (1950*b*), 'Points of Modern English syntax, XII', *English Studies*, 31: 153–7.

—— (1959/60), 'Points of Modern English syntax, XXXVIII', *English Studies*, 40: 462–3, 41: 58–61.

Fillmore, C. J. (1968), 'The case for case', in E. Bach and R. T. Harms (eds.), *Universals in Linguistic Theory* (New York: Holt, Rinehart and Winston), 1–88.

Foley, W. A. and Van Valin, R. D. (1984), *Functional Syntax and Universal Grammar* (Cambridge: Cambridge University Press).

Fraser, B. (1974), *The Verb–Particle Combination in English* (Tokyo: Taishukan). Reprinted, with corrections, by Academic Press, New York (1976).

Freed, A. F. (1979), *The Semantics of English Aspectual Complementation* (Dordrecht: Reidel).

Givón, T. (1979), *On Understanding Grammar* (New York: Academic Press).

—— (1984), 'Direct object and dative shifting: semantic and pragmatic case', in F. Plank (ed.), *Objects: Towards a Theory of Grammatical Relations* (London: Academic Press), 151–82.

Green, G. (1974), *Semantics and Syntactic Regularity* (Bloomington: Indiana University Press).

Hall, R. M. R. (1970), 'A note on *Will* vs. *Going to*', *Linguistic Inquiry*, 1: 138–9.

Halliday, M. A. K. (1967), *Grammar, Society and the Noun* (London: University College London).

Halpern, A. M. (1942), 'Yuman kinship terms', *American Anthropologist*, 44: 425–41.

Hasegawa, K. (1968), 'The passive construction in English', *Language*, 44: 230–43.

Hooper, J. B. (1975), 'On assertive predicates', in J. B. Kimball (ed.), *Syntax and Semantics*, 4 (New York: Academic Press), 91–124.

Hopper, P. J. and Thompson, S. A. (1980), 'Transitivity in grammar and discourse', *Language*, 56: 251–99.

Householder, F. W. (1981), *The Syntax of Apollonius Dyscolus* (Amsterdam: John Benjamins).

Huddleston, R. D. (1971), *The Sentence in Written English* (Cambridge: Cambridge University Press).

—— (1984), *Introduction to the Grammar of English* (Cambridge: Cambridge University Press).

Jacobson, P. (1982), 'Comments on "Subcategorization and grammatical relations" by Jane Grimshaw', in A. Zaenen (ed.), *Subjects and Other Subjects: Proceedings of the Harvard Conference on the Representation of Grammatical Relations* (Bloomington: Indiana University Linguistics Club), 57–66.

Jespersen, O. (1909–49), *A Modern English Grammar on Historical Principles* (Copenhagen: Munksgaard; and London: Allen and Unwin).

Keenan, E. L. (1981), 'Passive is phrasal (not sentential or lexical)', in T. Hoekstra *et al.* (eds.), *Lexical Grammar* (Dordrecht: Foris), 181–213.

—— (1985), 'Passive in the world's languages', in T. Shopen (ed.), *Language Typology and Syntactic Description,* i. *Clause structure,* (Cambridge: Cambridge University Press), 243–81.

Kiparsky, P., and Kiparsky, C. (1970), 'Fact', in M. Bierwisch and K. Heidolph (eds.), *Progress in Linguistics* (The Hague: Mouton), 143–73. Reprinted in D. D. Steinberg and L. A. Jakobovits (eds.), *Semantics: An Interdisciplinary Reader in Philosophy, Linguistics and Psychology* (Cambridge: Cambridge University Press, 1971), 345–69.

Kruisinga, E. (1927), 'Contributions to English syntax XVI: Retained accusative in passive sentences', *English Studies,* 9: 38–40.

Lakoff, G. (1970), *Irregularity in Syntax* (New York: Holt).

Lakoff, R. (1971), 'Passive resistance', *Papers from the Regional Meeting of the Chicago Linguistic Society,* 7: 149–61.

Langacker, R. W. (1972), *Fundamentals of Linguistic Analysis* (New York: Harcourt, Brace, Jovanovich).

—— and Munro, P. (1975), 'Passives and their meaning', *Language,* 51: 789–830.

Leech, G. N. (1971), *Meaning and the English Verb* (London: Longman).

Lipka, L. (1972), *Semantic Structure and Word-Formation: Verb Particle Constructions in Contemporary English* (Munich: Fink).

McCawley, J. D. (1979), 'On identifying the remains of deceased clauses', in *Adverbs, Vowels and Other Objects of Wonder* (Chicago: University of Chicago Press), 84–95.

—— (1988), 'Adverbial NPs: bare or clad in see-through garb?', *Language,* 64: 583–90.

McDavid, V. (1964), 'The alternation of "that" and zero in noun clauses', *American Speech,* 39: 102–13.

McIntosh, A. (1966), 'Predictive statements', in C. E. Bazell *et al.* (eds.), *In Memory of J. R. Firth* (London: Longman), 303–20.

Menzel, P. (1975), *Semantics and Syntax in Complementation* (The Hague: Mouton).

Newmeyer, F. J. (1970), 'On the alleged boundary between syntax and semantics', *Foundations of Language,* 6: 178–86.

—— (1975), *English Aspectual Verbs* (The Hague: Mouton).

Ney, J. W. (1981), *Semantic Structure for the Syntax of Complements and Auxiliaries in English* (Mouton: The Hague).

References

Nickel, G. (1968), 'Complex verb structures in English', *International Review of Applied Linguistics*, 6: 1–21.

Noonan, M. (1985), 'Complementation', in T. Shopen (ed.), *Language Typology and Syntactic Description,* ii. *Complex constructions* (Cambridge: Cambridge University Press), 42–140.

Olsson, Y. (1961), *On the Syntax of the English Verb, with Special Reference to* HAVE A LOOK *and Similar Complex Structures* (Gothenburg: Elanders Boktryckeri Aktiebolag).

Osborn, H. A., Jr. (1967), 'Warao III: verbs and suffixes', *International Journal of American Linguistics*, 33: 46–64.

Palmer, F. R. (1979), *Modality and the English Modals* (London: Longman).

Perlmutter, D. M. (1970), 'The two verbs *begin*', in R. A. Jacobs and P. S. Rosenbaum (eds.), *Readings in English Transformational Grammar* (Waltham, Mass.: Ginn), 107–19.

—— and Soames, S. (1979), *Syntactic Argumentation and the Structure of English* (Berkeley: University of California Press).

Poutsma, H. (1926–9), *A Grammar of Late Modern English,* Part II. *The Parts of Speech*, section iii. *The Verb and the Particles* (Groningen: Noordhoff).

Prince, E. (1972), 'A note on aspect in English: the *take a walk* construction', in S. Plötz (ed.), *Transformationelle Analyse* (Berlin: Athenäum), 409–20.

—— (1974), 'English aspectual constructions' (Ph.D. dissertation, University of Pennsylvania).

Pullum, G. K. (1974), 'Restating doubl-ing', *Glossa*, 8: 109–20.

Quirk, R. (1957), 'Relative clauses in educated spoken English', *English Studies*, 38: 97–109.

—— and Greenbaum, S. (1973), *A University Grammar of English* (London: Longman). (In USA titled: *A Concise Grammar of Contemporary English.*)

—— —— Leech, G., and Svartvik, J. (1985), *A Comprehensive Grammar of the English Language* (London: Longman).

Radford, A. (1988), *Transformational Grammar: A First Course* (Cambridge: Cambridge University Press).

Ransom, E. N. (1986), *Complementation, its Meanings and Forms* (Amsterdam: John Benjamins).

Rice, S. (1987), 'Towards a transitive prototype: evidence for some atypical English passives', *Papers from the Annual Meeting of the Berkeley Linguistics Society*, 13: 422–34.

Riddle, E. (1975), 'Some pragmatic conditions on complementiser choice', *Papers from the Regional Meeting of the Chicago Linguistic Society*, 11: 467–74.

References

Rosenbaum, P. S. (1967), *The Grammar of English Predicate Complement Constructions* (Cambridge, Mass.: MIT Press).

Ross, J. R. (1972), 'Doubl-ing', *Linguistic Inquiry*, 3: 61–86.

Sapir, E. (1949), *Selected Writings of Edward Sapir in Language, Culture and Personality*, ed. D. G. Mandelbaum (Berkeley: University of California Press).

Schmerling, S. F. (1978), 'Synonymy judgments as syntactic evidence', in P. Cole (ed.), *Pragmatics,* (Syntax and Semantics, 9) (New York: Academic Press), 299–313.

Sinha, A. K. (1974), 'How passive are passives?', *Papers from the Regional Meeting of the Chicago Linguistic Society*, 10: 631–42.

Stockwell, R. P., Schachter, P., and Partee, B. H. (1973), *The Major Syntactic Structures of English* (New York: Holt).

Strang, B. M. H. (1970), *A History of English* (London: Methuen).

Svartvik, J. (1966), *On Voice in the English Verb* (The Hague: Mouton).

Sweet, H. (1891–8), *A New English Grammar, Logical and Historical* (Oxford: Clarendon Press).

Thompson, S. (1973), 'On subjectless gerunds in English', *Foundations of Language*, 9: 374–83.

—— (1987), 'The passive in English, a discourse perspective', in R. Channen and L. Shockey (eds.), *In Honor of Ilse Lehiste: Ilse Lehiste Pühendusteos* (Dordrecht: Foris), 497–511.

Urmson, J. O. (1952), 'Parenthetical verbs', *Mind*, 61: 480–96. Reprinted in C. E. Caton (ed.), *Philosophy and Ordinary Language* (Urbana: University of Illinois Press, 1963), 220–40.

Van Der Gaaf, W. (1930), 'The passive of a verb accompanied by a preposition', *English Studies*, 12: 1–24.

Van Ek, J. A. (1966), *Four Complementary Studies of Predication in Contemporary British English* (Groningen: Wolters).

Vendler, Z. (1967), *Linguistics in Philosophy* (Ithaca: Cornell University Press).

—— (1972), *Res Cogitans: An Essay in Rational Psychology* (Ithaca: Cornell University Press).

Vissler, Th. (1963), *An Historical Syntax of the English Language*, part 1. *Syntactical Units with One Verb* (Leiden: E. J. Brill).

West, M. (1953), *A General Service List of English Words, Revised and Enlarged Edition* (London: Longmans).

Wierzbicka, A. (1982), 'Why can you *have a drink* when you can't **have an eat*?', *Language*, 58: 753–99.

—— (1988), *The Semantics of Grammar* (Amsterdam: John Benjamins).

Index

Sample members of Verb and Adjective classes have their TYPE or TYPE/SUBTYPE indicated in parentheses. Note that occurrences in the Preface, Appendix and References are not indexed.

Index

379

Index

Index

385

Index

Index

Index

Index

Index